D0979078

. . . . . .

DIFFERENCE AND SUBJECTIVITY

. . . . . .

Difference and Subjectivity

Dialogue and Personal Identity

. . . . . .

FRANCIS JACQUES

Translated by Andrew Rothwell

. . . . . .

Yale University Press

NEW HAVEN AND LONDON

Originally published as *Différence et Subjectivité: Anthropologie d'un point de vue relationnel* by Editions Aubier Montaigne, Paris, © 1982.

Designed by Barbara Werden.
Set in Bauer Bodoni type by G & S Typesetters, Inc., Austin, Texas.
Printed in the United States of America by Vail-Ballou Press, Binghamton, New York.

Library of Congress Cataloging-in-Publication Data

Jacques, Francis.
   [Différence et subjectivité. English]
   Difference and subjectivity : dialogue and personal identity / Francis Jacques ; translated by Andrew Rothwell.
      p.   cm.
   Translation of: Différence et subjectivité.
   Includes bibliographical references and index.
   ISBN 0-300-04830-0 (alk. paper)
      1. Philosophical anthropology.   2. Individual differences.
3. Subjectivity.   4. Interpersonal communication,   5. Interpersonal relations.   I. Title.
BD450.J24I3   1991   90-46661
126—dc20   CIP

10   9   8   7   6   5   4   3   2   1

CONTENTS

. . . . . .

NOTE ON THE ENGLISH TRANSLATION

THE GUIDING principle adopted in this translation has been to remain as close to the French text as possible without sacrificing readability in English. In particular, every attempt has been made to respect the wide stylistic range of the original. In rendering certain technical terms, the expedient of creating clearly comprehensible cognate neologisms is almost always preferred to that of lengthy and less satisfactory paraphrase. Quotations from secondary works in English are given in the original language, those from other languages are taken from the standard English translation, where one was available (see Bibliography). When no such source could be found, and in a few cases in which it did not prove possible to reconstitute incomplete references, the translations are my own. At the author's suggestion, a number of paragraphs in the Preface have been reordered and additions have been made to the Bibliography.

Because *Difference and Subjectivity* seeks to build bridges between formerly divergent philosophical traditions, it is clearly important that any terminological overlap between "natural" translations into English and the vocabulary of Anglo-Saxon philosophy be conscious and well understood. It is therefore appropriate here to set a number of central terms in their context and explain the translational choices involved.

Dialogisme/dialogue/interlocution. "Dialogism," as defined by Francis Jacques in *Dialogiques 2: L'Espace logique de l'interlocution* (1985), refers to "the internal structure of a discourse functioning transitively between two uttering agencies in an interlocutive relation, with reference to a world to be said. The production of meaning then comes about by a conjunction of agencies in the position of speaker/listener, for the benefit of the dyad of persons engendered by the relation" (181). "Dialogue," on the other hand, is "the trans-sentential form which, by bringing about an equitable pooling of meaning and referential value, determines both the semantic-pragmatic structure and the syntax of a statement (here, a message), and whose sequential organization is governed by pragmatic rules which ensure a property of convergence" (217). Finally, "interlocution" is not just the fact of speaking to someone; it is a foundational condition in its own right. Dialogism is thus a condition of all discourse, while dialogue is a particular form of discourse, and interlocution is the transcendental function of dialogue.

Enonciation is translated throughout as "(the process of) utterance" (and similarly for its derivatives: *énonciateur* = "utterer," *agence énonciative* = "uttering agency" etc.), while *énoncé* is rendered as "statement." The word *énonciation,* introduced into French linguistics by Emile Benveniste, is increasingly being used as the French translation of "speech act." However, the two concepts are far from interchangeable. In particular, speech-act theory takes no account of the relational component which makes énonciation a key concept in Francis Jacques' philosophy. While énonciation stresses the joint role of speaking subject and listener in an act of language use, in speech-act theory this role is subsumed into the semantic content of the statement, by way of the rules through which speaker and listener are integrated into an adequate context of utterance. Illocutionary logic is therefore constructed from the point of view of the linguistic object rather than of the speaker, and so tends to reduce the differences between delocutive and allocutive registers stressed by Benveniste. By undervaluing in this way the paradigm of communicability in discourse analysis, current pragmatic philosophy has run into difficulties with concepts such as "reciprocal intentions," "rule," "convention," and "norm," which the relational theory of énonciation is designed to handle.

Esprit ("mind," "spirit") is translated throughout as "spirit," "spiritual," to avoid any confusion with "mind" as used in English-language philosophy.

Sens/Référence. The distinction between "sense" and "reference" as used in the present book overlaps with two other classical oppositions, both relating to concepts, namely those between extension and intension and between denotation and connotation. In the case of sense (meaning) and reference, an expression in language includes both a sense, which is a function of the language system, and a reference to a nonlinguistic object in the world. The *extension* of a concept is the class of objects to which it applies, while its *intension* is the set of attributes which make it up; a concept *denotes* the objects to which it applies, but it *connotes* certain features or characteristics of them.

Finally, I should like to take this opportunity to thank Professor Jacques for his helpful discussions of the translation in the course of its preparation. I am also most grateful to Jean Khalfa for his valuable technical advice and numerous suggestions for improvements. Any errors that remain are my own.

ANDREW ROTHWELL
December 1989

PREFACE TO THE ENGLISH EDITION

WHILE PREPARING the present edition, I felt that it would be useful to set down a number of remarks which would make the book more accessible to English-speaking readers. These remarks will relate principally to my chosen subject area, the nature of subjectivity today and its role in the future. But I will also discuss the appropriateness of this text as I see it from my position in France, in late 1990, as well as its place within the series of works of which it forms a part.

Several of my remarks will be in the form of caveats, relating to terms that might give rise to involuntary confusions and misreadings, the sort that an author prefers to clear up on the threshold of the work itself. As the book progresses, the reader will find his or her attention drawn to a number of questions that are here left unresolved, but which I have tried to answer in later publications. My main wish is to invite the reader most cordially to examine what I am saying in a critical light, to watch out for the crucial conceptual distinctions as they emerge along the way, and to be aware at all times of the order of reasons upon which, as always in the radical but informal discussion that we call philosophy, the sense of my argument depends.

Today, in philosophy worldwide, we see subjectivity making a difficult return to the agenda. *Difference and Subjectivity* seeks to put forward a con-
structive solution to one of the major aporias that have emerged from the
ongoing contemporary debate. The origin of this aporia lies in two equally
extreme and equally unacceptable ways of regarding the subject. Either the
ego is held to be constitutive, even omnipotent, as in the phenomenology of
Husserl and the various egological models constructed by his successors; or
else it is seen as an empty form, a nonentity, as in the Sartrian vision of the
self as an agency of utter nothingness, or as in more recent poststructuralist
deconstructions of the subject. Another way of expressing this dilemma is to
say that we are obliged to choose between a humanistic valorization of human subjectivity and antihumanist efforts to undermine subjectivity by presenting it as simply a structural side effect of the play of signs.

My contention is that the subject does have a valid role after all, but only
on condition that we reconceive it on a new basis. *Difference and Subjectivity* undertakes just such a radical process of reconception. I am not sure
whether its title is well calculated to catch the attention of English-speaking
philosophers, but in French at least it brings together in an intriguing way
one term, "subjectivity," universally scorned and rejected, with another,
"difference," which until recently was hailed as a cure-all, a fundamental
value without which philosophical thought of any kind was impossible.
However, the title was not meant simply as a gesture in the direction of a
now-declining fashion. It accurately expresses my project in this book, which
is to found a conception of subjectivity on relations between persons. The
conventional field of subjectivity is so full of traps that I found myself
obliged to shift my ground entirely and begin from a different angle. This I
did by treating the relation as a primordial reality, a reality which constitutes one of the very conditions of possibility of meaning and which is prior
even to *I* and *you*.

The book sets out from a premise that I demonstrated in an earlier work,
that our *self* is a function of the communicative interaction which occurs in
dialogue. This interaction takes place on the level of "utterance," a term that
expresses the fact that what the speaking subject is saying depends on the
interlocutionary context of communication. In *Difference and Subjectivity*
this interaction is itself taken back to the originary relation from which it is
derived, a relation that links the "co-utterers" to each other in a dynamic
way. Note that dialogue does not demand any real consensus, although some
sort of simulated consensus, at least, is required even if one is to express one's
disagreement without giving rise to misunderstandings.

My work since 1979, whether it be best referred to as a philosophy of dialogue, of relations, or of communication, has developed along the dual axes of continuity with the Kantian critical tradition and openness toward English-language analytical thought, refusing to sacrifice either approach to the other. My aim, in an age of multiple discourses and texts difficult to reconcile with each other, an age when it is no longer possible to rely on any preexisting universality or rational homology, has been to arrive at a new, relations-based concept of the transcendental. Mine is therefore a philosophy for the scientific age, an age in which problems of innovation in meaning and the textualization of thought are, or will be in the near future, at the forefront of our concerns. But at the same time I am not averse to writing in a style, and involving the reader in a manner, typical of the French philosophical tradition.

In order for my position to be properly understood, let me set it briefly in the context of the other work I was publishing around the same time.

Dialogiques I (1979) sought to develop a theory of "being-as-speaking" (*l'être-dit*) according to which the object of discourse, on a metatheoretical level at least, only becomes fully established through deliberate exchange with others. Around this central thesis I constructed a model of referential dialogue, that is, dialogue in which the sharing of information allows the existence and identity of the referent to be determined (for example, the discussion between Oedipus and Jocasta over who caused the plague at Thebes). By linking dialogue in this way to the more familiar notion of reference, I was able to analyze the process of exchange between interlocutors by which new information is constituted.

I introduced a non-monological conception of dialogue—something which, curiously enough, had not been done before in philosophy—derived from the basic concepts of *dialogism* and interlocution. One error, which goes back at least to Plato, constitutes an epistemological barrier to the understanding of dialogue that should not be underestimated. Far from expressing the essentially dialogical nature of thought, Plato in fact constructed the first monological model of speculative dialogue. It seems somewhat paradoxical that the philosophical significance of dialogue should have been undervalued for so long because non-dialogical conditions were being imposed on it.

In defining dialogism as "the distribution of the message between two uttering agencies in present relation with each other," my aim was to contribute to the foundation of a pragmatics-based theory of language. I was able to introduce a number of key concepts, including *co-reference*, or the identification of the real by reference to the possible worlds pertaining to a shared propositional attitude, such as a belief or a piece of knowledge; and *back-reference*, or the process by which interlocutors refer to themselves and offer themselves each to the other's understanding as the dialogue develops, using the same mode of assent by which they become conscious of themselves.

Because "satisfactory speech" functions in this way, the cooperative element can serve as a basis for divergences of view without necessarily overcoming the competitive element entirely. In putting together epistemic logic and game theory and adapting them to form a model of discursive strategy, my intention was not only to articulate modalities of statement and modalities of utterance, but also to accommodate and reconcile within a single overall conception of meaning a theory of truth in the tradition of Alfred Tarski and Donald Davidson, and a theory of usage in the tradition of P. F. Strawson and H. P. Grice.

Difference and Subjectivity, published in French in 1982, seeks to develop a theory of the "being who speaks" (*l'être qui dit*) based from the start on relations. What I call the *primum relationis* principle, which I argue is both logically and transcendentally irreducible, allows the intersubjective field to be occupied in a nonphenomenological manner, without granting the Same anything but a marginal privilege over the Other. The basis for this theory was actually the notion of an interlocutive relation, rather than that of dialogue or even dialogism. It was then up to me to show its pertinence for a descriptive account of misunderstandings, secrecy, desire, and love, which for a long time now have been the preserve of orthodox phenomenology.

An indirect result of this communicational approach to subjectivity is that it rules out the ego's narcissistic claim to being the sole instigator of meaning. In their reviews of the book, the French critics realized at once the extent to which this result decenters the ego, a decentering which follows from, and is doubtless just as radical as, those performed by Freud, Nietzsche, and Marx. My book of 1982 was thus able to address the critical problem of how it is that we are able in general to communicate through signs, and to launch the idea of a communicational a priori which, as the "formal" counterpart of a "transcendental" reality, is the only effective and *originary* way of reconciling the referential and the interlocutive relation.

My strategy was simple: it was important above all to detach subjectivity from self-consciousness, and to link it instead to the more fundamental problem of personal identity. The second reason for publishing this book in English is that it espouses a position of communicative pragmatism, which relates to a general renewal of interest in pragmatism in the United States. I thus found myself working in the direct line of descent from C. S. Peirce, alongside Wilfried Sellars, Richard and Amélie Rorty, and Richard Berstein. My personal approach has been to take together the questions of difference, subjectivity, and the interpersonal relation. My conjecture may be summarized as follows. Schematically, the subject will succeed in constructing his or her self-identity to the extent that he or she manages, across all the communicational interactions in which he or she becomes involved, to integrate the three poles of any communication act: by speaking to others and saying *I*, by being spoken to by others as *you*, or by being spoken of by others as a *he/she* that the subject would accept as appropriate. In this process, the basic principles for a logical analysis of which I set out to establish, the subject is not defined by any substantive reality or transcendental function, but by his or her ability, or competence, to act as a threefold communicative agency. This analysis brought my position close to certain remarks of a psychoanalytic nature made by French authors such as Edmond Ortigues, while distancing me from other continental European thinkers, such as Mikhaïl Bakhtin, Emmanuel Levinas, and Martin Buber, who might otherwise seem much closer to my concerns.

Indeed, my position must be dissociated from a number of attractive but deceptive commonplaces whose inadequacy can be demonstrated by reductio ad absurdum arguments. Buber was influential in promoting the somewhat rudimentary idea that human beings only become *I* in contact with a *you* from whom their own interiority is derived. In the same way, according to Levinas, we should not speak of another person in the accusative or the dative, as *he/she* or *him/her*, but only in the vocative, as if *to you*. But I ask: how are we to reconcile this position with the overwhelming fact that we do all speak about each other? Delocutive discourse about a third person is no less valid for attributing personal predicates to that person, however we choose to define properly personal predicates (as the reader will see, my definition is not the same as Strawson's). A human being only becomes *somebody*, only acquires a personal self, after passing what one might call an additional he/she test, the test of other people. Thus alterity as I conceive of it—relational alterity—is a multifocus problem.

What is new here is the idea that there can be no personal identity without a certain relationship to an absent or distant third party. This is why I had to rework existing accounts to show how the allocutive, or interlocutive, register could be reconciled with the delocutive one, and the other close at hand with the other at a distance. This meant taking account of the third person and integrating it into the identificational process, as a third, but a person nevertheless. For when one speaks of someone else, *he/she* is not the same as *it*—a point that neither Buber, nor Gabriel Marcel, nor Levinas appreciated. The third person is relative to the first two in the circuit of their conversation, in relation to which it is precisely a third entity. According to the traditional model, in the communication relation the second person is the one who is going to take over the speaking role, and is therefore considered as virtual. In my definition, the third is the relatively absent person. This *he/she* is not a person outside all possible communication, for that would mean being nobody. He or she is first and foremost a specific other, a third person who is still to some extent privileged by the fact that one of the other two has already spoken, or will one day speak, to him or her, or might at least have done so in the past. *He/she* does not stand outside the interlocutive process, but is simply not present at the moment when it is happening. In short, therefore, the answer lay in reconciling presence and absence in the same model.

He/she is not the *you* of this you who is my partner, another person's other, but instead is a person in his or her own right, because even if he or she is not a participant in a presently lived relation, he or she still retains a relationship both with a communicational past and with that invocation by others which gives him or her a future. By the time my "deduction" of the third person is complete, that person finds itself bound up with the other two in a process of identification in which all three are interdependent. In comparison, most of the formulations of personal alterity to be found in the work of other philosophers can be seen as mutilations of the real situation. It is clear that the relatively absent other is not passive, like an object; nor should an author who discovers the vital role of our address to the listener, or the importance of our being summoned by a *you*, rush into imposing on that fact an emotive or exclusive coloration which will obliterate the rest of the interpersonal structure that is at issue.

"Which of us two created the other?" wonders the poet Paul Eluard. The answer is neither, for personal identity is a structure much richer than any specular relationship. Once we accept that persons have an essential ability to act as three agencies at once, personal identity becomes a process of great logical complexity. Correctly employed, this ability allows us to account for the hazards and crises of personal identity as difficulties in the process of mapping the three agencies of communication. In my view, certain problems in the psychoanalytic genesis of the ego can be reconstructed as the results of what one might call pragmatic prematurity.

Thus it is vital to appreciate that although the interlocutive relation of communication is binary, it engenders in each interlocutor a tripersonal structure that needs to be put into practice empirically.

Another frequent source of confusion is the difference between *individuals* and *persons*. The criteria for personal identification are different from those for individualization. If we are to understand the process by which personal identity comes about, we must abandon the old language of individual properties. Such notions as the permanence of our own bodies, or subjective memory, will be of no help to us. Persons are not just jumbled up in the world like peas in a can; they are always already linked to each other, both allocutively and delocutively. *I* does not have to search out *you* as an equal, nor still less to hunt *you* down as an adversary, as happens in the Hegelian western, where each consciousness seeks the death of every other. However, it is not enough simply to draw these distinctions; we need to articulate the concepts of *individual* and *person*. I trust that the reader will find this articulation in this book's order of reasons, or by exploiting its systematic structure, for the distinction between individuals and persons is in fact closely bound up with another distinction, that between the *vehicles* and the *terms* of a relation.

After producing a theory of reference and a theory of the subject, it was perhaps appropriate for me to turn back and assess the implications of both for language itself. This I did in 1985 with *Dialogiques 2: L'Espace logique de l'interlocution,* which invites the reader to rethink the nature of language from the perspective of discourse, and discourse from the perspective of communication. I needed to talk about communication as a philosopher, rather than simply as a linguist or a telecommunications engineer might do. All too often communication is reduced to a transfer of information, a view which does justice to only one of its dimensions, that which I call *communicativity*. My contention is that a place needs to be found for another dimension that philosophy throughout its history has underplayed, and that I call *communicability*. This refers to the possibility of a process by which what was not originally common to both speakers can become so by virtue of having been produced by them jointly. It follows from this that linguistic communication in the full sense of the term is not merely the exchange of fixed and reified meanings laid down in the language code (this aspect is derivative), but is more fundamentally the possibility of speakers instigating new speech *between themselves*. How is this process to be described? And first of all, how is it possible?

These questions are still pending. In their most radical form, when they are taken back to the level of language, they open up an even more fundamental problem: how is it possible for anything at all to be said between us? In essence, what we need to understand is how a meaning can succeed in making itself communicable. This is where the notion of a communicational a priori, which I first put forward in 1982 in *Difference and Subjectivity*, comes into its own. This a priori is part of the originary situation of communication, and it provides a basis on which more complex processes can be described. In a number of later articles (including "De la Signifiance," which appeared in the *Revue de métaphysique et de morale* in 1987) I have shown why the three constitutive conditions of communication may be expressed by the key terms *difference, reference,* and *interlocution.*

I leave it up to the reader to discover for him or herself what implications this has for a reevaluation of the Kantian problematic of transcendence. If Kant did not raise the question of communicability in the *Critique of Pure Reason* (though he did refer to it as "Mitteilbarkeit" in the *Critique of Judgment*), it is because he was legislating under the assumption of an initial agreement between understandings. The challenge now is to integrate conceptual divergence and discursive disagreement in such a way that they regain their semantic productivity. The central idea in this undertaking is no longer communication between consciousnesses, but the commensuration of discourses, for example in metatheoretical debate between experts on the foundations of a given science.

It has been said that I am the French philosopher with the closest affinity to the Frankfurt School. I am happy to concur. My only reservation is that in my books published from 1982 to 1985 I have been concerned rather to reconstruct some of the Frankfurt philosophers' most generally endorsed conclusions, relating for instance to the acceptance of rules by the individual (Karl-Otto Apel) or the problem of consensus (Jürgen Habermas). We were in fact all able to discuss our respective positions at a seminar that took place in 1989. In my view, it is vital that we give full weight to an irreducibly relational component at the very foundation of pragmatics (hence my critique of H. P. Grice), and return to a less irenic view of communication, notably by granting a much greater philosophical role to two realities that stand outside consensus. The first of these, *controversy,* is epistemological, involving as it does a battle over the possible meanings of words, while the second, *conflict,* has moral and political implications. We live in an age in which universalizing discourses are on the decline and the commensurability of categories between discourses cannot be taken for granted. But rather than regarding differences of opinion as irreducible conflicts just because there is no common rule of argument, as Jean-François Lyotard suggests we must, a more positive approach is to reconstruct the controversy according to the underlying meta-rules that allow the real issues to emerge. At that point, the interlocutive space becomes a space of scientific and cultural exchange.

My latest work has led me to the threshold of a general theory of textuality, which will probably be published in 1991, in French. I am most grateful to my American friends Hilary Putnam, John Searle, and the late Max Black, who will be sadly missed, for their kindness in discussing parts of it with me.

Autumn 1990

. . . . . .

PREFACE TO THE
FIRST EDITION

> Individual differences present within a relation . . .
> should be considered as products of the active process
> of that relation, and not as the first cause of relational
> phenomena.
> —DON D. JACKSON

IN THIS book I shall not attempt to go back over the crisis, and the doubtless definitive impasse, into which philosophies of consciousness have run. Our age not only must come to terms with the narcissistic wound inflicted by Freud's discovery of the unconscious; take notice, after Marx, of the structure of relations of production; and accept anxiety syndromes and other perverse psychological effects. It must also open itself up to the full implications of communicational and linguistic reality. We have learned almost too well the lesson that language games are, to say the least, a necessary condition for the integrity of the social fabric. Wide-ranging interdisciplinary programs are now based around a communicational component.

Communication is becoming more crucial every day in our increasingly computerized societies.[1] The effect of all this, which has not yet been properly understood philosophically, is that knowledge and even meaning itself are becoming more and more dissociated from the human subject which, until recently, was seen as the source of meaning. The idea of a subject that imperiously calls itself into existence as the giver of meaning,[2] a sort of self-founding foundation, has become quite improbable. If, then, we are to bring subjectivity back into the picture, it must be in a profoundly modified form.

I am quite ready to believe, as did Maurice Merleau-Ponty, that once subjectivity has been introduced into philosophy it can no longer be ignored. The resurgence of problems everyone thought were over and done with, the necessity we now feel to put them back on the agenda, is most significant. Even, and especially, thinkers who intend to leave subjectivity behind altogether will undoubtedly still have to face up to the problem.

What attitude have philosophers taken in the past forty years? Should they make one more attempt to grapple with this protean force? Instead, they have decided to extend further the range of possible alternatives. This time, the very existence of the ego has come up for discussion. Should phenomenology be allowed to restore it to its place as a founding absolute? Or, after a series of cumulative steps toward disinvesting the subject, from Wittgenstein to French structuralism and the system thinkers, should the idea of subjectivity finally be abandoned altogether? Killing off the subject is easier said than done.

From Montaigne to Pascal, from Rousseau to Kierkegaard, from Descartes to Husserl, subjectivity has undergone astonishing philosophical development. Rather than any continuity, we have seen the discordant celebration of a disparate reality. This is not so much because Montaigne's treasured self was hateful to Pascal (and the selves of other people even more so), but because the way the ego was constructed swung from one extreme to another in a disconcerting way. Thus Descartes' "je pense," which he claimed necessarily apprehended itself in the instant, was soon undone by the subjective series of ideas in the mind, as conceived by Anglo-Saxon philosophers. At the same time, the free negativity of the Sartrian *pour soi* seems to undermine Maine de Biran's vision of a full and incarnate subjectivity.

If the present position of subjectivity is so new and different, it is because the role it is being asked to play requires the total reinvention of the way we conceptualize it. In consequence, an acceptable model of interpersonal communication will also have to be constructed. As many have pointed out, in the planetary, data-linked society in which we live, everyone stands in an impersonal relation to everyone else. Each of us feels both lost and alone. My working hypothesis is that the status of subjectivity changes when a society enters the postindustrial phase, but that the concept retains a certain consistency[3]—on the condition, however, that our conception of it is constantly and relentlessly subverted, a subversion I shall simulate here by subjecting the concept to systematic and consistent analysis. In today's world, the communicational approach can provide a new and bolder way of looking at subjectivity.

Given the new position of subjectivity, what happens to the consistency that we cannot help but attribute to the so-called conscious subject? Under the title "Difference and Subjectivity," I shall be trying to pick up the threads of the philosophical quest for the subject. Can the search still be based on some ancient paradigm forgotten by the main philosophical tradition? The reason I set out to construct in tandem my solutions to the twin problems of personal identity and difference, with the more general aim of outlining the principles of a relational anthropology, will become clear.

What is principally at stake in such an anthropology is a concept of difference, difference of the sort that matters—between persons. The initial motive for my search was irritation at the clichés about alterity, or otherness, of which contemporary literature is so full. Intolerance of differences, be they of custom or culture, of age or sex (or even species), ethnic or ideological, is so painfully felt that there is no need to say much more about my ultimate motivations. Difference excludes, and it leads to violence, in speech as well as action; the real intolerance it creates is an almost insurmountable obstacle to dialogue between cultures.[4] No doubt because it is not enough just to try (as they say, time and again) to discover the other person, or listen to his or her point of view, while our concept of his or her alterity remains a *negative* one, based on its difference from our own self (this is how adults see children, men see women, normal people see the insane). Even worse, though, is the thought of the other as an outsider or a barbarian, cut off from us by an originary, innate difference.

In the present study my thesis is that the twin problems of difference and personal alterity must be linked, but in a new way. Most writings on the subject converge around a number of quite powerful positions, so that, for instance, the other is often seen to be structurally present within the self. However, most of the formulae that have been put forward drastically oversimplify and mutilate the interpersonal structure. Discovering the undoubted importance of an address to the allocutee, or conversely, of an interpellation by the *you*, a given author will attribute to these words emotive connotations that mask the logical complexity of the overall structure. For the other who is present to the self is not just the proximate other to whom I am speaking directly; it is also an absent and distant other *about* whom I speak using the term *he/she*. We can therefore assume that understanding alterity in its positive yet relative difference will involve me in articulating the three agencies—*I, you,* and *he/she*—that make up the other's personal identity, as well as my own, and without privileging any one at the expense of the others. It seemed to me that we should get rid of the false perspective that leads us to treat the Same and the Other as separate categories—but also, much less trivially, to regard the other person as an Other in relation to a Same (ourselves).

As long as the fact of difference invites us to take a monadic self as our point of departure, the other will be constituted with a meaning that refers back to that self. Once the self is seen as the basis of our relations with others, the way we designate these others (as nonbelievers, Gentiles, blacks, Jews, and so forth) ceases to be innocent. Even with the greatest humility in the world, there is one privilege we are not prepared to give up: we do not mind making sacrifices for others, as long as the sublime initiative for so doing comes from us. Whatever we might say to the contrary, the real typology of our relations with others is therefore based on the monotonous dialectic of assimilation and its mirror inversion. Either I assimilate myself to the other person by identification, or I assimilate the other person to myself by imposing my own image on him or her. But whether I move closer to the other person or further away, or remain instead neutral and indifferent, or whether I subjugate or submit to him or her, it comes down to the same thing in the end. Literally the same, for in each case the Other is no more than an image conceived, imagined, or fantasized about on the basis of my Same: understanding others allows me to take them over or exclude them, sometimes even to destroy them. In that case, understanding other human beings immediately gives me a hold over them, allowing me to judge them from the outside, to speak of them delocutively and to impute to them individual but ultimately nonpersonal predicates.

This is why I argue that the problems of difference and subjectivity need to be solved together, and that our theoretical structure for dealing with them must be completely rebuilt from the foundations up. The structure I am talking about is personal identity. Instead of seeing subjectivity as primary, or conversely as null and void, I have shifted the emphasis toward the question of the interpersonal relation. As the reader will see, this is more than just a shift of perspective: it is a complete change of strategy. If an alternative solution does emerge, it will be because all the data will have been restructured according to a perspective dictated by a different anthropological paradigm.

I spoke of an anthropology from a relational point of view. Martin Buber was the first to put forward this idea, but he did so in a form that left out logic and language: "Man exists anthropologically not in the isolation of the self, but in the totality of relations between one person and another." I shall need to modify these intuitions whenever I come across them in the course of my argument; often I shall radicalize them. Taking communication as an anthropological starting point represents a greater commitment than Buber thought. In my view, though, this is the only way to make subjectivity meaningful again in philosophical terms, while putting a new, positive valuation on differences between persons.

With that end in view I shall develop an argument that crosses over between different theoretical domains, while using complementary strategies. The reader is warned that he or she will not find ideas or analyses that can be isolated and used in other contexts; the meanings of such ideas would suffer if they were detached from the book's overall trajectory, which covers questions taken in part from the rapidly developing field of the linguistics of utterance and in part from literary criticism, but also from psychoanalysis and theology.

Why this cross-disciplinary approach? Because concepts as notorious as "person," "subjectivity," "individual," or "society" often either overflow the boundaries of the empirical sciences, or find themselves relegated to marginal status within them. This approach provides a convenient means of eliminating the most difficult questions, which can be divided quickly between several disciplines, each of which annexes a part for its own purposes. Or, even worse, when such questions cease to be discussed in a particular research field it is easy to imagine that they were only illusory in the first place.

My central conviction will be expressed through investigations of a concrete nature into silence and loneliness, desire and love, character, the individual and the person, indiscretion and secrecy, weakness and betrayal, and that strange form of self-avowal that is autobiography. But I shall also be discussing what it is to have one's own face and voice, and what speaking means for the ego—not only speaking to other people but (a point that has recently been reduced to a trivial commonplace) communicating with them in their differential and positive status as persons. As the situations I shall analyze correspond to expressions in the language in which communication takes place, it goes without saying that my concrete investigations will be conducted in that language.

On this point I shall not follow Bertrand Russell. He declared that dependence on natural language was one of the main obstacles to progress in philosophy. On the contrary, the very possibility of philosophy appears to depend on a positive attitude toward natural language. Whereas science puts much of its effort into constructing an autonomous language with operative-type intelligibility (with meanings produced solely by the language's mode of operation), philosophy's energy is expended in a different direction. It remains rooted in the resources of everyday language, which is the universal metalanguage. The aim of philosophers is to articulate an interpretation of their experience as a whole. They attempt to bring about a process of semantic extension within various domains of ordinary discourse. Their own difficulty is how to put forward a coherent and overdetermined interpretation of experience using a set of interdependent metaconcepts. Philosophies that strive to systematize are always categorical, that is they tend to present a single interpretation with only a limited range of variants.

I have explained elsewhere why the philosopher's strongest guarantee lies in respecting the authentic, pragmatic rules any language of communication must have.[5] All the concrete investigations that will be put forward here follow from my logical work on dialogue and its transcendental counterpart, the interlocutionary relation.[6] In that earlier work I outlined a relational conception of knowledge and communication. The present book represents a thematic interlude during which I shall aim to set that conception on secure foundations.

The reason I look at existential phenomenology in terms of a comparison with the type of philosophical logic done in the English-speaking world will soon become clear. I shall be using it negatively, to demonstrate that the relation I am pursuing (and which philosophical logic was doubtless unable to construct properly due to its egological premises) is irreducible to particular properties. My aim is to provide a genuinely logical justification for the interlocutive relation, by way of transcendental and descriptive arguments. However, the debt I owe to Anglo-Saxon philosophical analysis is too great for me to intimate any ingratitude. Even if its limitations are now clearer to us today, it has made no small contribution, through some undeniable results of its own, to illuminating those very limitations. This is an illumination that only someone who has pursued its disciplines for a time can fully appreciate.

Logicians are well aware of the impossibility of translating relations into properties. Whatever Leibniz may have thought, if a man living in Europe has a wife living in the Indies who dies unbeknown to him, the change undergone by the man at the moment of her death is not intrinsic but relational.[7] In this case, the immediacy of the description is supported by the irreducibility of the logical point of view; both give the relational aspect, and the interlocutive relation in particular, its due weight and primacy. They make it a good candidate to take on a foundational function.

This is a crucial point, and one which cannot be overemphasized. For this reason my aim is not really to undermine the reader's confidence in the classical way of conceiving of the ego, or to track down the Cartesian heritage of the Cogito. On the contrary, I am trying to arrive at a positive reevaluation of those elements of both traditions that can be preserved. But this is where something new comes in: the attempt to construct a philosophy of the person based on the concrete experience of standing in a relationship to others, a relationship maintained by communication—that is, a philosophy conceived from a directly relational point of view. This fresh approach should allow the fragmentation inherent in ordinary ways of thinking to be overcome, leading in turn to an extraordinary division of human experience and thus to a new human truth.

Only a short time ago subjectivity oscillated between an excessively lofty and an excessively lowly status, between exclusion and exaggeration. Having often been left out of any account by post-Saussurian linguistics, the concept of the subject was ruled out altogether by the structuralist anthropology that followed and modeled itself on Saussure. During the same period, in legitimate protest, Husserlian phenomenology tried continually to bring the ego back in, if not as a foundational absolute, then at least, with some provisos and limitations, as an autonomous force of reflection and evaluation, one hidden behind all the signs of culture. It is significant that subjectivity as act and as presence is found today, thanks to Roman Jakobson and Emile Benveniste, among the metatheoretical premises of the French school of utterance-linguistics.[8]

There is something worrying about an oscillation of such amplitude. It points to an urgent need to transform the problem of the subject, a philosophical undertaking not without its importance for the human sciences. People have realized that however crucial relations of production or the determinants of the unconscious might be, they do not dispose of the reality of the person as a subjective speaking entity.

The reduction of the person to subjectivity, and of subjectivity in turn to consciousness, was the central lesson of idealism. The discourse of the "metaphysics of subjectivity," which today has been thoroughly discredited, was one of its triumphs. Merleau-Ponty suggested resorting to the idea of *institution* as a remedy against such a discourse. The theoretical advantage seems obvious: beyond the fact that an "instituting" subject will be able to coexist with another person without reducing that person to a negative image of itself, the concept of institution guarantees that they both belong to the same common world. It builds a kind of hinge between them. As a positive model for action, institution creates an organized system of original ways for us to satisfy our most common needs. It works in the kitchen to help us satisfy our food needs and in marriage in the service of our sex drive; it encourages brutality in warfare; and, above all, it works within language to promote communication.

Now one aspect of the "linguistic turn" taken since the beginning of the century by Anglo-American philosophers, whether in Oxford or Cambridge, in Princeton, Harvard, or Stanford, has been to turn the problem on its head and to put forward a new, quite radical remedy from within the institution of language. Some people believe that this movement is now running out of steam. On the contrary, it is only after having given it the considerable credit due it that one can explain why it now needs to be given a slight change of direction, with language being taken in the sense of discourse, and discourse in the sense of communication.

Searching Descartes' *je pense, donc je suis* for anything at all that might be the object of rigorous certainty, Nietzsche concluded: at the very most, the fact that I am speaking. It is tempting to add: and not even that. There is nothing to prove that I am the originator or even the effective producer of the words I speak. The speech of madness, and the banality of much everyday language, more often tend to suggest the opposite. "And what can we say about the self (*le moi*)? It has become a fable, a fiction, a play on words:* it has stopped thinking, feeling, willing, altogether."

Hyperbolic criticism is always provocative. It cannot take away the fact that it is hard to eliminate subjectivity from the ways we think. Who can restore us to the relationship with being that we enjoyed before the introduction of self-consciousness? The myth of pure subjectivity is, admittedly, like all philosophical myths, substantially linguistic in origin. Not in the Wittgensteinian sense of deriving from an illusory (or metaphysical) use of the words of everyday language, but in the sense that the individual self and its qualities are only correlates of a certain discursive practice, a past act of self-avowal. I therefore make the following hypothesis: what if subjectivity, the individual, permanent self, with its determinations and their mode of belonging, were no more than a translation of some leftover ideological representation? The self would then correspond simply to the demands or the pragmatic distortions[9] of a very particular form of discourse, one that claims to speak about the subject and produce the truth about the speaker. It would then be the result of a curiously stable combination of grammatical illusion, category mistake, and manipulation of the mechanisms of utterance.

This would show that the most ordinary discourse about the self sometimes emanates from pragmatically curtailed speech; at which point it confirms, rather than invalidates, the essentially relational condition of the person. As for proving this directly, I shall ask how far an analysis of utterance—that is, the declaration by which the speaking subject makes a statement meant to be understood by a listener—can provide information on

---

*As well as meaning "self," "ego," *moi* in French is the emphatic form of the first person singular personal pronoun, "me."

the conditions of personal identity and therefore on the consistency of subjective experience. For in my view it is the *pragmatics* of discourse, its mode of operation, rather than a system of representations dealing with the self, that makes the decisive contribution to determining, in turn, the fundamental characteristics of subjectivity. From this point of view the history of subjectivity could be rewritten as the history of various discourses about the self. A full treatment of this idea would be impossible within the scope of the present book. It would involve asking what confessional discourse, what iterative mechanism, makes it possible for us to invest the ego with possession of its qualities, with responsibility for its actions and the consistency of its ideas, its desires, and even its amorous intentions. And also asking which discourses have allowed us so insistently to confuse subjectivity with character, individuality, and the type of figure that appears in morality tales, thereby jeopardizing contemporary research seeking a true system of criteria for defining the person.

The question of the extent to which a balanced analysis of utterance, in the widest application of the concept, now allows us to confirm that subjectivity is real, is one I would like to delay answering for a while. By reflecting on the conditions under which utterance is possible in the communicational situation, I shall try to show both that subjectivity is a strongly derivative idea and that it is far from lacking consistency: there certainly exists on the one hand an activity of personal identification—the subject (*subjectum*) is that which is found to be identical to itself in different circumstances—and, on the other hand, something like a subjective effect. By preserving these, and articulating them in an innovative manner, we may be able to make a dispassionate assessment of the problem of the person.

The time has come for me to stand by certain problematic commitments I made in *Dialogiques I*. This book, by creating its own problems, pointed the way toward the research that has kept me busy over the past two years. I wanted to extend the things I had already shown about the reference or object of discourse to cover the discursive subject. How does philosophy's discovery of communication change our conception of the speaking subject? That is the precise technical subject of the present work. Apart from any moralistic intention, this is what underlies my main argument.

The establishment of the subject, a question raised throughout the tradition of the Cartesian Cogito, should be set at or just before the moment when language appears, and not somewhere outside it. It is not enough simply to juxtapose a vague phenomenology of speech with a rigorous linguistic description of the language system; a minimum requirement is to demonstrate the establishment of the subject in the act by which the virtual system of language becomes the present event of discourse. But this is a deceptive minimum, for the act in question is really an interaction. As we shall see, *I* is not established contemporaneously with the expression "I," despite what linguists often like to suggest. A speaker is only established as a subject in an originary relation with an interlocutor, and not by opposition to him or her. The formation of this relationship is primary in relation both to him or herself and to "his or her" utterance. Which is to say that the establishment of *I* is only announced and truly achieved with the assistance of a highly complex process of structural integration that needs to be described. This is where theories of a new type start to make their appearance.

As soon as the relation is perceived the way it really is, which is the way a logician sees it, the novelty of this idea becomes clear. People will probably not like it, for the simple reason that a new idea is unlike anything else. We are not used to understanding, observing, and describing relational phenomena in any other language than that of the individual and his or her properties and roles. The whole description has to be rebuilt; in particular, it can no longer be phenomenological, for there is no question now of relocating phenomena on the famous axis of intentionality. Nor can it be positivistic.

My overall strategy is simple: above all, I want to detach the problem of subjectivity from self-consciousness, so as to link it to the more fundamental problem of the person; this problem in turn can be examined through a communicational approach. Utterers are subjects to the extent that speaking consists for them in identifying themselves during and through the different communicational situations in which they are participants. This strategy contains a method: stating the problem of the person in terms of another problem, that of personal identity (a subject of wide debate in English-language philosophy today), in line with the principle "no entity without identity." My own choice has been to look at this problem in terms of the personal agents of verbal communication.

As this book progresses it will become clear that my approach runs parallel with, and to some extent corroborates, certain quite recent analyses that have vied with each other to dispossess the ego of its will to mastery, its autonomy, and ultimately any importance it may ever have had. Once we agree to transform the concept of communication by introducing an interlocutive relation, my own disinvestiture of the subject will doubtless be different from the various types carried out by Freud, Marx, and Nietzsche. But there is one claim I am not afraid to make: this disinvestiture represents the most radical attack possible on philosophies of the Cogito. Even when I try to give its due weight to a person's undeniable ability as a user of discourse to set him or herself up as a speaking subject, I shall be forced to relativize this ability in terms of certain dialogic conditions of discourse, and likewise to call radically into question the status of the ego within utterance.

As the proposed solution to the problem of personal identity was part of an entirely new philosophy of dialogue and the interlocutive relation, it had to be constructed from scratch. I decided to follow the classical golden rule of never doing more critical deconstruction than is required by the job in hand and by the risks of the construction process. In the plan of the book there is an evident alternation between chapters that elaborate the argument (1, 3, and 5) and critical chapters that bring out their negative implications for certain traditional positions (2 and 4). The final chapter (6) is then able to establish how the being of subjectivity might be articulated in its positive difference, according to the three categories required by a new philosophy of the person.

Paris
Spring 1982

Introduction: A Communicational Approach to the Person

Can we not envisage a philosophy
diametrically opposed to solipsism?
—WITTGENSTEIN

THERE IS at least one clear difference between traditional philosophy and philosophy of a type more relevant to our age. On the one hand lies the old conjecture that everything can be looked at from a purely subjective (or, conversely, a purely dogmatic) point of view; on the other, the more and more widely held (but as yet little tested) belief that the originary and authentic condition of our understanding is intersubjective communication—and that all the most basic questions will therefore have to be examined again from this new angle. The important new role now being given to subjectivity, be it the subjectivity of a person carrying on an everyday conversation or that of an expert engaging in metatheoretical debate, is taking the concept into a completely new phase of its history. We now see subjectivity essentially in terms of the speaking person (or better: the person capable of discourse), operating in a situation that we today regard as exemplary—that of verbal communication.

As soon as we begin to think about it, subjectivity seems deeply bound up with linguistic communication. It is as if language had solved in one stroke the twin problems of communication and subjectivity. Can we not then say,

I

suggests Emile Benveniste, that by instituting a category of mobile signs and a large and specific formal apparatus of "utterances," language "allows each individual to declare him or herself as subject"?

In one area Benveniste is doubtless correct. Language seems to have solved at least three problems left open by simple perception: the universality of statements, communication, and subjectivity. Leaving aside the first, and without claiming to exhaust the scope of the other two, let me now list the most clearly evident ways in which subjectivity is present within linguistic communication.

Benveniste, and many others after him, stressed the need to distinguish between what is said—the *statement* (*l'énoncé*)—and the speaker's act of presence within what is said—the act of *utterance* (*l'énonciation*). According to this view any discursive sequence bears the mark of its utterer, but in different ways and to varying degrees; all statements are to some extent marked subjectively. This marking may occur explicitly, through the direct intervention of the signifier *I* or its variants, or it may occur implicitly, in subjective formulations that are not acknowledged as such. A systematic study could be made of all the places, or instances, within language where the speaking subject—considered, most important, in a general way as the subject of the speech process—is present. Such instances may be found in expressions of affectivity (something is poignant, or funny), evaluation (I hate it), praise (it is magnificent, useful), interpretation (she is an intellectual), or modality (I feel that). Subjectivity is certainly not ruled out by the Gorgon's gaze of linguistics.

No less topical is the logician's point of view, in many respects complementary to the linguist's. When logicians look at types of statements that appear to have cognitive content alone, they will point out that these too are subjective in a number of different ways. One type of subjectivity is visible in the indicative mode of a sentence such as "the earth revolves," which posits a relationship between what is said and reality; another in the subjective mode ("he doubts whether he will come"), in which what is said is linked to the state of mind of the speaker; still others may be seen in the interrogative and imperative modes. Different, and no doubt less familiar, lines of enquiry involve the logician in determining how subjectivity is present in those sui generis forms of predication that we might call *circumstantial*, in such sentences as "he (the person of whom I am speaking) is bald," or "it is raining" (at the place and time when I am speaking). These statements are *occasional* because it is impossible to determine the referent, and therefore to attribute the predicate, independently of the circumstances of utterance. It is a short step from here to suggest that as the act of utterance is caused by the utterer, he or she can therefore be used to define the parameters of the spatiotemporal indices.[1] We should note that for the logician the occasional statement "it is raining" is still either true or false: it is an assertion, just like "sin $\pi/2 = 1$," though it has no permanent truth value.

Nor is that all. Any statement which refers to propositional attitudes such as "believing," "knowing," or "doubting" also shows signs of subjectivity. We can take our analysis further by distinguishing between the statement "A believes that p" (which, although it describes someone else's subjectivity as a fact, can also be given a truth value by the provision of a suitable referent); and "I believe that p," in which a propositional attitude is expressed in the first person of the present tense. This implies a certain commitment to accept the logical consequences of the speaker's present belief, but only insofar as the speaker is aware of them.

This last type of statement also makes a certain claim to empirical truth. However, it does not rule out the possibility of error, unlike other statements which bring out the presence of subjectivity in still different ways and which leave no room for doubt. Such is the case with "I have a toothache," as Wittgenstein realized. He was able to dispose of this category of statements once and for all as evidence for the subjectivist cause.

That, in highly schematic form, is the present state of the debate. The reader will have realized that not all of the so-called philosophies of subjectivity look to the same mode of inscribing the subject within language. Some in particular have chosen to examine only statements with an apparent cognitive content, showing that every possible assertion is bound up with subjectivity. Descartes' theories provide a marvelous illustration of this approach; for him there is always a potential gap between a state of affairs and its truth, a space in which doubt can lodge. But the Cartesian model of evident truth depends upon isolating with complete certainty a propositional attitude, namely, "I think." In this respect Kant, by reaffirming the true modal status of the Cogito ("I think that . . ."), can be seen to have moved the analysis a decisive step forward: by making the original synthetic unity of apperception the condition of all possible experience, he put forward a paradigm, a theory of the transcendental field in which subjectivity has the *ultimate* founding authority and in which it is constituted by the *ego*. Its presence is required, as it stands as a necessary precondition for any possible knowledge of the object.

What happens if we now carry this transcendental problematic across into the logico-linguistic domain? The foundational function of subjectivity lies in its ability to act as an agency of utterance, rather than in that sense we all have of being ourselves. In this light, speaking means telling someone

3

what we mean, and language is seen as the instrument of the process. The speaking subject would then be someone seeking to deliver a message who selects a particular lexical item or syntactic structure from his or her store of linguistic aptitudes, with no constraint other than what he or she wishes to say and the meaning he or she wishes it to have. According to this widely invoked orthodoxy, the subject of the utterance supposedly

1. says what is said
2. is such that what is said can be directly attributed to the ego's intention to mean
3. knows everything it says (at which point it would also be saying what it means).

There is no need to think very hard to see that these three assumptions combine to form a highly improbable doctrine, according to which the subject of the utterance is seen as the master of meaning and pertinence. If the ego speaks, according to this view, it does so quite simply in order to say what it has to say. It knows what it wants to say, while the listener does not. It is not difficult to guess what the identity of the subject amounts to in the light of these three assumptions: it is recognized as the source of all its utterances, the sovereign authority over its own speech.

We might doubt whether experience would confirm these three simplistic assumptions. My aim in this book is to call the first two into question from several different angles, to see what consequences such an enquiry has for the idea of subjectivity. I shall also mention the third: as we will see, it involves the whole problem of the unconscious.[2]

At the other extreme, it might on the contrary be thought that any equation of subjectivity with the discourse-producing agency is radically unthinkable. But if this is so, and if this agency is not to be rooted in some substantial or sense-giving ego, the extreme relativity of the *empirical* conditions that influence and determine the situation of utterance would seem to make the search quite hopeless. For Bronisläw Malinowski the "situational context" includes all of the circumstances affecting the act of utterance: not only who is speaking but also, in ever-widening circles, the whole historical and sociocultural conditioning of the speakers.[3]

In fact, this dissolution of the problem into empiricism is overly hasty. Any productive line of critical enquiry must impose limits on dogmatism (that goes without saying) and, as well, on the discovery of types of conditioning that incline us toward pessimism. Are there not certain conditions of *communicability in general* which stand above the infinite diversity of utterances? Having seen the birth over the past twenty years or so of a pragmatic approach in linguistic science, we know very well that such conditions do exist and that their generality (not to say their necessity) provides ample scope for a new type of philosophical enquiry.[4] According to the following hypothesis, which has implications in turn for the speaking subject, it might well be possible to define subjectivity as either competence in or mastery of the conditions of communicability, when we ask under what conditions communication through language is generally possible. There is a good chance that a subject of this type, able to enter a communicational universe as a possible interlocutor, will turn out to be the ego for which people have been looking. But the concept will have been profoundly transformed: the ego now has the status of a person. We are beginning at least to suspect two things:

1. that the discourse-producing agency cannot simply be naively identified with the speaking subject;

2. that the question of the personal self is no longer to be confused with the classical problem of subjectivity, precisely because it needs to be approached from a communicational angle. In its standard form the old notion of subjectivity involved a confusion between the notions of self, individual, and person, which are undoubtedly all different entities.

A hypothesis along these lines was to be expected: if there is no ready-constituted or originarily constituting subject, there might, as we have said, still be a process by which the speaking subject is instituted as an agent of communication. When he or she uses discourse to communicate things about the world and human experience, such a subject is certainly not expressing his or her inner being. Yet he or she continually defines him or herself as an agent of communication, and thereby realizes him or herself: he or she achieves recognition of his or her anonymous status as a human being because he or she occupies a certain ideal speaker-listener position, but also because he or she possesses the personal and nominal status of empirical subjectivity by virtue of having a certain place within the socially instituted communication system.

The foregoing hypothesis coincides with an insistence in the recent philosophical literature on discussing the criteria of *personal* identification, rather than those applying to the identity of the character, the individual, or the subjective self. By making this distinction philosophers aim to cast a new light on human action in a communicational context; here again, therefore, the concept of the person is emerging as dominant in present-day philosophical enquiry.

Let us now return to contemporary work in linguistics: what does it say about the reality of the person as a subjective, speaking entity? Both because of the desire for objective precision and as a result of some debatable epistemological decisions, this question has become rather crucial: where does the subjective element fit in when one tries to define the discourse-producing agency as accurately as possible? Benveniste's reading of subjectivity in language, together with the work of French utterance-linguists,[5] still has considerable truth and relevance. For many thinkers these are now seminal texts, defining the avenue down which future investigations must begin their travels.

It must however remain a broad avenue and not become just another rut in which philosophy can get stuck. The claim that utterance—in the precise sense of the activation and application of the linguistic system by a deliberate act of the speaker—installs subjectivity within discourse is clumsy and, in the final analysis, inaccurate. It needs to be qualified and given nuance.

For the language user does not immediately establish his or her subjective reality simply by saying *I*. The meaning of *I* is not created at the moment when the speaker appropriates the first-person singular pronoun to designate him or herself, and thereby bear witness to his or her presence. To believe otherwise would be to forget that the speaker's activation of language conventionally occurs within a dialogue. In other words, at the moment when language's potential for conversion into discourse is realized in the act of utterance, what is inserted into the statement is not the speaker alone but the speakers, plural. Or better: what is created is the completely inescapable interlocutive relationship which links them together and constitutes them as co-utterers. It is the task of my analysis to prove that this is so. I shall have to begin by regarding the notion of utterance as a concrete product of verbal interaction rather than as the "activation of language by an individual act of language-use."[6] It is beginning to appear quite strongly that the discourse-producing agency can no longer be straightforwardly identified with the speaking subject. I propose to show that it is in fact to be found in the interlocutive relationship, the origin of effective verbal interaction in linguistic communication.

What does this mean for subjectivity? Benveniste had of course already said that as soon as the subject speaks, it necessarily implants in its discourse a *you* capable of speaking in its turn.[7] But, beyond the fact that this type of remark tells us nothing about the deeper semantic significance of what is said, simply to suggest that utterances have a "dialogue structure" is insufficient. What is needed are effective definitions of the different categories of linguistic communication,[8] from which to draw conclusions about the extent to which a speaking ego really exists. As soon as we begin to lay bare its relational and interactional nature, the intersubjective act that is the founding source of discourse shows itself to be much more complex than it seemed at first.

According to my theory, the speaker no longer stands at the center of the utterance process, manipulating the linguistic apparatus in the service (or to the advantage) of his or her speech. The typical situation of utterance is no longer egocentric, even though the function of the speaker as referential center might be marked by deictic terms such as *I, this, now*, etc. If the role of speaker passes from one participant to another in the course of a conversation, taking with it the center of the deictic system, is this not in reality a marginal shift? For a statement to be acceptable—correctly formed according to the rules of utterance formation—it must be spoken in a common interlocutory context. It therefore follows that:

1. Utterance is not simply (as is usually assumed) "the linguistic activity performed by the speaker at the moment of speaking."[9] It is just as much the activity performed by the person who listens, to say nothing of that other basic fact of verbal communication, that the speaker can if he or she wishes listen to what he or she is saying with the ears of the other person. In short, utterance is then a joint discourse-creating activity in which speaker and listener are the terms of a real-time relationship.

2. This joint act of discourse creation in turn implies a *pooling* of the meaning of statements, which is essential even to establish a disagreement during a conversation or an argument. The present term *discourse* is particularly appropriate for referring to real language-use activity. It corresponds to the figurative sense of the Vulgar Latin *discurrere*, "to run about"; discourse implies following a path through an interlocutive situation. If we now add a logico-argumentative dimension to this path, we can see how the process of discourse creation necessarily involves a dialogic framework. The very first sense given by the *Littré* dictionary for *discourse* is "discussion," "conversation." This meaning is already present in the Latin *sermo* (*serere*, to plait) as well as in the Hebrew *patal*, which also means to plait or weave and is the root of the name Nephtali, given by Rachel to her servant-girl's son: my struggle, my plea, my entangled conflict.

3. Though they remain distinct, speaker and listener are virtually in the same spatiotemporal situation. Linguistic time is created within the act of discourse-making proffered by *I*, but the temporality which governs the discourse must at the very least be acceptable to the interlocutor. Equally, the relative proximity of the object designated by *this* or *that* cannot be assessed in relation to the speaker alone: the object must belong, at least potentially, to a sphere of common interest. Thus even those less frequent uses that indicate a dissociation between the relative distances from the speaker and from the listener introduce a differential meaning, which can only be interpreted by reference to a common framework.[10]

Unlike, for instance, evaluatives or modalizers, which differentially reveal

7

certain peculiarities of the cultural or ideological competence of the speaker, the use of deictics depends on a consensus operating in a given interlocutive situation. Far from each being able to speak only in his or her own present, the interlocutors are pragmatically obliged to adopt a common temporal framework, a multipersonal time scale that in a sense joins them together in the same speech act. My today only becomes your today if you can link it with your own time scale by yourself becoming a speaker. As Wittgenstein pointed out, asking ourselves how we learned a particular word allows us to dispose of a number of wrong ideas. We need only look at what happens with children: we first have to get them to agree with us on the meaning of "to-day." Otherwise, "my" today is incomprehensible to them; indeed, it only remains "mine" so long as they do not understand it. It can be shown in the same way that interlocutors are co-uttering agencies by virtue of the fact that they share a certain number of presuppositions that place them, at least partially, within the same semantic frame of reference.[11]

The foregoing observations confirm a well-known result in genetic psychology, that a person's perceptual system depends directly on his or her ability to understand space and time. The acquisition of pronouns, and particularly of the first-person pronoun, comes after mastery of the spatiotemporal framework, which in turn depends on the interlocutive relation. Most descriptions agree on this point, including those of Henri Wallon and Jean Piaget.

It is beginning to be clear why Benveniste's account very much overstates the case. It has the virtue of bringing *utterance*[12] and the subject to the forefront of a linguistic approach (post-Saussurian structuralism) that was initially resolutely hostile to the notion of utterance. But there is something badly wrong with it; the essential point which has been missed is that the speaker does not in fact have the power to appropriate language for his or her own use. Our linguist sometimes writes about subjectivity in the same way that Hobbes (*Leviathan*, chap. 16) did about the person: "A person is someone whose words are considered either as *belonging* to him or as representing the words or actions of another, or some other reality to which they are attributed by a true or fictitious attribution."

In fact, the act of saying is indeed present in what is said, but the trace of that act does not refer back exclusively to a speech-originating ego, as the proprietor of its own message. The message does assign alternating positions to the interlocutors but always within an interlocutive relation (and, as such, a verbal interaction) that involves a cooperative semantic transaction. Each of these points will have to be established and developed.

For the moment, suffice it to say that this type of intersubjectivity can be assumed to be poles apart from the notion of a transcendental intersubjectivity given currency by phenomenology. We shall have to look for a rigorous foundation for the paradox that whereas the pronoun *I* might well refer to the person who *speaks*, it no longer belongs to the one who *says*. It is doubtless I—the speaker—who speaks. But I am not, correctly speaking, the utterer: it is *we* who say. Neither is it possible to elude the primacy of the interlocutive relation merely by pointing out that encoding operations are partially determined by the *image* the speaker has of the listener. Whatever marginal asymmetry there may be between them, the *presence* of the listener is crucial. It is inscribed not only by the use of "appellatives" or "vocatives," such as "Uncle Paul" or "Mr. President," which refer explicitly to the social relationship between the performers of the utterance, but also by the use of general terms whose lexical meaning is assumed to be shared, as well as in particular terms referring to individuals assumed to be known or familiar. In every case the listener's presence is productive. It can be seen in the choice of the argumentative apparatus employed and ultimately in the whole range of linguistic material selected with a view to mutual understanding. From the language spoken to specific language acts and the determinants of utterances, everything seems to vary according to the relations between *I* and *you*.

The conceptual implications of this simple hypothesis, which needs further refinement, are considerable. What happens to the philosophical status of the person if we replace the individual's *cogito* with the proposition "I speak, but we say"? The assertion "I do not exist" was held to be refuted by the thought or the act of discourse that it performed. I should add that the same is true of the assertion "you do not exist," unless we consider our communication act to have failed—a point to which I shall return later. At the very least, we are led to a different view of the discourse-producing agency, taking account of the fact that speaker and spoken-to are from the first only defined as such in relation to each other. We then have to revise the agreed philosophical sense of the common expression "I mean" (*je veux dire, Ich meine*). Accuracy obliges us to do away with the illusory hegemony of the subject, and to strip it of any monologic privilege over the other agencies of discourse.[13] It is now evident that the ego's philosophical position can no longer be taken for granted. The nonautonomy of discourse is a condition of communication.

Moreover, it is not true that "language alone founds in its own reality, which is the reality of being, the concept of the ego." However close may be the link between the philosophical experience of subjectivity and the forms of language that determine subjectivity, it is not entirely reducible to these

9

forms as a pure linguistic category. Even if each speaker only establishes his or her personal presence when he or she begins to speak, subjectivity, however we choose to conceive of it, remains an extralinguistic presupposition of the speaking act. The pronoun *I* is no more able to free us from this realization than the demonstrative *this* is able to abolish the world to which it points. If empty signs such as *I* and *this*, available in language, are to be filled and given referential value in the institution of discourse, then we must assume a reality outside language; the world made manifest, the speaking subject establishing its presence. This type of search for presuppositions opens up a new line of enquiry to those who wish to compensate for the excesses of the "linguistic turn" in Anglo-American philosophy. The irony is that it should be the pragmatic approach, in the direct line of certain investigations into language, that provides the means of doing so. This is the point of departure for my main argument.

By *pragmatics* I mean everything that involves the relationship between discourse and the most general circumstances affecting the production of a communicable meaning. In my view, it is by taking to its logical conclusion the pragmatic approach to language phenomena[14] in function of the *primum relationis* in the theory of language use, that we are led to make the ego the seat of communicative competence and of the responsibility for exercising it. In this way subjectivity once again acquires solidity and reality; at the same time, however, it now depends on the relational condition that is constitutive of the personal self.

The proponents of discourse linguistics are eager to reintroduce the subject and the communicational situation into their work, as both had been largely excluded in the name of the immanence postulate. In my view, however, this double reintroduction cannot be brought about unless both the idea of utterance and the basic conception of subjectivity in language are modified first.

I shall not be proposing a restrictive conception of utterance. For it seems to me that to define it as the language activity performed by the person who speaks is to impose a considerable distortion on our study of the process of discourse creation. This is where the point of view of philosophers of language diverges from that of linguists. The latter can envisage limiting their investigations to the identification of units that function as indices of the speaking subject's inscription in the statement; they can deliberately restrict their enquiry to describing the linguistic procedures (e.g., shifters, modalizers, evaluative terms) by means of which the speaker imposes her mark on the statement, inscribes her presence in the message, and situates herself in relation to it. This is particularly true as it is easier to question a speaker about her intentions than it is to link her statements with the relation in which the interlocutors stand to each other. Do not all theoreticians have a tendency to limit their theories to the realm of what they know how to do? [15]

But the perspective of philosophers is different. Their aim is to establish a consensus on the form to be given to the problem of subjectivity as it really appears in discourse. In that case they cannot simply search for the dominant parameter under the pretext of delineating the most visible aspects of the problem, thereby giving up any hope of grasping the communicational circuit as a whole. On the contrary, their task is to reveal the preconceptions underlying the current description of utterance, in relation to what they believe to be the mode of existence and the consistency of subjectivity. Philosophers no longer have any reason to privilege the most obvious types of meaning or to promote them to the rank of fundamental parameters in relation to which their account of usage might be organized. That is why, convinced by the convergence of at least three approaches (logical, descriptive, and transcendental) to the important and irreducible interlocutive relation, I am in favor of an extended linguistics of utterance. Such a linguistics can include features reflecting the relationship the speaker entertains with the listener, as well as the relations that link a given statement to the communicational framework. These, too, are parts of the interlocutive situation—that is, of the circumstances governing the process of discourse initiation.

This choice of strategy should help to explain a new intelligibility being forged unwittingly in the human sciences, despite the fact that certain of their presuppositions remain rooted in a metaphysics of subjectivity. But giving up the central role of the speaker, with his or her intentions and expectations, clearly does not make the question of subjectivity in language any simpler. On the other hand, it does allow a more comprehensive statement of the problem. Suddenly *I* is not, in itself, a person; in other words, no personal positional value in discourse, be it *I, you,* or *he/she* is sufficient to complete the reference to the person. The *I* is not something substantial or structural. If it manifests itself, it does so not by itself but relationally and in dynamic interaction; action and speech intersect. We should now be able to bring these diffuse themes, which used to belong firmly in the moralist's or the anthropologist's domain, straight back into the field of primary philosophy. It is remarkable, the pragmatic linguist will observe, how the apparently highly personal pronoun *I* is in reality neither just an abbreviated way of speaking of the self—a substitute for the proper noun—nor the means by which the speaker seizes the apparatus of language for his or her own advantage at the moment of discourse initiation. It is remarkable that this pronoun obliges the speaker to designate him or herself with the same word that the interlocutor uses, while he or she will be addressed as a *you*, or potentially de-locuted (and addressable) as a *he*.

Let us therefore be clear about the marks of utterance found in statements. The *I* and the *you*, which are revealed retroactively in discourse, figure as two alternating agencies within the allocutionary process. In this way, the ego ceases to be a fixed point; the *I* is something we pick up with the role of speaker. For me to be excluded from the interlocutory relationship is sufficient to make me a *him*. But I have to be included in it in order to be included in the *we* of interdiscursivity, where the *I* and the *you* form a constitutive alliance. As this *we* is the only relatively stable point in the logical space of interlocution—the only invariant—in relation to it *I* and *you* are nothing more than provisional and differential nodes of enunciation.

It is certainly clear now that using "I" is from the first a relational and differential exercise. Who am I for you who are speaking to me? Who am I for him, he who is speaking to you? The *I* only discovers itself in the process of allocution toward a *you* and in its delocution by others. Overall, the relationship with the other precedes the self's experience of itself. This "personal" pronoun marks as present within the discourse one of the agents of communication, rather than the subject of the saying process. As such, the pronoun really occupies the threefold position of representing the one who speaks, the one who is spoken to, and the one who is spoken of. While the object of discourse, the referent, is constituted cooperatively by progressive accretion of the messages exchanged, what about its true subject? My answer is that the relational agency is the effective discourse producer; I shall have to establish and justify my conclusion—that this agency is only accessible a posteriori—from the reflexivity of discourse. It results from the reciprocal process by which each partner in the joint task of meaning-creation is constituted.

When a proposition, *p*, is uttered about the world, each partner undoubtedly performs an action, which is to utter *p* with the help of, and in relation to, the other. The whole question is, how can this cooperative semantic transaction make it possible for us to respect the positive difference between our own person and the person of the other, while at the same time maintaining a marginal asymmetry between the protagonists in the interlocutive relationship? This is where the central theme of difference comes in; it is a theme to which I shall give the importance it really deserves.

Mine will therefore be a communicational approach to the person. But what type of communication are we discussing? The reader will have gathered that I want to renew this concept, too, essentially in order to give the interlocutive relation its rightful place and to take into account the highly significant fact that there is bilateral participation by the agents in a single mediation process. The other is not the target of communication; he or she is, like me, a fundamental part of it.

The interlocutive relation and its dynamic effects were the crucial element missing from classical communication theory. That is hardly surprising, as the standard schema goes back to information theory as developed by Claude Shannon and Warren Weaver, which was constructed for telecommunications engineers, by telecommunications engineers.[16] Their terminology was later adopted by psychologists and linguists. Those among them who—like John Lyons[17]—pointed out some of the weaknesses of the theory missed the objection of principle: communication is not just about sending information or transmitting a message; it is also, precisely because it involves an interlocutive relation, about pooling as far as possible the meaning and the reference of one's discourse.

I aim to prepare the ground in a positive way for a later contribution to the metatheory of the communication sciences. I base this approach on an essentially *critical* conviction. Assuming that a transcendental philosophy is still the most likely to give a satisfactory account of the person, it must renew its critical position as a matter of urgency by assimilating external reality as a determinant of communication. One thing is certain: the classical ego can no longer be allowed to take over the central transcendental role. But a purely linguistic theory of the formal aspects of the problem is not acceptable either.

It is already possible to draw up the program for a transcendental philosophy of the person, to which it is my intention to contribute here. Its aim will be to construct the concept of person by articulating two types of relations: between human beings and things as referents, much as in the concept of the subject as seen until recently; and also between one human being and another, in the interlocutive relation. So significant is the pragmatic approach for philosophers that it will even lead them to what has for so long been the private territory of semantics—the problem of reference. In *Dialogiques i* I was able to show that reference as it is usually understood (particularly in the case of singular terms) can be regarded as a reductive abstraction of an interdiscursive act of reference performed within a community of speakers, without undermining the conventions that subsequently neutralize the pragmatic dimension to bring it within the bounds of an established scientific theory. Since then, I have gone deeper into the philosophical inspiration of a theory of language based on the paradigm of communicability, carrying over onto the transcendental plane the idea that the relation between language and the world is mediated from the first by interlocutors who have interacting needs and projects. I shall continue to show the reasonableness of this program in much the same way we can demonstrate movement—by walking.

13

1 Num Quid et Tu?

The I, the I, that is the deep mystery
—WITTGENSTEIN
Blue and Brown Books

THE HUMAN sciences have ascribed the disruption of the person to the ill effects of a mis-integration, or even disintegration, of the subject. A number of studies have linked these effects to disturbances in the communicational schema, and especially to systematic distortions of it. Accounts of this type have prepared the way for a long overdue, genuinely conceptual investigation of personal identity. They also allow us to characterize its opposite—the illusory subject.

Methodology

The problem of method is important for our present purpose, as well as for the foundation of the human sciences. What difference does the discovery of communication make to our conception of the subject? What type of underlying consistency should we try to maintain within the dispersal that communication brings about? The problem is how to institute a speaking subject that is now conceived of as an agent of interactive communication, and what sort of reality can be granted to subjectivity within a problematic of communicability. To put the question another way: what happens to the concept of the self as a speaking individual, if it can only be grasped differentially in the context of the interlocutive relation, to the vicissitudes of which it remains exposed? This is not a psychosociological question. I am not asking how individuals are produced socially as subjective entities. I am attempting to base my conception of the person on the category of the relation, thereby turning upside down the order in which the question is usually approached.

The Disgraced Self

In looking first at the present state of the debate, we see that the problem of subjectivity appears highly unstable. Modern philosophies systematically promoted the idea of a *being* of subjectivity which was not a lesser form, and which might even be the absolute form of being, the negative whose role was to make manifest or modify all positivity. Descartes saw subjectivity as a thinking substance; Kant saw it as a formal a priori structure of all experience, and Kierkegaard conceived it as a fundamental relationship to being. This notion is a datable cultural fact. Humanism was certainly a Hellenistic invention. The Greeks made man divine in his own limits. But they did not conceive of the possibility that the being of the soul or the self might constitute the canonical form of being. At the other end of historical time, our contemporaries are now deconstructing the ideology of subjectivity and denouncing the vague charms of interiority. They are announcing the death of man, while we experience it firsthand.

The discovery of subjectivity took many different forms, even among those thinkers regarded as most closely related. The Cartesian ego is reflexive; the Kantian ego is pure form; the Husserlian ego is intentional. There has been much hesitation about how to constitute the self. Equally, we know the philosophical disgrace into which the various types of self—as substance, structure, or, more recently, person—have fallen.

The psychologists are equally embarrassed:[1] there are a multitude of different terms for subjectivity, from self-image and concept of self, to self-representation or self-recognition, and of course to self-consciousness. These are by and large the available options, but how can a choice be made if it predetermines the answers to the question asked?

If there is recognition going on, it involves not so much an image, a concept, or a representation as a certain identificatory integration of the self in relation to the world and the other. Indeed, there is nothing to be gained by stating the problem in the static terms of the presence or absence of a particular representation (at what age is a child able to recognize its image in a mirror?). If we do that, we limit our account of subjectivity to a naturalistic description of the process of chronological maturation, perceptual organization, and even the development of specific categories, which is what we see in the ordinary approach used by cognitivists.

The greater part of contemporary discussions about the identity of the self revolve around the relative sufficiency of criteria such as the permanence of the body-self or of subjective memory. Even if these fairly traditional criteria do correspond to necessary conditions, they are insufficient to construct a coherent concept of person. They are limited to rediscovering the notorious psychophysical unity of the human composition.[2]

It is in everyone's interests to go beyond this way of stating the problem. Let us consider the recognition of the body. This is not only a matter of the images that make it up, but also of mastering the relationship between gestural space and object space: the body cannot be identified by the subject if it is not situated. That requires both a motor accommodation with the world outside and a communicational accommodation with the world of others, which *is* the outside world.[3] These requirements, I might add, are simultaneous.

It has been a long time now since psychology took consciousness as its starting point or its explanatory principle, as Henri Wallon pointed out. Instead, psychologists chose to work on "the long series of reactions of which consciousness is only the final outcome."[4]

As the problematic of the conscious subject gradually starts to lose its prerogatives, the body-self suddenly comes to seem much more interesting. I am not talking now about the objective body studied by anatomists, which can be seen, dissected, and analyzed. Nor do I mean the body as perceived by artists, that physical surface others see as our body, whose form is reflected in mirrors. This is the body beloved of Narcissus, the body that love sees and wants to grasp. No, I am speaking of the body-self, something so insistently *ours* that it is confused with the feeling we have that there is a "substance of our presence." The body that I am is not the body that I have. And our body in the first sense is on the way to becoming for each of us the most important thing in the world. It is felt no longer as an opaque or hostile mass, but instead as the locus of a type of intimate attention through which we can work on ourselves in the pursuit of a cult of greater well-being. In our anxiety about our image, we try to make our physical heritage flourish; this is another type of narcissism, that of vigilance rather than fascination. To please has become essential for us. It is noticeable today that, with the increasing elision of the subject, the object of individual investment has been displaced toward the body.[5] Not without a curious exchange of metaphors: we now speak of the body's deep awareness, of its intimate changes, and even of a type of inward contemplation of the self which can take the form of physical investment.

The remarkable thing about this is that the interlocutive relation was the determining factor in the acquisition of this image of the body. More generally, work in genetic psychology has shown that the interlocutive situation speeds up the phenomenon of identification of the self. A child begins by naming other beings and things in the third person and including itself among them. It is only later that the child learns to differentiate its own bodily identity from the background beyond itself, when it is able to contrast it with a privileged element of that background—the other who speaks to it and to whom it learns to speak in turn. At the "mirror stage," when the child plays at making its image appear and disappear, it experiences itself as something situated in space. But Freud emphasizes that the child under observation was playing at being present or absent *for its parents.*

This is far from the complete acquisition of a sense of the first person, however. Pronouns stabilize late in the child's language, "I" coming later than "me." The first-person marker does not appear until there is at least some mastery of spatiotemporal relations, and most likely a first notion of time. Two of the arguments I shall be putting forward later are that the personal self is identified in time, and that knowing the self means constructing it through a process of identification.

Outside the psychoanalytic model, which sets out to account for all human motivations, and the behaviorist model, which sees in the person (or the individual?) a set of behavior patterns reducible to the relations between stimuli and responses, analytic studies of the development of personality converge with cultural factors to suggest that the person is not a substance that exists independently of the natural and human context. It has no existence outside various "networks of relations."[6] What makes it possible for us to find in the person (or the individual?) a set of traits that can be integrated into a specific unity is the fact that relations of this type are formed between behavior patterns and attitudes. Traits are thus a secondary translation, mediated by a whole series of correlations of such patterns and attitudes.

Character, Individual, Self, Person

In the English-speaking countries the philosophical debate about personal identity, bordering on the territory of the social and psychological sciences, is of course in full swing. It seems to me that it will not reach a conclusion without preliminary work being done to sort out the different concepts, themselves always changing, which have been laid down by the long history of studies into subjectivity. Let me explain.

We today have inherited a certain number of terms like *self,* and also *character, individual, person, figure.*[7] Disparate they certainly are. Each comes to us embedded in its own idiom, which we will have to reconstruct if we want to be sure of understanding it correctly. But the problem would already be much clearer if we agreed to accept a certain number of implications and distinctions, some of them far-reaching. If this allowed us to characterize the type of discourse into which they are inserted, we would perhaps be able to delineate the current state of the problem of personal identity.

Without thinking too hard we can pick out a number of traits that contribute to describing identity on the most immediate level. Let us begin with *character*. If we think of the magnanimous or the meditative person, we have two definite, quite closely determined types. They possess qualities that are the predictable manifestations of certain dispositions; these serve in turn to identify them. "Characters" are notorious, by definition public, people; even their private lives take on a sort of typicality. Their occupations and roles seem to derive from their character as if it were their "nature"; they *are* their nature. In contrast, let us look at what we call the *individual*. We think of individuals as undivided, singular people who count only on themselves (the famous self-reliance so dear to Emerson). We imagine them as crucially important to themselves, though they may be insignificant, nonentities, in almost everyone else's eyes. For individuals are centers of integrity, and as such they are the focus of inalienable rights. That said, there are actually countless numbers of such singular people.

The *self* puts a different slant again on the problem. People nowadays place great importance on certain qualities and capabilities, as if they were all properties or possessions belonging to the self. A self is likely to insist on making the most of its own abilities, though not, paradoxically, without assuming that it is bigger than any set of qualities by which we might try to define it. The *person* is different again. Rather than being a collection of qualities, like the self, or a certain configuration of traits, like the character, the person is traditionally defined by its ability to assume responsibility and, I would add, to respond to others as a possible interlocutor. In line with the two historical sources of the concept of person—one legal, the other theatrical (as in, dramatis personae)—what demands are made of persons? We ask them to play a wide range of different roles with grace and aplomb, but above all to allow us to judge their choices, actions, and words in terms of what we see as their distinct destiny. This is not quite the same as what we expect from exemplary *figures*, like Adam or Christ, or the "naive" character or the female "confidante" in a classical French comedy. Such figures are determined by their place in a given drama, and they declare themselves progressively as it unfolds.

In the light of these few differential characteristics it is already clear that problems of identity do not arise in the same way with persons, individuals, characters, and figures. In the first place, any coincidence between their respective classes is purely accidental. If we take a particular biological individual, he or she can be regarded as one major variety of personae, each of which is a distinct and unified agent, the ultimate center of responsibility for a whole register of actions and words spoken. On the other hand, in certain circumstances the class of persons no longer coincides numerically with the class of individuals. In Roman law it could sometimes include corporate bodies or, in the case of the family, institutions, so that for instance a woman could not initiate court proceedings against somebody else—it had to be done for her. What responsibility she had was conferred on her collectively, by virtue of her belonging to a family.

Our own experience confirms the fact that we are always able to regard ourselves in competing terms: as an individual, a character, a self, or a person. This situation is not without conflict, for the different terms all occupy different intellectual and emotive spaces. And that has a bearing on the powers we see ourselves as having, on our relations with others and our freedoms, right down to our conception of society, which varies according to whether we see ourselves as individuals or as persons. As an individual, I feel that my rights have been hard-won from society; as a person, I see them enshrined *in* society. Whereas a character can be content with having a continuum of personal abilities or gifts, the self typically requires an all-or-nothing evaluation from others around it. The self is therefore the most likely to engage in spontaneous or elicited confession. We shall see that the types of confession prduced by the self and the person are different; they lead to two different sorts of autobiography. Nor is that all: a "character," such as a grouse or a misanthrope, chooses his words in function of his nature; Miranda, as a "figure," chooses them in function of her story; while a person constitutes in his or her own right a unified center of choice. On one condition, though: that the person is able to unify (and first, doubtless, identify) him or herself.

This is the crux of the matter. Identification, and identity crises, mean different things in each case. How can you be what you are? It all depends. We notice that when we ask what we are, and what it is to be the same, the stage is set in each case in a different way. Let us start with the self. The criterion of identity is generally held to be the conscious possession of experiences. And since continuity is established in this case by memory, any difficulty with the identity of the self will relate to the transmission or alienation of memories. The self ceases to be itself when it loses its sole possession—memory. In the case of the individual, the question changes. How could an individual have an identity problem if hers is an indivisible identity that resists reduction to a type? It is the exact opposite for the character: as the tendencies that constitute it can be identified, their configuration can be reproduced. In which case, there is no particular expectation of identification, and no need for it either: no identity crisis. Look at the characters of Theophrastus: as they have been predesigned and predetermined, the events of the story will never alter them. But for persons, the situation is obviously reversed. Unpredictability, delay, conflict, and all the other obstacles to identity are an essential part of the truly *personal* self. The search for what is at the heart of the person ceases to be a matter of psychological curiosity and becomes a quest for the principles according to which choices are made and responsibilities accepted.

It is now clearer why the philosophical debate today is more concerned with the criteria for identifying persons than with those for characters or individuals: identity is constitutive of the person. Or better; the person results from a certain labor of identification.

To conclude on this point: the criteria do not coincide. Those that are useful in identifying the self do not work when we want to define a character. Both are different again from the criteria that allow the recognition of individuals and persons. In cases when they appear similar, their meaning and importance will be different. As we well know, these various concepts are forever offering us in our own lives widely differing norms against which to judge ourselves and others. If it is a question of finding guidelines for our behavior, we are hard pressed to do justice to all these archaeologically distinct layers.[8] They are impossible to integrate into a single concept. How can we be at one and the same time a rounded self and an admirable character, an exemplary figure and a unified person? The latent conflict between these models is part of our experience of living. We therefore adopt toward them certain ironic or sentimental strategies, if we do not actually play them off cynically one against the other.

If these concepts are so difficult to articulate, it is probably because they are sensitive to the discursive or textual games within and by which they are discussed. They are dependent on, if not engendered by, a certain mode of discourse. Take self-confession: it occurs (a point to which I will return) within a largely manipulative discourse. Take characters, such as we see portrayed in a specific type of novel, the sort written by Dickens rather than Kafka. Balzac needs characters, whereas Dostoyevsky uses figures. Novels of the person are different still, with their quest for unification, their discovery of responsibilities. This is because persons are linked to each other by a complex communicational field. And, as we shall see, they are linked according to a variable regime of communication; the language of properties is no longer suitable, so what is needed is a language of relations. Different again are "figures," who are obviously textual beings. As they are designed to illustrate certain recommendable ways of living, their physical characterization is more or less accidental. The figures of the pilgrim and the Savior in Christian drama, the ingénue and the traitor in the morality tale, all lend their support to a particular intepretation of human actions. For me, Stendhal's Mme. de Chasteller is an example of a figure of this sort, and a most delicate one. Individuality, on the other hand, is conveyed by certain comic or grotesque forms which establish the individual's right to uniqueness. On occasion this can be taken to absurd lengths, as in the final whirlwind in *Finnegan's Wake* in which, it seems, the individual voices, each with its own timbre and respiration, are stirred up together by the fury of the story.[9]

Subjectivity is clearly not to be equated with any of these concepts, all waiting quietly for someone to analyze their necessary and sufficient conditions. It has undergone extremely dramatic changes in the course of its history, which could be redefined as a history of different discourses on the self. Different discursive games, rather than a gradually revealed system of representation, are what have determined the fundamental characteristics of the ego. This is something we shall have occasion to remember.

Validity of the "No Identity without Entity" Principle

As the foregoing distinctions will doubtless have convinced us, the person is not something that *is*, but something that is *produced*. Or rather, for the person, being is self-production by gradual self-identification. It is a process working directly on the self, an activity that refers back to itself in order to prevent us from making a substance out of this activity that refers back to itself. . . . So that the only philosophical problem that is at once complete and concrete becomes that of personal identity. The question is what criterion to use in recognizing persons in their identity. But how should we approach that question?

We do not recognize a person in the same way that we recognize a familiar object as being the same. Let us think back to the traditional problem of Theseus' boat. If I replace the wooden deck, plank by plank, with an aluminum one, is it still the same boat? If I continue until the boat ends up being made entirely of aluminum, would we argue that we are still dealing with the same (wooden) boat with which we began? We would have to make a deliberate agreement to do so. Whereas, when a person is considered to be the same because his or her identity has persisted despite change, the question is rather different: a person differs from a boat in that there is also a sense in which the application of the binary predicate "the same as" or "identical to" is not dependent solely on a convention.

In some cases, of course, we might say: "So-and-so is no longer the person you knew." Well then, how great must be the changes for such a statement to be made? It is tempting to reply, with Bishop Butler: "As you like it."[10] It is again a matter of convention. It all depends on whether it suits you to use the expression "So-and-so is still the same as he always was." The application of this public law of language is in your hands.

In fact, however, the sense in which identity is being used here is extremely vague.[11] Our ability to regard as true such first-person psychological statements as "I am hurt," "I am moved," or "I remember" cannot be explained on the basis of this sort of criterion. I am convinced that if we say that a person who exists at time t is identical to a person who exists at another time t', we are taking the expression in a much stricter sense. Indeed, there is nothing to be gained by weakening the sense of identity, because this weaker sense is unacceptable on logical grounds. Suppose we say of a person: "A is no longer the same as he or she was," we certainly do not mean that A has ceased to be identical to a certain entity. In other words, we are in no way implying the existence of certain entities x and y such that at a given moment x is identical to y, while at another moment x is no longer identical to y. This is proved by the fact that we are not expecting either to have to call A by a name other than "A," or to reply to questions of the type "what has happened to A?": it is all too clear that A has neither died nor disappeared. All we mean is that A has become a different person. We still need to understand what we mean by saying this.

If there is a type of change that is not just the product of simple succession, two terms in that process must have something in common. If then x becomes y and is not simply replaced by y, x and y must something in common. Equally, if y becomes z, then y and z must have something in common. But why should there necessarily be anything in common between x and z? The common element between x and y might have ceased to exist before the common element between y and z began. As Anthony Kenny points out in another context,[12] it would be creating a sophism by displacement of the quantifier to infer from (i) to (ii) here:

(i) in any process of change there must be a common element between the two terms of the change;

(ii) there must be a common element in the terms of any process of change.

As a result, when we state that so-and-so has become such-and-such, a first approximation to what we mean is that so-and-so now possesses a particular quality he or she did not have before. For that reason, it seems that we must presuppose the identity of A through time in some other, philosophically stricter sense than the traditional sense of A being a unique subject persisting against the background of change, and acting as the possessor of qualities.

One prerequisite: as Locke pointed out, the identity question cannot be determined in isolation from the entity involved. We cannot avoid linking the concept of identity to some substantive notion such as a boat, a tree, or a person, if this concept is to be applicable. What makes us say of a given entity that it is the same seems to depend on the type of entity it is.[13] This then raises the problem of unity: an entity of a given type can only remain the same through changes insofar as these changes are precisely characteristic of that type of entity. Over the years a tree may double in height and volume but remain the same tree, because changes of this sort belong to the concept of tree under discussion. But what about persons? What sorts of change can be allowed in their case? Is the "no identity without entity" principle applicable? The foregoing analyses seem to indicate that it is not.

How Do We Recognize Ourselves as the Same?

Classically, this question is stated in monadic terms. If we want to deal with the identity of the person, we ask ourselves about the self, and we do it from the point of view of simultaneity or change. And we immediately assume the problem can be solved by recourse to consciousness. The conscious self has a linking and grouping function. It can act as a permanent substrate:

> Mysterious Self, yet you still do live,
> You will recognize yourself at the rising of the dawn
> Bitterly the same. . . .[14]

Or it can act as a transcendental subject. But whether it is one or the other, the essence of subjectivity is separated from the exterior reality that changes it and breaks it down. The search for a permanence *through time* constitutes the foundation of any reflection on the self. We shall come up against it again as something we cannot ignore in the problematic of the person.

The self represents subjective awareness of empirical experience, the awareness of changes and fluctuations in something that is invariable. The basis of the answer is well known: even when we feel that there is a dissolution of the personality, and particularly when we say "I have a double self," we are misusing the metaphor. We are *one* because there is only one center of consciousness, the single I that is the subject of all thoughts.

"I travel indefinitely through my own mind. Not a color, a scent, the taste of a fruit, a smell, can resist this movement. . . . The interior man holds the sea in the hollow of his imaginary hand." [15] This holds true whatever struggles or splits there might be, and whatever may be said about personality disorders. For in each of us there is a single soul, "which has in itself no diversity of parts," according to Descartes. Thus—so runs the conventional argument—there is no experience of alienation that is not still secretly presided over by the *I*. "I was out of my mind" is merely an excuse, always insincere.

Beyond the Metaphysics of Subjectivity?

When put to the test, the monadic solution I have just sketched out in fact refers us back to two quite distinct problems. This is because it assimilates the substantive self to a structural self manifesting the formal presence of an *I*.

"The 'I think' must be able to accompany all representations." [16] Kant is here making no claims about the actual existence of a transcendental consciousness, nor is he saying that it inhabits all our subjective states. He is raising the critical problem of consciousness: the "I think" contains the set of conditions necessary for the existence of a subjective consciousness. If—in true Kantian orthodoxy—these conditions are met, I could consider my perception and my thought to be mine.

But is the *I* that we find in consciousness made possible by the synthetic unity of our representations, or is it the thing that unifies them? This problem of the actual existence of the *I* in consciousness is quite a different matter. Only a descriptive study of the way in which empirical consciousness constitutes itself can provide an answer. This was the aim of phenomenology as a descriptive "science" of consciousness. It matters little here that we are dealing with a science of essences: the formal presence of the *I* as Husserl discovers it in the process of reduction [17] is no longer a set of conditions in principle, but an absolute fact. The *I* or transcendental consciousness inhabits as a matter of fact the empirical consciousness of our psychic and psychological self: it becomes personal. I can say "*my* consciousness." The unifying *I* individualizes and creates interiority. My consciousness constitutes a synthetic whole unified in time, but isolated from others and incommunicable.

I shall not ask, as Jean-Paul Sartre does, [18] whether the transcendental *I* as a structure of absolute consciousness still has its place in a phenomenological conception of the problem, because it seems of itself to make possible both the unity and the personalness of the *I*. It is sufficient for our purpose to underline the fact that in any event the Cogito is personal. In the "I think," there is an *I* which thinks. Whenever we grasp our own thought, we therefore apprehend an *I* belonging to the thought we have grasped, and it is a personal *I*. All my subjective states come equipped with an *I* which, as a reflecting consciousness, establishes them as reflections of a consciousness. And this *I* is characteristic of the person. What Sartre calls the "de facto guarantee of Kant's affirmation in principle"[19] is doubtless such that as soon as I grasp a representation through intuition or memory, the personal *I* appears immediately: "The fact that man can have the idea 'I' raises him infinitely above all the other beings living on earth. By this he is a *person:* and by virtue of his unity of consciousness, through all the changes he may undergo, he is one and the same person."[20]

He could not have been clearer. And as it is impossible in principle to think of the person conceived of in this way as an object, we tend to think of a subject yesterday who is analogous to the subject today, a subject who cannot lose his or her consciousness of himself. We know a priori that an experience that broke the unity of the self would not be able to enter his or her consciousness. Furthermore, the *I* is not knowable because it knows.[21] No objectivization, no representation of the subjective in this sense is possible, since any representation is objective. Something that is a condition of the possibility of an experience cannot be represented. The type of introspection that claims to treat the subjective objectively is misguided from the start. But even if I cannot know this *I*, I can still be conscious of it.

To achieve a thoroughgoing grasp of the *I* of representation was the ambitious program of what was called the metaphysics of subjectivity. In its foundational drive, and in line with the original sense of the term *subject*, this approach looked to the subject as its founding agency. The aim was to develop a theory of consciousness that could found the acts (perceptions or thoughts, desires or feelings) that belong to consciousness. As the central focus of these acts, the ultimate core of these different figures, the subject was granted the power of synthesis and the final unifying function. The whole of reality was conceived of as something that could appear to the subject. The metaphysician started with this founding agency and worked to unfold reality from it. As for discourse, it was now no more than the secondary appropriation of reality as so conceived through language.

The whole enterprise took the form of an attempt to constitute experience, and through it, reality itself. In its most complete form, this constituting discourse that took its own foundation as the basis for reproducing reality, by making the whole of what is appear as a representation of the subject, succeeded in overcoming the old oppositions between subject and object, between foundation and essence. For this to happen, subjectivity had to be regarded not as being affected by essences from outside, but as modifying itself through the determinants it creates. It is the subject that introduces difference into itself and, in producing itself, reproduces the totality of what is. It establishes determinants in the process by which it assigns its own content to itself. The completion of the constituting enterprise, then, coincided with the full manifestation of subjectivity.

There is nothing to stop the metaphysics of subjectivity from extending beyond simple perception all the way to scientific objectivity. The language of science was admittedly communicating a universal vision, rather than particular experience. But then the agency that conditioned its possibility was the pure subject, seen as the founder of all the systems studied by science, whether they were formal, material, or living. At the same time, this pure subject was held to be internal to the operation of any concrete subjectivity, which itself was resolutely assimilated to a singular person, with a real location in space and time, possessing its own qualities, and standing as the center and origin of its own limited experience.

This metaphysics of subjectivity has been more or less thoroughly condemned from all sides; more important, it has been dismantled. It was realized that it must be possible to examine the *I* in a different way from an object, and even from the subject of representation. In the *Tractatus* Wittgenstein strove to save the metaphysical subject at the expense of the subject of representation. No true subject could be the limit of the world and still exist in the world; nor could its thoughts, which would remain simply events in and of the world. A subject of that sort remains an *I*; it has already ceased to be an *I think*. It is simply a focal point from which the outward projection of reality through language occurs. For my part, I shall seek to put forward a critique of such subjectivist discourses, and to show that, in the foundational order, being-as-subject is derived from the notion of person, rather than defined by self-consciousness. If consciousness is implied in the development of the person, it does not follow that it is its essence.

Formulating the Problem of Personal Identity

The solution to the problem of personal identity that I intend to put forward will not be the same as the one suggested by classical thinkers, which depends on an illusory equivalence between individual, self, and person—or rather, between their respective modes of identification. We have become so used to this point of view that we have quietly turned into accomplices in a deception. Its variants were broadly contemporary with Western society's discovery of the ideology of *individualism*. By allowing human relations to be ignored altogether, individualism encouraged the atomization of analytical rationality.

Thus an awkward type of self was constructed which was able with a perfectly clear conscience to direct toward the perceived "other" an attitude characterized as "suspicious, calculating, and demanding."[22] Its demands

27

were presented as no more than its due, an intrinsic possession of which *I* could be seen as the beneficiary and titular holder. Individualism stretched friendship to the point of paradox with its singularly demanding logic, which is that of the *autos* and its absolute autonomy. Bourgeois liberal individualism was apt to consider human relations as passively experienced by each of us and conditioned by various forces. It hoped to be allowed to apply to human relations the positivistic laws of exteriority; according to these we are all subject, in absolute separation from other people, to the historical conditions of our relations with them, the forces and imperatives of the age, and the relations established by earlier generations. It becomes virtually impossible to conceive of authentic friendship within the bounds of this bleak horizon. Simone Weil puts the point very concisely when she sees in such friendship a miracle by which the ego "agrees to look on from a distance, without approaching the being that it needs like a food."[23]

We might agree with the common-sense position that the significant thing about personal identity is actually identity. But *personal* identity—leaving aside for a moment the cases of the character and the figure—must not be confused with the *individual* identity of an empirical self. When a child first asks itself "who am I?" it is not displaying a desire to learn its age or its nationality. It has the feeling that there is something important, unique, and continuous that goes beyond a simple list of individual data (which it already knows perfectly well), something that corresponds to the pronoun *I*. An *I* that is intangible because it eludes apprehension, like my shadow around my head, but from which I can never free myself.

Let us again ask ourselves the naive question: how do we recognize ourselves as the same? This is an old man's problem, strange but inescapable. Just who are you? Formally, it seems that we can only conceive of ourselves as identical to the extent that we also think we are self-repeating. Even, and above all, when we say: "I have changed." Identity does not have to realize itself tautologically: personal identity is precisely that by which we judge ourselves (and are judged by others) to be one and the same, here and there, yesterday and tomorrow, whatever we may have become.

To that extent, we can understand the fascination exercised by the notion of a substantive self. *Self* was the term used by the conscious subject viewing itself as a single and permanent object, a psychical unit able to transcend the whole of its lived experience. And able also to make the distinction between this object and everything that is the nonself, as well as other foreign "selves" (on condition that the "selves" in question be of the same type—i.e., identifiable objects whose integrity is threatened by the alienation of the qualities they possess).

28

There are few who do not believe in the realism of immediate experience. The principal objection to it is an epistemological one. My criticism is that it leads quickly to a sterile metaphysics which blocks off further research rather than encouraging it. A collection of characteristics might allow us to put together an identity card; they certainly do not give us a personal identity. It is one thing for us to convince ourselves that we have a certain type of individuality, and quite another to ensure that we have our own identity. But in that case, could we not simply make the self into a principle for the structuring of experience by reference to our biological individuality?

The very etymology of the word *individual* makes it a negative concept. As a living individual, the self is the minimum level of being that cannot be further fragmented without losing its characteristics. As has often been said, my heart beats for me, my blood flows for me, it is for myself alone that I breathe and in myself alone that I suffer and die. Here then is the ultimate element, the final foundation, the vital minimum of *ipseity*, of sameness. But this elementary being at the very edge of nonbeing involves inevitable reference beyond itself, to a wider being with which it stands in a relation of continuity.[24] It might be objected that the consciousness of this individual is likely to tend toward a unitary organization of its experience, by attaching itself to certain social markers such as the proper name, which supports a multiplicity of roles. In fact, this too is an illusion. It is striking how the task that psychoanalysis has set itself coincides on this point with philosophy's critique; both aim to dissipate what was rightly called consciousness's fascination with the self. There is indeed an imaginary and mendacious "self" able to disguise itself as a personal subject.[25]

In trying to describe the recent state of the question, I might begin with the following assertion: far from possessing an identity by nature or configuration, or by some advantage of sociobiological individuation (man is the product of man as wheat is of wheat), the person is in essence condemned to acquire its identity through its own efforts, by striving for identification. "To identify oneself" (*s'identifier*) is an active, reflexive verb. Personal identification is not a process by which the Same is identified in a self equipped with its various qualities, or in an individual in the psychosocial sense. The identificatory action of the Same takes place "as a *sojourn* (*séjour*) in the world. The way of the I against the 'other' consists in *sojourning*, in *identifying oneself* by existing here *at home with oneself* (*chez soi*)."[26] In such a world, the self is at home, it has power, and, despite its dependency, it is free. An independent self surrounded by the alterity of things—we are back once more in a highly traditional situation.

A self of this type discovers the Same and the Other by assimilation to

29

the other subject, and by assimilating the object to the category structures of its own thought. This is an idealism parallel to the sort that seeks to derive the autonomy of the personal sphere solely from the initiatives of self-consciousness.

We shall have to abandon once and for all the idea that the ego is a complex representation, as Pierre Nicole believed in the classical age.[27] I cannot identify myself through the immediate coincidence of a representation with what is represented, which would give me an image of myself. An idea—or idol—of this sort would be the futile ghost, the mere illusory form of a fantastical self, of an alienated, fascinated subjectivity that is much closer to the social self than to the *I*. Unless I suffer from neurosis or regression, my task is to identify myself by a slow, steady process of construction. I need the sort of patience that most autobiographers lack.

In this way the personal pronoun *I*, whose function is both to designate the speaking subject reflexively and to refer to the logical subject of the utterance, often masks both of its subjects. We should be legitimately suspicious of the "I" in statements, because spoken and written language make it all too easy to confer on it an objective status when what we are dealing with in reality is an imaginary self. The analysis must therefore be redone so as to take into account the oppositional structure linking personal pronouns, and the interplay that exists between the function of the subject in statements and the function of what we have agreed to call the subject of the utterance.

The first thing that needs to be understood is that a person does not sit among other objects in the world like one apple in a basketful of others; he or she is linked to them both allocutively and delocutively. I must be capable of receiving an address or an interpellation from someone else who calls me *you*, otherwise I shall not be able to call myself *I*. If I am the person to whom reference is being made in the second person, this *you* must then be me. Who could deny it? At the same time, I must be able to recognize myself as the object of a discourse about me in the third person; this *he* is once again me. There is thus an unbreakable link between the three agencies of discourse— I, you, and he. The result is a structural unit of enormous logical complexity: the person.

The Trans-Agential Capacity of the Person

Let us pursue the hypothesis in more detail. I will succeed in constructing an empirical self-identity if, across the range of my communicational performance, I manage to integrate the three poles of the communication act— whether I am speaking to others while calling myself me, or being spoken to by others as a you, or being spoken about by others as a him which I can at least recognize, if not entirely accept (since people wish to be recognized in their acts, but doubtless more important in what they say).

I, you, and he or she are the three positional values in any communication act. They are not inventions of grammar. In one form or another, according to Benveniste, an oppositional structure between *I* and *you* on the one hand, and that "personality correlation" with *he/she* on the other, exists in every language. It imposes its mark on all communication, and as a result it plays a constitutive role in the concept of person. These values must not be confused with their corresponding identities, mine, yours, or his or hers. We can start to define the subject not as some substantive reality or some transcendental function, but by this very *trans-agential* function that it has.

The problem of personal identity coincides in a precise and, above all, more complex manner than is usually realized, with the problem of alterity. Let us start with the closest commonplace to it in contemporary philosophy. We might say that it is by speaking to the other that I attribute to him the quality of being a subject comparable to myself: the other is another I. We could then add: so long as I myself am not totally alien to everything that is not me, as in Rimbaud's *je est un autre* (I is an other).

Such formulae are inadequate if we interpret them solely on this basis. By extending them to suggest that an ego without a second person would not even be a first person (it would not be any kind of person at all), or, more abstractly, that there can be no sense of ego without alterity, we are already moving way outside the range of what they can explain. But even this new, much stronger thesis is still not adequate. The least we can do is to clear up this mystery of the self in two persons and, in order to carry the analysis forward, think about the precise way in which the two agencies *I* and *you* overlap. Even that is not enough, however. There can be no personal identity without a certain relation to an absent or distant third party. It will therefore be necessary to take account of and integrate this third person.

The Three Agencies—I, you, he/she—and Their Mutual Dependency

Saying "I" is a way of introducing myself before having been introduced. Saying "you" is in no way enough to involve me in reciprocal relations with someone else. That sort of "you" is just a direct address. The other person must also address me. Independent of my ability to receive such an address, without a corresponding initiative from the other person I could not possibly be myself. The other as *you* acts as a virtual person, i.e., one capable of addressing me in turn. Only then (and it sometimes happens in a moment) does allocution become interlocution: a relationship comes into being.

This prerequisite invalidates any unilateral opening-out by the *I* into the other's "transcendence." Interlocution alone is not able to set up the I as an I and the you as a you—and here I diverge from Martin Buber's concept of interhuman relations expressed in the key term of the I-You (in that order).

This remark also rules out a fortiori any confusion between the inter-locutive relation and the image each person has of the other. Until such time as the relationship has become established and operative, we can lose our-selves in questions: who am I to speak to him or her like this, who are you for me to speak to you like this, who do you think I am for you to speak to me like this? In fact, it is possible to address another person without having any prior image or experience of that person. Equally, it is difficult to identify with the image the other person has of you, and to say, "I am not the person you think I am." It is when the other person is missing from the relationship that I become attached to his or her image. The image of the other has the same sort of obsessive but fluid consistency that characters have in our dreams; no less, but no more either. An amorous relationship cannot feed on images alone. There is nothing more dreadful than the realization that one's feelings are directed solely at an image. Moreover, whatever may be the psy-chological cause (and the frequency) of our tendency to forget that relation-ships are relational, this forgetfulness is above all logical: an interpersonal relationship with another person cannot be made to emerge from the other's experience of the Same. The French verb *vivre* (to live) is, like the German *erleben*, transitive, but such superficial grammatical facts must not be al-lowed to mislead us. It is one thing to speak with a real interlocutor and an-other to speak to the image we have of that person, or again to fit what we say to the image we imagine the other person to have of us.

Frequency has nothing to do with it. An effective relationship experienced nonreflexively is a quite different reality from the reflexive image each person has of it. To confuse the two—as psychologists do all the time—is, whatever they may say, to commit a category mistake. Everything lived by the self is then called experience, *my* experience, even relations with others, which can alternatively be claimed as collective experience. Linguists are the ones who have remained most faithful to relational realities by adopting the paradigm of communicability: they are concerned to trace within the most singular types of language use the relation that both opposes and binds us one to an-other in verbal exchange. Such an enterprise is even more demanding than the already meritorious one of trying to trace the other's discourse within my own, or, on the level of principle, to identify the other that is supposedly con-stitutive of the self.[28] In any event, putting real interlocutors into relations with each other is a way of short-circuiting the vague images we have of the other—images that hinder our speech and end up blocking it altogether. As

32

we shall see, once it has been established, the reciprocal relation that makes possible the attribution of *I* and *you*, and then the first stages of personal identification, appears in the form of a union and an alliance. As a result, it cannot be appropriated; to say that a mutual alliance is mine or yours is inevitably to usurp it. An alliance is *ours*.

Once I have acquired this ability to respond to the address of a real other, there is nothing to stop me from addressing myself, in a kind of intimate division process, in the same way that the other person addresses me. But we will have to show that the real other precedes the virtual other in me, something philosophers who work on such reflections are too apt to forget. Yet this is precisely where the philosophical difficulty, and interest, lies. The effective responses others make to my messages are what modify my presentation of myself. I am led to see myself differently, which puts my self-esteem to the test. We can see then how much of a battle it is for each of us, every day, to ensure that our concept of self continues to coincide with itself. I do not simply have to treat myself as the object of my own consciousness, as a *he*. Communicating with oneself is not just reflecting back on oneself; it means entering into relations with oneself. I need the other in order to accomplish my personal identification. And you, who do you say I am? I am neither the first nor the only one to stress this point. But instead of saying that the other is indispensable to the accomplishment of my totality as a *consciousness*, my claim is that the other must play a role in my relational mapping as an agent or protagonist of communication.

Sometimes I am unable to communicate completely with the other person. Paradoxically, this is also because I am not communicating properly with myself. A number of authors[29] confirm that the feeling of being alone even originates in an inability to enter into relations with oneself. Once again, there is no dissymmetry here. Moreover, it is precisely those writers who deplored the impossibility of communicating with others—Paul Valéry, Marcel Proust, Stéphane Mallarmé—who were able to create the most vibrant evocations of imprisonment in solitude, like the swan in a world of ice.

Let us now move on to the problem of mapping the third agency, *him/her*, against the other two, *me* and *you*. This theme is new. As will be seen, it is sufficient on its own to distinguish my approach to personal alterity from the various phenomenological approaches, and it also provides a direct polemical thrust against idealism.

Buber thought that man only becomes an *I* through contact with a *you*. From that contact he derived an interiority, a personal being; for him, the love felt for another person founds and constitutes the first person in return.

In fact, although this is undoubtedly a necessary condition, it is not sufficient. A person only becomes someone, an *I*, under the extra test of what we
may call the *he/she:* the other not as an allocuted *you*, but as a *him* or *her.*
According to Emmanuel Levinas, I should not speak of others in the accusative, as *him/her*, but only in the vocative, as if to a *you.* In reality, the
fact that we do all speak about other people is undeniable and doubtless legitimate: under certain conditions, a delocutive discourse about another person is valid. Moreover, speaking about someone else as a *him/her* is not ipso
facto the same as calling that person *it.* We must therefore revise the usual
analysis to reduce this predominance of the nearby over the distant other, of
presence over absence. Normally, when we look to grammatical forms for
support in our efforts to describe the status of persons, the third person is
regarded as a purely negative notion. Thus Benveniste sees it as the category
of the "nonperson." In his view, it is only used to refer to other things or
people different from the speaker and the listener. The *he/she/it* value* is
then divorced from the two participants in the verbal exchange, the speaker
and the spoken-to, both linked by a present interlocutive relationship.[30]
Moreover, the third person often remains unidentified.

It is quite true that certain languages seem to give no explicit recognition
to the third person; instead, there is simply an absence of the formal markers
for the first and second persons. But the tendency among linguists is to stress
the heteogeneity of the three persons.[31] In my perspective, the third person is
in a way relative to the first two, figuring as a third entity in relation to the
circuit of their exchange. The value *he/she* is indeed separated from the *I*
and *you* values of the participants, but it nevertheless remains in a certain
relation to them.

The Dyadic Nature of the Interlocutive Relation

What sort of relation is the interlocutive? What I call an interlocutive relation is an intersubjective relation established symbolically. Suppose that *I*
and *you* are currently in an interlocutive relation. Our natural language suggests by its system of pronouns—the so-called "third person" pronouns are
entirely different in nature and function—that *he/she* is a third party in relation to us. Even in modern languages in which the personal pronoun is
obligatory and "he/she" seems to have equal status with "I" and "you," the
symmetry is no more than formal: apart from the fact that "he/she/it" can
combine with any object reference at all, and never reflects the agent of dis-

---

*Translator's note: in French the third-person pronouns *il* and *elle* (masculine and feminine) refer to both things and people.

course, this pronoun is incompatible with the paradigm of deictic terms such as "here" and "now." [32]

For their part, logicians have underlined how difficult it would be to extend to a relation with three arguments the properties of a dyadic relation like the interlocutive one. C. S. Peirce, whom Alfred Tarski recognizes as the inventor of relations theory,[33] indicates that an authentic triadic relation can never be constructed as a complex of dyadic relations.[34] All that can be done is to break it down into its three arguments and then build them up two by two into dyadic relations. According to Bertrand Russell it is impossible to carry out the formal reduction of a triadic relation to dyadic relational terms, even if the reverse can always be done.[35] As for the idea of defining a property of interlocutive reciprocity for a triadic relation, the task is not an easy one. Although the power of general relations theory has been recognized, only the theory of binary relations has as yet been properly developed.

Experience supports the positions adopted by linguists and logicians. A group of three people, unlike a dyad, is weak and unstable. Leaving aside cases in which the third party is virtually excluded from the conversation, perhaps even rejected outright and thereby excommunicated, it is very dificult for the third person to enter into a stable triadic relationship. On the other hand, that person will try to situate him or herself in relation to the two others. Either by playing the role of witness or mediator between them, in order to bring them together in a (dyadic) relation while remaining in a (dyadic) relation with each one of them; or, more commonly, by trying to disrupt a relationship that already exists. A third possibility is that the other two take a joint attitude to the third, which may be one of rejection or exclusion.

In the case of most interest to us at present, I should stress that *he/she* does not represent the person shut out from all possible exchange, who would not be a person at all. Instead, someone different, someone privileged in a certain way by the fact that one of the two others has spoken, will or at least might speak to him/her, or could have done so. This he/she about whom I am speaking to you is virtually addressable by you and by me.

This is proved by the fact that in a number of languages the personal pronouns "he" and "she" are determined in relation to the indefinites "someone" and "one" (*on*).* He/she is not just any determinable individual whom we choose to leave undetermined; nor is he/she just any representative of the group of others. Still less is he/she the anonymous and impersonal *on* who is placed right outside the situation of utterance, and who could be anyone at

---

*Translator's note: *on* more often corresponds to the English "they," "people."

all. Compare: "Whatever will he/she say?" and: "Whatever will people (*on*) say?" He/she does not stand outside the allocutive movement: it is just that he/she is not currently present in person.

These last two characteristics must remain linked. It is crucial for the third person to be a potential partner in an interlocutive relation, to be able to be reactivated. In the absence of this contrastive virtuality, the *he/she* changes status and slips out of the tripersonal system of overlapping agencies, leaving behind that strange, partially diminished (and in compensation, elevated) *he/she* which refers to a dead person. This change of status whereby a relative absence becomes absolute probably accounts for much of the pain felt during the mourning process. The dead are only to be spoken about with care, precisely because they are excluded from speech as a matter of principle; they cannot reply. This verbal deficit is experienced reciprocally by the partners in the exchange. The dead person is defunct to the extent that he or she no longer has any point of his or her own to make, and can neither speak of us nor address him or herself to us.

What are we to think of this absence of the third person? Traditionally, it is the second person who is held to be *virtual* in the communication relationship. The person who is spoken to will take over the speaking role in his or her turn. But now we are starting to define the third person as *relatively* absent. This other seen as a *he/she* is not just anybody, but a variable third party whom we could address, and who gives us access to all possible others, even when they are strangers or at a distance. Rather than being simply a spatial distancing, absence is one more form of personal existence; it is presence elsewhere. To say that someone is absent amounts to saying that his or her existence is attestable to by other people, while excluding him or her from the present exchange. "He/she" can just about be used as a form of allocution toward someone whom one wishes to remove from one's present personal sphere. Suppose there were someone whose existence was not attestable by anyone: the person would not only be absent, but he or she would not exist at all. The presence elsewhere of the absent person is attestable to in the future or the past to the extent that he or she has been or will be in an allocutive relation with us. The other as a *him/her* only exists for me as a past memory, or as my partner in some future activity.

What is it that still makes the relatively absent him/her a person? After all, it could be argued with some plausibility that this him/her has the passivity of an object, as long as he or she remains absent. Whereas "I" designates the person who is speaking, and sometimes also the logical subject of the utterance (e.g. "I am walking," "I say that I am walking"), a person is designated as "you" by an "I" who at the same time imputes to him or her a predicate ("you are walking," "I say that you are walking"). In the case of the third person, the form "he/she/it" calls down an indication onto someone or something. But *he/she* and *him/her* nevertheless refer to a person, the so-called *third* person. This is not because *he/she* is *you* to the *you* who is my partner, the other's other. But because to make a third, it takes two others in a present relation, two others in relation to whom he/she is a third. But he/she remains a person because, while he or she is not a participant in a presently lived relation, he or she continues to maintain a double link with a communicational past and with an address from someone else which gives him or her a future. The plurality of contexts of life and their successive interlinking are essential features of human reality. The third person has spoken in the past and is likely to do so again one day, becoming once more its own *I*.

As a result, *he/she* is neither just a mediating third party between you and me, nor a pure delocuted *it*. We should only conceive of a third party as a person to the extent that he or she might have the opportunity to assume responsibility him or herself for the things which are said about him or her. The ambiguity arises from the fact that the first- and second-person pronouns refer to present human beings, whereas those of the third person concern someone with whom we may have dealings, who has been or will one day be in an allocutive relation to us. Failure to realize this would lead us to see the third person literally as an object, instead of simply as the object of our discourse.

The personal pronoun "he/she" in the delocutive register and its grammatical flexions ("him/her," "to him/her") allow the attribution of certain predicates: in that case, the third person is delocuted as well, taking the objective position of active or passive participant in the action expressed by the verb in the statement. In the end, therefore, any reference to persons brings into play concurrently the delocutive and the allocutive registers. This is because, as we shall see later, a person can be recognized in two different ways, both in his or her status as a person (through his or her speech acts, or as the allocutee of someone else's) and by his or her *personal* status, as a carrier of determinants in the social community.

At the end of this process of "deducing" the third person, let me again stress the fact that it is deeply involved with the other two in the whole business of mutual identification between persons. That is the crucial thing. I myself need only to be excluded from the present interlocutive relation to become for others a *him*, a third person. At that point, as the third is the absent person in the sense that we have just examined, and as a complete self must be capable of becoming a him/her, we should stop thinking of the reality of self in terms of the restrictive dichotomy of being and nonbeing; a personal self is absent or present according to the position it has in the communicational act.

Character: Limits of Delocutive Discourse about the Self

It is important to realize that if I am "I" for myself, I am simultaneously "you" for the person speaking to me and "him" for the other who is speaking about me. The ego will of course only ever be a person if it is capable as a "self" of saying "I," but also of being the one who is spoken to and spoken of. This is where we come up against the difficult question of personal predicates, which will be examined later. For the moment, let me deal with the better-known problem of character and its particular mode of identification.

We might say of the ego, for instance: "he is affable enough but easily annoyed," or "he is capricious," "he is a spendthrift," or again, "he is a slave to his creature comforts," like La Bruyère's Hermippe. And we expect the ego to be like that. What we are doing in the end is attributing to the ego a character—but not just any old character.

Everyone would probably agree that I can choose, up to a point, not to contradict the character attributed to me by others and to accept such descriptive traits as these, which undoubtedly correspond to external appearances. However, I am not obliged to act the boor or the pretentious fool just because others believe me to be such. Nothing can make me limit myself to what others describe, from outside, as my character. Quite rightly, we call character that which tends to be imposed, imprinted, from without, according to a predicative relation. Look how one's character seems to become fixed within the circle of family and friends. People often say they are misunderstood. It is not necessarily that judgments about us are wrong, but rather that they close us off once and for all. Nobody deserves to be put down forever as selfish, or unscrupulous, or ambitious. The question is, how far should I go along with judgments like this? It is an epistemological as well as an ethical question.

It is quite clear that nobody is forced to affect the character ascribed to him or her by others. The proof of this is that those who impute a particular character to us are the first to criticize us for giving in to it ("Don't give us your annoyed look again"), or conversely, to congratulate us for showing it. Anyone who tried to claim her character for herself, as absolute and different in nature from those of other people, would be accused of affectation. I suspect that there is a good deal of conventionality involved in the notion of character.

Let us take a closer look. A certain naturalizing, objectivizing type of psychology, as is its job, regards character as a set of specifications or dispositional qualities that determine the individual. These are not connected with age, sex, race, time, socioprofessional background, or pathology. They are seen as an underlying psychological structure, an unvarying mental pattern that emerges in childhood and continues into old age,[36] revealing itself in attitudes and ways of behaving. "He's still the same . . . he hasn't changed," we often say. I can believe it; it must be true because I hear it said so often. Try lending a hand with something if you are reputed to be lazy. People will not expect you to be of any use: as Alain noted, the moment you jump up to help someone, you are in the way.

It is significant that this facile naturalism, which does not hesitate to make the character a sort of *hyle*, a form of the ego itself on the properly psychological level, has long been aided and abetted by literature. A character will typically remain stable from beginning to end, like Prospero in *The Tempest*. Cécile, in *Les Liaisons dangereuses*, remains "silly and sensual" throughout, and Valmont is permanently fickle. If a character does undergo a major change, it will either be through a process of gradual development, as in Rastignac's case, or at the end of a grave crisis, as in that of King Lear. Which means that even breaks in the continuum have to be justified within the laws of character.

But there is more than one view of psychology, and more than one type of literary convention. Flaubert and Henry James began the fashion for a dramatic type of writing that shows characters acting, speaking, and constructing themselves before our eyes, in line with the development of their mutual transactions and without any prior, arbitrary attempt by the author to describe or evaluate: there are even novels in which the author does not see fit to intervene at all. It is only one step from here to the complete dissolution of the conventions of character, a step taken by Joyce. This move was then reinforced by a certain form of structuralist criticism, which admitted the existence of differential traits but saw them as a system of codes and cultural stereotypes. If these were naturalized at all, the process was performed a posteriori by the reader, in a secondary language which he or she was free to choose. It was up to the reader to invent his or her own delocutive discourse about the individual homogeneous character. This marked a break in a tradition which, since Theophrastus, had made character portraits a literary genre in their own right, and one which, incidentally, its best practitioners had understood as humorous. This is all very well for portraying the absent-minded individual, the flatterer, or the fool:

A blockhead is an automaton, a piece of machinery moved by springs and weights, always turning him about in one direction; he always displays the same equanimity, is uniform, and never alters; if you have seen him once, you have seen him as he ever was, and will be; he is at best but like a lowing ox or a whistling blackbird; I may say, he acts according to the persistence and doggedness of his nature and species. His least visible aspect is the soul; it has no action and no influence, and is always resting.[37]

But what of the Marquise de Merteuil, she of the eagle eye who in the last analysis has no character at all beyond her passion for liberty? It is precisely this passion that makes her an archetype, a figure of cloak-and-dagger fantasy. And yet, what is my real nature if my nature is constantly to pretend, and I display conflicting passions and contradictory weaknesses? There is a paradox here, one admitted by the same La Bruyère who translated Theophrastus: "Men do not have characters, or if they do, it is the character of not having a consistent, non-contradictory and recognizable character."

How then can "my" character be me if strictly speaking I do not *have* a character? At most, all I have is my own personal way of making choices and choosing to be what I am—a way, of course, that I do not choose. Shall we say then that in its immutability, a character is a sort of mode of being of one's liberty? In fact, I am regarded as short-tempered if that type of behavior is noticed in all my relations with another person, and if it seems to determine all my reactions in my various transactions with the world and with others. It is still necessary that I accept this descriptive discourse as applicable to myself. The alienating power of the discourse that describes me is measured by the extent to which I agree to adopt it myself. Such is the "confession" of character; it breeds compliance and consent, as I adopt a character as mine, of my own free will. On the other hand, the conditions of the agreement are broken if I fail to behave in a certain way in at least some of my relations with others, or if I am not prepared to admit to the presence of a given trait in a descriptive discourse of my own. Prospero is a tyrant with Caliban and Ariel; with his brother's usurper he shows himself to be a just sovereign.

Under certain variable conditions, nothing now prevents the ego, which speaks in the first person, from being mapped against what others say about it. After all, what people say about me is no more wrong (or right) than what I would say about myself, though it probably has a different sort of wrongness (or rightness) about it. I only identify myself as a person if in some way I assume responsibility for what people say about me as a "he," or what they want to make me say about myself; assume responsibility for, agree with, consent in my own appearance. Then again, doing that is not so much having *a* character as simply having character, period. Consenting in your own appearance can sometimes become an advantage or a weapon. Having a character means having qualities on which you can depend and to which you can stick despite the temptation to change them. *Being* a character means having some recognized qualities and overdeveloping them to the point where they are allowed to dominate all the others.

So this "him" is indeed me. And we can see that grammar is right to give the subject a nominative pronoun, but also a direct and indirect object. It is because each of us has the power to recognize him or herself concurrently as *I, you,* or *he/she* that we are able to identify ourselves. In common with everything else in the world, we can become objects of perception and discourse. But my knowledge of the other is only able to be stated delocutively if I have once entered allocutively into a relation with him or her. It is because each of us normally has the opportunity to identify him or herself through the three positions in the communicational act that there is no contradiction between the words "person" and "object."

Not that the integration of these terms is easy to achieve, or is always complete. The desire, requests, and expectations addressed to me for approval will sometimes be incompatible with each other. Conflict, with its oblique, alienating, and depersonalizing effects, is never far away. Which again goes to show that the problem of personal identification is a far from trivial one.

By affirming that personal identity operates through a mapping of the self against the three positions in the communicational act, we can avoid falling into the trap of idealism. Let us be clear about this. Idealism is a doctrine that sees everything that exists, or at least everything of whose existence we know, as nothing more than a conception of the mind, an idea of the individual subject. This completely disregards common sense, which suggests that the sun and the moon, the sky and the desert, are quite different things from the ideas and views of the mind. And yet we know how difficult philosophers of representation have found it to refute idealism. That things appear to us *as if* they were external is certainly something we have no need to prove. To that extent the problem of sensory evidence is meaningless. But we can still question whether these things are simply phenomena inside us, mere determinations of our self, or whether they relate to something genuinely external. Kant considered it one of the scandals of philosophy that there was still no irrefutable proof, sufficient to convince the cynic, of the necessary existence of things outside ourselves, and that this crucial point had to depend on belief alone. Kant's own proof is fragile. It is based on the fact that the original essence of time implies, in addition to change, something permanent. His argument goes as follows. I am aware of my own existence as something determined by time. But for a multitude of representations to persist in the way in which they do in my mind, something permanent is necessary. As this permanence cannot be an intuition in me (the principles by which my existence is determined are representations that require there to be something permanent and distinct from them), if we want to say that changes in those representations are determined, we need to posit the persistence of something outside me. In short, our experience of the temporality of representations could not imply something "changeable" in me without including something "permanent" outside myself.

One objection has often been raised, and justifiably so: the opposition contained here between consciousness and the external object does no more than repeat another opposition, between empirical and transcendental consciousness. Russell, a philosophical realist, follows G. E. Moore in pointing out that just because we have the *idea* of a thing in our mind, it does not mean that the thing itself is located there. At most, an idea about the thing can be said to exist in the mind so long as we refer to it using our propositions. Without putting forward in turn my own formal refutation of idealism, let me stress that the communicational approach places us in a better position to avoid once and for all mixing up what is in the mind with the reality which the mind finds laid out before it.

Indeed, communication is a process for developing jointly the semantic means that allow us to refer to something else. For each of us, that something is not bounded by our representation of it. When communication is defined as a pooling of sense and reference, it becomes a bilateral process of participation in the identification of the referent about which we are speaking, itself now a co-referent. Whereas in the case of simple representation reality could not be taken as given, are we now treating it as a necessary mediating force independent of the speakers, beyond what can be apprehended by the consciousness of each? Whether in the case of an external object seen as an *it* or another person seen as a *he/she*, the world will exceed the representation that every possible interlocutor may have of it. The referent is henceforward a part of the communicative process, acting to mediate the relation of reciprocity. It is that permanent presence outside ourselves that founds *a parte rei* the possibility and the dynamism of communication.

The Tripersonal Structure of Communication

The object that Martin Buber calls the *it* is in fact our co-referent, or inter-referent. In the final analysis, the everyday world we all share, and the universe that scientists study, are derived from a relation of knowledge between *I* and *you*. For relations to objects are not independent of interpersonal relations. The ego is not in direct relation with any variety of *it*. It is the task of communicational activity to engender the ordinary world of our co-references, and even, through the theories constructed within the community of experts, the very objects of science.

Let me return to the tripersonal structure of communication which, as the reader will have realized, is full of implications. We will now give up thinking of the *he/she* as a *you*, as Levinas does, and then the *I* as something addressed by a *you*. The double opposition between *me* and *you* within the "I/you" correlation on the one hand, and the presence and absence of the person as *he/she* on the other, determine exactly three persons. There is no room for a fourth, except perhaps as a witness to the fact that the rules of exchange have been observed. We return to this same schema whatever the number of interlocutors. The speaking community must fit itself into this tripersonal structure in every case. In order to do so, it will have to combine the grammatical categories of number and person: the three personal positions will each have both a singular and a plural. People will be able to agree to state a common belief by making a statement in the first person plural; it will be possible to address a number of others simultaneously as *you* plural, and several absent people at once can be spoken about using the third person plural.

One way of grasping the pragmatic significance of dialogue is to notice that it deploys the interlocutive relation and the communicational structure of persons for their own sake. We have seen that the first is of necessity dyadic, while the second is triadic. Persons in a dialogue are obliged to situate themselves canonically in one of the communicational positions, to take over and hand back the speaking role, and to give their opinion on the propositional attitudes (knowing and believing) expressed by the other parties. Dialogue is the opportunity for each person to aim, as far as possible, to integrate the three positions. The same invitation is issued by the dialogism inherent in all ordinary discourse. As real dialogue by definition adds something to discourse, it has an irenic virtue and can count as a spiritual exercise.

Genesis of a Personal Self

If the foregoing analysis is correct, the first and greatest paradox is that the ego, like the spirit, has no existence on its own. If it does exist, it must be as a being which (sometimes) manages, after much effort, to identify itself as a person. Let me for the moment put off examining the question of how real the ego actually is. For now, let us just assume that this is a difficult undertaking, full of illusions for the unwary. Later on I shall have an opportunity to detail some of the subtle and protean forms these illusions can take.

43

Illusions of Personal Identity

The principle is simple. In my particular perspective, there are illusions of the person because there are illusions of personal identity that arise during communication. A rudimentary typology would suggest two types of communicational illusion, total and partial, both equally serious.

The illusion will be termed primary or total when there is no functional mapping at all between the self and the discursive agencies. In all walks of society we find an abundance of peremptory people (who speak to make the other person speak to them, or for fear that the other person will do so), as well as timid types (who listen intently to avoid having to speak), and touchy people who cannot stand being spoken about in any terms whatever. Pascal, himself touchy on this point, remarks in substance that nobody would be entirely happy to hear what their best friends say about them behind their backs. Whether among clerics or the laity, technicians or philosophers, there are assuredly very few great persons. And yet, however difficult and painful it may be, it is my duty to attempt the identification of myself as a person. To a third party, I always seem different from his or her model of me, constantly changing, and he or she may find this picturesque or ridiculous. Unlike me, however, the other is not in charge of my personal identity. The self is both the craftsman and the final result in a responsible labor of self-identification, which has its own singular history.

The illusion is partial or secondary when what little functional mapping is achieved proves to be illusory. The psychoanalytic listening process has managed to reveal all sorts of displacements and masks in the ways in which people address and delocute others. Verbal interactions in the present show distortions that can be explained by earlier psychological damage; these strongly influence our spontaneous identifications. It remains the responsibility of each of us not to be blinded by these opaque aspects of our experience. The task of personal identification is never completed, especially because communication that is easy with one interlocutor can be precarious with another, straightforward today but uneasy tomorrow. There is something obviously provocative about the methodological principle adopted by the Palo Alto school, which privileges interactions in the present or from the immediate past. Paul Watzlawick refuses to resort to the conscious or unconscious memory of people involved in the present system, for whom a more satisfactory homeostasis is to be found.[38]

Difficulties in Functional Mapping

The wealth of evidence accumulated by studies in genetic psychology, as well as the strategies of psychoanalytic anamnesis, can make a useful contribution to the debate. We now know that before a child comes to exist in and for itself, it exists for those close to it. The parents' desire (or lack thereof) and what they say (or do not say) are reflected onto the child. It stands as an objective pole in many different relations; from its gestation on, and sometimes before, the fetus is spoken *about* by others. It is a far-reaching truism that my existence has already been tried and judged, found innocent or guilty, before I come into the world. Those around me have more or less assigned me a place in my family and in their own plans; a fore-name already identifies me with my grandfather, unless I supposedly take after some more distant figure.* In short, I am thoroughly *delocuted* by everyone, in accordance with the inherent relationship structures of my culture and the particular idioms by which they are actualized in my family, which are simply different ways for the group to understand that it exists within a social space. All of this is also in accordance, as Jacques Lacan continually insisted, with a powerfully determining semiotic structure.

There is no question of denying effects like these, whether on the level of relationships or on that of the signifier; the relations between the subject and the other who speaks about him or her do indeed form a structure. The autonomous self that must spring up and be able to defend itself will of necessity arise as part of a system. But that is not a sufficient condition.

The work of personal identification is a long-term task. Metaphorically, we might see it as a sort of itinerary, with the self immediately being thrown into the uncertainties of a journey. Each time this *viator* imagines the end has been reached, it will turn out to be an illusion. We cannot foresee all the dangers of this journey, but we can guess that somewhere along the way we shall come upon alienation, diverse and fascinating, and even self-impersonation. Each time, the high cost of this fascination will be that communication is broken off.

The ego must eventually learn to deal with inputs from the stereotypes applied to it. As we shall see, such data bring about a quite remarkable kind of "symbolic prematuration." The mother's discourse is obliged to anticipate the *I* in the child's psyche, if only to translate its gurgling cries into a call for attention. This is a moment of characteristic violence, both absolute and necessary, yet one that is regularly misunderstood. Earliest childhood is typically a time when relations with adults are blatantly unequal. Humans as linguistic animals suffer when they are unable to formulate any of their stronger affective drives in language. Each encounter with another person presents the child's psyche with an excess of information.[39] In other words,

*Translator's note: traditionally, in France, a saint from the religious calendar.

45

the child's capacity both to anticipate and to react is literally overwhelmed by contact with its adult entourage, whom it is not allowed to "answer back": "Never, before today, have I seen grown-ups cry, and I cannot understand why grandma keeps repeating: 'Say goodbye to your father, you won't see him any more, poor man; he died too soon, before his time'"[40]

There is here an excessive supply of meaning. The devouring mother's words are vitally necessary for the child's physical and psychic survival, but they do the child "primary" violence by anticipating by far and so forestalling its ability to understand their meaning;

> Hiding behind a chest, in a dark corner, I watch my mother writhing on the ground, moaning and grinding her teeth. My grandmother kneels beside her, telling her in a gentle, happy voice: "In the name of the Father and the Son! Be patient, Varvara! O Most Holy Mother of God, our protectress. . . ." They frighten me. They drag themselves about the floor beside my father, brushing against him with shouts and lamentations; he, motionless, has a grim smirk on his lips. They thrash about like this for a long time.[41]

The mother's supply of meaning prejudges her child's demand for it, which she formulates in lieu and instead of the *infans*. By articulating both a desire (her own) and a demand (that of the infans), she in a way monopolizes both the listening and the speaking roles. This is a remarkable pragmatic short-circuit. When does the danger of excess, the threat of alienation for the child, appear? Milan Kundera tells us that Jacomil's mother had decided even before he was born that he would be a poet, a second Rimbaud. This bitter woman hoped thus to have her revenge against fate. She had chosen a name that means "he who loves the spring": "When Jacomil spoke his first word, which was 'mummy,' his mother was deliriously happy; she thought to herself that her son's intelligence, which as yet was composed of only one single concept, was entirely taken up with her alone, and that in the future this intelligence would grow, ramify, and enrich itself, but she would always remain its root."[42]

When the mother takes unfair advantage of the situation in which she has to satisfy the child's elementary needs, making it the object of her own desire, she is hoping to perpetuate a situation that should no longer exist. Particularly at the moment of language acquisition, she is deliberately subjecting the child to a dual constraint, that of thinking for itself and that of thinking as she thinks. The mother does everything she can to encourage the child to think and speak, but she finds it hard to accept the autonomy of its thought; she considers herself to be as indispensable to its "proper" thinking as she recently was to its proper digestion.

From a genetic point of view there is no doubt that it is first of all the other who speaks and addresses me. As a child, I only gain access to language by entering into the game of listening and speaking which everyone else has always played before me. The initial pragmatic situation is not one of two people standing in front of each other as equals, but of a child lying on its back and looking up at a grown-up. From the first, the other encourages me to respond. He or she signals his or her expectation that I will occupy the position of speaker, even if only by replying to my cries with words, and by taking care to behave toward me as he or she would toward a speaking subject.

In this situation there is therefore a real risk of excess, which becomes even a temptation. All it takes is for the relation of dependence to become firmly established, and for the child to take its own image directly from the adult giver. Soon the child will signify only that for which the other is the spokesperson, and of which he will be no more than an insignificant echo. The child's situation is such that discourse addressed to it (and discourse about it) overwhelms it with excess and frustration. The defenseless child is assailed by verbal violence, a violence that does provide the ego with its first identificatory landmarks, but which the child must fight in order to assert its own identity: for the self, this is the heroic period.

Pragmatic Prematuration

That said, I would claim that this state of prematuration offers a genuinely pragmatic starting point. This is a metatheoretical decision that the foregoing discussions have begun to justify. The analyses that follow will start from this presupposition.

The Notion of Allocutive Ambiguity

It is clear that well before its birth, and often before its conception, the child is a focus of different attributes. When we say that this leaves its mark on its "unconscious," what does that mean from our present point of view? Above all, that not all aspects of communication itself are accessible to the conscious mind, particularly in the case of a child, in the sense that it is preceded and preformed by the other's discourse. The network of family relationships forms a structure of expectation into which the child is fitted. A name, which is both a concrete and a symbolic condition, is set aside for it. As we have just seen, the reasons for this preformation are to a large extent pragmatic. It is a fact that the individual starts off small and incapable of speech, and that he or she is a being in the rapid process of becoming, in an opaque world which speaks. The world as he or she finds it is one in which people speak to him/her and in which he/she cannot reply.

47

In my view, insufficient emphasis has been placed on the difficulty of this allocution process, for which there is one very general explanation. Like any other being who is rapidly evolving, someone for instance who is sick or dying, the child is an ambiguous, unstable allocutee. It lives with its future as much as its past. No one quite knows who it is. It therefore follows that errors of address are constantly being committed. In other words, the language addressed to the child contains what might be called an allocutive ambiguity. This provides a basis for reinterpreting many phenomena which until now have been explained by the notion of a double bind. Up to a point, it is impossible to eliminate this ambiguity from the adult's discourse to the child. "Be independent" is a recommendation the child can understand. A recommendation is not an order. Normally, when its mother advises it to be independent, the child will take what she tells him on two different levels: obey me now; be free later on. The whole problem is to find an appropriate and fair mode of communication with a rapidly developing being. The fault, or rather the pragmatic error, is for the mother to want to preserve the status quo of infantile dependence in her rational behavior toward the child.

In the end, the weakness of the childish ego's being can be put down to a particularly obvious lack of personal identification. This problem can only be resolved in principle by a normalization of communicational activity. Until this norm is attained, it is easy to imagine the disturbances and distortions that can disrupt and slow down the child's development. Things happen very fast. Genetically, a babe in arms will have occupied the position of a "he/she" in the parental discourse before it becomes a "you," when people start to speak to it like a real allocutee. It is only much later that it will come to occupy its place as a personal self, when it emerges from the relational status quo of the infans and gains access to the specific temporality of the child. But before that can happen, it must go from being a delocuted *him/her* to a speaking *I;* it must learn its first lesson in contradiction, and reject the omniscience in the name of which the other claims to speak.

Uncertainties and Delays in the Child's Self-Integration

It is easy to see how difficult this is. Almost impossible, if the other refuses to allow his or her discourse to be questioned in the name of a reality which, even for an adult, remains inexhaustible. First, however, the child will have to learn to identify itself with the way in which others address it, by speaking of itself in the first person.

In short, the child's integration of the three positions is subject for a considerable time to uncertainties, delays, and conflicts. Particularly as the ego acts as a focus of subjective relations long before it becomes the center of personal integration. Even when it is used in context, the statement "I am speaking to you" is not sufficient to establish the intersubjective reality of the speakers. The condition of neurotic pseudology provides ample evidence that this is true, and it is confirmed by the genetically very late acquisition of those most personal of pronouns, "I" and "you." The child hears itself referred to by name, sometimes followed by the third person. The breakthrough is not so much the occurrence of "I" in the child's discourse (which incidentally also marks the achievement of personal identity), but rather his or her ability to distinguish between the agencies "I," "you," and "he/she," to employ them in a relational way, and to use an integrational mapping of all three for his or her own benefit. Only then will back-reference to the self occur in the child's discourse, and always with difficulty, as it is at once mediate, indirect, and postponed. Mediate, because it operates through shifters encoded in the linguistic system; indirect, because it can only come about reflexively within a statement made jointly with an adult about the world; and postponed, because between personal identity and its linguistic mark various masks and mendacities interpose themselves and interfere.[43]

The self sometimes remains overwhelmed for life by the different types of "he/she"s and "you"s used to refer to it, with their lasting, often permanently precessive resonance. Correctly speaking, prior "he/she"s and "you"s are never completely reabsorbed. Freud tells us that a woman's dearest desire is often to make her partner into something like a son. We are marked by the chance conditions of our triple birth. On this point, reports of analysis sessions show that the present attitude of the parents is a good indicator (though one that needs to be interpreted) of their objective relations with the child. These pragmatic distortions are a necessary, if not a sufficient, condition for a proportion of our neurotic illness.

For when distortion of the communicational regime becomes systematic, we enter the pathological domain of neurosis. One step more, if the pragmatic competence itself is affected, and we arrive at psychosis. The schizophrenic is someone who has lost (or who never acquired) the ability to enter into the type of balanced interlocutive relationship that conditions the very possibility of discourse. As a result, at the very least certain signifieds strike him with obsessive force, first in relation to the material of the signifier (any symbol at all can call up the same signified, by substitution or association), and second in relation to the referential context (the signified ceases to be contextualized, loses all pragmatic pertinence, and becomes incomprehensible to any other speaker). Examples of this abound. In the case of the subject afflicted with delirium, we find this same inability to contextualize meaning, but contrary to the schizophrenic, for this person a given signifier can refer back to any signified at all. Thus the patient will find the thing he or she calls an attacker or persecutor everywhere around him or her.

It is therefore obviously not a matter of indifference whether my mother spoke *of* me during her pregnancy as an inconvenient or parasitic object, or *to* me from the start as a complete person. And later, whether or not she refused to listen when I attempted to speak, thereby making me like someone who becomes a liar by force of being misunderstood. If other real people have refused to listen to it, the child runs the risk in turn of becoming a bad listener, by repressing its internal listening faculty.

Let me now state the problem that the child must solve in its psychological development. It must above all break the vicious circle of its dual or mirror relationship with its mother, by mastering the system of the three positions of utterance. Its desire doubtless relates in the first instance to the mother; other authors have stressed the fact that incest comes first in the child's affective development. But it must be understood that the incest taboo demands a painful renunciation. It is also a necessary obstacle. Only by accepting the incest taboo, and later the law, can the child become itself.

In that enterprise it has one ally, a symbolic actor within the family structure: the father, whose function is precisely to differentiate the distinctive status of each person in a ternary structure. The father's place is that of the third party who conditions the possibility of a stable system of positions of utterance. At the same time he represents the general rule of communication beyond the pleasure principle. As we know, Freud made the phallic image of that which the mother does not have into a blank marker of the third party's position. This castration image, which is found in all mythologies, is experienced as an anxiety about losing the differential indicators necessary for personal identification.

It will be appreciated that the integration of the three positions in the communication act that conditions personal recognition will be facilitated by the pragmatic attitude that others strive to adopt towards the infans. There always remains the danger of becoming locked in a self-reflexive system. It is common knowledge that the role of the oedipal complex is one of relational differentiation: that is what helps to open up a breach in the fusional relationship with the mother.[44] We therefore have to revise our idea of intersubjectivity in a determinedly concrete direction. It now refers simultaneously to an intersubjective relation and to an objective question of structure; it of course connotes the relation to the other, not as someone like me, but as someone who is different and initially beyond my grasp.

In general, a child is in a precarious position. To begin with, everyone agrees that he or she does not speak. This is an inveterate belief; parents tend not to recognize the child as an uttering agency, i.e., as a virtual participant in semantic interchange. The fetus, the infant, and even the child are considered to be neurologically and symbolically premature human beings. More radically, if in fact all speech in earliest childhood emanates from the other person, the human offspring is regarded as pragmatically premature. At this point my interpretation coincides with the classical reading of the problem. Freud showed that the child is invested by its parents in a way that reactivates their old oedipal situations. These are presented to the child at the start of the process by which the child constructs his or her own oedipal complex. Here lies the source of many later communicational distortions. The interlocutive relation into which the child is about to enter will be vulnerable to all sorts of dissymmetries, preemptive behavior, and abuses of authority. The pragmatic attitude people adopt toward him or her is rarely the canonical one; for we should not forget that the interlocutive relation is symmetrical in terms of rights, with each participant learning through the other how to see him or herself as a *he/she* at the same time as a *you*, without renouncing his or her right to speak in the first person, and encouraging the other to do the same.

We may therefore infer that personal identity will remain precarious in the face of the constraints weighing down the communicational schema. This is a frequent and, as will have become clear, far from negligible danger; an identificational conflict underlies most neuroses. In such cases both personal identity and the communicational regime are disturbed simultaneously. For that to happen all it takes is for me to be no longer able to withstand my own objectivization, which occurs when others look at me, of course, but also (and more significantly) during verbal exchange, particularly if the present pragmatic situation echoes the earlier situation of the infans which is felt as intolerable ("persecutory," in the terminology of Melanie Klein). How often do we see interlocutors commenting on the doings of a third party as a diversion, because one or the other of them cannot stand the delocutive objectivization implicit in the address itself? The conversation shifts compulsively toward the absent person, who, like a sacrificial beast at an initiation ceremony, bears the cost of establishing the momentary atmosphere of harmony. The partner is often asked to take sides, and inevitably becomes an accomplice.

Ego Sum?

However precarious may be personal identification and its product, the identity of the ego, we can see why the temptation toward subjectivity is still so strong. As we have seen, the ego must always experience and grasp itself without having any possibility of self-representation. Narcissus is unable to provide himself with a self-portrait. He fails to grasp the fissures and distortions that compromise his being as it is transformed by becoming. His existence is never achieved, but instead it is suspended and in a sense proleptic. Just because the self has been denied its chance of identification in the present, this does not mean it can fall back on old positions, which are constantly shifting. Integration of the three positions, on which personal identity is conditioned, is problematic; so too is the reality of the ego.

From a Logical Point of View

Suppose nevertheless that integration is achieved: what then is the meaning of the phrase *ego sum?*

From a logical point of view, how are we to analyze the existential statement "I am"? I shall do no more than make some preliminary remarks here. In post-Fregean logic the *sum* cannot be interpreted in the classical sense, where existence is not a predicate and its expression is an existential quantifier. The existence of subjectivity must at least be taken in the sense of effective reality. In the same way, Frege often draws a distinction of emphasis between *Wirklichkeit* and existence, expressed in such terms as "there is such and such a thing" (*es gibt ein*). The prevalence of existence in its logical sense in treatments of the problem by Frege, Russell, and Quine should not blind us to this distinction; otherwise we would be committing the grave sophism of confusing concepts on different levels.

As P. T. Geach quite rightly points out, reality can be attributed to individual objects, whereas existence cannot.[45] When we ask whether there is such and such a thing, we are asking whether there is anything that belongs to a particular class of objects, or in other words whether there is anything of that sort. And of course we can never reasonably affirm or deny the existence, in this sense, of an individual object, including the ego[46]—any more than we can reasonably ask whether a particular thing or individual is numerous or frequent.

Frege did not explore existence in the sense of reality at any length. No doubt this was because he was interested in the foundations of arithmetic, and strictly speaking numbers are objects, not realities.

The difference in logical status will be seen immediately if the following negative existential statements are compared:

1. Pegasus does not exist
2. The golden mountain does not exist
3. Abel is no more.

In (1), if I do not make the proper noun Pegasus a simple abbreviation of a definite description, "Bellerophon's Horse" (Russell), the statement relates to a certain usage of the proper noun, which serves to deny that "Pegasus" denotes anything at all. Here I am not using the proper noun; I am just speaking about its usage. Of course, this occurrence of "exist" is not predicative.

In (2), the statement no more concerns the golden mountain than the first did Pegasus. The grammatical subject is a predicating expression which I am affirming does not apply to any object: there is nothing which is "the golden mountain." More generally, if F is a predicating expression, saying that F exists attributes existence neither to an object nor to a predicate, but predicates the property F to something. As for "exist," here again it is not a predicate.

In (3), on the other hand, the occurrence of "exist" does encompass a predicate, as when we say that an individual is real, meaning that he or she still exists, or has begun or ceased to exist. We can no longer claim that we are not speaking about Abel, but only about the meaning of his name. We are saying that some misfortune has happened to Abel. Here, "is" means "lives." For a living being, "exist" means the same as "live." As we can see, the fact that the verb "exist" is not a true predicate in (1) and (2) in no way prejudges the outcome of our analysis of a type (e) proposition.

It is in this sense of being that we say that something continues, or has ceased, to exist. And for a living being, continuing to exist means remaining the same X for a certain time, where X represents a conceptual term (what Frege calls a *Begriffswort*). And this in turn means the persistence of a living being in the conceptual form expressed by the predicating exprssion X. We should note that this is the way in which a man in his biological individuality exists or continues to exist, so that child, young man, and adult are declared to be the same individual.

The word "be" has been eroded by its frequency of use to the point where it is often reduced to insignificance. When speaking of the verb "to be," we should not forget that beside its syntactic function it contains a lexical notion, "to really be somewhere," "to be truly present." This notion can play its role to the full without trespassing on the logical function of the quantifier. For "to be" is the ultimate verb of condition. It designates the state of being that defines a being which is something. By specifying that something belongs to a particular domain of objects, "to exist" links the existential quantifier with the categories that define a given sphere of existence.

But then what sort of existence, or reality, can a human being have when he or she is seen as a person? Is it the same sort that he or she has as a biological individual? In that case, to say that a living being exists is to grant him or her reality according to a criterion that may be stated as follows: X is real if and only if X acts, or undergoes change, or both, where by "acts" is meant both mental activity and activity that transforms the environment.

Let us then consider the following statements:

4. The ego does not exist
5. I do not exist

Statement (4) has metalinguistic or metacommunicational status. It is saying something different from (5), which is one of those statements that are necessarily false when made in a present context, and that create a pragmatic paradox, as we shall see. On the other hand, statement (4) is a dubious proposition that belongs to speculative language. For us to analyze it we find that the distinction between existence and reality is indispensable, though not sufficient. The ego is no longer a thing that can be described, even if that thing were a living individual. It is actually a person.

Existence and Reality

Persons are, horses are, numbers are, God perhaps is. Everyone understands what these statements mean, and realizes that not all those things *are* in the same way. Numbers do not exist as an electron or a tree does. A person does not exist in the same way as a tree or other living beings. As for how to think about this difference, the problem is neither a trivial nor a hair-splitting one. In particular, in the subject function it is impossible to replace expressions referring to persons (proper names, definite descriptions, personal pronouns) with expressions denoting physical bodies. Apart from the fact that when we desginate a person as a subject, that subject is assumed to be indivisible (X has a particular feeling, rather than his head; Y has done something, rather than her hand), identical (X whom I see here is the same as the one I met there), and re-identifiable (the person who performed an act yesterday is the same as the one who will take responsibility for it today), we should be aware that the process of reference by means of personal pronouns (*I, you*) is complex and needs to be studied in its own right.

At that point, the reality criterion for individuality stated above ceases to be appropriate. Like any living being, the personal ego has a propensity for action; but at any given moment it is both action and the product of action, an indefinite product. As we shall see, it possesses both status as a person and personal status. Equally, the distribution of the autonym "me" shows that it can both act as the antecedent of a personal pronoun before a verb, as in "me, I am traveling around," and stand in identifying position before a proper noun, as in "me, Gabriel, I am traveling around." The ego is both the agent and the result of communicational activity. We can therefore advance the following provisional explanation for the reality of the ego:

> X is real if and only if X is capable of performing an act of synthetic identification in the course of the communicational situations in which he or she may become involved.

Note that this criterion is redundant, because there are many communicational situations that do not lead to any reidentification of X.

From a philosophical point of view, this is the first confirmation that the phrase *ego sum* cannot have the obvious meaning that philosophers of consciousness give it. In particular, it is impossible to conceive of the self as pure presence to oneself. I have just shown that the self is not a being whose personal identity is naturally given, or conferred by awareness of some spiritual substance residing within or linked to it, as though self-discovery meant simply a descent into one's own mind.[47] Nor is it enough to recognize oneself in a loved one, a privileged other, as one eye sees itself in another, a tiny silhouette, a pupil.[48] For the self is a being that sometimes manages and sometimes fails to constitute itself as one and the same, through all the confrontations in which it occupies a formal position or an institutional role from which to communicate.

Personal reality is the human mode of existence. The fact that I am is a fluctuating reality which can be sustained and determined only by action. This is what is expressed, despite its inadequacy, by the phrase *ego adsum*. In communicative activity the self either truly discovers itself or slips away and conceals itself. We can see that this activity might be compromised or suspended by an opposing and rebellious process of de-identification, once I refuse to play the role I am called upon to play by my position, a particular institution, or my reputation.

As we can see, the identification of the self as a person, which it is the ego's job to bring about for its own advantage, depends in the most direct and incontrovertible way on the relation with the other. We can go further: loss of this relation entails the loss of any synthetic idea of a personal self. The condition is therefore a necessary one. But my thesis is stronger than that. Its claim is that the idea of a personal self is compromised as soon as the different relations in which I engage with other people cease to work together to form a coherent system.

One thing is sure: the certitude of self is anything but primary. If we still want to talk about our experience of self, we can say that it is discursive before ever being existential. The following chapters will indicate how that experience can be traced through the logico-linguistic marks it leaves behind.

2　Man without Qualities

How beautiful you are, my dearest.
O how beautiful.
Your eyes are like doves.
—*Song of Songs*

I HAVE set out to defend and illustrate the reality of the interpersonal relation. But it is a characteristic of the most basic facts that they are philosophically irreducible and tend therefore to be misunderstood and misrepresented. As such, their recognition involves painstaking work, unending polemical activity. Ultimately, what needs to be shown is that all attempts at conceptual reduction fail in that they presuppose that which they propose to reduce.

In view of the ego's personal mode of reality, can we speak of the self at all, and if so, how is it legitimate to do so? For Montaigne, such questions were far from academic. In one sense such an undertaking is extravagant, with a complexion far removed from that of everyday experience.[1] In another, it is something we do all the time. And yet, how are we to speak about it? Indeed, what discursive form can the confession of a personal self actually take? We have fallen into the habit of using the possessive in connection with the empirical self, so that we talk about my feelings (which I describe to you), my beliefs (which I state for you), my actions (for which I take responsibility), and my memories (which I tell you about); we seem to relate all of these to a first-person subject as if it were a man with real qualities. Ordinary grammar thus allows me to speak of the qualities (and faults) of the self. This speech, however, is not without paradoxes, as will soon become clear.

Desiring

Many of our contemporaries subscribe to a thesis on personal identity which, though weak, seems plausible. It includes positions that today are clichés but only recently seemed new and exciting: the identity I see myself as having cannot be divorced from my identity for others, its actualization depends on other people without whom I cannot survive, and so on. In such views the other person acts no longer simply as rival, adversary, or enemy, but as the vital witness to my existential self-recognition. We know very well that a man needs a woman to confer on him his identity as a husband; that a woman can never be a mother unless she has a child; that a man in love who had no one to love would only be a potential lover; etc.

All this is only too clear. Everyday discourse tends to replace Socratic self-gnosis with a *loqueris, ergo sum.* Theatrical discourse, too, has seized insistently on the theme. Beckett, Pinter, Pirandello, Losey, Ionesco, and Albee all show us beings engaged in a search at once anguished and grotesque for a self that constantly eludes them, a quest for identity full of sound and fury because it is always condemned to seek the sanction of others, of witnesses.

Counting for Somebody

In reality, personal identity demands a stronger thesis than this. It is not only that we want to see our view of ourselves confirmed by others. The real problem is that if the other does not respond, he or she introduces a complete emptiness and powerlessness into our notion of what we are. So much so that any meeting at all can appear as a kind of oasis in the desert of some people's lives. Striking back against frustration by destroying the other in one's imagination is no solution. All that does is to close the vicious circle, for the greater the other's inability to accept me, the greater is my need to destroy or exclude him; but the more I exclude him, the more I feel my own emptiness and powerlessness.[2] It becomes a never-ending race to catch up with myself. As soon as I attempt to eliminate the other as a way of being certain of my own essence, I start to endanger my own identity.

This process of reciprocal implication is so total that the road to frustration and despair is soon the only one open to us. We can see from this that a relational conception of personal identity has certain general implications for everyone. If A is in relation with B, then B plays a part in the definition of

A, and vice versa. For unlike need, desire is carried by our relations with others.

In abstraction, the central idea in a relational theory of desire is not difficult to formulate: A desires to contribute in some way to defining B, and wants in turn to be defined by him or her. This is shown clearly enough by the frustration mechanism associated with the process. Nothing is more frustrating than being unable to count for something in someone else's eyes, i.e. to *make a difference* to him or her. Failure to do this results precisely in what we call indifference.

A relational or dialogical theory of desire disposes of a number of unfounded commonplaces of the following type: my desire is different from yours; it accommodates itself to or intersects with yours; it is a desire for your desire. As though desire could be determined simply by reference to the ego. In my view, it must be seen as a function of the relation itself; we need to understand how it is that we can be in a desiring relation.

To do that we must find a path between two extreme ways of looking at the problem. The first is typical of the Hegelian idea of desire. It is centered on the self, from which desire proceeds outward like the movement of appropriation, or even negation, by which consciousness strives precisely to become self-consciousness. As if the activities of those around us were only designed to increase the feeling we have of our own personal life. The second approach, on the contrary, refuses to consider desire a natural necessity. It sees desire simply as an ethical awareness of being separated from the other person, a form of respect for the other as such, in all his or her magisterial and irreducible dignity. The reader will perhaps have recognized here the position defended in France by Emmanuel Levinas.[3] According to this view, desire tends toward that which is absolutely other. It is an opening-outward with no return to the self, and therefore no link with pleasure. No consummation, no satisfaction, no fulfillment.

A Dialogical Theory of Desire

A dialogical theory of desire will be founded on the relational principle. Desire is not lust, any more than it is need. The ultimate goal toward which it tends—its *ariston* as well as its telos (to use the language of Aristotle)—is that which is good. We know that there are always stumblings, failures, and misunderstandings along the way; you want a turtledove but you catch a woodpigeon. But what we are pursuing in these refracted images is always that which is supremely desirable. I suggest that, for a person, what is supremely desirable is to be able to live out one's relational condition to the fullest.

For I do not believe that desire in its essence seeks to realize itself in its identity with the Same, as would be the case were it governed by the pleasure principle. Nor do I believe that desire is some indeterminate search for satisfaction, always straining toward the appropriation of its object in the object's negative difference, and thereby its destruction. However, neither does desire aim to experience itself in another concrete consciousness, enjoying the pleasurable intuition of a unity between two different awarenesses of self. Instead of this type of effusive unity, all that is felt is once again frustration. Hegel is right: the soul that does not recognize itself in its own operation becomes an enigma to itself. Just when it thinks it can grasp life, it looks on death, and decides that "the world is badly put together." Equally, the idea that the soul seeks pleasure from the very start, out of a kind of natural concupiscence, is a typically abstract and puritan one. It is also highly ambivalent, as one's desire for self-affirmation would immediately clash with the same desire in others, so that each person's self-esteem would soon engender hatred of the other. This type of conception is typically monological; it completely misinterprets the struggle for recognition.

But I do not believe either that the original vocation of desire was to feel the pull of an absolute Other. Without wishing to lower the high-minded tone of the debate, or attack the context in which Levinas has chosen to situate it, let us take sexual desire as our touchstone. According to Pierre Aulagnier,[4] a heterological conception of desire gives quite a good account, in its very asymmetry, of female eroticism. When a woman talks about her desire, he explains, she is really talking about the man's desire; as if all she wanted were to offer herself to the desire of the other. Beyond the fact that this asymmetrical view can be put down to particular cultural circumstances (the fact that pleasure is codified by men), it does explain why the experience of femininity is a problematic one. But let us now ask ourselves what happens to the man, now firmly established as a desiring being. We have to assume that he at least is able to feel an autonomous desire, that he is its master and first subject. At the same time, the essence of the woman's desire will have turned back on itself, toward the fantasy form that she adopts in order to offer herself to the other's gaze. Quite obviously, we have now come back to the polar dialectic of the Same and the Other.

In their needs as in their desires, people stand in a relationship to absence and lack. There are indeed extravagant illnesses in which desire resembles a need. "Beautiful desires," exclaims Gide, "I shall bring you crushed bunches of grapes, I shall fill again your enormous cups." But to have needs is not the same as to have desires. Need is what I live off as an individual at the center of my environment. Need invites us to overcome the alterity of that which we need to live, in order to preserve the integrity of our individual self. This alterity is that of the Other—be it food or shelter—constituted by the world on which I depend, and from which I free myself through work. Needs move centripetally toward the Same, to ensure its permanence and security. They are therefore ordered as pairs of opposites. People need food, but they also need intervals of activity, rest, etc., between meals. In contrast, desire is not projected toward what is desirable without becoming an invitation to live a relationship with someone else. It therefore moves centrifugally, out toward others.

> My desire
> Your desire
> Conjoined by a leap into the in-breathed void
> Break against the awning of our eyes[5]

Whereas the satisfaction of a need suspends the alterity of the thing that is possessed, desire is something not to be satisfied, but to be experienced—so that my personal identity can be constituted by a mutual relation of myself and the other to that which we lack. My claim is that sexual desire, even when blurred by anxiety, is undoubtedly grafted onto the relation with others. Which is to say that it cannot be called up by some absolutely irreducible difference from the other person, in the face of whom the desire should remain infinitely inadequate, indefinitely frustrated: the necessary condition of desire, it seems to me, is really that it makes a positive difference to the other person as soon as I enter into a relationship with that person. Our desire exists contemporaneously with that relationship.

In that case, there is indeed a sense in which a person either is or is not capable of desiring. What does this new desire seek? In fact, this great desire, which now wants to give rather than take, to thank rather than ask, does not seek anything at all. Like happiness for Montesquieu, it can be seen in this perspective as an aptitude, as the fruit of our relational maturity. Its final aim, whether for the giver or the receiver, is to make a difference to someone else. In methodological terms, whether the problem is to explain frustration, immaturity, dissolution, or other psychological side effects, our starting point is no longer the subject's originally asymmetrical relation to his or her desire; on the contrary, the positive difference that desire seeks can now be explained as a differentiation caused by the desiring relationship between persons. And that in turn is the starting point for an explanation of both frustration and perverse effects.

There is nothing more frustrating than being unable, despite great expenditure of energy (libidinal and other), to make a difference to the other person. But this type of difference *presupposes* the establishment of a relation. Otherwise, the door is opened to perverse effects. Female frigidity, and by analogy male impotence, are easy to reinterpret in this light. The former often goes hand in hand with a refusal to allow the man to triumph over the self on the pretext of "giving satisfaction." Conversely, the latter is often determined by the man's refusal to give the woman the satisfaction of satisfying him.

There is nothing more perverse than desiring everything one desires non-relationally, i.e. *for oneself.* In that case, the very movement of desire is perverted. How is it possible? The quality of unreflecting desire is to transcend itself in the direction of the object, by grasping in it an embodiment of desirability. Desire is thus seen as centrifugal, as if the desirable were moving the desirer. But if the awareness of desiring turns back on itself, this first movement becomes perverted. Desire knows itself as desire. Affectivity is something that is given for itself, and with it appears the possibility of an egotistical life.

We cannot exclude the possibility that a particular process of reflection will bring about a fundamental change for the worse in desire of the naive kind: as I watch myself desiring, I might replace that which was desirable by my desire itself; this desire I then substitute either for the desired object, or for the desiring relation that links two people. What can be the nature of this reflection that so poisons desire?

First Experience of the Spirit

The French moralists of the seventeenth century tracked down the elusive self (*le moi*) at work within a wide range of human activities—from feelings and desires to actions—whose very structure became a constant reminder that the self was monadic; they gave that self the name *l'amour-propre*—literally, self-love. Whatever the question, self-esteem always has the same answer: Me (Moi). Such is the basic mechanism of ordinary egotism. Now, if what the psychologists of l'amour propre say is true, these feelings originate in our reflexive experience. At least (and this is a point to which I shall return), this is true if reflection is seen simply to establish empirical consciousness as a pleasant or an unpleasant state, which can then substitute itself for what is desirable and become a motivator of desire in its turn. Thought preoccupies itself with the frontiers of the body, busily assessing pleasures and avoiding pain. Desire plays wily games with its apparent meaning, something Dostoyevsky explored to its absurd limits. Even a feeling of humiliation will do, when thinking about it turns into a pleasure in its own right: "It came to the point when I felt a sort of small, secret pleasure, abnormal and vulgar, in returning to my hovel on one of those nasty St. Petersburg nights, realizing perfectly well that I had done something disgusting . . . and gnawing at myself, biting and sucking my own body until the bitterness turned into shameful, accursed pleasure and then, finally, became a definite, serious delight. . . ."[6]

Just as the possibility of lying is implicit in consciousness itself, and stands as a measure of both its greatness and its pettiness, so we are starting to see that a certain way of thinking about the self, far from exemplifying human greatness, can instead prove people base, if not actually cursed. Moreover, the monadic self—with its capacity for self-idolatry and ability to live out its fantasies—should be sought not in the actions, desires, and feelings of everyday, unself-conscious life, nor indeed behind them as their cause; it makes its appearance only with reflexive thinking, as the central pole of the infinite series of conscious personae reflected by such thought.

Fortunately, the sort of reflection that poisons desire is quite different from the sort by which the desiring person seeks to grasp his or her own image through a genuine relation of desire. We should not mix up two different things here. The bad type of reflection *precedes* the subject's involvement in communication; its centripetal movement impedes the thrust of desire and insults it. The good type also involves a turning back toward the self, but only *after* communication has been established. As we have always known (and as I shall shortly confirm), reflection in this last sense helps the process of identifying a personal self. Our experience of this undoubted aspiration to identify ourselves through our desires, feelings, and actions is relational in nature. But it is just as much "spiritual," too. And since the word is available, I shall say that this is the first experience of the spirit.

There is a second one: the work of identification that takes place within the communicational game has its counterpart in the process of dis-identification, undergone either with or without the individual's consent, which appears in crisis situations. Any crisis, be it social, doctrinal, or familial, poses a threat to personal identity. As Cicero noted, someone involved in a court case occupies three different positions and sees things from three points of view: the position I am defending is always perceived in opposition to those of my adversary and of the judge.

At this point it is no longer enough to suggest, as Martin Buber does, that a society is human only to the extent that its members mutually confirm each other's identity. This thesis is just too weak. It still implies some sort of dialectic between ego and other, both substantially autonomous. We need to go so far as to think of the *I* as its own goal and issue. The ego is not simply a task, as people have repeated ad nauseam. The *I* consists in that particular competence of a tactical nature which Saint-Simon and Stendhal were so successful in elucidating. Tactics, the wartime art of adopting the best position, is a serious game in which each participant allows him or herself to be recognized by the other in a certain position, with personal status. The communicational game then comes into play within a ready-constituted system. This system can always be shifted a little, but the smallness of the range of possible shifts doubtless gives a measure of the humanity of a particular institution. Within its bounds, everyone feels obliged to institute him or herself in function of the largest possible number of interlocutors; or at least (in response to a sense of failure, or perhaps of one's own nobility) of the small remnant of some happy few.

The Theological Paradigm

> The Great God, He who is Begotten of God, the
> All-Shining (Apollo, the Spirit)[7]

Whether they be operating in a particular pragmatic position or, more profoundly, aspiring to create for themselves an ideal situation, *I, you* and *he/she* endlessly reflect each other. As Paul Valéry wrote, "The self says *I, you* or *he*. In me there are three persons; the Trinity. One calls me you; another, he."

It is indeed tempting to regard the doctrine of a three-way relation within the deity as the preeminent and noncontroversial paradigm of personal identity. It is not the key to the mystery, but a convenient way of thinking about it. There is no question here of converting articles of faith into units of lay philosophical meaning, nor even simply of making them explicit and accessible to reflection. In spite of the appalling misuse to which the great name of *God* has been subjected, let us not speak ill of dogma. The doctrine of the Trinity in particular has powerful heuristic possibilities. It provides an enigmatic, and in part negative, formulation of the mysterious force linking the three divine persons within the being of God. Gregory of Nazianzus explains it as follows: "It is the difference of manifestation, or rather the difference of relation, which causes their difference of Name. This is then a way of rescuing the distinction between the three Persons in the unique nature of the Divinity. The Son is indeed not the Father, since there is only one Father, but He is what the Father is. The Spirit which comes from God is not the Son, since there is only one Son, but It is what the Son is. In terms of their divinity, the three are one, but this unity is a Trinity from the point of view of its qualities."[8]

Unless, that is, it is a theological transposition of a fundamental relational phenomenon. If we were not all afraid of the sublime, I would say that human persons, just like the divine "Persons," are quite literally secondary aspects of a primary relation, a fundamental agency. Through this agency individuals become persons, subjects in the legal sense of the term; they are capable of speech but also, as Hobbes later noted, of assuming rights and duties. Like divine Persons, human persons are "divided without division, and united in division."

A Relational Intelligibility of the Person

Shall we have sufficient simplicity and strength of mind to place ourselves within the Christian mystery of the trinitary relation? In it, the three Persons are no longer named separately but understood as a unity. This "one and trinite" God is not *triplex* but *trinitas*. We might debate the nature of this unitary simplicity; we could attribute it to a unity of essence or call it, as Duns Scot did, a formal characteristic. Or again, we might grant a trinitary reality the relational unity of three persons. It is this solution that I shall attempt to trace in the works of Saint Augustine. He begins with a unity to which he brings back the three Persons, each of which is known separately through Revelation, but whose reciprocal relations and unity of operation (*opera ad extra*) he also stresses.

Whenever one of the divine Persons acts, the other two also act: this is a logical consequence, for Augustine, of the unity of their nature. He then must solve the theological difficulties this poses. How can the Son become man? How can the Holy Spirit appear as a dove, or as tongues of fire? How can the Father make His voice heard at Christ's baptism? [9] Let us take careful note of Augustine's solution, as we shall see a remarkable application of the paradigm later on. The divine Persons manifest themselves *separately*—and that is how we learn of their existence in the New Testament—but they act jointly. *Inseparabiliter Trinitas operatur.* [10] The Son is indeed the only one to have made himself visible to men through the Incarnation. But his personal union of the Word with human nature was the work of all three jointly, in the unity of their divine nature. On this point Augustine was a pioneer, showing how trinitary operation could be reconciled with the Incarnation of the Son alone. [11] Whereas Gregory of Nazianzus liked to say of the Old Testament theophanies that it was impossible to determine whether the whole of the Trinity had manifested itself, or just one of the three Persons, Augustine is more methodical, showing that the Bible did not allow such manifestations to be attributed to one and the same person, as all the Persons are consubstantial.

He had therefore to construct the concept of a trinite unity. The New Testament had certainly revealed the divine Persons in concrete form. But Augustine could not find in the natural order either the terms or the concepts he needed to speculate about them. It was not enough to claim that on the subject of God thought was truer than discourse, and reality was truer than thought.[12] Until an adequate way had been established of conceptualizing these things, using a tried and tested vocabulary, theological thinking would continue to drift, unable to arbitrate among the heretics, who sometimes applied the attributes of the Persons to the divine Nature and sometimes did the reverse.[13] It was important for Augustine to be able to distinguish conceptually between what belonged to the divine Nature and what belonged asymmetrically to each of the Persons.

I shall not say anything here about Augustine's efforts to conceive of a trinitary reality from book 5 on, except in so far as they anticipate and provide an important illustration of my theory of personal identity.

Note that he does not entirely give up using existing terms and concepts. When he asks which categories of human thought (predicaments) might in some way apply to a one and trinite God, and then examines how far the doctrine of predicables (universals) might shed light on His nature, Augustine's partner (or adversary) is clearly Aristotle. But at the same time he does attempt to create some new concepts.

Leaving aside the insurmountable problems the predicaments posed him, let us look at his analysis of the relative predicament of the relation. Against Aristotle, he argues that it is false to say that all relations are accidental and imply change. We say of God that He is Father, Son, and Holy Spirit; we do not thereby wish to express any link with ourselves or with His substance, but we simply indicate certain reciprocal relations existing within Him. These relations are not symmetrical: therefore, it is not because of his relation to the Father that the Son is equal to the Father. And yet he is equal to Him in an absolute sense. We therefore need to conceive of the divine Being as both an absolute and a relative. The relative character of Father and Son is obvious. That of the Holy Spirit is revealed not only in his own name, but also in the explanations of him offered to us in Scripture: he is *donum Dei* and a link of love between Father and Son. This can be expressed well enough by reference to these distinctive properties, but we must not allow ourselves to be taken in by words. For he is certainly the spirit of the Father and the Son, but without their being conversely the Father and Son of the Holy Spirit. Rather, it is the Father and Son together who are the giver of the Holy Spirit.[14]

As we can see, what Augustine is trying to develop is a whole doctrine of trinitary relations—paternity, filiation, procession, and so on.[15] In this way, he puts the respective positions of the persons in an order that relates them to each other within a single nature; each remains clearly distinct from the other two but not from the divine nature itself. His intention was to show that if God is a Trinity, it does not follow that we must believe Him to be triple, or that the divine nature must be seen as a sort of fourth Person, to be placed alongside the other three.

The difficulties Augustine encountered in trying to apply the doctrine of universals to God are no less instructive. He decided it was impossible to consider the relationship between the three Persons and the unity in God, which they all have in common, as a relationship of genus to species. Otherwise, we would have to say that the concept of person was also common to all of them: "The Father, the Son, and the Holy Ghost are three; so we ask: three what? and what have They in common? . . . If they are three Persons, They have in common that which makes a person."[16] However, this something they have in common cannot be numerically one thing, either. For if it were, it would have to be what constituted the Father. Otherwise, the three would be the Father to each other, just like friends who stand in a reciprocal relation. Nor are there three Sons, because neither the Father nor the Holy Spirit are Sons. How then can we conceptualize this something in common that allows us to speak of three Persons, without at the same time speaking of three essences, let alone three Gods?

Augustine has no answer to this question. Thomas Aquinas later returned to it, putting forward a solution in scholastic terms: the person, without being a *communitas rei*, could be seen as a *communitas rationis*.[17] But this meant giving up the attempt to conceptualize the relational unity of the person. Aquinas went on to develop a notion of the person which could be applied both literally and by analogy to men and to God, but in which the relational aspect remained secondary; it remained extrinsic to the notion of person, becoming identical to it only in the case of God. The distinguishing principle of the human person was that it was *this* body and *this* soul. In the case of the divine person, the personal properties of the three were to be distinguished by relations.

Of course Augustine too, falling into line with the usage of the Roman Church,[18] had never really seen the term *person* as anything more than a fairly arbitrary extrinsic name: "The Scriptures may not speak of the three Persons, but they do not contradict the idea, whereas to speak of three Gods would be directly against the Scriptures." Saint Augustine adopts the term "person" without much enthusiasm and in fact with some reservations.[19] It comes in handy, he says, if we want to express the way in which we should conceive of the Trinity, ". . . and not be absolutely at a loss for words when we are asked what the three are, since, by our own admission, there are three of them."[20]

66

Speaking of the three Persons relative in God, Augustine was on the way to understanding that while a person is not a relation as such, it is essential for him or her to be in reciprocal relations with others. Gregory had already said something similar: "O you so clever men! The name Father signifies neither essence nor action, but indicates a relation, that between the Father and his Son, or between the Son and his Father." [21]

Father and Son are differentiated only by their mutual relations and their respective positions. Each is only what he is by relation to the other. The Son is he who gives his *you* the name of Father. Now, this relative attribution (*ad iliud*), while not identical to the essential attribution of the predicates common to the three—the attribution that defines the divine essence—is nevertheless equal to it, since at the same time each term of the relation, considered with reference to itself (*ad se*), expresses the divine essence: "By the term person was meant an absence of diversity [*diversitas*], not an absence of individuality [*singularitas*]. . . . If for God being [*esse*] and existing [*subsistere*] are different [because being is an absolute term, whereas being the Father is relative to the Son], then it follows that God exists in the form of a relation." [22]

The Most Beautiful Mirror of the Trinity

Overall, it seems that Augustine failed to construct a notion of the person capable of accounting for the extra meaning that the concept of existence takes on in everyday usage when we speak about the person. In order to do that, he would have had to step outside the monadic conception of human persons and look at creatures in general. It is of course true that around his time the word was acquiring a technical and legal sense in the language of administration and the law which tended to confirm the self-sufficiency of persons. In consequence, it had become rather unsuitable for expressing the mystery of God. Augustine makes the point himself: "The three persons are a single essence in God, whereas each man, on the contrary, is a single person." [23]

It seems paradoxical that Augustine should have come close to a relational understanding of the person, based on a quite remarkable trinitary model, without ever having thought of applying it to human persons. This is particularly so as he saw the communion of men in the Church as a consequence of the communion of the Trinity. [24] And also because he had imported into theology a term borrowed from everyday usage. It was not until more modern times that such a conception became a part of anthropological thinking. In the intervening period Christians tended rather to support a monadic view of the person, which was arrived at by a well-known route.

Thinkers of the Neoplatonist School, such as Porphyrius, had conceived the idea of a substantive individuality, which introduced the concept of the *persona* (first meaning mask, then actor, and eventually social role) into the ontological vocabulary. For Thomas Aquinas, a person is "the individual substance of rational nature." A person is being *in itself*, i.e., autonomous and self-controlling, self-possessed and incommunicable. Just like the individual, the person is different from other beings. Its goal is immanent in itself and attained by its own activity. It is therefore also being *for itself*. Unlike God, in whom each person *is* for the other two, the person never *is* for others. After the discovery of subjectivity during the Renaissance, the notion came into conflict with the conscious ego, capable of being present to itself. From then on the idea of person took on a dramatic density, as the language of ontology and the language of liberty were combined: it came to mean freedom of position and the creation of self by self.

It is therefore not surprising that Saint Augustine, in his great desire to discover analogies for the trinitary mode of existence, should have found them more readily in being in general, in human rational activity or the structure of the human soul, than in the relational structure of the person. To be sure, no analogy could really do justice to the mystery of the Trinity. But the analogy with the person was reasonably accurate. It might be argued that Augustine did not have the same reasons for looking in this direction that we do. Yet he saw that the Bible was discreetly inviting him to discover analogies between the life of the spirit and the life of God. Better still, he set out to study self-knowledge after knowledge of God.[25] It was to be self-knowledge modeled on knowledge of the true God—a clear answer to the Delphic precept, "Know thyself."

In addition, according to Augustine, the human soul knows itself as an image of the reality of the Trinity: "We are speaking not of the supreme Trinity (. . .) but of its inadequate image, though image nevertheless, which is man; perhaps that image is something more familiar and more accessible to the feeble lights of our mind."[26]

The human soul's immediate presence is not that of a being already present to itself in solitary reflection, an insular subject immediately given to itself in the solitude of consciousness. Without going into the details of the Augustinian analogy, let us say that this presence, which excludes any inference or idea, could have been that of a *relation*. Such a conception, which frees us from the soul as object, is in agreement with Kant's critique of the first paralogism of pure reason.[27] In my opinion, the personal identity of communicating persons is the most beautiful mirror of the Trinity: when a human person turns to look at herself, she is present to herself as a trinity (I, you, he/she).

Just as what God is in Himself is revealed by the fact that Father, Son, and

Holy Spirit are at once distinct in relation to each other and each other's equal in relation to themselves. Thus the identity of human persons is revealed by the fact that they are able to differentiate themselves from the other persons in the relation in which they are involved, while still remaining each other's equals. But communication is what frees us from the "soul as object"; more specifically, linguistic exchange about the world outside—in the form of a delocutive and co-referential act of discourse—makes the speaking subject present to him or herself reflexively, as an *effect* of his or her status as a person engaged in an interlocutive relation. Each new communicational commitment partially composes, decomposes, and recomposes the concept of self. One's voice originates, or is returned, from elsewhere. Here then is an important consequence of the logico-semantic premises I established in an earlier work.[28]

Despite the reservations formulated above, the paradigm of the Trinity is eminently valuable from a heuristic point of view. What essential lessons has it taught us? If we stop and take notice of the appropriateness and splendor of what it is saying, we learn that the Trinity founds within the divine Being itself nothing less than the relation by which persons are constituted. Metaphysically, how can this be? I shall go so far as to say that God Himself *is* relationally. God is He who is, the One who makes relations possible, because He Himself is a relation. It is the Word that makes us men because that primary relation is constitutive of the Word. The doctrine of the Trinity casts a disturbing light on depths that human reason finds it difficult to penetrate.

The important thing to understand here is that the doctrine of the Trinity, which I have taken as the archetype (expressed in theological language) of a tripersonal humanity, is intended to found the hypothesis that the human person is basically relational on the level of absolute being and absolute value. Even in the case of God, the causality of self by self is not that of an absolute self. Admittedly, the search for being, with the help of transcendental notions such as these, is a way of responding to what is today increasingly seen as the hopeless desire to renew contact with the most fundamental and necessary realities. If it were not my intention to give a critico-transcendental role to the notion of absolute being. I would therefore be led back into a kind of onto-theology. But my concept of a relational *anthropology* is intended to pull this process of philosophical regression up short at something like a condition of the possibility of sense and truth. That condition is none other than the interlocutive relation.[29] Augustine for his part proposed to give it a theological foundation. But we have seen that it is not unrelated to the preeminent value that the philosopher is led, by his or her own method, to place on the relational principle in anthropology.

Before I conclude my thoughts on theology, let me make a few remarks of metaphysical import. Far from diverting us or turning us away from human relations, this way of looking at God opens up the possibility of any relation with that other which is the person of someone else. God is not man's rival. The ultimate relation, which determines how being is made manifest, is also fruitful in human terms. It is given to us as a relation of reciprocity. There is no question of trying to claim that being as a neutral idea is in any way prior to the existence of individual beings. Our relation to someone else (another being) does not have to be subordinated to some prior relation to that person's mode of being, for the simple reason that the relation is about the very being of God.

Now here is the same argument in technical language: by accepting the equality of essential and relative attributions (and therefore the convertibility of ad iliud and ad se relations), Augustine is able to introduce the relation alongside the notion of divine simplicity, and to reconcile an ineffable God with His manifestations as Father, Son, and Holy Spirit. The result is not only that what God is in Himself can be revealed and made manifest; the Trinity also shows that being consists fundamentally in communion between persons. God as Word creates all things in such a way that they are in relation each with the others. By right, the human person only exists because God places it in existence, by an act of love (awakening) both benevolent and free.

The human person in its turn is capable of manifesting itself during its relational existence,[30] and in the first place of receiving that revelation from God. To have brought into existence a creature capable of accepting such a revelation is the highest achievement of creation. In this sense faith, for the created creature, is an encounter with an Other whose otherness, so to speak, is felt as radically different. Such a conjunction of the dogma of creation with the dogma of the Trinity is an impressive achievement: the two problems of being and man's relation to being are presented in dogmatic terms and brought to a joint resolution. Man is a relation to Being, which itself is a relation. The meaning of that relation, which man makes explicit by reflecting, is always of significance for the relation itself. The dogma of creation remains tied to the dogma of the Trinity, and the latter seems to me to owe much of its power of persuasion to an interpretation of a linguistic schema. The obvious clarity of the three positions I, you, and he/she, linked to the quasi-contradictory formula of a trinite unity, does much to increase the mysterious prestige of the dogma of the Trinity. Some people would say that this historical model retains its strength of conviction because it derives from a formal, anthropological structure.

Thomas Aquinas compares the Holy Spirit to an effect, to the flower that comes forth from the tree in an act of vitality.[31] In much the same way, we might say that when *I* and *you* are in an interlocutive relation, *he/she* emerges likewise from their joint speech. It must of course be pointed out that the formal structure (I, you, he/she) is much more general than its theological paradigm, and it allows more varied interpretation. Proceeding from it to the structure of trinitary relations is a transformation in several stages. We can say, for instance, that divine persons are specified and assigned a place in a world of genealogy and filiation (Father, Son, Holy Spirit). I shall not embark here on a study of these changes, and others which would be needed before the trinitary model was reached.

However, the Trinity—which for Christians is the first and greatest mystery—was on more than one occasion anticipated, or at least prefigured in its most general outlines. Heraclides of Pontus and Porphyrius both report a famous oracular pronouncement of Serapis: "Everything at the beginning is God; then, Word and Spirit: three gods jointly engendered and brought together as one." The Pythagoreans, too, knew the excellence of ternary concepts. We might add that Chaldean theology also contains the triad Father, Logos, and Power. Without faith (philosophical, at least) we are substantially incapable of seeing ourselves as creatures made in God's image. But however sceptical one may be about the Trinity, it is hard to be equally sceptical about the notion of *trinitariness*. And we have seen that it would in many ways not be wrong to see our own trinitariness in the image of the Christian Trinity.

God as a Person

With its tripersonal structure, communication is so essential to man that we can easily suppose it to have been the origin of his being. We left psychology behind and were washed up on the banks of theology. And the Catholic dogma of the Trinity allowed us to see this communication at work within God Himself, before showing us that it was the founding principle of creation.

As a result, the criterion of personal identity can quite naturally be extended to a trinitary God. The nominalists were right about the trinite God: He is one and unique. Even though there are three names, there are not three Gods. But do we have to go along with the realists who concluded that He correspondingly has one essence, rather than three? I shall not get involved in this theological quarrel. I shall simply remind us that in the case of a religion of personal salvation, the theologian is wont to identify the divine as a person. This avoids a sort of neutral way of thinking about God as anonymous, as simply being's mode of being. Admittedly, at first sight we might envisage identifying God by means of the sort of criterion which might be used to define individuality, such as His type of power or modus operandi.

71

That is the position taken by Thomas Aquinas in his *Treatise of the Names of God:* God is the One who brings about the creation of the world and the redemption of man. The name given to Him will therefore have the sense of a verb such as "to create" or "to redeem." But my hypothesis allows us to be more precise. We have indeed seen what the theology of revelation commits itself to once it sets out to give God the reality of a person, rather than that of a philosophical concept whose existence can then be tested, as happens with rational theology.

Religious anthropology confirms something else, too: with the progress of science, religion has come to concern the personal lives of believers much more than the knowledge and control of events. Every believer has to confess his or her faith. In a religion of personal salvation, he or she refers to God as a person. How significant is this analogy? In the first place, I believe that it can be shown to be much more than a simple anthropomorphic transposition: it is a principle for analyzing religious contexts, rather than for reading sacred texts.

Let us consider one of the persons in the Trinity: the Father. From public or private worship, to devotional literature, to sacred writings, religious contexts are indeed diverse; so are the utterances made in them, be they expressions of praise, requests, offerings of thanks, exordia, admonitions, commandments, or judicial proclamations. But referring to God as a person implies the ability, in principle at least, to identify Him, in the context of the whole network of biblical texts, as a unified person.[32] And this person is "called" different things. The "I" of prophecy is balanced by the "thee" of the Psalms and the "He" of narrative. For the Father is "named" equally in the story of deliverance and salvation that tells us about Him, in the prophesies that speak in His name, and the commandments that identify Him as the source of the imperative, as well as in hymns and Psalms invoking Him in the second person. This of course in no way implies that there is no difference or disproportion between the eminent Person of God and the personal reality of the human ego.

Next, the above analogy shows how we are ready to say *that* God is personal, without knowing *in what way* He is personal. Through biblical revelation we have a partial knowledge of the trinite God. At least this is so if I believe that the divinity in all His confidence is calling to me and that I must respond with all my fidelity. Such is faith in a personal God, something comparable to a loyal commitment.

By reading the Bible we can determine which analogies are suitable for the name of God and which are not. This is true of the person. We would not say that God was personal in the sense of possessing intelligence and will, like a human subjectivity. Rather, we can see Him as the identifying focus for the agencies of communication within Himself and in relation to men. Admittedly, we know only one type of personal identity—the human type— and one type of spirituality, which is associated with our existence as persons. But from there on, anyone can read the Bible and use analogical language to capture the resemblance between the Creator and His creature without prejudice to this central difference. When we say that God is personal, at the very least we exclude the possibility of His being impersonal. Thus the language of the Bible can hardly be seen as a *via negativa*. When Jesus speaks of God as his father, he does not modify his statements negatively. God is personal in a concrete and useful way. Use can therefore only be made of the negative way when it is supported by a positive voice.

—But no term, whether it be that of person or any other, can be attributed univocally to God and man. Is God not universally positive?

—The person is still not a predicate like any other.

—Would you say it could be attributed to finite and infinite beings indifferently?

—On the one hand, as God is infinite, all the finite analogies by which we know Him in other things will have to be denied as soon as they are applied to Him. On the other hand, the biblical texts ask that we apply these same images to God positively.

—Then you would be stuck in a dilemma.

—You should look rather at how I am disposed to apply those images.

—How do you mean?

—Indirectly, in a way supported by the revealed doctrines of Creation and Incarnation, and more generally by the manifestations of the trinite God; at that point, we can speak of the Creator through the creature. And it is precisely this relation to the creature that guarantees both the resemblance and the difference between human and divine persons, and so justifies the use of analogical language.

The Dilemma of the Self: Pascal's Paradox

What is the ego?

. . . does he who loves someone on account of beauty really love that person? No; for the small-pox, which will kill beauty without killing the person, will cause him to love her no more.

And if one loves me for my judgment, memory, he does not love me, for I can lose these qualities without losing myself. Where, then, is this Ego, if it be neither in the body nor in the soul? And how love the body or the soul, except for these qualities which do not constitute *me*, since they are perishable? For it is impossible and would be unjust to love the soul of a person in the abstract, and whatever qualities might be therein. We never, then, love a person, but only qualities.[33]

My commentary on this famous text will be brief and limited only to its implications for my present thesis.

If by *self* we understand our concrete, psychic, and psychological totality, what can we say about our experience of self? It is so opaque that we cannot speak about it directly, but only through paradoxes of this sort. Such is the stubborn truth of the paradox that it wrecks our attempts to dominate the problem conceptually within the framework of the traditional system. It makes it inaccessible to any common-sense view. What then is the ungraspable subject which on its own possesses all these qualities, while exceeding the bounds of any particular predicate? This paradox of the self is directly linked to the object of our enquiry. It calls our attention to the fact that the term *self* definitely does not function as a generic expression signifying "a set of qualities." If the term has any meaning, it must refer to the "individual personality." But if we are to explain this notion of personality, we shall have to start by calling into question the substantialist conceptual framework.

Point two: apart from a paradox, Pascal's text contains a dilemma and a difficulty, which are interrelated. The self cannot be reduced to its qualities—which are all fragile and perishable—and defined by concepts (so that they are interchangeable). Neither the integrity nor the disintegration of the self is dependent on the preservation or alienation of its qualities. But neither can the self be defined as a neutral substratum of body or soul, which would give an abstract subject.

Pascal's argument comes to a disappointing end. He concludes that the self is a figment of the imagination, and that the love of God alone is not illusory. As a figment of the imagination the self is hateful not in one or another of its modes or ways of being, but in its being pure and simple. For Pascal, then, the remedy lies not in some kind of modification, but in conversion.

At least he states the problem correctly. As for his eschatological solution, it is put forward only because of his substantialist preconceptions. These are what we must dispose of now. I shall avoid having recourse either to the cynical superficialism of appearances, or to the rather summary alibi of the absolute. When Pascal confronts us with the dilemma of either loving nobody, or loving nothing but qualities which are not the person, in my view he can equally well be seen as inviting us to reject the presupposition on which the dilemma is based. While the dilemma is untenable, the paradox is intolerable, for it is most definitely persons that we love.

From Grammatical Appearances to a Category Mistake

Paradoxes and dilemmas are signs, at the very least, of an inadequate mode of expression. There is nothing wrong with any mode of expression as long as it does not lead to insoluble philosophical problems.

But the difficulty with this language of the self and its qualities is that it quickly leads us into such problems. One suspects that the irritating tautology "I am what I am," even more irritating because it is usually offered as an excuse, contains a real category mistake. Combined with its role as an alibi, this suggests that its use reveals a form of self-indulgence. It also flies in the face of the most elementary and obvious fact that the self is not some indivisible monad, always in agreement with itself. It is never wholly present here and now. I am not referring to the emotional rents of the heart or the illogicality of feeling, but to an overall disparateness that cannot be reconciled with a monadic self. Such a self has to believe with its heart what it denies with its intelligence; it must detest with one part of its soul what it cherishes with another. These apparent realities cannot be assimilated in the same model.

However, Pascal does open up other avenues of enquiry. If we follow the thread of the Pascalian paradox, it leads us to reflect on the implications for the self of a privileged interpersonal relation such as love. This is unexplored territory for primary philosophy! It does not immediately lead us to separate our psychological self from some meditating subject which, to our reflexive consciousness, would appear as the ultimate source of all objective affirmations and justifications.[34] We will only arrive at that particular problematic after a somewhat longer detour.

In the text quoted above, a remark about love first enjoins us to dissociate the notion of a self made up of qualities, logically untenable, from the notion of a personal self and its own particular mode of identification. It was the first type that Pascal's contemporaries among the moralists described as self-idolizing, skillfully evading its determinations and slipping away from its signs. For La Rochefoucauld, such a self only "settles on a subject outside itself as a bee does on a flower, in order to draw from it that which is proper to it." As we see, this essential process of imputation to the self and self-love are one and the same thing.

This same avenue of enquiry also invites us to conceive of the reality of the personal self in a different way. It allows us to overcome the paradox not by modification or by conversion, but through a certain trans-agential renunciation with which we are already familiar. The notion of person must be made compatible with that privileged interpersonal relation (we might even call it the interpersonal relation par excellence) which is love. This is the principle: the ego is not a person, but it becomes one when it loves or speaks to another person. By abandoning the traditional presupposition underlying Pascal's paradox, we renounce once and for all the substantialist principle according to which a self which can be loved would be to its determinants as a substance is to its properties and qualities, and as the ego's being in itself is to the things it has for itself. The paradox only disappears if we make a clean break with the point of view that grammar—or superficial logic—attempts to impose on us. The naive objection "but I know very well that I have certain qualities," can be answered straightaway by asking: "What type of proposition is this? Is it one about real experience, or a sort of grammatical tautology?" I shall come back to this point later. It still remains true that we love people not for the qualities they might possess, and which we could speak about in the delocutive register of language, but because we are living with them through a happy relationship that we want to maintain.

If the language of relations is still difficult to use, and stumbling in its expression, it is first because we speak interpersonal relations directly in the allocutive register, when we address and converse with another person.[35] We know how poor is the vocabulary for expressing amorous relations as such, as a result of excessive modesty or simply lack of imagination. If we absolutely have to talk about them, we generally get around the difficulty, as Montaigne did when speaking of his friendship for La Boétie, by avoiding any description based on attributes or on adjectives: "If I were pressed to say why I loved him . . . I feel that it is something I can only express by replying: 'because it was him, because it was me'."[36]

However clear the reasons for loving ("because . . .") might be, the lover could always put forward good reasons for not loving ("despite . . ."). Except in the case of conscious second thoughts, or some previous cause of resentment, an incomprehensible necrosis of feeling always prevents him from actually doing this. For love owes nothing to justice, and precious little, in the end, to esteem. It is only to third parties that it appears as an unfair preference or a predilection based on favor, and, in his exasperation, to the disdained lover himself. Thus in the mad relationship between Alexis and Pauline, what is given painful expression is a hurtful and ambivalent resentment: "Wherever I go I see only you and nothing else matters to me. How and why I love you is a mystery to me. You know, you may not even be beautiful at all. . . . Your heart is undoubtedly bad, and your mind most probably lacks all nobility."[37]

The truth is that people only love in the silence of a certain discourse—the discourse of justification. If love were justifiable, it would be prescribable. What do you see in him or her that I haven't got? We do not have to explain. Listing qualities is a rationalization after the event; it uses only the delocutive register of language. We might see it as following, rather than preceding, the establishment of a relation of predilection, an exclusive relation between persons. But even then it remains extremely difficult to determine with any pertinence the pragmatic situation in which the discourse of justification might itself be pertinent.

Love begins for no particular reason. I suspect that the reasons that occur to us afterward are not exactly reasons at all; in any case, they seem to be invented by the heart from nowhere. As retrospective discoveries made after the event, they are more akin to hymns than to an explanatory narrative. If they provide any justification at all, it is in the eyes of a third party; they have no foundational status. Otherwise, they would make people replaceable. A lovable quality is only an objective and secondary stabilization of a loved one which I use in her absence, when I have brought myself to talk to you about her. In him or herself, the loved one is the correlative of a primary, active relation. Any attribution of qualities to the loved one is a kind of poetic license, a deliberate category mistake. Predilection for someone then takes on a metaphorical value—that of beauty, for instance, which is a promise of happiness. It is also the most commonly accepted form of the lovable, but the secret reason is that love beautifies both the lover and the loved.[38]

The Predilection Relation

I have just attempted to sketch out an indirect description. In the case of the predilection relation (but neither more nor less so than in any other), such a description immediately poses problems when we try to reconcile it with the traditional conception of the ego.

A substantive ego recognizes in its surroundings, and even in its relations with others (including those of friendship and love), only its own adjectives. For it, love is one state of mind among others, a sweet inebriation or inspiration of the heart. This is not far from being a complete logical dead end. We are misled by grammatical appearances into making the whole of the love-relation dependent on one of its poles, the first person in its loving intentionality. As for the other, it is simply the accusative of his or her love, his or her target; it is the direct object of the verb to love, the second person, You. Even where the object of love is imaginary, the subject is supposed to derive a form of interiority from it.

Neither Egocentrism nor Allocentrism: Love Begins in Itself

The foregoing description is widely accepted. Yet who cannot see, after a moment's thought, that if it is true only egocentrism can be declared as an elementary and positive value? Others can only be loved if one first loves oneself: *prius te diligis.* I love you because you are like me—so goes the classical theory of love. A friend is only another version of oneself, as Pylade is for Orestes. It is doubtless always possible to escape the obviously tautological nature of self-love, but only by adopting the most unlikely strategy of abnegation pure and simple. If self-love is natural, how can one renounce oneself? Love for others becomes paradoxical, a pretense. Unless we choose to make it simply a modality of self-love; the other becomes dear to the self, its friend. This is Aristotle's theory, which we never quite cease to find astonishing: I love him because he is me. Which suggests that loving another is once more to love oneself. Love for others is, in a sense, nothing more than an extension of egotism.

On the other hand, this does mean that self-love is conceived of as the center from which well-wishing and the desire to seduce diffuse out toward the loved one. We know well enough that intending to love someone has something forced and risible about it. As for intending to seduce someone, this is clearly a most debased form of love, and quite enough to take away all its magic. If the ego is a substance, man constitutively loves only himself. He cannot help loving his neighbor, by existential project and by analogical projection, as himself.

"Your neighbor, whom you must love as you do yourself, so that you appreciate him too for what he is, will come to have for you the same savour as yourself." [39] The loved one, by becoming another version of ourselves, here takes on an astonishingly increased importance. But what if the self were hateful? Would there then not be a certain irony in loving the other as ourselves?

It is true that we can always compensate for this reduction of the interpersonal relation, and more particularly for the predilection relation, by subscribing to a second one in which the values are reversed, and in which we give our support to what we shall soon see is an equally dubious allocentrism.

This time, my relation to the other is given as a centrifugal and spontaneous movement of the heart, a simple drive of the whole soul, unadulterated by any quest of my own. [40] It is a devotion like that of Heloïse for Abelard, an unfailing generosity which seizes me. This form of love has its sublime side. The other is now loved in every way for him or herself only, for him or her irreplaceable ipseity. I love him or her because it is him or her. The charm of the loved one attracts by his or her presence alone. The lover, a heart inspired, is drawn almost magnetically toward the one he or she loves. Understand if you can, there's no explanation to be given: because it is him or her. . . . That is not a reason. Now, the other has become my own center. The other causes him or herself to be loved; he or she has not become his or her own nucleus. Now, love and friendship raise no problems and are bounded by no restrictions, or they are simply a spontaneous inclination toward the loved one, an initial gratitude without cause, which does not even expect reciprocation. There is here a sublime of Goethean proportions: "If I love you, what does it matter?"

Once more, logical contradictions abound here. How is it possible for the other, rather than for his or her lovable qualities, to be the cause of love? It must be love itself that makes things lovable, as terror makes them terrifying. The other quickly becomes an indifferent cause of that which is lovable. To love the other person simply because he or she is an other and for no other reason, would be the action of a pure and disinterested love. I understand how edifying that would be. I also detect, in this amorous allegiance to someone else, this preemptive attraction of the other, a philosophically suspect mechanism: it seems to be caused by the impalpable fact of there being another person, similar but different, "monadically distinct from me, who is the cause of a love without cause." [41] As we are forced to admit, this is a paradox no less troubling than Pascal's.

Nor should we be surprised that this swing toward allocentrism should be counterbalanced by one in the opposite direction, confirming the primacy of self; so that from the start this swing was as exaggerated as it was insincere. I have always had doubts about the good faith, or rather the good sense, of those who are happy reading a Treatise on Pure Love. Here they are, claiming that we emigrate into another self and, like all-sacrificing heroes, elect to take a You as our true self. This effusion is admittedly not seen as a property, but it does remain linked to the self; however absorbed the ego might be in self-forgetting, the specific movement of intentionality remains primary. We cannot help but accept that in the last analysis the effusion depends on a certain quality of intention by the ego and the dynamism of its disposition to love. *Amo ut amen.* [42] In the end, in this view it is the intention of loving that makes the loved one worthy of love.

This is then a straightforward inversion of the terms of egocentrism. Allocentrism has no more need of explanations than does its opposite number. Each has something unconditional about it which looks very much like grace. In egocentrism, what I lavish on the other is not things that are mine, but rather my own *self*. In the allocentric view, we would be giving up what we *are*. It is true that the gift would be compensated for by the effusive exchange; the gift of self is balanced by the other person's gift of *him* or *herself*. As if a love shared were a love doubled.

Actually, the sudden reversal of egocentrism into its strange opposite has the air of a speculative lurch from one extreme position to another. We seem to be accumulating edifying paradoxes as a way of avoiding the difficult task

79

of describing a basic, relational fact. This difficulty is one of which Thomas Aquinas was well aware. He at least took a moderate approach, without making a definite choice between the Same and the Other. He sometimes stresses the lover's affectionate impression of the loved one, and sometimes the latter's gravitational pull. He calls the first affection, or immutation; the second he calls inclination, or influence over a subject who is, in any case, seen as capable of loving.[43] Incidentally, in the case of God he also recognizes a single act of love as common to the divine Persons, so that the Father loves the Son and the Son the Father in the simplicity of a single operation.[44]

I am resisting here the pull of two ideas that are in a way symmetrical. The first is the hypothesis that amatory relations are something "to which we are subject"; according to the second, they can be assimilated directly to the love "object." In both cases, the relation is broken down and made simply into an image of itself. I shall look at each idea in turn. The first seems to me to be logically and affectively suspect, for the simple reason that when love enters a human heart it opens it up to the demands of a new relation (unless, that is, it breaks the heart instead). Which implies that we learn to love by loving, as we learn to want by wanting: as a relation, love can only begin with itself. The imputation of love to the person who loves or is loved is always a descriptively facile, not to say logically confused step. On the other hand, if we are really to understand the apparently trivial fact that the accords or links formed by love are relational, we must put an end to the swing between a dogmatism that makes love into a conditional truth and an idealism that sees it as a free option open to the subject. For the former, love is as the loved one makes it, good if he or she is lovable, bad if not. For the latter, it is possible to love, virtuously and unilaterally, a person unworthy of love. The dogmatic approach is highly reasonable, but the idealist hyperbole remains most doubtful. It comes down to saying, in a manner more troubling than it is accurate, that the other cannot be regarded as the cause of love. Especially as the effusive movement of love can be described as an illness.[45] An illness we find treated in the works of Stendhal: there are different remedies, a friend can bring relief, etc.[46] Proust's characters, too, dream of a cure: "He told himself that when he was cured, whatever Odette might do would be of complete indifference to him. But in the morbid state in which he found himself he feared such a cure like death itself."[47]

In Dostoyevsky, this illness is often fatal and passion is so ambivalent that it can swing between ecstasy and the lowest degradation, even tending at times to fulfill itself in murder: "I only have to remember or imagine the feel of your dress brushing against me and I am ready to wring my hands in remorse. Why are you angry with me? Because I declare myself to be your slave? Go on, take advantage of me as your slave! Do you know that one day I shall kill you? Not out of jealousy, or because I have stopped loving you. No, I shall kill you simply because there are days when I feel I could devour you."[48]

All this seems to suggest that love is first and foremost not an emotion, but a process of feeling. It is not because there is no love in the loving subject that love is a state of the subject. Love is not primarily about feeling; it is simply the perceived form of a real relation. Of course, the relational movement can always turn inward and become centered on the self and its stratagems. The works of Proust contain several examples of the way we bluff others into loving us by a pretense of detachment and indifference: "Just as I used to tell Albertine 'I do not love you,' so that she would love me more; 'I forget about people when I do not see them for a while,' so that she would come and see me often; or 'I have decided to leave you,' to forestall any idea of a separation . . ."[49]

The novelist remains bitterly aware what a poor subterfuge this is: "At the somewhat disillusioned age which Swann was now approaching, an age when one knows one must be satisfied with being in love for the enjoyment of it, without asking for too much in return . . . one seeks in love above all a subjective pleasure."[50]

Affectation, the ruin of affection, is not far away here. Even if it is almost impossible to love without watching yourself loving, I do not believe, unlike Vladimir Jankélévich, that self-indulgence is a necessary part of love, except in those who are emotional invalids.[51] Unless, that is, we mix up the transitive feeling of love with our ambivalent attempts to control it, or with a clumsiness that compromises and spoils it. "If I dwell too long, all is lost," wrote Joseph Joubert.

I shall then separate love from the self-indulgence which ebbs back toward it like an echo, when the amatory relation takes stock of itself and becomes fixated on one of its poles. It hardly matters that such indulgence is psychologically inevitable, for it remains a parasitic phenomenon, a kind of supernumerary grimace. In real love we each feel as if we are constantly escaping ourselves, overflowing the bounds of our being in a tireless inventiveness, richness of experience, and consideration for the other person that we are not responsible for creating. Nor does this spontaneity of existence have anything at all disturbing about it. The amorous relation does not emanate from the *I*, but rather it flows toward it, as well as toward the other person, linking them together and transporting them; it quite literally grabs them both and elevates them into an awareness of their own personal existence.

Loving: The Relation as Feeling

We should therefore remind ourselves that love is a relation, and that it is neither a modification of the ego, nor something called into existence by an appeal from the other, nor even some magic trick which induces a mutual fascination. (I am of course talking here about love without lust.) The conjugation, the number (first or second person), matter but little: in parallel to my relational conception of desire, I am putting forward a relational idea of love. To put it in more decisive terms: far from the feeling *amo* being exalted and redoubled by an external *amor*, the relational condition of love is what makes it into something immediately bilateral, if not exactly symmetrical. For those who had not yet realized it, this sets some of our earlier paradoxes on a much sounder footing; it is now scarcely a surprise that neither the other, nor his or her wonderful qualities, should be the cause of love.

Anyone who says that the other is the *cause* of love is making a category mistake, because love itself is an experience (always full of pathos) of a positive relation with someone else. Again, it is no surprise that love should continue: if it ever did come to an end, in all due rigor it must be either because it never really existed, or because one person or the other sinned against it.

On the other hand, it takes a long time for a relationship to reveal the state of disintegration into which it has fallen, and for its inanity finally to be realized. The longer things go on, the more worthless an unkept promise turns out to be. At a given point it is broken simply by the passage of time. If many people remain together instead of separating, safe in the protection of a legally binding contractual intimacy, it is often because they have died without realizing it. How can this intimacy be restored if it was never really established between them in the first place? Or if it has been damaged beyond repair? Conversely, it is hardly surprising that I should not wait to be loved before loving someone else. A person who resigns herself in advance to a time when she will no longer love, and a fortiori one who waits before loving, cannot genuinely be said to love. In matters of love, people like Alceste in Molière's *The Misanthrope* are setting off on the wrong foot.

The claim that it is impossible to love without being loved would be contrary to what happens in the vast majority of novels. And yet, I am indeed intending to suggest that something of the sort is true. I am not sure whether it is true that the most important thing about erotic literature is what perverts have said about it.[52] My suspicion is a more measured one: what if novelistic fiction did present the truth, but the truth inverted?

It would be a mistake to push the asymmetry of amatory relations too far. It is never as frequent as it seems in books. If you want to be loved, we often read, do not fall in love yourself. Of course, any such essential asymmetry in human relations does seem astonishing to us: one person commits himself to another to the extent of putting his life on the line, while the other remains quite free, seeing love simply as a contingent way of living. But this degree of frivolity (or ferocity) merely travesties love. Asymmetry is also the order of the day with great passions. They are loves which have turned back on themselves and become self-feeding; they are loves in which a certain fear or distrust can be seen deep down in the eyes. These can quite easily be identified by the type of discourse they produce: whereas the speech of love is happy, suffused with a kind of elation and a drive caused by the presence of the loved one and the ease of relations with him or her, passion for its part speaks in monologue. Its words admit of no reply, are not understood with any certainty, and need to be often repeated, as we see in the suspended and poisonous lines of Racine's tragedies.

Except where it is imaginary, in cases when the loved one is nonexistent or inconsistent, love at least proves the existence of a happy relation. Through it, I am immediately linked in one way or another. Love is always at least in both parties.[53] But this is still not going far enough. Logicians would remind us not to mix up the dyad with the binary relation that created it.

On the other hand, it is true that not all reciprocal relations are symmetrical. The objection might be raised that it is sometimes possible to love someone whom you have never seen close up, or who does not know of your existence. Have there not been cases of people sending love poems to someone over the course of several years, without ever worrying about receiving any sort of reply? Baudelaire imagined a frigid wife becoming the passionate lover of her dear departed. But in all these cases, one of two things happens. The first possibility is that this nonreciprocated feeling withers away, or even becomes denatured. The other person becomes represented as something dear to the lover, an imaginary portrait, linked directly to him or herself. This is what makes all jealousy suspect. The very dialogue form into which the unreal imaginings of jealousy slip is proof that reciprocity is indeed at the root of love. In the alternative outcome, on the other hand, one comes to suspect that one's love is no more than a fiction, a fantasy without relational existence, which is being heightened by memory and suggestion. It has become—we might as well say it—a state of mind.

It is a mistake to take harebells for passionflowers, as the novel genre so commonly does. How in the world did I fall in, then out of, love? Such is its ordinary text. One character is taken with his own emotion, another savors her power to fascinate, a third looks on at what the novel alleges to be his own abandonment of self-control, while yet another wears her distinguished sentiments on her sleeve. The novelistic text always welcomes the increased complication afforded by anecdotes on love's vicissitudes. It describes the

83

birth of that curious state of mind and love to which the amorous relation is so often reduced, but also its advances, retreats, and intermittent resurgence, until it reaches the sordid decline that precedes the death of the liaison, after which forgetfulness finally closes over it like the sea.

This conception of love has provided a wealth of literary material. The feeling, in its most immature forms, has been constantly reinvented over the centuries. In the lighthearted mythology, one love comes, another goes—though not without determining, as it disappears, the form of the one that follows. Courtly games, games of chance: the lady who allows her heart to be conquered by valor, the hard-hearted prince whose feelings are touched in the end. Obstacles and differences of feeling are the stuff of fiction. Poets and novelists alike make the loved one into either an object to be conquered, or one that remains inaccessible. In both cases we find the same image:

> This fearsome and indomitable enemy
> Offended by respect and angered by pleas,
> This tiger, whom I could never approach without fear,
> Docile and tame, now recognizes a conqueror:
> Aricie has found the way to his heart.[54]

When by some mischance the fascination is not mutual, there is a whole stock of pathetic and luxurious asymmetries: we may not always know when we are loved, but we certainly know when we are not loved. According to Proust, commonplace is the point of view that love is necessarily an unhappy experience: "At first one dreams of 'possessing' the heart of the woman one loves. Much later, feeling that one possesses a woman's heart can be enough to make one fall in love."

Hence the extreme disparity of tones, everything from euphoric confabulation, to happy burlesque, to anguished melancholy, to idealization of the image from which the lover is separated, and idealization's rapid decline into anxiety, then suspicion. Now we are shown love as a joyous devil drumming at the door of the heart, and we see Juliet's shudder of anticipation as Romeo approaches. Now on the contrary it is a passion repressed, grasped on the very edge of ultimate catastrophe: an absurdity to be looked straight in the eye, love without hope. In Racine's *Andromache*, such is the impotence of Orestes before Hermione, and Hermione's own inability to exist in the eyes of Pyrrhus, when she bursts out in the full fury of her love for him: "I loved you when you were faithless, how much more so had you been faithful?" Indeed, how is it that Racine is able to make this novelistic hell into something human? He does so by describing not so much the passion that refuses to let go, a furious wave whose immense but futile power spends itself in foam, as that static, contained passion that is unable to rise above the wall of another person. When the person we love neither sees us nor hears what we say, when we have no existence at all for that person. Thus Hermione will discover that Pyrrhus is not even listening to her. But by what misunderstanding about feelings, by what extraordinary perversion of the heart, can Nero or Roxane one day say to those who are dear to them: "Love me or die?"

Mad love: that is what it really is. Having a project: to go mad. Why not? Or is it rather vague love? We might be captivated by such hyperbole; we might also have our doubts about this nonrelational fury in love. Writers are people with the ability to write down their daydreams in a form which both fixes them for posterity and liberates the writers from them at the same time. Only a Romantic man of letters would claim that this is not true, while only an early phenomenologist would be surprised by it, and celebrate the divergence of a pair of intentionalities, or their miraculous concordance.

The Ontological Function of Love

The truth of the matter, which most of the moralists and fathers of the Church did no more than touch on, is both humbler and more discreet than this: because of its fundamentally relational nature, the reality of love has as little to do with the lover's gracious homage as it does with the loved one's merits or charm. That is why the very smallest degree of hope can be enough to fuel love.

It is one thing to say: "I could fall in love," but quite another to say: "I love you." Every love affair faces the same problem: do I want you to exist for yourself, or through me, or better, *with me*, through the reciprocal relationship that binds us together? This relational and ontological feeling is ascribed derivatively to the other person. Loving someone is then no longer loving *what* he or she is (still less what he or she has), but loving the fact *that* the other person is, and exists (just as hating someone means being unable to stand his or her existence or presence). The most curious and remarkable thing is that if I want the other person to exist with me, through our relationship, I am not only taking him or her as is, I want him or her to be as she or he is.

Love, the brightest and perhaps the only light, gives being to people in love. Love is what makes us believe in the existence of other human beings as such. And in our own. It is literally true that living without love, we are deprived of the most indispensable thing of all: existence. "I may have the gift of prophecy, and know every hidden truth; I may have faith strong enough to move mountains; but if I have no love, I am nothing." Thus we read in St. Paul's canticle on love (1 Corinthians 13). This privation which takes personal existence away from us is no trivial one. But neither, conversely, is the joy of being in love, as it is identical to our feeling of reality. Love, like poetry, can neither be deliberately created nor forced. It always begins with itself and is, by its relational nature, the *causa sui*. By fostering our concern for others, it makes us exist.

> Throw your love on the common fire
> What is there in it that you should care about . . .
> Only, let it give forth a flame
> Like a rose on a rose-bush.[55]

In this sense, the only contact there is with being and life is through love. When an individual submits to its universal law, it begins to mold him or her into a personal being. And first of all, it raises him or her up, like Lazarus. The ontological virtue of love is so great that it is often considered valuable enough to render death unacceptable or, on the contrary, acceptable. The reason is that the sign of real being is found in an equivalence of the highest order: it is as strong as death.

Even though we only rarely experience its power over our lives, there is something epiphanic about love that makes it *the* happy ontological and poetic relation above all others. By poetic, I mean that which is most real of all, and only completely true in the other world—the world of the here and now. A happy, privileged relation; in fact, it is the archetype of all human relations.

However far away from it we choose to go, the norm remains the norm. It gives a measure of our divergence; it indicates when we start to slip out of humanity altogether. It has nothing to do with frequency. I am well aware that most people only give when they have already received. In barter and exchange the same rule applies: what will you give me in return for what I have given you? And so on. We can also, in jest, reduce the paradigm of our species to its inverted image, the parasite, who receives but never gives, living entirely at the expense of the partner on which he feeds. But what unhealthy spirit of mystification leads us to say that man is a wolf (or a flea) for man? Only someone in real distress, or with the humor of Rameau's nephew, could avoid insulting humanity by saying so. Inability to follow a straight line is of course no reason for proclaiming the virtues of the curve. But the idea of a unilateral relation is a most curious one, and not just for Alice. As we will remember, it is a notion devoid of meaning, a kind of logical monster.[56] If it came up in a philosophical theory it would prove either that the theory was psychological, or that it was confusing psychological problems with logical ones.

On the other hand, there is nothing paradoxical about the observation that certain human beings seem mysteriously to give what they do not yet have. As we know, love by its very nature does not need to have before it can give. If in the process of giving it creates something, it is because having is not what matters. Our embrace with someone else frees us from the sordid reciprocity of mercantile exchange. Love, the miraculous creation of our empty-handedness, is the living relation, the relation as feeling. Which is why it gives fulfillment.

Of course, there are few cases of such an absolute predilection. Jacob loves Rachel, but he is also Leah's husband.[57] It also sometimes happens that one amorous experience points the way to another which then overwhelms us. We might then ask: but what are these two loves that live deep in the unconscious of each of us? We must avoid treating simple things in too simple a manner: a complete predilection would be one in which each partner, totally bound to the other, experienced the happiness of being utterly him or herself. It would correspond to an exclusive interpersonal relation, an intimacy with no respite. An exclusive relation is not a totalitarian one; the latter excludes all relations on the pretext of containing them, whereas the former allows other types of relation but demands the right to organize them, by a privilege of ultimate metacommunication over all others.

We have more than one friend—and friends of quite different types—by choice, but also out of necessity. Some people prefer them not to meet, or hope secretly that they will not get along. Should we say: he has as many friends as there are different persons in him? Or: there are as many persons in him as he has friends? Clearly, neither; instead, we say: his personal identity is presented with as many problems as he has friends—not all of which are insoluble.

The predilection relation, just like the relation that is constitutive of full speech, basks in the warmth of reciprocity. In fact, love given and received is in that way just like speech addressed by one person and received by another. Who gives and who receives? It is impossible to tell; so close is the reciprocal link here between giving and receiving.

In my view, the two problematics of full and pacific speech, and love, are entirely comparable in that both derive from the interlocutive relation. Both illustrate the paradigm of an interpersonal relation. Like full speech, love is able to create everything positive within the soul, everything that is communicable and yet unique. I see one sign of this in the Spanish word *conversar*, which means both "to converse (among several people)" and "to be friends." Oscar Wilde was sent to prison and exiled for the offense of criminal conversation. . . . Just as love cannot feed on images of the loved one, so speech that is addressed to the image of an interlocutor, without proceeding from an interlocutive relationship with him or her, remains null and void. If I am not able to speak when my turn comes, and *with* you rather than *to* you, then the fact that I am being spoken to is already a form of intimidation, an enemy discourse. The business of speech is not to break the silence but to interrupt violence. A communiqué is not communication. A person who holds the floor has possession of everything important, leaving for others only the crumbs, the role of listener.

I notice that in Platonism the preeminence of the lover over the loved one is paralleled by the preeminence of the speaker over the listener. Socrates and the stranger play the game of pseudodialogue (just as the act of loving always overpowers the loved one): is it better to suffer injustice or to commit it? Questions like this are Platonic. In each case, what is missing is any conception of the relation. Our philosophy, like our morality and our politics, often does not have the supporting logic that it deserves.

Me Ames Non Mea (Love Me, Not What Is Mine)

The experience of a true relation is ours for a short time only; it has the eternity of the rose. Thinking about it, we realize that even the truest love cannot maintain itself in the actuality of such a relation, if only because it lasts. A thing that lasts is one that persists through alternate states of actuality and latency. Of course, the loved *you* never becomes an *it*, i.e., the sum of certain qualities; but it does become a *he* or *she;* thus the other becomes absent. I could now speak delocutively of his or her tone of voice, or their particular type of intellectual generosity, or any other such predicate. How is this possible?

From the Possessive to the Relational

Let us return to the subject's being. As we might guess, the language of relations, which is already difficult enough to sustain and master in the context of interpersonal relationships, in which we use it to express friendship or love, is a fortiori very hard to use when we want to speak about ourselves.

Montaigne, who is fond of referring to himself in the first person, imputes qualities to himself as if they were so many personal determinants. This is perhaps the result of an unwelcome solitude: " 'Tis a melancholic humor, and consequently a humor very much an enemy to my natural complexion, engendered by the pensiveness of the solitude into which for some years past I have retired." [58]

The pronoun "I" functions both as one of the indices of the act of utterance and as a conventional symbol within the statement, or, respectively, as the subject of the utterance and the subject of the statement: "I have a free and open way that easily insinuates itself and obtains belief with those with whom I am to deal, at the first meeting." [59] He presents our being and his own as fissured, and held together, by unhealthy tendencies: "Ambition, jealousy, envy, revenge, superstition, and despair have so natural a possession in us, that their image is discerned in beasts." [60]

Let us admit it; it is difficult to circumvent this way of talking. It is clear that the grammatical possessive makes it possible for the self to become involved, or meddle, in anything it wants: my butcher, my friend, my God. There is nothing quite so sincere as this *my*, the my of certain believers who say: my Lord and shepherd. "The Lord is my shepherd, I shall not want." [61]

After all, we say my belief or my hat; as if, in the words of Paul Valéry, "between a God and a self there were no room for anyone else." The self first appears as a kind of primary superstition, which gives in to the appetites that play upon it, and gives great authority to its desires and propensities. It goes around displaying *its* mood, affects the character others believe it to have (*its* character), and attributes qualities to itself, all of which it sees as belonging to it, but which are more or less fake appendages of the *ipse*, of everything marked by the possessive. The self, this false subject, not only takes itself for *someone;* it also makes everything into an infatuation, to be used as a weapon. This is because the *ipse* has become mixed up with the *idem*, the self identified with the Same.

It still remains to dispose of the recurrent illusion that the self's determinants, and even the relations in which it is engaged, are by their nature possessive. For despite its evident falsity we always come back to speaking the easier language of qualities and faults, above all in the context of interpersonal relations. Love, like friendship, is to a high degree not hypothetical, not unmotivated. On the contrary, both are creative relations. A relation is not an object that can be spoken about in the same—albeit relational—way as a quality: it does not belong to the same logical type. I shall return to this point. Nor is a relation an object that can be perceived as a property. A property can be either accepted or doubted. It is far more difficult to decide about a relation. The naive belief that our own perception of such an interpersonal relation is the only right one, because that is how we feel it to be and the other person must be quite mad or evil to believe otherwise, is manifestly illusory. In this domain there can only be individual prejudices, condemned to remain discordant. The whole delocutive discourse on the relation is as fallacious as it is inoperative:

—Have you got something against me?
—Not at all; you always misinterpret what I say.

We move laterally toward the definition, rejection, or redefinition of our relations with others. [62] Or explicitly, on the metalinguistic level, by communicating with each other about communication.

Most of the time, we see people in terms of the qualities that are imputable to them. We think that one of the things that happens when I become aware of myself is that I recognize past or present experience as mine, in the sense of a quasi relation of property. This is because language uses the same sign to express both possession and the relation, thereby encouraging our category mistake. "My Lord" refers to the guardian of my prosperity and my life, Him from whom I expect personal protection. But the same type of formula can also mark the elective relation man establishes with the divine: if You have chosen me as an individual, I choose You as God. Whereas for Plutarch the divine belongs to no one, Isaiah emphasizes the link of belonging that ties God to His People. Reciprocal belonging: the God of Israel is "our" God. The Lord is my Judge and my Avenger. He is my help, my light (Psalm 26).

Between themselves, people constantly attribute experiences to each other through speech. For instance, there are our indispositions, our particular illnesses, of which we often imagine we can only rid ourselves by *giving* them to somebody. In the language of flowers, the hawthorn says: my heart is cast down. The lily says: my heart is pure. Then there are your states of belief, which I immediately compare with mine as soon as our first words are exchanged; there are also his or her actions, which follow him or her around and on which we comment between ourselves. If, in addition, we attribute to each other motives and intentions, then wrongs and virtues, it is primarily because assigning responsibilities to persons is a practical necessity. Human agents comment on events of which they claim, and are seen by others, to be the instigators. They interpret their own actions in terms of motives, and they interpret the causality of their actions—in relation to those of other people—in terms of influence. The question of exactly what can legitimately be imputed, and to whom, lies in the domain of law rather than moral philosophy. But the question under what conditions such imputations can be made is one on which the entire program of the human sciences can feed.

—How is your chest complaint, Casimir?

How problematic these imputations are. The idea of contrasting the self with what belongs to it certainly comes up against no small number of objections of principle, which I shall now examine and test.

Doubtful Appropriations: My Beliefs, Actions, Projects, Memory

Above all, we must not be fooled by words. How in fact should we react to the possessive? Even if we stick to the traditional grammatical view, it by no means always marks possession.

Like the genitive case, the possessive does not necessarily convey the value of belonging. It indicates any sort of intimate relation with the grammatical subject. From this point we can trace the inflation of its role in language. In some cases the genitive replaces the possessive, and what is true of one is true of the other. There are genitives which are purely attributive, with no trace of possession, such as: "the ladies' gallery." Others have a more locative value. For instance, *un camp de prisonniers* (prison camp): not something they own, but the place where they are, unfortunately for them. In the parallel case "his armchair" (i.e., the one in which he parks himself), the pseudopossessive conveys an agential value; "the speeches of the new members of parliament" and "my speech" designate respectively the speeches they make and the one I am making, myself. Then there are final genitives, as in *un comité de soutien* ("support committee"), and others that specify, such as *les papiers de voiture* ("car documents"). Others again indicate measure ("a distance of a hundred meters"), or time (*un travail d'une journée*—"a day's work"). In all these cases, the genitive has lost all of its possessive value.

Anyway, in many cases the possessive in fact behaves exactly like a relative pronoun. "My father" designates the person who stands in a relation of paternity to me; "her husband" refers to the man to whom she stands in the relation of wife. More manifestly still, "my enemy," "my thief," "my judge," in no way designate possessions, but instead respectively designate the man whose glance turns away, the one who wants what I possess, and the one who has the right to judge me. Equally, "his funeral" denotes a ceremony that is related to him in the sense that it will see him off for good.

The possessivity of the expression "my God" is more apparent than real. It is the link, the alliance relation between Israel and the revealed God, that is essential. "My judge" does not indicate any type of property; the Eternal stands as a judge in relation to me, and I meet Him as such. The God of Abraham is the one whom Abraham met. More than all the divine names which can be said in the possessive, the Tetragrammaton is the name par excellence. Grammatically, it is a sort of absolute name that cannot be declined.

Moreover, in some languages all these possessives or genitives would translate quite differently into French; the English term "men's club," for instance, becomes "a club for men," while "a summer's day" becomes "a day in summer." In fact, we can go so far as to say that the possessive only rarely serves to mark possession. Even "my house" designates both the house that I own and the house in which I live.

We can now see how wrong certain philosophical investigations into ownership and possesion have been to rely on grammar for their evidence. The same might be said of certain literary works (such as those of D. H. Lawrence) in which authors who think they are developing a moral theme are actually giving expression to their obsession with jealousy and possessiveness.

However diverse the values of the grammatical possessive and genitive may be, the similarities and differences shown up by surface grammar are not always a reliable guide to the facts. Even if we suppose that our bodies, actions, and beliefs are related to the self, in the best possible case they give us no more than an image of it. To say that the terms "me" and "my body" do not have the same distribution is as banal as it is incontrovertible. There are contexts in which first-person pronouns simply cannot be replaced by expressions such as "my body," "my head," or "my speech."

Certain things that belong to us may give an image of ourselves, but not all (e.g., my cat, my place in the sun). And even this sequence of images is in any case specious in itself. Proust deplored the successive images that, in his opinion, were all that we "saw" of other people, and others of us: once again, there is no dissymmetry here. A logician would quite rightly object that the grammatical and the logical forms cannot be equated, with the propositional form differing according to whether I am speaking about "my body," "my actions," or "my beliefs." Let us for a moment concede that the notion of *what is mine* informs us about the personal self by providing a representation of it. This is then a mark received from outside the self, one that is immediately unstable because of its dispersion and the fact that it is mediated by, and as it were shot through with, relations to others.

The image that these attributions, assignations, or imputations give of the personal self is a sort of mark received from outside the self. If we look at it more closely, we shall see that it is always involved in a relational context.

What then about the rights I insist are mine? In substantialist language and the surface logic that goes with it, *my* rights are something entirely positive: I have a right to my rights. They precede and condition my duties. As myself, I am the beneficiary of my own rights. This is the loud and clamorous discourse of demand. Everyone has rights, and so do I. The discourse of protestation is a shadowy one, born of a collusion between the norm, whose origin is obviously relational, and a monadic instinct for self-preservation. There is also an absurd, fallacious reciprocity at work here, according to which your duties are the inverted image of my rights, and as such serve to give them further substance. Other people's obligations are thereby annexed to my duty. This appearance of harmony is quite clearly a fake. Let us not waste time in dismantling it.[63] The possessive language of a self on the defensive is a clear sign of moral vulgarity. Don't waste your precious youth trying to sort out what is mine from what is yours.

What are we to think of the imputation of propositional attitudes, in the

form So-and-so doubts whether . . . , or I believe that . . . ? This is something we do all the time; yet just try to relate one of your own beliefs to yourself. It will be hard, if not impossible, to detach what you believe from the
protocols by which you came to agree with one particular interlocutor or disagree with another. If you do it sincerely, you will find yourself in the position
of a spokesperson who is reporting a belief shared by a small group of people.
If you still have some memory of the origin of your opinion, you will agree
that it cannot strictly be said to be an individual one. Diderot used to say:
"My ideas are my whores!" I am not sure that this is the best way to put it.
Ultimately, an individual opinion or idea is practically unsayable. Both tend
toward insanity. Of course there are moments when we affirm a belief using
the first-person form, particularly when it poses a problem for us. In such
cases, the belief is given without anything being accepted in return, as the
response to a threat: yes, *I do* believe in democracy. In fact, it is being not so
much affirmed as reaffirmed here. Even if I think I am putting forward such
a belief in my own name, I am actually offering myself as the representative
of a grouping of beliefs or opinions.

Again, if I find I have to speak about *my* illnesses, they must be considered
in the light of the relational modifications they bring about. No disorder is
pathological in itself. As has been said before, normality can only be judged
in relational terms.[64] Even the most organic of illnesses that I believe myself
to have involves in part an implicit link with at least two subjects: the patient
who has the illness, and the doctor who is looking after him or her. An intersubjective process with several participants always plays an essential role in
defining a pathological disorder.

It seems harder to resist imputing actions and patterns of behavior directly to the self, almost as descriptive attributes. This is because the link
between an action and its agent has long been the most stable and general
fact to emerge from all the attempts to construct a semantics of action.

Classically, actions are interpreted in terms of motive or legal responsibility. The language of psychology and law overlaps here: governed by norms
(or—as with patterns of behavior—by institutions), actions express initiatives or interests that involves an agent and a "patient." Sometimes we can
also become the executioners of our own actions, carrying them out uninten-
tionally in response to a powerful inner compulsion. In this view, our acts
attach to us very much as the glow does to phosphorus. And we are caught
out by our own faults. But my question is precisely whether this classical
schema, in which actions are attributed to agents and processes are predi-
cated of nominal agencies, can in fact be applied anywhere outside the conventions of monadic psychology and civil responsibility.

Contrary to appearances, "I did that" (past tense) is not a descriptive statement. Its main role is ascriptive, on the model of "this is mine" (present), which serves to claim a right of ownership.[65] And we know that ownership is no more of a descriptive concept than is appropriation. Such ascriptive statements in many ways resemble those that lawyers use to make accusations and imputations, or to deliver a verdict. The judge's role is not to provide an accurate description of the facts, but instead to decide and pronounce on the charges or the defense pleas. We need only infer from this that the appropriation of an action is not a fact that is given, but instead results from a problematic process of imputation, accusation, or confession. Many philosophical difficulties are caused by the refusal to see the ascriptive nature of the concept of action and the failure to examine the transactional conditions governing its imputation or appropriation: "I did x" or "You did x" are primarily expressions by which we admit or impute responsibility. And, in the first place, by which we ensure that someone else admits action x and imputes it to him or herself. We use this type of language not to describe something, but to conclude a complex transaction. If we find ourselves talking about one of our actions, it is implicitly in response to questions of the type: "What did you do? Why? With what aim in view? What led you to act like that?" This question game is part of a much wider scenario of transactions between one agent and another.[66] An action is just as inseparable from the system of interactions and transactions within which it occurs as it is from the person who does it or to whom it is done.

But, people will say, at least there are plans. Cannot the plan of an action exist before we make even the slightest move to carry it out? In this connection, I speak all the time of *my* plans. Ask someone else: "do you know what you want to do?" The answer will often be: yes.

> —But is there not something unusual about such an admission that you have plans? The declaration of an intention or a plan is actually a quite remarkable linguistic instrument. What is it for, and how have we learned to use it?

I was planning to . . . This is not the memory of an experience, or of some internal process. I am retrospectively the person who conceived of a particular plan, the one who will take the consequences and shoulder the responsibility. It was said that in Michigan people considered Ford quite heretical when he planned to build a car for all Americans; there were fifteen million Model T's sold from 1908 to 1927. But would there have been any sense in making a plan (almost) on his own, and then telling people about it, when others were patently implicated in it—if this project of "his" were not a response to "their" demand? Leaving aside the associates, engineers, workers, shareholders, bankers, customers, and—most closely involved of all—the co-inventor of the project and loyal agent of its fulfillment.

—Is it not conceivable for several people to have a plan and carry it out together, without any one of them having the idea individually?

—Of course, but then the verb that signified it would not be synonymous with my "I planned to. . . ." We must therefore to some extent reappropriate the plan to the person who claims to have made it.

—In what sense? Not in the sense that she will necessarily act as she is supposed to be planning, or intending, to do. Her action will be caught up in the flow of interactions and conjunctions between one agent and another.

As can be seen, we have to distance ourselves from Stendhal's idea that to act is to bring to light something called "my" plan or project. Such an idea fits in so well with our familiar techniques of self-confession that we are predisposed to believe in it: Julien Sorel's project leads us straight back to him as its source. Julien defines himself absolutely as the other person that he will be, with the actions he will perform according to the plans he will make; when he gambles on a future that will bear his mark, and boldly takes a mortgage on what he will become, he is behaving as a novelistic character. Just like Rastignac. Imagine, however, a historian relating the same actions and describing the same character: it is clear that real actions, deriving from real plans, never enter into the traditional novel. On the other hand, what defines the novel is a certain relationship between actions and plans. The everyday games we play with our language of plans and projects are much less exciting.

You say: I am planning to go away to the islands. You agree to forget the genesis of the project, the interactional content, the participation of other people in conceiving it or carrying it out. Your expression remains splendidly abbreviated, recapitulative, elliptical. "I should like to go with you" is more like it; it gives more adequate recognition to the part played by the ego. For the conditional tense of attenuated affirmation indicates that I am not projecting myself toward my particular goals by some movement inherent in me, nor regarding my goals as completely separate from yours—and you, if need be, as simply a means for attaining them. Sartre suggests in fact that I am now integrating the other's plans into my own, with each of us moving so as to become integrated into the other's project.[67]

If we take to its logical conclusion the idea that a separate project and individual goals are no more possible than a solitary action, there is a further twist. Making a project one's own is actually a process of secondary reappropriation of the part that the agent has played, and has been allowed by others to play, in its realization. For me to plan something is to anticipate an action in which I am involved with someone else, an action which must be undertaken jointly if it is to be realizable. As a commitment for the future, "my" project is the fact that I undertake personally to anticipate and take responsibility for an action (or set of coordinated actions) directed toward a goal which involves, in however small a degree (but one that remains real), the participation of others. In this differential sense we can certainly be said to have our own projects, in the same way that we have our own desires and interests. We intend to have a role in what is to happen; we imagine what it is to be and declare as much to others, so that they will agree to it and recognize our right to do it.

It is clear that, for most of the time, the process by which we appropriate our projects is a dubious one. While we will rarely be challenged when we mention them to a third party who is not involved, our appropriation quickly comes under discussion when we try to defend it in the face of other participants. It takes a certain aplomb and a great deal of humor, or some neurotic complaint that makes us slip gradually out of the human sphere, to disentangle our part in a goal that has been jointly adopted, or that calls at least for some form of joint realization. We certainly feel that the more personal a plan is presented as being, the more chancy or gratuitous it is, and we all tend to apologize for our frivolity is disclosing "our" plans.

The rest is literature. The characteristic fiction of the classical novel is the continually stressed link by which actions serve the advancement of projects, in a life in which everything is willed—even passions and crimes—to the point of distress. The analytic link is tightened by the approach of misfortune, a misfortune that is chosen and loved. That never happens in real life, as historians well know. As a result it is naive to ask whether the story is true or not, and whether the author has changed much in it; what is important is the power of the fiction. The novel of romantic individualism projects itself as the poem of free will, using the convention of a central perspective, that of the main thinking or acting subject, with whom we are invited to identify for the duration of our reading. We know everything about the character's plans and the feelings that acompany them. The thoroughly novelistic thing is the confidence of these plans: acts always fit the plan, as though action were the sister of dreams and gave them consistency, instead of negating them.

These remarks are not intended to eliminate subjectivity as such completely, but to find the exact limits of the appropriations, imputations, and attributions we make in relation to it. My question was: what does it mean to impute to a subject an action, a belief, a project, or a statement? I have resisted the temptation to see the personal self as the source of its own decisions, as a nonproblematic unit of intention, planning, and action.

But, the reader will doubtless argue, is there not in fact a limit to your enterprise of strategic dis-imputation? Is it not still the subject that is responding to its own relational questions? And the reply to them certainly seems to bring in memory, with its own duration. This in turn apposes the precious seal of continuity on the personal subject. Why should not the inherent particularity of a given personality, which no doubt cannot adequately be accounted for by any set of priorities, in fact derive from the possession of one's own past?[68] In that case, the term "personality" would not be a general expression, it would actually mean "individual personality." The memories of my actions, which are by definition individual, or at least the unique series of such memories, could then serve to individuate me.

No doubt the best response to this objection is to say: "what then?" The question is how we might conceive of a specific personality in terms of memories. On one point at least there need be no hesitation: far from constituting personal identity, memory in fact presupposes it. Who was it who said that we only ever remember ourselves? If I claim as my own first one set of memories, then another, I am precisely absolved of all doubt about my personal identity. What stranger phrase is there than "my memory"? In fact, what does it mean when we say that someone has a good memory? I say he or she has a good memory as if it were a thing, when I am unable to explain his or her behavior purely by reference to his or her present state. Conversely, suppose I am able to understand the exact situation at any moment during a chess match simply by looking at the present positions of the pieces on the board: I have no need to record earlier moves; in other words, I have no need to preserve their memory. We should not be fooled by the reified term: "memory" is only a shorthand expression for designating a particular form of the relations in which I am engaged. And we are more or less conscious of all these relations—not just some—however we may then tend to reify our consciousness of them.

In addition, I remember what I call my past to some extent in order to explain and even justify it to myself, as Rousseau does. When I set out in search of my past, it is not my internal myth that I seek. If it were, the past would have to be woven exclusively from my own duration in time; it would have to constitute a germinative succession of choices made by me. This is not the case.

Take two speakers, s_1 and s_2. First, everything s_1 tells s_2 about his or her past is closely bound up with the present relation between s_1 and s_2. Next, we only remember what we were to the extent that we were actively; of the things that were done to us, we remember only those that were obstacles to our own action. But these actions which are supposed to make up "my past," when I remember them, cannot be related to the ego alone. "My" past is intrinsically made up of relational events, the experience of which has immediate, indeclinable intersubjective meaning. I forget nothing that is important to me. But what is important to me embraces people other than myself. Let us think about our memories of the insults, the good deeds, and the various small confrontations that have marked our daily lives. As soon as I remember them, I find myself obliged to split the Same from the Other in my mind. When I look again at my "memories," I perceive that this other is involved in a relation with me, i.e., in an agency that no more belongs to him or her than it does to me.

Of course, anyone can discover him or herself within such a relation, and reemerge as a self. As we have seen, this is the price of personal identification. Anyone can at least reconstruct certain acts, if not actually demand them directly, as his or her share in the interactions and transactions of everyday life. It is this second, differential reprise or reemergence, which may or may not be spoken about after the event, that establishes an act or idea or feeling or memory as something personal, something admitted and recognized as ours, or on the contrary something refused us, disavowed by others. Note that our speech after the event recapitulates in the first person what was originally a tacit communication from ourselves to ourselves, which gives a new meaning and role to the concept of interiority. An act, idea, or feeling will only be admitted and recognized as personal by the discourse that comments on it if it has already received the appropriate qualification from an internal review of this type, i.e. a commentary derived from communication between self and self. What Augustine and the whole biblical tradition call "the heart" would then be the place where everything, figuratively speaking, takes a personal turn. Moreover, some texts draw subtle distinctions. The good man speaks to his heart (cf. Hebrew, "*el*," "to"): "And the Lord said to himself, never again will I curse the ground because of man." [69]

There is an internal dialogicity here which seems lacking in the wicked man, who expresses what is in his heart (cf. Hebrew "*be*," inside) as though he were swamped and lost in himself: "The wicked man scorns the Lord in his heart, and leaves no place for God." [70]

Which shows that his perversity is caused in part at least by an illusion as to the essence of the self. In my view, Nehama Leibowitz's idea of preserving the distinction between the Hebrew prepositions *el* and *be*, a distinction lost both in French and in English (where both are rendered by *in*), is a most suggestive one. [71]

The Question of Personal Predicates

P. F. Strawson has proposed that we divide the predicates attributed to persons into two classes. The first could equally well be applied to material bodies: these he calls M—predicates. The second would imply the possession of states of consciousness by those to whom they are applied: these are P—predicates.

I would not wish to challenge the particular sense in which a human being is conscious of his or her own identity, but I do not believe that consciousness is such a primary fact that it deserves the commanding role in an all-inclusive dichotomy of this type.[72] The dissymmetry we experience between the interiority of self and the exteriority of others is one thing, but the principle we adopt for the attribution of personal predicates is quite another. Whether it be to you or me, the assignment of a state of belief or the imputation of a particular action should not privilege any of the three persons; otherwise a category mistake is being made. Differences of decision criteria are just about tolerable, so that for instance we might allow that self-consciousness is sufficient for a person to recognize him or herself as him or herself.[73] But a so-called personal predicate should not change in meaning depending on whether it is being attributed to me or to someone else. This suggests that we might look for the nature of personal identity in the direction of certain public traits, which in any case are distinct from the physical characteristics assignable to bodies. Whatever logical form is selected for personal predicates, their attribution should be identical for the Same and the Other.

A certain dissymmetry is indeed brought into the investigation by performative verbs occurring in the first person. But in an interlocutive context a dissymmetry of this sort remains marginal because it is provisional and reversible. As long as my language acts alternate with yours, their illocutionary force is not privileged. And as long as they convey a real message, this illocutionary force remains a communicative one.[74]

Speaking of Persons

Let us not have any illusions about the language of psychology, which has remained monadic and retained memory, attention, and perception as independent concepts. They are considered as psychic functions with which the subject is equipped, and studied under artificially isolated conditions.

I recently showed, and perhaps proved, why the natural and primary mode of relating to a person is not the delocutive register (he/she), but instead the allocutive one.[75] The reason is that persons relate to themselves as uttering agencies by a specific process of back-reference, while giving symbolic expression to their selves in the movement of discourse, by which they compare and contrast their different propositional attitudes to the object of the discourse. The world in which I find myself is always effectively constituted as a *common* world with the participation of the other person. This world is the set of our co-references, and as such it is effectively shared with others. Persons bring each other into existence in the process and for the duration of their communication together about the world. By which I mean that the centripetal mode of referring to persons is only gradually acquired by speaking individuals as they learn to relate more to the world, in a more or less successful, direct, or postponed attempt to establish a system of co-references.

Note that reference to persons as uttering agencies comes about as it were simultaneously between them. Each interlocutor can grasp his or her own specific differences by back-reference, within the agency of discourse that constantly expresses the partial pooling of the utterance. This analysis, which I have pursued in detail elsewhere, has new implications for the problem of the Same and the Other.

We tend to want to treat certain determinants as qualities or properties, and to treat these in turn as images of the self, for us or for others: my wife, my children, my beliefs, my body. We have already seen how mistaken these images are. From a simple grammatical point of view they have the appearance of descriptions, something that tends to be seized on by philosophers who grant an obsessively privileged status to a narrow range of schematic, half-analyzed examples. From a logical point of view, each case needs to be analyzed separately. Thus "Scott" and "Scott's body" are not interchangeable *salva veritate* in every context. It is then reasonable to suggest that the identity of the body with its spatiotemporal continuity is not a sufficient condition of personal identity.

The symbol used to represent the self is probably the most complex symbol of all. It is manifestly impossible to use it as a generic expression. Negatively, it therefore follows that the self cannot be reduced to the possession of a set of characteristics, as the substantivized pronoun (le moi) might seem to imply. In particular, it is clear how artificial is the supposition that the personal pronoun *I* is related to an enduring, unique mental entity equipped with attributes. Once self-consciousness ceases to be a primary datum, experiences are no longer intrinsically marked as "mine" by their common relations to this entity. They will rightly be distinguished as my experiences only in relation to those of other people, all in the context of the external world formed by our co-references. In that case, self-knowledge can no longer be identified with a Cartesian-style Cogito which empowers the ego to know itself by immediate intuition. Still less can it be identified with a Kantian *Ich denke,* which postulates a self that is always the subject of consciousness and never its object, a self-sufficient subject that accompanies all possible experiences regarded as mine.

If we are to avoid presenting a fantastical image of man, we must take account of the fact that the real status of the term "me/self" (moi) is not substantive, but pronominal. While the "I" can be properly understood as a mobile first person that alternates during communication, "me" clearly results from a process of construction that is a complex mix of confluence and accretion. There was recently a proposal to make it into a separate subsystem on another level, a constellation of symbols rather than a single one in its own right.[76] If one then adds, as I shall be led to suggest, that the self as person is the seat of a pragmatic competence,[77] it is easy to see what obstacles analytic logic will face when it tries to give this notion an operative value. Not to mention the additional difficulty of linking together the various elements of personal identity that emerge from the analysis.

In my opinion, the whole discussion of "personal predicates" suffers from a number of confusions. Are they individual traits, dispositional differences deriving from character or from whatever it is that characterizes persons uniquely? Or are they predicates that we attribute to persons as such, in our delocutive discourse about them, or on the contrary, ones to which we claim they are admitting in the first person ("I am in pain," "I am bored")? Or, more generally, are they just verbs subjectively marked as evaluations of propositional attitudes—I am afraid, I hope, I desire—which actually imply a speaking subject who assumes responsibility for them?

Let me restate the problem in a different form. By specifying the contexts in which personal predicates must appear, we will gain some idea of their nature. If the foregoing analysis is correct, so-called "personal" predicates should be thought of as deriving from the notion of personal identity, rather than the reverse. In other words, ways of being can only be imputed to persons on the basis of a language expressly used in a communicational situation. That is actually the most general condition of the perception of someone else as a person: I only see that person as such to the extent that I can engage with him or her in communication through language. The same language that assigns to each interlocutor a position in the communicational act founds simultaneously in each the possibility of saying "me" (I who am speaking) and "you" (to whom I am speaking). And also the possibility of differentially imputing to each other propositional attitudes such as beliefs, feelings, or judgments.

This approach will allow us to avoid attributing to the person things that only apply to individuals, such as somatic differences or particular social roles, or others that serve only to characterize the monadic self, such as acts or states of mind. It is logically impossible to attribute to a person in a communicative situation predicates that could only be attributed to the subject or object of a statement in the delocutive register. Such confusions, incidentally, also have a moral connotation, for they are the origin of the things we say about people behind their backs.

So if we wish to speak about people as persons, we must be prepared to reveal our relationship with them in what we say. It is difficult to characterize inductively the particular style of someone's mode of being in a relation, for the good reason that we too are participants in it and any extrapolation from the communicative situation is dubious. Hence the understandable prudence of the Talmud in recommending that we give up speaking about other people altogether, even in praise, because praise soon leads to the pseudo-objective reduction of the person, if indeed that is not its aim from the start. Real praise consists in bearing witness to and celebrating a person's achievements, and not in imputing things to him or her. It is quite wrong to see the other as someone to whom we can sovereignly attribute a given character trait or individual difference, as though it were a personal trait. This is a category confusion. The reason is that the person in me and in the other can only come into existence in the course of communication. As our conversation unfolds, I gradually perceive the other in his or her propositional attitudes (beliefs) and language acts (assertions, questions), just as I gradually come to perceive myself in relation to him or her. The Same is in no way privileged over the Other. I shall not return here to the originality of a process that conditions the manifestation of a personal being, at the same time that it conditions the assignment of its status as a person.[78]

Once these initial conditions are accepted, how can we then define genuinely personal predicates? The difficulty is that they may only be imputed to persons if the relations in which the persons are engaged are taken into account. Personal predicates must qualify either persons as they are in given relations or their general way of being in relations. Thus personal predicates can first of all qualify the propositional attitudes that arise in the communicational situation: I shall speak to you about your beliefs. This is possible to the extent that each speaker is able without misunderstanding to perceive him or herself within the interlocutive relation—allowing him or her to declare and keep a dynamic check on his or her states of belief, while allowing the other person to comment on his or her own role in their formation—and to perceive him or herself in function of his or her inalienable share of the semantic initiative, which the other person freely concedes.

I do not deny that research in this area has a long way to go, or that it is a logically highly complex field. Of pertinence here are all those verbs that denote types of speaking behavior, under the dominance of the archi-lexeme "to say": these include locutory verbs like "declare," "ask," "criticize," and "reply," which incidentally can also convey evaluative-type presuppositions (as in the case of "claim"). Then, on a different language level, I would suggest that some personal predicates are expressed in the vocabulary we use for talking about the aptitudes of persons for entering into and maintaining relations with others. The poverty of the description ordinarily given of relational phenomena is well known. These phenomena are denatured by being dealt with—either for want of anything better, or through a desire to exaggerate—in the language of dispositions, i.e. once more in a monadic manner. In themselves, they are seen to characterize the exclusivity or, on the contrary, the polyvalency of a relationship, its strength or its weakness, or its rigidity.

From the foregoing analysis we may now expect there to be in theory as many possible predicates of the person as there are forms of interpersonal relation between the three positions in the communicational act, as they are realized two by two. For instance, the speaker might appear "peremptory" to the listener if he or she refuses to allow objections or remarks about what he or she is saying. This judgment reflects his or her tendency to take over or refuse to relinquish the speaking role, thus usurping the semantic initiative. Or he or she might be seen as "indiscreet," a predicate which marks an annoying tendency to want to make people give away or listen to confidences. When qualifying a person's attitude to being called upon by someone else as his or her allocutee, we might well describe that person as painfully reserved, meaning that he or she has a delicate ear or is frightened of contact. If reticence is a personal predicate qualifying a peculiar reserve in relation to allocution by others, it is not the same thing as taciturnity: it is a reserve of the ear, rather than of the mouth. In the opposite case, a person can be open to everything another might say, listening to the other's words and taking the person seriously to the point of indulgence. This is the reproach that Alceste makes to Philinte during his relations with him, accusing him of treating the worthy man and the fool in the same way, and of being indifferent to no one:

> I spurn the indulgence of a heart
> That will not set merit itself apart.[79]

The predicates that Molière hands out with great accuracy throughout the comedy are genuinely personal ones.

Finally, in his or her attitude to someone else as a third party, a person can suspend any delocutive discourse straightaway by using greater discernment, which is the first step toward benevolence. On the other hand, that person might appear as a mocker, or on the contrary indulge in a perverse form of commiseration. As for the way in which he or she reacts to what others say, he or she might be "thin-skinned," over-prepared to take what others say as the truth. Or he or she might seem "blasé," taking hardly any interest in the image other people may have of him or her.

To conclude with one important remark: the vocabulary for describing persons is much poorer than that which is available to define individuals or characters. In addition to describing stereotyped or rigid attitudes, it should also be able to qualify particular inabilities, such as the failure to allow a relationship to develop into intimacy by being too distant. But the most difficult thing remains how to give a positive characterization of the ability to enter into and maintain interpersonal relationships, throughout their vicissitudes. I repeat that rather than grasping the stylistics of interpersonal behavior, people are generally content to fall back on a lexis of excess and fault that is more applicable to the individual or the self (which are then brought strongly back into the picture) than to the person.

Grievances: Normal and Perverse Forms of Self-Confession

Both the normal context in which personal predicates are imputed and their particular nature provide criteria for defining normal forms of self-confession. Only careful examination will show the invalidity of the arguments that supporters of a monadic self like to base on certain (perverse) forms of confession.

"Admit what they are accusing you of." We all know this type of absolute imputation, which occurs when the appropriately coded action is reputed to be both mine and reprehensible. Psychologists have no trouble in explaining why we normally react badly to accusations of this sort, in which the slightest suspicion is hurtful to us, or even why reproachful behavior is totally lacking in some people. Be that as it may. The important thing is doubtless that accusations, always unwelcome, tend to be challenged by those against whom they are made, and seem metaphysically false coming from the person who makes them. Between people who were once linked, or supposedly were, by a relationship, any absolute imputation is unfair, and often it is the fact of the accusation rather than its substance that is so forcefully rejected. What does it take for the accusation to be felt as anything other than intolerantly direct; what does it take for the grievance to be accepted? No doubt an exceptional accuracy in the attribution of the act, and consummate tact in dividing up responsibility for it; the grievance must be put forward in a marginal, differential way. But still, who is in a position to impute it? And in what conditions can a confession come about? It is the same question in both cases.

The pragmatically normal forms of self-confession occur in the canonical communicative situation. The condition of the personal self is relational. As we have seen, very particular precautions are necessary when assigning personal predicates to the self in a confessional discourse. Even more so if someone is being expected to vouchsafe a confidence about himself, or admit to what is about to be imputed to him: after all, this is precisely an attempt to take the relation back to a fixed origin, or assign to one of its terms something (a belief, action, or idea) that occurred in the relational situation. Or again, we might demand of someone that he undertake a confession unilaterally, a common enough operation requiring at the very least a communication of the self with the self, and a kind of recycling of previous communications with other people.

If it were properly understood and conducted, it is not impossible that confession, freely made on demand before an arbiter, might contribute to the construction of personal identity by giving a new solidity to subsequent relations with others, as a response to the need for reassurance and the need to speak impartially about oneself. In theological terms, we could say that confession and the expression of repentance reestablish the integrity of our relations with God, at the same time reconciling us with ourselves by restoring the rectitude of our reciprocal relations. Note that in confession, the arbiter has the right to know on what basis I accuse myself; however, I remain the judge of this, although this judgment is tempered by another, between me and myself. This explains why Christian confession, when all these precautions are taken, is supposed to lead directly to forgiveness and reintegration into the community.

On the other hand, such precautions are lacking in perverse forms of confession which, in my view, follow from a deliberate manipulation of the utterance protocols. But a statement of this complexity needs to be analyzed in more detail.

Michel Foucault, much inspired by perverse modes of confession, traces their structure back to the law, medicine, and even amatory relations. He reconstructs them at length.[80] According to him, the centuries-old yoke of confession can be seen as a power structure immanent in procedures for the production of a certain discourse. This structure goes back to the thirteenth century, when the Council of Latran in 1215 drew up rules governing the sacrament of penitence by which Christians were obliged to kneel once a year to confess their sins—"in detail" demanded the Council, so that the priest could judge the person who was thus admitting that he or she was a sinner.

Foucault finds this same structure at work in Christian confession and in the methods of investigation, the interrogations, practiced by the Inquisition. He sees maleficent confession everywhere, disseminated in a variety of forms, from interrogations to medical consultations, and wherever the vast written archives of the self are transcribed and filed, or made public and critiqued. This is a major ritual from which society expects the production of a certain truth about the self, and in which its power system takes a keen interest. It is also so deeply ingrained in us that we no longer feel the effect of the power that forces us to submit to it; worse still, we believe that confession liberates, as if the truth of subjectivity were only waiting for a chance to express itself before emerging.

Perverse self-confession is then, in this light, the result of a vast process by which the West has forced people generation after generation to say what they are, what they have done, what they remember, what they have forgotten, and what they prefer not to think.[81] Perverse, because I end up confessing, of my own free will, something that should not be said; I confess not because what I admit to is true and must be revealed, but in spite of the fact that it is not true. How can we be stupid enough to confess our own situation, and yet sufficiently conditioned to "come clean"? Our language itself carries traces of this conditioning. "Admitting" or "confessing" p implies that p is true in the eyes of the speaking subject, while indicating that his illocutionary act is delayed, or hindered, by certain reticences; particularly as the object of his confession is evaulated axiologically. Natural language contains the evidence of this: what is being confessed, and what is the subject being asked indiscreetly to confide? That which is hidden, of course, that which he would do better to keep secret, his weaknesses and his guilt. And of course his love: "It was in a little wood full of flowers that he confessed his love," etc. The myth of expressivity, supported by the myth of the interiority of the self, is confirmed by a postulate of latency. The self will reveal itself, through confession, in all its qualities and states of mind; it will reveal everything within itself that is hidden, and expose its private parts.

I am quite prepared to agree that this type of confession of the self in no way commits its true being. It may sometimes be in the interests of the power systems in society to take over and exploit certain procedures of individualization, in the same way as a lawyer may exert undue pressure on a witness. Theoretically, there can be no subject in the politico-legal sense of the term unless the psychological subject has been forced into acting as the owner of its own actions, ideas, and qualities. This constitution of the subject in the two senses of the word is doubtless part of the wider political history of subjectivity. It is important to know *who*, otherwise universal disorder reigns. It is important to find the guilty party (ultimately, any guilty party will do), rather than leave an anonymous evil floating about in the world. Not that the source of the evil must necessarily be imputable to an individual; but whatever it is imputed to must have a name, be it a spirit, an ancestor, or the community. If this nameable entity is the individual self, it is appropriate that the archives of the self should be held by the state.

Do the facts bear out Foucault's theory of penal truth production? If so, the judges of old France must have been either negligent or biased. What do legal historians have to say on the subject? At least as far as the exercise of criminal justice from the sixteenth century onward is concerned, their first results contradict a good proportion of the picture. L. B. Mer, for instance, is struck by the variety of the recorded statements and the natural, unforced quality of the speech reported by witnesses.[82] Even if there had been legal pressures in serious cases, they would have been condemned to failure by the wide range of testimony heard. Interrogation, usually conducted in an entirely routine manner, was as likely to lead to an acquittal as to a confession. In the end, adds my informant, it was a relatively ineffective tool as the confession rate remained low.[83]

Even supposing that certain forms of confession were indeed shot through with power relations, what in fact is the role of theory here? In my view, its more fundamental task is to establish precisely under what conditions, in what form, and through which type of discourse, the confession of an authentically personal self can be expected to occur. At the same time, by examining deviations from this norm, we would be able to observe the pragmatic mechanism governing perverse confession, and we would understand how the normal ways of imputing personal predicates to the self can theoretically be hijacked. And that is the real point.

Personal predicates, as we have seen, cannot be used in a context in which the other is entirely delocuted. On the other hand, they can appear in contexts in which the delocutive and allocutive registers are associated in a controlled way. Certain contexts are conducive to their appearance. In polite society, for instance, it is not done to speak of those who are absent, while to speak of those who are absolutely absent (i.e., dead) without engaging in some elogious ritual is felt to be quite impossible. How impoverishing it is no longer to be able to speak *to* someone, but only *of* that person! Other contexts are more or less explicitly unfavorable. The military and even medical institutions place a premium on delocution. An example is the case of a patient in a hospital surrounded by doctors talking about *her:* even if they do address themselves to her, because she is lying down they speak differently than they would if she were on her feet. It is probably a property of any institution that it introduces additional constraints and acts as a filter that privileges certain language games, whose predominance, selection, and rules are precisely characteristic of that institution.

For personal predicates to be attributed to persons without privileging one at the expense of others, an equitable communicative situation is required. That is the initial condition. As we know, in certain cases of blatant asymmetry a dominance relation grows up, producing a distortion that is stable. This is why an accuser stands provocatively at a distance when he demands a confession. The subject who confesses certainly coincides with the subject of the statment, but if he speaks in order to confess or avow his self, he does so in function of what is demanded of him. The agency that demands the accused person's confession is not simply an interlocutor, but an invested authority, an "established power." Is its aim to make the accused tell his or her version of the truth, or to prevent it from being told? The difference is not pertinent here. The first aim is always to strip the accused of his or her share in the joint process of sense-creation, by suggesting to him or her that it be invested instead in an established and reserved communicational regime.

This explains why a whole ritual is required before a confession is obtained, i.e., before a person who is supposed to possess, express, and be responsible for the truth about him or herself tells it to whomever it may concern. The search for a confession has nothing to do with the giving of confidences. An extreme form is seen in witchcraft trials. The astonishing thing about them is that the accused is interrogated in (and indeed by means of) a state of repression, and yet the accusers never stop hoping for a confession of the person's fundamental truth. Better still, they see the size of the obstacle to be overcome by the accused as an indication of the value of the confession. But, in hypocritical homage to the correct imputation of personal predicates, only the person who is induced to confess can give full meaning to the charges against him or her, through a confession which is in itself a ratification. But if what the accuser says about the accused requires authentification by him or her, a cunning ritual is needed of the sort that we find in today's trials by media. The agency of utterance must be maniplated in such a way that our ascendency over the accused is preserved, with due attention to his or her own code and context: these include the person's real relationship to his or her actions, thoughts, and gestures, so that the person can be made to fit the partial account we intend to give of him or her, and which the person will give of him or herself.

We might go along with Foucault's suggestion that there is a power structure immanent in all confession. It is certainly true that confession is induced in too asymmetrical a manner for it not to be a violent process; there is an obsessional drive to prove too much, to produce a confession as perfect as a mask. But a description given in pragmatic terms is both more precise and more fundamental. It shows up the machinery of incitation, the powerful injunction to say what one intrinsically is, what one has done (and therefore what one has to answer for, and remember). The aim is to make another person tell you in your code about things that concern him or her, so you ask him or her to impute them to him or herself through confession.

Self-confession is something that is provoked, because it occurs within a manipulative discourse. How can this discourse be characterized? It consists in a discursive action by a speaker who intends to produce in his or her interlocutor a verbal reaction, in this particular case the admission, confession, or imputation of actions and intentions. This verbal action can only be provoked if certain changes are also brought about in the interlocutor's beliefs about him or herself. Like any manipulative undertaking, the accuser's discursive action triumphs when it succeeds in inducing a sincere confession; it can only be completed by the *sponte sua* of the accused. In short, the accuser's aim is then to make the accused do something by modifying his or her own self-conception, by making him or her *be* different.

This is what separates manipulation from straightforward lying. Lying is also a maneuver, for the liar keeps control of his or her duplicity. But the peculiarity of manipulation is that it also induces actions, on top of everything else, and this is what makes it truly scurrilous. The person who provokes someone else to self-confession is at the same time a manipulator of the mechanisms of utterance. The subversion of discourse this manipulation introduces is far more profound than that produced by an incorrect statement. Manipulative discourse, deliberately one-sided, is a truncated form of speech. Except on the most superficial level, where the manipulator puts his message across in a perfidious discourse, he is in no sense a unit of communicative interaction. Nor, a fortiori, does he have a dialogical role: it is a matter of principle that the agent-listener is changed without any reciprocity by the agent-speaker.

Therefore, whenever the words of the accused seem wrongly coded to the accuser who is manipulating him, they will be picked out, rejected as obscure, and duly reinterpreted. This other, who already knows about you what you do not know yourself, reserves the right to decipher your words and restore them where necessary to their true meaning.

Even the hesitations and reticence shown by the accused are held against him as contradictions in his story. We should study the pseudo-dialogue by which people are interrogated in court to see how it forces them into a particular frame of reference, and the whole apparatus which the masters of legal pertinence construct around the accused so as to incite him to produce "his" truth in conformity with theirs. Look, our group is strong, its code dominant, whereas yours is inconsistent and no one else shares it (anyway, you are on your own). So tell us our own truth about you, in front of those who are witnesses and who are asking us to hear it from your mouth: if you do, it will intrinsically prove you innocent or guilty. And we shall become stronger. Only those whom our group has excommunicated shall be regarded as excluded; their number does not matter.

The Case of Psychoanalysis

I find it hard to believe that authors of confessions, or intimate journals, or egotistical memoirs, are indulging in forms of confession shot through with power relations. Let us think about the pen and the person holding it. She is writing the confession of someone else, purer, blacker, livelier, and above all more natural and real than she was before she had the idea of writing it. This form of confession is doubtless practiced for specific reasons, perhaps from a desire to be unlike everyone else, to be the singular being par excellence.

Nor do I believe that what Foucault calls "psychoanalytic confession" takes a discursive form remotely comparable to that of the provoked confession of the self. We do not find in psychoanalytic therapy the same obvious manipulation of the apparatus of utterance as in the latter case: you will speak of yourself, at our request, saying what we ask you to say, and imputing it to yourself according to the preestablished interrogational code; kindly reply in the terms in which we ask the questions, and speak of yourself as the origin of acts, intentions, and memories which are imputable to you. And certainly not, of course, as the agent of joint actions caught up in a network of interactions and transactions. The psychoanalytic situation is quite different. At the start of the therapy, the discourse about me is requested by me from someone else. The analyst in any case takes care not to defer to this first request from the patient. And, at the end of the cure, it turns out that I myself have been able, with the help of someone else, to speak about myself, and more or less to become the holder of the code that allows me to give a unique interpretation of myself.

Let us go back a little way. Entering into psychoanalysis commonly involves calling on someone else as a way of finding out who one is. Needing someone to listen is often the first symptom: it realizes the metaphor about "lending an ear" to a person's problems. It matters little that the subject of analysis experiences things as if he or she were being asked to confess: that is definitely not the scenario we have here. The rule of free speech is simply designed to ensure that the thought object, whatever it may be, can be expressed without any checks or precautions as to the pertinence of its content. So instead of wondering about whether self-confession in psychoanalysis is normal or perverse, let us shift the question: under what psychoanalytic conditions can the attribution of personal predicates legitimately be made?

Let us recall the key principle. The only legitimate way of speaking about others is to say only what we could also say directly to their faces. From which a demanding maxim follows: "Always treat the person of others, in your discourse about them, as a potential allocutee as well." Thus the other person will end up recognizing at least that he or she is the one being spoken about, even if the person does not see what is said as a faithful portrait of him or herself. By regarding someone purely as a delocuted *he/she*, we make it virtually impossible for that person to realize the identificatory mapping of his or her self. Whereas if we always see the person at the same time as a virtual allocutee who could substitute his or her own questions for those of our present listener, we provide the person with an indispensable continuity of context.

A first approximation in pragmatic terms would be to say that the unconscious intrinsically qualifies the subject of the utterance. It would therefore be of the order of what is hidden between me and myself, a secret we keep from ourselves, either because we do not want it, or because we do not know how to reveal it. In fact, we find that this so-called unknown aspect is actually merely misunderstood. The subject is not initially a good receiver of the messages he or she puts out: for him or her the link between meaning and understanding is broken. Then the so-called unknown is gradually revealed by the other person, who knows how to understand it. Finally, and crucially: thanks to this special type of interlocutive relation in which one person speaks more than he listens and the other listens more than she speaks, what for the subject of analysis was unknown eventually ceases to be so. It does not remain unsayable. For the analyst who is interpreting it as a symptom it is already something perfectly sayable, of which the speaker must become the co-utterer.

Thus the thesis of the unconscious actually relates to interpretative *delays* within a quite specific interlocutive relation, operating in a particular type of discourse. The therapy makes us participate in a form of communication that is not so much precarious as out of phase, one in which the patient's words reply to implicit questions which the patient is incapable of asking himself, (in a code he does not know), but which the analyst is able to reconstruct bit by bit. In this way, the subject is gradually able to listen to more and more of what he does not yet understand; one person's relative deafness is thereby overcome by another's acceptance of a purely listening role. It is as if the patient, whom others had not been able or not wanted to understand, had become unable to hear the interiorized other within him; having repressed this internal listener, he then needs an external listener to bring it back into use.

Now, time is essential for this restoration process to work. The things said by the subject's voice are not initially recoverable by him as concerning him, but they can be recovered by someone else. Conversely, even if the analyst tells the subject delocutively what he wants to hear, he will be unable to recognize himself in what she says before the cure is complete. This point of completion could equally be defined as the moment when what is proffered by the patient becomes recoverable, i.e., when it can once more be integrated into an interlocutive context. People often stress the idea that the therapy is over when one is able once more to speak in the first person, as the originator of one's own words. Here I will stick my neck out a long way and say that this point is actually reached when I come to hear myself. The patient then starts to listen to what he or she is saying with the same suspicious ear as the practitioner. Thus as far as a (partial) pragmatic description is concerned, analysis always aims to reestablish a communicative competence with the self. In this sense, analysis is always somewhat didactic—just as any didactic analysis is to some extent therapeutic.

Once again we see how a special kind of discursive interplay can gradually lead to a knowledge of the subject, of his or her psychological predicates, obscure depths, and everything that takes the subject for a time (and sometimes for good) out of him or herself. If the attribution of personal predicates in discourse occurs legitimately, in function of the interlocutive relation by which persons are constituted, it must not privilege any one person at the expense of others. Hence the difficulty of the process. Apart from the fact that the logical forms of such predicates vary widely, it is essential to overcome the persistent illusion we all experience—that there is a dissymmetry between the interiority of our own self and the exteriority of other people. Once these conditions are accepted, we can begin to define the real meaning of the personal status of the self in such a way that it conforms to the personal status of the person (I shall finish defining the status of the person later on). But it is already clear that we can no longer simply use pronouns of the personal register, such as "me," "you," and "he/she," to designate delocutively the identity sometimes of the self, sometimes of the other, without taking certain precautions. These pronouns also belong to the allocutive register; they cannot refer in the same way as either a proper noun or a definite description.[84] Nor is it any longer possible to claim that subjectivity is defined by lack of knowledge of the self.[85] When thinking about subjectivity, that elusive beauty, we can do better than talk about its lack of reality. For it is the role of communication, in its ceaseless ebb and flow, to engender the reality of persons by back-reference to the speaking subject.[86] This is how persons construct and reconstruct themselves.

Let me now sum up. From the foregoing analyses we can see that there are two different modes of identification of the self, of which one—wherein the self is enclosed within the circle of the Same in order to make it homogeneous to the concept—has been shown to be illusory. According to that model, the self is a subjective, individual, and permanent notion; this illusory metaphysical conception appears to accord with a "natural" reality (it is a standard idea), a cultural reality (the imputation of actions is important both to the law, and in society generally), and a grammatical reality. Language is unable to give proper recognition to the apparently unique position of the self as the center and origin of its own experience in the world. How could it, without giving the same privilege to every speaker? And yet traces of it do survive in language, in the purely formal grammatical inflation of possessive expressions. The difficulty we encountered was in disposing of this grammatical monster without appearing to deny its expressive value.

For four centuries now the legal experts, in alliance first with the theologians of the Counter-Reformation and then with psychologists, have been working to enclose the field of human nature. That is why I chose to pursue the investigation of concrete phenomena such as desire that I began in the previous chapter, and extend it to cover the predilection relation, i.e., love. Moving from a typology of grammatical forms to a study of usage, I tried to understand the real meaning of expressions in which the self appears to give a description of the experiences it has had. I concluded that when we describe what we mean by using expressions such as "I have qualities" or "I have memories" in real situations, the description contains nothing corresponding to the fact that I have them.

In the first place, I contended that statements in which "I" appears do not thereby necessarily allude to a particular individual. Second, however striking the forms in question may be, there is no place for a relationship of possession between the self and any of its subjective experiences. Except insofar as we are the victims of an inveterate grammatical habit, psychological predicates do not require a subject (or any other type of support), nor do they need to be regarded as states or properties of anything at all. A detailed analysis of this point will be found later on, in the context of my reply in principle to subjectivist discourses about it. A further reason will then emerge, which is that when I say that I am the only person who can have the experience I am having, it is far from certain that I am saying anything very meaningful at all.

Conversely, this chapter has again shown the legitimacy of the second mode of identification of the subject, in which the sameness of the self is derived from a personal identity gained in and through communication. In this view, there is no concept corresponding to the existence of the self. It presupposes the crucial possibility of integrating the alterity of others on the basis of a reciprocal relationship with them on which I embark in the act of communication. But it also presupposes my own alterity in the eyes of others when they speak about me. In short, the person is an intersubjective, communicational, and diachronic notion. The implications of this are important, for psychology's reduction of the self to a monad was doubtless more serious than its subsequent reduction to a set of mechanisms. We need not only to bring the self out from the limits of its cut-off singularity and egotism, but also to help it to emerge from an ontological illusion.

3 Primum Relationis

Only those universals which are named by adjectives or substantives have been much or often recognized, while those named by verbs and prepositions have usually been overlooked.
—BERTRAND RUSSELL
Problems of Philosophy

IN THIS chapter I shall adopt in turn a logical and an aporetic point of view, before setting off down the freer path of description, to show how the three approaches converge. We shall see that experience confirms the conclusion reached by analysis, that the relation is a fundamental and irreducible given.

It is true that people only exist for each other in a given set of social circumstances, and as a result all relations between them are historical. But while history may determine the content of human relations, it is definitely not responsible for their existence; rather, the reverse is true: what makes possible the constitution of a group or society is the permanent presence of human relations at any moment in history.

Whatever the most appropriate explanation for it might be, my lived experience cannot help but make me see my life in relational terms. And our understanding of being as something relational is probably what distinguishes people from other beings, which are content simply to exist. All our affirmations and attitudes imply such an understanding. If what constitutes the human being is his or her relation to being, and if that being is itself relational, then everything about people, their knowledge as much as their everyday lives, will be in some way connected with it.

Other people change as I look at them. If I smile at a child, it will smile back. A timid person will intimidate others, although if I refuse to be put off he or she will gradually gain in confidence. The deep reason for this is that the other person is immediately linked to me. Human relations are established and confirmed in such a way that deception follows close on the heels of suspicion, whereas we tend not to suspect someone who is confident. Readers will be able to supply their own evidence that this is so. We find it easy to lie to someone who regards us as a liar, and we would be prepared to strike a person who is convinced we are brutal. My enemies remain such because I will not pardon them for being my enemies.

Being sure that someone is speaking to me and (on a sub-linguistic level) that he or she is feeling unwell, doubting whether this is so, and so on, are all *immediate* ways of being in a relation to that person which do not derive from some prior cause such as a joint activity or some particular social praxis. Human relations undoubtedly do have individual specificity, but the relation in general is an inherent component of life itself. An animal has a sense of the relations that link it to other living beings, a fact that struck Gregory Bateson when he observed the antics of otters. As someone who was trying to introduce into ethology a number of ideas of great simplicity, elegance, and power concerning the relational nature of communication, he began to wonder how it was that apparently aggressive behavior in otters could be immediately perceived by them as play; in the face of all this provocative biting and chasing, thought Bateson, they must somehow know from the start that it is only a game. As Montaigne had already noted, who knows, when I am playing with my cat, whether she is not in fact playing with me? We play with each other. A person who holds back from a relation with any living being shows that he or she is incapable of a certain relativity. Rightly or wrongly, we assume that he or she will behave in an equally unrelational way with other people.

Interhuman relations have the status of an ultimate reality. Without referring to them in some way I could not say that someone else was hard to reach, or speak about solitude, or the ramified levels of connivance. The interlocutive relation is the most immediate form of relation, for it is one of the most basic: "Caring for, treating the part that hurts when someone else is ill, and not just oneself, is a basic form of behavior."[1] Although, Wittgenstein also observes: "Commanding, questioning, recounting, chatting are as much a part of our natural history as walking, eating, drinking, playing."[2]

Language as an interdiscursive praxis is founded on a practical relation between one person and another. Conversely, such a praxis is always linguistic because it cannot come about without signifying itself. Language can no more have occurred to people by chance than the relation can; each supposes the other. For someone to suffer from isolation, he or she must be constituted as a person by his or her relations with others, as expressed in and through language.

But in the first instance we must look to logical analysis to help us avoid mistakes and confirm the conclusion drawn from experience, that the human relation is indeed primordial. Logic and experience here go hand in hand. The relation is independent of its components, and in principle it even takes priority over them. This is not just the independence from its members of the whole which is made up of the beings it relates.[3] It is the priority of the relation itself that is at issue here.

To what does this commit us? First, to regarding the interpersonal or interlocutive relation as just as real as its terms. Next, to giving a precise definition of what those terms are. And finally, to understanding in what sense the relation can in a general way be primary.

From a Logical Point of View

The idea that there is a specifically relational reality is not entirely new in philosophy. But it is by no means self-evident. One of Bertrand Russell's greatest contributions was to introduce consideration of verbs and prepositions, which convey relations, alongside nouns and adjectives, which deal with substances and properties. As he himself noted, "such an omission has had a major influence on philosophy; it is scarcely an exaggeration to say that the greater part of metaphysics since Spinoza has been influenced above all by this state of affairs."[4]

The Irreducibility of Relations

But could not relations be conceived of in a different way? Let us examine the relation in intensional terms. Is there no way of reducing it to a property? In fact, people have been trying to do this since Aristotle. It was Russell who managed to extend the conceptual domain to include polyadic predicates, and who demonstrated their specificity. With C. S. Peirce, he laid the foundations of logical thinking about the impossibility of this type of reduction; it is similar to imagining what it is like to be thirsty when you are not.

It was Russell who first saw that the preposition *with* is just as real as *before* and *after*. I do not want to challenge the existence in the real world of terms that are not relation-dependent. In certain cases relations can occur between such independent terms. This is what happens, according to Russell, with relations of order, which are "external."[5] But I believe that there are also relations that change their terms, and even that constitute the terms themselves.

One example is the interlocutive reciprocity relation. This is a case in which Russell's opposition between internal and external relations is no more than a formal one. It is a relation that grabs hold of *individuals;* that happens to them and, as a result, makes them into *persons.* We could say that the individuals exist before the relation that grows up between them. But the same cannot be claimed for their personal identity. The relation of mutuality takes hold of individuals, but only in order to make them into agencies capable of communicative speech, so that they may then acquire personal identity, sui generis. This identity can therefore be regarded as a secondary consequence of a primary reality, the relation of mutuality.

Thinking about relations from a philosophical point of view, we are faced with a preliminary choice: should we regard them as external to their terms; or, stressing their internal incompleteness, should we put them on the same level as properties, the only difference then being the number of terms and the manner in which relations are inherent in them?

Russell called this latter choice—by which relations, like properties, are seen as inherent—the "principle of internal relations." It presupposes that a subject or foundation is related to a term of which it is the ordinate. The relation then consists in the reference to this term. In a sense, the nonsaturation of relations is even greater than that of properties. A relation without its terms is a pure abstraction, intrinsically incomplete, while a property—such as color or softness—can only be sufficient extrinsically. In fact, the relation is linked to a body or an extension, etc. By relation in this sense is meant simply the fact that the terms are presently linked (relatedness). The terms are presupposed by the relation: they are the foundations on which it is entirely dependent. That is why Alexius Meinong, who expresses this traditional conception quite well, makes them into objects of a higher order, *superiora* that depend on two or more *inferiora* whose existence presupposes the existence of the terms.[6] The inferiora are prior to the objects constructed upon them. In this sense there is no reason to exclude the relation from the nature of objects—or to include it, either.

When it came to examining the reality of relations, classical thinkers found themselves having to accept one of three positions. The first option is to define the relation as being *in re,* i.e. absorbable by its terms; it is then internal, and can be expressed by a generative property—in which case it is, as Leibniz put it, a well-founded phenomenon. This foundation is given by the fact that the category of the relation depends on another category, such as quality, that is less extrinsic to reality.

Alternatively, it can be seen not as a "real" relation in this sense, but as simply a rational relation founded in our faculty of abstraction. This is the case with the identity relation, which operates *quoad nos*, or with respect to us. I am the one who knows that *a* is identical to *b*. Third, there are epistemological relations whose terms correspond to each other on the model of the knowing subject and the object known. In these terms relations are neither real nor rational, but rather a mixture of the two, because they are real in relation to their first term, knowledge, but rational in relation to their second, the thing known. This type of conception was called for by the realist view of knowledge as an image or a representation of being. For if an idea appears to us as the picture of a thing, the nature of the thing will not be much affected by the representation of it.

In the case of real relations, what are we to think of their dependence on another category? Logically, this involves the reduction of the relation to predication: if *a* loves *b*, the amorous relation will consist in certain states of mind of *a*, rather than being something genuinely relational. Let us leave mixed relations aside, as they pose a problem: being unilateral, they have no real converse.[7] This leaves the relation as something that we have, and as a result our understanding of it tends to be based on the notion of a "relational property." This is in line with Leibnizian monadism: any proposition aRb in which R is a relation can be reduced to two propositions, ar_1 and br_2, which give predicates to *a* and *b* respectively that are then supposed to be equivalent to R. The result is to attribute properties to *a* and *b* by which they are intrinsically distinguished from each other.

The doctrine of internal relations is particularly inapplicable to asymmetrical relations such as "*a* is prior to *b*" or "*a* is to the left of *b*," i.e. those that occur from *a* to *b* but not from *b* to *a*.[8] If we were to try to explain *a*'s relational priority over *b* in terms of predicates of *a* or *b*, we might say for instance that the date of *a* is a property of *a* as the date of *b* is a property of *b*. But that would be no help because we would still have to say that the date of *a* is earlier than the date of *b*; this is therefore not a way of avoiding relations. The order in which the individuals *a* and *b* occur in the statement "*a* is prior to *b*" cannot be subsumed into their nature as individuals. As Russell stated,

> "There are facts such that *x* has the relation R to *y*, and such facts are not generally reducible to or inferable from a fact concerning *x* alone or *y* alone."[9]

Being Related, Being in a Relation

The only reducible type of dyadic relations are those that have the properties of symmetry and transitivity. In such cases, a relational proposition can be reformulated as one affirming the fact that a predicate is held in common.[10] In other words, a statement constructed by a reference to a relation of equivalence may be reduced to one constructed by the attribution of a property. For example, it is legitimate to translate "x is parallel to y" by the conjunction of two statements, "x is D-directed" and "y is D-directed," where the monadic predicate "D-directed" is the directional property of a straight line, which is the defining property of the equivalence class to which x and y belong.

But in general this is not possible, and it is better to regard relations as external to their terms. As Russell put it, "These relational facts do not imply that x and y have any complexity or intrinsic property which distinguishes them from an x or y which did not have the relation R. That is what I mean by saying that relations are external."[11]

As long as relations were seen as dependent on their terms, for one term to be related to another meant that there was a link between them. Following Russell, however, we see that relations are not about being related, or linked, in this way, but about being in a relation. According to the principle of external relations, a relation is established between two terms. It is like a third between them, a mediating, included third. It relates like a third party between the other two; in short, like one extra. A relation thus becomes as real as its terms. Its role is to put individuals into order, and give meaning to that order, when the individuals themselves are strangers to it. Relations introduce into the universe something that cannot be reduced to the individuals x and y, or absorbed by them: that something is a universal.

For Russell, the irreducibility of relations proved that they included an ontological commitment. Something that exists in the abstract imposes on things an order that they do not have in themselves. The autonomy of relational propositions still remained to be guaranteed, however. They gained their philosophical independence with the *Principles of Mathematics*, which showed not only that relations are logically irreducible to properties, but also that they play no part in defining the terms they relate. We should remember here that Russell's theory of types does not allow analysis to separate the related relation from the relating relation, i.e. to separate the relation from its arguments.[12] The unity of propositions is intelligible because each relation is conceivable independently of the relationships it seems to imply by its links with the terms it brings together.

Objectors to this view may point out that there have been a number of attempts to construct an extensional analysis of relations in terms of sets.[13] Thus Quine himself, in his "New Foundations,"[14] introduces relations as classes of pairs; though he is still left having to define what he means by a pair. Any acceptable definition must allow the pairs (x, y) and (z, w) respectively to be identified in all cases except when x = y or y = w. The first definition fulfilling this requirement was put forward by Kazimierz Kuratowski: [15]

$$(x, y) =_{df} \{\{X\}, \{x, y\}\}$$

In so far as the *definiens* and the *definiendum* have the same mathematical properties in set theory without relations and in the theory derived from the axioms of ordered-pairs calculus, this definition provides a way of dispensing with pairs in favor of the clearer notion of sets. The familiar notion of order seems to have been swept under the carpet here, though in fact this is not the case. What this explanation actually eliminates is the notion of an ordered pair, because practically everything that can be done when speaking of the ordered pair (x, y) can also be done while referring to the set $\{\{x\}, \{x, y\}\}$.

Should we conclude from this that relations of order taken extensionally have been reduced to sets? I should also point out that Kuratowski's definition treats the pair as a class made up of two other classes, one of which is composed solely of x and the other solely of x and y. According to that definition, $\{x\}$ and $\{x, y\}$ must therefore be regarded as the names of entities underlying the operation "take the set of." In a sense, then, this is a reductio ad absurdum of Quine's position on relations, because order can only be reduced to absence of order by quantifying on classes, i.e. by committing ourselves to the relation in the very sense implied by his criterion. In a different sense, Russell's commitment to relations can be seen to be perfectly compatible with the criterion.

The same type of proof or presumption can be produced in support of an ontological commitment to the reality of relations as it was for an ontological commitment to sets. The same metalogical reasons can also be invoked. A commitment to sets corresponds quite closely to Gödel's theorem on the property of completeness in calculus,[16] while a commitment to recognizing the reality of relations fits in rather with Church's theorem on the presence or absence of algorithmic decisions in calculus.[17]

Quine based his ontological division on the level of quantification and justified it by claiming that a theory that only allows for individuals as quantification variables does not have the same metalogical properties as a theory that also allows for classes: the former is complete, while the second is not. However, this ontological division can be seen to be inadequate, something Russell's recognition of asymmetrical relations had the merit of anticipating: a theory that only allows monadic predicates involves a decision-making procedure, whereas one in which polyadic predicates are allowed does not.

Russell's hypothesis fits in quite well with the idea that the dividing line between elementary logic (a logic of monadic propositions and predicates, roughly as used by the ancients), and general logic, runs between monadic predicates and relations. However, Quine's logic also corresponds closely to the cleft between a general logic of first-order predicates and a higher-order logic.

On the Interlocutive Relation

Such was Russell's approach to relations. His decision to grant them an irreducible reality was made from an unassailable logical position. After careful consideration, however, it seems to me that his approach can actually be made more radical.

Indeed, a relation no longer has to be conceived of only as an emergent reality, one derived to a certain extent from the terms from which it emerges; it can also be seen as primary. In that case, the relation calls its terms into existence, constituting them and establishing them on either side of itself. *Res hactenus ignota* (something hitherto unknown). We could then say of relations in general what we have always known about amorous relations, that they are their own cause; or about the interlocutive relation, that it in some way precedes the interlocutors. This is a difficult notion.

Supports and Terms of a Relation

Let us dwell on the case of interlocution, which will serve as a paradigm. Asserting that interlocution is primary obviously does not mean in terms of set theory that the relation, taken extensionally, is prior to its terms. On the other hand, it does imply first that the concept of interlocution is a primitive one, whereas those of locutor (*locuteur*) and allocutee (*allocutaire*) are derivative. Second, these two concepts cannot be assimilated to particular empirical beings: locutor and allocutee are agencies brought about by and in discourse, and not concrete individuals—even if in the real world they can secondarily be attributed to individuals.[18]

In particular, the locutor must not be confused with the speaking subject, from which it is explicitly distinguished, for instance in indirect discourse. Equally, the allocutee must not be confused with the listener, a particular real individual who overhears the discourse or eavesdrops on it when it was not intended for his or her ears. Furthermore, just because an utterance is addressed to someone, this does not automatically make that person the allocutee. The direct addressee, or "intended recipient" (Lyons) is not yet a partner in an interlocutive relation. If I do not understand the words you are saying to me—poor me—I am only their recipient and not your allocutee! Utterance must involve the transmission of a message that is implicated in a process of mutual understanding. If we do not understand each other, what have we to say to one another? As we can see, the terms of the interlocution—the agencies, or positions, of utterance—are determined in the first place by speech, for their determination forms part of the meaning of the proffered messages. It therefore follows, rather than precedes, the establishment of the dialogue.

Once the principle of the *primum relationis*—or primacy of the relation— is defined in this way, we must resist the immediate temptation to ask: relation between what and what? The category of the relation as so conceived establishes the rule that the relation spans its terms. But the terms themselves are not there. It is the interlocutive relation that constitutes them; not that it is entirely unsupported by anything else. Personal relations are established in the present between living individuals; it is therefore also they who form the medium for the interlocutive relation.

The important thing is to distinguish between the media which support the relation on the one hand—its elementary and unspoken condition, a sort of ontic vital minimum—and its terms on the other. This elementary condition should not be underestimated: it is obvious, for example, that before someone can love, he or she must *be*, i.e., be alive. The supporting medium is an anchoring or mooring point for the relation in an otherwise impersonal world. Being and living in this sense is hardly a very demanding condition: being comes before love as the individual comes before speech. But if we separate the medium from the terms of the relation, we realize that the opposite is also true, that as love grants being, loving comes before being, just as it is necessary to be in an interlocutive relation before one can be a speaking subject. Such is the significance of individual being, the ultimate component of all sameness, the condition that conditions all others and yet on its own remains no more than a negative authorization.

Of course we cannot afford to neglect it. If individuals are so strongly attached to their own lives, in the biological and social senses of the term, this is probably why. For one thing, our body is a constant source of surprises to us. One moment we despair of ever getting back on our feet, then we are up; we are full of confidence, then all at once our life falls to pieces; then we start to hope again, and so on. Through these various vicissitudes the individual supporting medium of our personal life imposes itself on our concerns.

We sometimes confuse the supporting media with the terms of the interpersonal relation because they can be structured in similar ways. On the one hand there are interindividual relations in which a person as a social being enters into social relations with others, and on the other interpersonal relations marked by their special quality of reciprocity. Each type also finds expression in particular forms of behavior: social relations structure the social activities of individuals, a sphere in which being is a sociohistorical notion; more radically, personal relations structure the symbolic and signifying activities of persons.

This is not the place to ask how these two types of relations overlap, where they intersect, or whether they are causally linked. I shall not even attempt to establish whether they are structured in different ways. Let me instead illustrate the problem by means of an elementary and fairly commonplace comparison. Take a jigsaw puzzle. It is an assemblage of cutout fragments. Nothing in the puzzle is other than fragmentary, just as nothing in the person is supported directly by the medium of an individual. Each fragment of the puzzle is related in space to all the others by the way they are cut out; similarly, each piece of individual behavior is related to all the others in ways that can be studied by social psychology. However, we can also adopt a different point of view: instead of looking at how fragments of the puzzle fit into the part already assembled, we could examine the relationship between the image-fragments and the overall picture as it is beginning to emerge, thus introducing a very different type of structuring—that of the image itself. Just as it would be absurd to explain the structure of the image on the basis of the way in which its material fragments were cut up, so it is pointless to try to explain specific relations between persons on the basis of relations between individuals. In fact, it is the image that is primary, and its figuration is what guides our assembly of the material fragments, even though it bears no logical relationship to the way the puzzle is cut out. Interpersonal relations are primary in the same way; they guide our understanding of interactions, transactions, and joint actions, which are the only pertinent elements of primary personal activity.

Applied to persons, the primacy of relations implies that the personal subject can in no way be regarded as a sufficient and solitary subjectivity that constitutes its own reality, but must rather be seen as the seat of a certain number of powers, abilities, and relational checks that allow it to come together with others in a creative interspace and maintain itself in relations with them, or on the contrary to grasp its own identity in a reflexive way. We need to define how it manages to do this and why we are able, to a certain extent at least, to walk with our own legs, work with our own hands, and think with our own heads.

As we saw earlier, in love we always feel as if we are constantly escaping from ourselves, overflowing our own limits in a process of tireless inventiveness and concern for the other person—without there being anything at all worrisome about such a spontaneity of existence that we have not created. The amorous relation does not emanate from the *I* but moves toward it, meets up with and grabs hold of this *I*, and establishes it in a brand new personal existence. Whether or not it is felt as a particular experience, of which we have an image, does not matter. An image manifestly presupposes the relational event. As for experience, far from revealing the relation, it is rather the process of living through the relation that constitutes the experience. The same is true of hatred, which is another possible relation between myself and others. Even if I experience and represent it as a moment of repulsion, hatred is too profound a relational upheaval for it to be confused with an instantaneous experience of that sort.

An Original Ontological Principle

It goes without saying that I am here positing a principle unknown in the self-sufficient systems of the Absolute, Substance, or Totality. The primum relationis is demanding. It brings to an end the whole metaphysics of representation. It goes against all our habits of thought, which tell us to conceive first one term, then another, before we can examine their relation. In this light, the relation takes on the ontological guise of a dynamic manifestation of absence. It confirms the fact that the Same is powerless to be without an Other. This principle demands that we think about everything, and particularly about beings, from within the relation. Is it not in the nature of thought that it is able to proceed in harmony with the voice of being? But this harmony assumes that thought will rediscover the true ontological difference between the fact of being and beings themselves.

However, I shall use the term *beings* to mean concrete individualities, whether or not they have the potential to achieve personal status;[19] whereas by the *fact* of being I mean the primordial relation of each being with all other beings and with itself. But how are we to define such a fundamental idea as this? The best we can do is agree on a description, but without forgetting that beneath the description lies an inalienable well of experience that analysis must seek to explain. To say that the relation constitutes the mode of being of individual beings is to refuse the subordination of being itself to beings, because being is what makes possible their community. The relation is not just something ideal; it has its own type of existence. And, as Octave Hamelin realized, we unhesitatingly grasp the relation of communicability that is in us and around us, even if its oceanic character gives us the feeling of being enclosed in a bubble and cast adrift on our own.

The difficulty is that being as a relation conceals not only itself, but also the very fact of its concealment. The important thing to appreciate here is that the interpersonal relation as such extends well beyond the boundaries of the self. In fact, it is always ontologically and logically prior to the constitution of a personal self. We can prove this by simply wanting to enter into a relationship; wanting has no power over the spontaneity of the relation. We all know that despite our best efforts, there are some relationships that just cannot be improved. A true relationship is no longer a subjective event, and self-love always has something strange, slightly shameful about it, for it is a pseudorelation which closes the self in on itself. But nor can the relation be interpreted as something to be apprehended objectively; it cannot be reified. It can only be grasped in its transcendental and metaphysical nature by logical and philosophical reflection.

It is transcendental because all relations to objects depend first on relations between one human being and another in the community of knowledge. Relations between persons underlie all objective knowledge. And the problem of being links up with the problem of the possibility of meaning and its interlocutive foundation.

Being is metaphysical in so far as being is that which constitutes the presence of present reality, and not the views, images, and representations we have of it. Giving fresh impetus to the problem of the relation also provides us with a new approach to the problem of being.

We must not take the Heideggerian distinction between being and beings too far, although it has been convenient to use it up to now. How is it that the world can be articulated in an infinite variety of schemata and figures? If the world is open to people, it is opened out not by some manifestation or given revelation, as Heidegger suggests, but rather by the joint production of meaning, and therefore of reference.[20] If a person is capable of discourse, it is not because he or she allows the language of the origins to resonate in his or her own voice, by making him or herself the locus of its manifestation, but because he or she is able to enter into a primordial interlocutive relation. And if meaning springs up from within it, it is because that relation is constitutive of being itself. I believe that our understanding of language is essentially linked to our transcendental understanding of being. But why? Because of course langauge does not function in a vacuum. Relative to the beings to which it refers, language constitutes itself as discourse anthropologically. But not on the basis of the individual speaking being: it is based rather on being itself, which—as a relation—brings beings together by the way that it constitutes them. In which case, language can indeed order meaning and knowledge.

The relation is an ontological event which in addition is able to grant being to its terms. The interpersonal relation maintains the integrity of the *I* and the *you*, instead of relegating them either to subjective singularity or to objective anonymity. If the relation occurs neither in the order of the subject nor in that of the object, it is because in it the act of being is in the process of realization. If the relation is the fundamental mode of being, the person is the locus where the act of being is enacted. So that each person only becomes a personal totality in virtue of the canonically controlled set of his or her relations with others.

According to the primum relationis theory, the terms cannot exist independently of the relation. We have seen that this was the case with the interlocutive relation. We discovered the priority of the relation within the theological paradigm of the Trinity. The "personal" properties that constitute the three Persons are a way of expressing their relations. For the true God is He in whom the relation produces Being. The Word made flesh with a terrestrial body and born of a woman. This union of Word and body is indestructible.

This way of thinking about relations, which sets up an absence or lack as the central principle of reality, can indeed prove its dynamism. It fits with my conception of interpersonal relations. Instead of appearing as a weakness, the lack of a relational order acts as an appeal, and a form of promise. There is no difference that a relation cannot bring about, no acquired differentiation that it is unable to enrich or call into question. It works to create the singularity of beings. Conversely, so long as philosophy sought its beginning in Being, and the category of substance, the only known type of lack was a lack of determinants; a richness of determinants was expected, and was simply postponed. This singularity of beings, their dissimilarity and difference, seemed to be nothing more than a provisional illusion, soon to be swallowed up.

An Aporetics of Personal Alterity: Existential Phenomenology

We would do well to accept all the consequences of this last option, which makes the problem of being and the relational essence of the human condition one and the same thing. But if we wish to explain our understanding of being and say what it means (rather than simply using it to live, work, do science, or talk to other people), phenomenology is probably not an appropriate way of bringing out the being-as-relation of the human being. Why not?

Giving priority to relations is a way for philosophers to avoid having to resort to any sort of explanatory or founding agency within consciousness or the subjective self. Martin Buber, who so often stressed the immediacy of our relations with others, said that he welcomed any philosophy of existence that left open a door into alterity. With one proviso: that he did not know anyone who had opened the door wide enough. As we shall see, that proviso perhaps applies also to his own philosophy, as well as to all earlier systems.

Hegel's attitude is a good example. His discovery was that it made no sense to speak of the self outside the relation with the Other. But in *The Phenomenology of Mind* he presents this relation as the result of two linked processes: "Self-consciousness has lost itself, for it has discovered itself to be another essence." [21]

If I find another self I am lost, since I have found myself to be, as it were, other. Yet as this works both ways, it means that consciousness "has thereby suppressed the Other, for it no longer sees the Other as an essence, but sees itself in the Other." [22] Hegel admits that the relation is still too unilateral if it is conceived of in this way: "This is a way of representing the movement of one self-consciousness in its relation with another self-consciousness as an operation of one self-consciousness only." [23]

Now what is needed, continues Hegel, is for the operation itself to be bilateral, for it to be the double and mutual operation of each consciousness. If I am to recognize the other person as a self (moi), it is vital that I see him or her doing the same in relation to me that I do to him or her. The two consciousnesses not only see themselves in each other, but they also see themselves as seeing themselves in each other, and at the same time they fail to grasp each other in a reciprocal, specular structure, thus: "They recognize themselves/each other as recognizing themselves/each other." [24]

What is clear here is that the relation has been reduced to the interweaving of two consciousnesses. This is a nonviable solution whose consequences— a struggle to the death between two opposing consciousnesses of self, leading to the master/slave dialectic—are well known. Its inevitable outcome is a turning-inward of the self and the virtual disappearance of any alterity; this makes for an unhappy consciousness, which absorbs the dominance/servitude relationship into its own being. Alterity becomes the superego. Consciousness judges itself to have sinned and finds itself guilty. Not that this play of mirrors ends up as an entirely blind alley; according to Hegel, it is on the contrary what opens up the very possibility of history. All these concrete figures are possible only within the perspective of self-consciousness. They are insane figures, repeated tragedies, from desire to presumptuous delusion. [25] In each case, one person is always content to be him or herself in the other person, and to exist through this very alterity.

If philosophers abandon any attempt to locate the founding agency within the self, they will also have lost the possibility of appealing to innate or a priori characteristics. Saying that the other is innate in the self, as for example Martin Buber does, would then simply emphasize the fact that the reciprocity relation can be dismembered, giving on one side an *I* with its innate *you*, and on the other the *you* itself. Which would bring us back to the duality of Same and Other. If it is true that each new meeting is for us an occurrence of the essential relation, then it is just not enough to say that in this relation each partner affirms and confirms the other. What we need to explain is how the relation itself has the power to confirm each person in his or her positive difference, through the fact that they are in a relation. And that is something quite different.

In addition, if the relation really is fundamental, as both a primary reality and a transcendental agency necessary for the constitution of meaning, then it would be inconsistent (and a technical mistake) to make the self into the subject of a relation of which, in fact, it is simply one pole—on exactly the same level as the other, with neither privilege nor dissymmetry between them. Martin Buber makes this mistake in his own work. To explain the notion of mutuality he has recourse sometimes to an originary communal instinct, a natural ability to confirm the other,[26] and sometimes to epistemological terms such as "innate" and "a priori," which mean very different things but are used as synonyms. Nathan Rotenstreich rightly reproaches him for this, saying that he oscillates between the primacy of the relation and that of the self.[27]

Of course there is no question of denying that the self can act, chronologically speaking, as a way into the relation. In fact, as we shall see, it is its responsibility precisely to provide a way in. But this self cannot be seen as the relation's absolute point of departure. Any more than the other can be regarded as the absolute expression of a radical heterogeneity with which it would be the self's improbable and laborious task to establish a relation. The person who is radically other does not concern me; he carries the threat of death. Equally, in the work of Levinas only the infinite, which is infinitely other, saves the world from being totally given over to violence.

A better way of demonstrating the absurdity of the concept of absolute alterity is to show that the quest for the other leads to a reinforcement of the primacy of the self. For if the other person is seen as infinitely different, infinitely separate, then he or she may no longer be *myself*, but is definitely still *a* self. Admittedly, Levinas rejects theoretical approaches that claim to grasp and to know the other, for by operating within the notion of the sameness of the Same, they end up assimilating the other to the self. Like Kant, he decides to replace knowledge by respect. But instead of founding this respect on a universal morality of which the self is the agent, he bases it directly on the solitude and individual transcendence of the other. The problem is that this approach overdramatizes relations with other persons, even on an ethical level.

I shall come back later to that most sublime and unlikely form of hyperbolic behavior—living for the other, who and whatever that other may be (everyone has rights except me; I only have duties). The descriptions so far put forward are surprisingly disjointed; it is as if the *ipse* could somehow be jolted out of itself in some gracious move toward the other, still seen however as heterogeneous; as if it could flow out of its envelope, leaving its own place empty and moving to occupy a different one, absorbing the difference between them and even substituting itself directly for the other person. In short, as if, by some act of voluntary reunuciation, it could live sometimes in itself and sometimes in the other.

The number of such descriptions is itself intriguing.[28] From a methodological point of view they all remain centered on the subject, quickly confirming the existence of the subject's inner being. In one and the same move they call into question the self-sufficiency of the ego and grant it strange powers, such as the ability to modify a relation unilaterally (although such a modification can in no way be seen as an interaction: it is real acts of communication that have the effect, among other things, of modifying the relationship between the communicating parties).

In my view it is not enough to conclude that existence for oneself also implies existence for others. I believe that we need to break once and for all with the philosophical narcissism of the ego, even where it is compensated for (and overcompensated for) by "good" impulses. Subjectivity is living neither for oneself nor for others; it is the originary ability to be in and sustain relationships. It is a most demanding skill.

This requires a complete change of philosophical viewpoint, in which things are no longer looked at from the angle of pure subjectivity, but in the context of a type of communication that from the first is intersubjective. If communication is indeed the original and authentic medium of our understanding, we must also grant it the initiative in the formation of meaning. This requires a genuine sharing of the semantic initiative that should not be underestimated: the need to renounce the self's privileged semantic initiative as the notorious "giver of meaning" is doubtless the most difficult thing with which philosophy must come to terms. Almost as difficult, as we shall now see, as accepting that the Earth revolves around the sun.

Overcoming the Aporia of Solipsism

Whatever forms it may take, and whatever may be its advantages, the approach to alterity taken by existential phenomenology is based on phenomenological premises that seem to me inadequate in principle to delimit the constitutive domain of intersubjectivity, once we set out to define it without privileging the ego at the expense of the *alter.*

As is well known, if subjectivity is defined in a post-Husserlian way as the intentionality of consciousness, we arrive at a relation between Same and Other such that the latter is determined by the former, and not the other way around. If, as is claimed, consciousness is a constituting force, it must be able to relate the alterity not only of objects, but also of people, back to the self; and this despite all Husserl's efforts to draw a distinction between the alterity of people and things (by saying, for instance, that people are not other in the same original way as things). Indeed, it is all very well for our consciousnesses to construct an in-between world in which they can communicate with each other; the question of whom that world is for still remains to be answered.[29] Even coexistence must be experienced by each participant. Such is the underlying stratum of existence for *oneself* that constitutes the Cogito: any affirmation or negation of existence, any project or construction, can ultimately be tested only in the domain of the ego. This aspect of existence for oneself, which crops up insistently as soon as the question of communication arises, seems to stand in the way of any reasonable solution to the problem of other people. Such solipsism seems impossible to circumvent.

Let us take a closer look, however. In what sense is solipsism impossible to circumvent? If we reread the closing pages of Husserl's *Krisis,* we can legitimately be severely critical of his position there, for he reduces all beings, even other people, to the constitutive noemes of intention that make up experience, noemes which phenomenological thinking must understand apodictically. Admittedly, the concept of a "consciousness of the world" does presuppose the existence of others: at the heart of the Cogito, Husserl discovers in the *cogitatum* something like a *sumus cogitantes.* The Other represents an important stage on the road leading to the ultimate *epoche* of transcendental consciousness, with the result that the act of reduction, in the case of other people, is forced to operate in a specific way. But, as Levinas has pointed out, if the egological consciousness is linked to the other consciousness in the intermonadic community, this is only a first stage, before it sets itself up in a grand and noble gesture as an absolute subject. If the ego's consciousness is linked to that of others, it can only be in terms of a "sympathy," or to put it another way, in terms once again of a certain structure of experience.

In the end it is not indispensable for the transcendental subject to have relations with others, for such relations have yet to be constituted. Other people, who first appeared as nonreduced nodes in the egological field in the fifth *Cartesian Meditation,* fall into the domain of the epoche, where in my view they are nothing more than intentional phenomena. Even the relations that the ego entertains with others come down to a monologue between one self and another, like the silent speech of the soul with itself to which Plato refers.

A Critique of the Husserlian Program

This method has obvious limitations. Husserl was certainly attempting to defend phenomenology from the charge of solipsism, and in order to do so he closely defined his problem: the transcendental experience of the other. We know how careful he is, in the *Cartesian Meditations*, to respect what he takes to be the alterity of other people. He asks himself what intentionalities and temporalizing syntheses lead to the formation of the alter ego. Which means that for him there is no question of measuring other people's being by the knowledge they have of themselves, but rather by the knowledge that I have of them. Husserl is quite willing to describe others as others, but only in so far as their irreducible alterity remains in some way clear to me.

Yet he admits that this entire question remains a painful one.[30] If it is to be made soluble, the problem of other people must be transformed. The other in his or her very alterity must indeed appear to an ego as its phenomenon. There is no need to insist on the fact that the movement toward other people leaves intact the distinction between the new sense of being other people take on for my intentional life, and their being "as a person." The being of others is constantly slipping away; they are he/she's revealed to me as absences. The only reality that remains is the *I*'s intention toward others. As J. T. Desanti lucidly notes, the being of others remains in them; in me it can only be meaning.

Then why appear to want to mix them up? We soon realize that this is not Husserl's real aim, and that he never had any real intention of breaking out of the ego's sphere of interest. He is certainly concerned to release the phenomenology of persons from the limits of the constitution of things. But with the fundamental aim of turning phenomenology into primary philosophy. The other person is therefore constituted with a meaning that refers back to myself. Far from being an attempt to gain access to the existence of others or to their specific temporality, the fifth *Cartesian Meditation* is rather a last-ditch effort to complete the structure of the ego's transcendental domain.

Before asking what happened to that attempt, I would like to conclude my remarks on the question of solipsism. Solipsism is not content simply with being given implicit recognition as the origin of experience. According to some linguists, this originary status is recognized by ordinary language, though they immediately add that it is an occasional privilege, because in discourse each speaker in turn takes him or herself as the center of reference.

Solipsism would like to be seen not merely as constituting one permanent center, preferable to many others, but as the *only* logically and transcendentally possible center, so that it would actually be meaningless to speak of any other. The conclusion that Husserl is a solipsist seems unavoidable.

Of course there is a (weak) sense in which he goes beyond empirical solipsism, for there is indeed nothing to stop philosophers from investigating within the transcendental sphere the specific mode of existence of the alter ego that manifests itself there, and establishing that at the very heart of this restricted phenomenological field there live the acts, syntheses, and modes of appearance of other people. But there is also a (strong) sense in which he remains solipsistic, as the transcendental sphere in question remains precisely my monadic field. It is not enough to counter this by saying that my concrete self is in no way privileged (as other people's selves appear in the world in the same way that mine does), or that the existence of others is just as certain as that of the world: solipsists have always admitted as much.

Husserl was resigned to this from 1913. Did he not give paragraph 49 of his *Ideen* the title "Absolute consciousness as the residue of the annihilation of the world"? It becomes clear, he wrote, "that the being of consciousness would indeed necessarily be modified if the world were to be annihilated, but that its existence would not be affected."

Few philosophical currents have described with as much conviction as has phenomenology the relational structure that links consciousness to the world and to the self, and few have worked so obstinately at its reduction. But phenomenology was never able to overcome the solipsistic illusion that all transcendence must necessarily be transcendence through the ego.

Could it ever have been otherwise? If we think about it, the only problem that Husserlian doctrine and method made it legitimate to investigate was the meaning of other people for me, and its only possible solution was to produce new versions of *Einfühlung* (empathy). How, indeed, could the other person ever come across to me as another constituting subjectivity, when any access to other subjectivities is closed in principle to the ego? It is unthinkable that I might explore operations specific to someone else on any plane other than my own. The modes of being of the alter ego must therefore be constituted in my transcendental field, which acts as their original source. And since Husserl is obliged to relate each noeme in the field without exception to a corresponding noesis, he finds himself in an even more unfavorable position than that of High Rationalism: unlike Leibniz, he does not have available to him any preestablished and infinitely repeatable homology which would allow the isolated universe of each monad to unfold; nor can he resort, as Descartes did, to divine truth. In a major obstacle to the phenomenological program, the meditating ego therefore proves to be incapable of constituting the original domain in which the movement of any transcendence must occur, because the being, if not the meaning, of other people escapes it completely.

Which Type of Transcendental Intersubjectivity?

But, the reader might insist, as a transcendental theory, Husserlian subjectivity is precisely intersubjective. Let us therefore try to see what type of intersubjectivity this is, and how ambiguously it is introduced.

On one point, this idea is an undeniable advance beyond standard approaches to the metaphysics of subjectivity. The object is no longer constituted solely by reference to the subject. Husserl attempts to show that our recourse to others conditions the way we constitute the world, which, as it is revealed to our consciousness, is therefore intermonadic. The other person appears in the world not only as an empirical reality, but also as a necessary condition of its unity, coherence, and objectivity. The constitution of everything down to the psychophysical self (because it too is part of the world) is conditioned by others. In which case, the general significance of other people cannot be derived by abstraction, or from some reasoning by analogy: others are simply a supplementary category that allows us to constitute a world.

This is the point: the other is not a real being who exists independently of the constituted world. We each really exist in our own interiority, which is accessible only to the meditating ego. Any knowledge of others as they know themselves is closed off. In fact, then, Husserl retains the transcendental subject. On the one hand, the mediation of the intermonadic community takes place within the egological sphere; intersubjectivity is constituted on the basis of an experience of the transcendental ego in the primordial sphere where it belongs. But on the other hand, the intermonadic community must in turn be constituted by the ego in the transcendental opening created by phenomenological reduction. Once the ego discovers that for cultural objects to take on meaning they must also be present to an alter ego, then a cultural horizon opens up which Husserl presents as a specific moment in the transcendental field.

But there is a difficulty of principle here which prevents the program of reduction from being carried to completion. It is instructive for our purposes. This specific moment is actually a present which mediates the passage toward other moments, all of which lose their unconditioned quality, contrary to the demands of phenomenological reduction. What unconditioned reality remains? In the end, the only one we are able to find is the structure of references between moments, which characterizes the transcendental field.

To reduce such a circular structure to one particular moment, as Husserl does,[31] would be to negate its foundational significance.

In such a situation, which we must first accept for what it is, the choice of where to go next is clear. We must leave the field of consciousness and locate somewhere else, for instance in interdiscursive praxis itself, the domain in which transcendental intersubjectivity is constituted. I am in agreement with J. T. Desanti that such a way out of the problem is closed precisely to a type of philosophy that applies phenomenological reduction. I would claim, however, that this does not apply to every transcendental enterprise. In particular, we can establish the conditions of possibility of the meaning and reference of statements in our language by tracing them back not to the speaking subject, but to the present relation between the interlocutors. I have already devoted two books to showing that this program was feasible, and making a start on its implementation.[32]

Let us therefore abandon once and for all the idea that we might find in an extended version of the Cogito some moment of consciousness that refers to others. Merleau-Ponty's early attempt to respect the reality of the other person as a close presence, while constituting that presence in one's transcendental field as the boundary of meaning, is not even a first step toward a solution. Technically, the conjunction of a descriptive and existential premise with an idealist and foundational one just does not work, and leads only to the ridiculous spectacle of a collection of consciousnesses all being solipsistic together.

Philosophical narcissism may hide behind different masks, but sooner or later it always shows its true face. When its practitioners decide to give a proper account of the notion of other people, its egological premises force them into intellectual contortions. Phenomenologists have been obliged to put a precarious slant on some of Husserl's ideas in order to bring into their thinking an unavoidable concern with alterity. It is on this subject that the disagreement between them was most marked. Let us examine the opposing positions of Sartre and Levinas.

They put forward two main arguments. For Sartre I meet the other person; I do not constitute him or her: "Formerly I believed that I could escape solipsism by refuting Husserl's concept of the existence of the Transcendental 'Ego.' At that time I thought that since I had emptied my consciousness of its subject, nothing remained there which was privileged as compared to the Other. But actually, although I am still persuaded that the hypothesis of a transcendental subject is useless and disastrous, abandoning it does not help one bit to solve the question of the existence of Others."[33] Apprehending the meaning of others in our own sphere of belonging allows their absolute alterity to be neutralized. Sartre then devotes more than a hundred pages to existence for others, following directly from Heidegger: "I discover the transcendent relation to others as constitutive of my own being. I need the other person in order to grasp fully the structures of my being." [34] But it soon becomes clear that this appearance of radicalism is deceptive. The idea that human relations result in "the immediate and continuous determination of each person by others" is safe enough, for it does not disrupt the egological principle. If the reality of others affects me in the very depths of my existence, it does so by its negative difference, in that it is not my reality. When one individual speaks to another, the words used "transport into me the other person's projects, and mine into them." But these projects, which are transcendent, nevertheless "remain separate." [35] The Sartrian image of the wall expresses the essential solitude of existence for oneself. Levinas' attempt, on the other hand, is both more radical and more interesting. For him, it is my neighbor whose singularity imposes itself on my attention, making itself of direct concern to me. The other person summons me (*m'assigne*) before I can designate him. [36] Even before I recognize who it is, he is sending me orders. I am under obligation to him, and he obliges me.

But let me repeat that in philosophy themes are less important than theories. The way to judge an author is on his or her theories and methods, their consequences, and the contradictions they generate.

Allegiance to Others and Original Difference

What happens to subjectivity in a body of thought whose significance is precisely to have introduced into philosophy the primacy of the Other? This is an excellent question. Levinas' work, apart from being the perfect antidote to egocentrism, is worthy of consideration in many other ways. He is one of those thinkers who puts all his speculative energy into testing the limits of inherited methods and accepted doctrines, in a highly instructive clash between intellectual courage and piety. As he says, "Our investigations are conducted in accordance with the spirit of Husserlian philosophy, the letter of which in our time has been the reflection of a universal phenomenology, elevated to the status of *the* method in all philosophy." [37]

For this gesture of loyalty is accompanied by a rigorous thematic opposition to Husserl—particularly, as most commentators have shown, on the question of alterity. On a first reading, I can see no reason to go against this interpretation. Levinas does indeed invite us to a fine celebration of the Other. And he is motivated by a higher loyalty, as well: "Respect for strangers and the sanctification of the Name of the Eternal form a strangely equal pair, and all the rest is a dead letter." [38]

Levinas' work takes the message of the Bible as its inspiration for introducing a rigorous allocentrism into philosophy. It presents itself from the start as a challenge to philosophical idealism, which has pushed the primacy of the transcendental ego to its furthest possible limits. Levinas is, then, obliged to define subjectivity as something other than the pure presence to itself of a sovereign consciousness.

From Digression to Compensation

On a second reading, however, the nature and extent of his gamble becomes clear. The outcome of his methodological challenge, and of his attempt to reconcile different aspects of his theory, is far from certain. How can a philosophy of the Cogito be maintained if the spontaneity of consciousness conceals an underlying heteronomy, if the Cogito itself become a contradictory configuration, an impossible spontaneity[39] in which consciousness, as a secondary moment, makes manifest the real world that constitutes it in the first place? And if phenomenological reduction no longer means, technically, reduction to noesis? For in the end, either Levinas' discovery (paralleling that of Freud) of the irreducibility of the other person is an unequalled subversion of the phenomenological approach, or the method established by Husserl, and firmly linked by him to egological premises,[40] will constantly lead him back to a paradoxical primacy of the self. How does Levinas set about preventing his dual allegiance from making him doubly inconsistent? From the start he seems to exclude the third party. But is there no way of avoiding this? If not, what are we to think of interpersonal relations as viewed by Levinas?

The author of *Totality and Infinity* sets himself against the author of the *Cartesian Meditations* to describe how the self is determined by the other. The most unusual idea of an allegiance to others inevitably introduces the theme of a self that is no longer the source of its own legitimacy. This is where his opposition starts to show itself. Husserl always saw subjectivity as the ultimate possession of the self, whereas for Levinas consciousness is already possessed by alterity. Not only the alterity of the world, but that of other people. Husserlian alterity was always relative to that of which my consciousness becomes aware. For Levinas, it is the other way around: our consciousness only acquires its identity, only appears to itself, through others. Thus ethics becomes primary philosophy.

There is no doubt at all that some of Levinas' arguements in favor of an uncompromising alterity are advanced with astonishing inventiveness and stylistic power.[41] Even if the other is that mysterious being with whom I am in a relation, yet who declares him or herself to be beyond all relations in the world. Here is a philosopher who is looking at interpersonal relations in much the same way that other thinkers look at the relations linking people and God. For example, speaking to God is generically different from speaking to oneself, but not from speaking to another human being. I only perceive speech, whether it be the other person's or God's, if I am in a position to reply. More precisely, Levinas transposes the relation between God and Israel, as he interprets it, into the sphere of interpersonal relations. Thus his questions about other people derive from his reflections on biblical exegesis. For Levinas there is no doubt that Husserl's enthusiasm for monologue would quickly be undermined by Israel's experience of faith, in which the divinity assigns me to my place and signals to me from the depths of His confidence and trust, while I am accountable to Him and owe Him a debt of fidelity.

Let me transpose this argument onto a different level. Within subjectivity, there is always a reference to other people in general. I am assigned to my place by others, including in my corporeal integrity, and painfully exposed to the alterity of the world. Then the other person reveals him or herself and becomes my law. The summons (assignation) of others demands a response from me. Levinas now opposes to Husserl his own fundamental precept, poles apart from idealist beliefs, which is that the self is not the source of the legitimacy of its own position. That position is made precarious by the alterity of the world, and even more so by the alterity of other people, which shatters the totalizing system that seeks to reduce everything to the Same.

"Such is the significance of proper nouns among all these common nouns and commonplaces. . . . Can we not then legitimately assume . . . that we would be unable to speak without them, and that otherness (i.e. other people) exists, and not just being?"[42]

The self must respond to, and take charge of, other people; so that now it is not only called into question, but invested with a responsibility. This is the point at which ethics comes in: subjectivity is irreducible because only it can take on this responsibility.

Let us leave aside the difficult question of whether for Levinas the irreducible and infinite alterity of persons other than myself is like the alterity of God, who is a positive infinity. It is paradoxical that another human being should be infinitely different in the essential finitude of his or her face, glance, and words. The important thing is that it is only possible to grasp the alterity of others through the negation of things in the external world. Levinas' arguments are well known. His break with Husserlian concepts occurs at the moment of confrontation when the separation and the immediacy of beings are experienced together. At that point the other's face conveys an expression, and becomes something not only that is seen, but also that sees, offering itself both as glance and as speech, in a unity between eyes and mouth. What, briefly, is the reason for this privileging of the face?

According to Levinas, the face is "the way in which other people appear to us, transcending the idea of the other that I have in me." It signifies without being signified, appears before any sign, as the carrier of a meaning that is prior to any meaning. Through his or her face, the other appears as a person. In the nudity of that face, the other person reveals him or herself as Other— in the fullness of an alterity which is refractory to any simple "thematization." It is something over which my categories and concepts can have no hold.

And yet there is always something excessive in the questioning, something exaggerated in the replies, that indicate to us that Levinas feels himself to be in an awkward position. He affirms the autonomy of the other, while at the same time subscribing to a highly solipsistic epistemology whose effect is to reduce the other's person by objectivizing it. Levinas, or phenomenology discomfited.

"Solipsism is neither an aberration nor a sophism; it is the very structure of reason." If this is so, claims Levinas, then any system (in the old etymological sense of the word) or any "totality" that makes a given being intelligible, traces out a schema of that being in the thoughts of someone else. A being thus known loses its alterity in relation to the self, which assimilates it. Conceptualizing the other means bringing it back to the Same, "doing away with or possessing the other." [43] The clear soliloquy of reason does violence to others by depriving them of a separate existence from mine. A being whom I subordinate to common concepts is one to whom I do violence: "Me, You, are not individuals of a common concept." [44]

The Face, and the Inconsistencies of the Via Negativa

Since Levinas has no intention of making a direct challenge to the epistemological egocentrism derived from Descartes, as a number of other commentators have already noted, [45] he is forced to undermine it from within. If he had remained less faithful to its precepts, he would not have found himself constructing an ad hoc metaphysics to neutralize its effects. We would not have seen him trying to escape by the via negativa, according to a line of reasoning which seems resigned to defying common sense logic. The reader is perhaps familiar with the following formulae by Levinas:

> "The face is infinitely distant, though infinitely present;"
>
> "The face expresses itself in the sensory domain, but also tears through it;"
>
> "In the epiphany of his face, the other person is present to me without my 'receiving' him."

In other formulae proximity and distance, presence and absence, are given simultaneously, without any sign that this sort of opposition between them can be resolved. Of course we might regard such a body of logical paradoxes as challenging conceptual difficulties. But we still need to understand: (1) the nature of the paradox. It is not enough to show by irreproachable reasoning that paradoxes lead to an absurd position; and (2) how to deal with it. A paradox remains unresolved so long as we have not understood why our reasoning is defective (and as long as the author who professes it remains consistent in his or her arguments).

If our logic seems unable to grasp other people, explains Levinas, it must be due to a weakness in our categories, as the call addressed by the other cannot be thought or spoken about without being in some way denatured. At that point others necessarily appear to us as absence; they do still appear, but as nonphenomena. If therefore the face, in which the other person is absolutely present, shows him or her to me as a person, it does so without revealing him or her. It offers and does not offer itself to my understanding; it manifests itself and withdraws from its manifestation. How should we respond to this surface, the most fascinating on Earth? For the face is a spatially localized body, and yet I can only designate the irreducible alterity of the other who shows him or herself to me through it by negating all spatial exteriority.

I quite understand that, by locating the face beyond the realm of essences and freeing it of any positive determinants, Levinas is not claiming to bring about a coincidence of opposites, but only trying to explain the ineffable through paradoxes. Negative theologies, with their litanies of the ineffable, have accustomed us to such paradoxes, for the discourse of the via negativa undoes all constructed discourses. Although they defy everyday logic, they are not necessarily incoherent for the contemporary logician who, by distinguishing between different levels of language, will avoid confusing negations concerning the face with negative predicates belonging to the object-language. Levinas' negations bear witness to the powerlessness of all object-languages in the face of a reality that transcends all determinants.

It is easy to see why Levinas should have been tempted by a stylistic approach of this sort, an approach that is supported by theology (not, admittedly, in its role as a science of origins, but as a discrete exegesis of the transcendental word). After all, once theologians decide not to compromise their position by contact with our all-too-human forms of logic, apophatism becomes the best corrective against dogmatism, a sort of genie in the bottle. Levinas, however, is speaking as a philosopher. Furthermore, as a philosopher of language he does not believe either that speech is a debased, fallen medium, or that it is essentially distinct from thought. For him as for Wittgenstein, thinking means speaking, as we are told in *Totality and Infinity*. But what does it mean when the ineffable turns up in the discourse of a philosopher for whom thought does not exist outside, or above, speech? What does his inscription of words like "face," which by rights transcend any constituted or constitutable discourse, actually mean—once he can no longer hide, like Descartes or Bergson, behind a view of language designed to strip it of its power?

Leaving aside this major difficulty, does Levinas manage to escape from the classical dialectic of the Same and the Other? By a remarkable inversion of arguments, he appears to go a long way toward reversing the privilege of the ego over the alter. He sees the self giving up its power so as to believe in the reality of the other. My obligations to the other come first, and are infinite, but so are the other's toward me, which makes this fiduciary pact something quite euphoric. The swing from one term to the other is compelling. But strategically, the insistence on the other is like a philosophical diversion which leaves the original principles intact. Let us try to see why.

For Levinas, there is a transcendental structure of alterity which allows the other to retreat into the secret of his or her originary difference. In particular, we believe in the absolute Other because we accept his mystery. We can never manipulate God, not even through prayer. In fact, Levinas soon corrects this displacement by saying that the radical heterogeneity of other people is itself possible "only if the Other is other in relation to a term whose essence is to act as a way into the relation, to be the Same, not relatively but absolutely." For, he goes on to insist, no term "can stand absolutely at the point of departure of a relation unless it acts as a Self."[46]

All in all, what I find here is an uncomfortable tension between a description for ethical purposes, often highly accurate, and a metaphysics that sees the condition of all beings as one of separation and radical exteriority. Levinas himself is a thinker with divided loyalties. In his best moments, this tension produces a balance, but sometimes the balance is lost and his work begins to oscillate from one extreme to the other. In any case, he is well aware that phenomenology is incapable of respecting the other and his or her real meaning, so that it remains a philosophy of violence. At the same time, one is struck by the slightness of some of his theoretical premises, which continue, more or less against his will, in the tradition of transcendental phenomenology and German idealism. "My presentation of these notions . . . remains faithful to intensional analysis."[47]

It is therefore not surprising that a certain conception of the relation derived from Aristotle can be traced, in more or less implicit form, through the theoretical premises of both Levinas and the existential phenomenology of alterity in general—a conception involving mixed or *modo intelligentiae* relations (with which I dealt earlier). The terms of such relations do not have equal status. It is knowledge—as an act of the intelligence—that is real, whereas the intentional object is unreal. Such relations are only founded *a parte cognitionis,* and not *a parte rei.* The same is true for theories of the intentional "relation." It is possible to assimilate the intentionality of mental states to the relation of reference to objects, which itself can be compared to a relational property. This model goes back to Franz Brentano.[48] If I think about *x*, my thought about *x* is a relational property of a mental type. The strangeness of this mental property derives from the fact that it is not engendered by a relation of adequation between a mental state and its object; on the contrary, such a relation of adequation would presuppose the relational property. It is not because my mental state is adequate to *x* that it possesses the relational property of being directed toward *x*. Again, it is the other way around: it is adequate to *x* because and to the extent that it has the relational property of being directed toward *x*. Logically, and whatever efforts may be made to separate it, that relational property is inherent in the self, in accordance with the logic of terms.

This is the usual view of intentionality as relation to others. If the absolute solitude of each being in its own existence is primary, as it is for Levinas, then any relation, any movement toward the other can only arise from the depths of that solitude.

Which means that difference is therefore seen as something originary. Levinas' philosophical itinerary leads him on the one hand to assume a clear separation between the Same and the Other—as a condition of his view of infinity—and on the other hand to locate the Buberian concept of responsibility within subjectivity. This importation of responsibility is judicious, as it provides a final alibi for an out-maneuvered phenomenology. Its effects, however, are extremely limited. It is as if for Levinas intersubjective relations always started from the self. In addition, not only does the self as point of origin determine the perspective, but it is also given value as the marker of an impossible totalization.

Overall, the phenomenological premises of Levinas converge with the demands of his own conceptual predispositions and his biblical inspiration to place a decisive emphasis on the original asymmetry of the Same and the Other. This increases the unilateral power of the effects of responsibility and concern for others: I am now responsible for everyone else, and even for the persecution that I suffer, even to the extent of expiating the sins of others.[49] The subject becomes totally subjected to others, and to their originary difference. For Levinas, the *sum* of the ego should be an *adsum*. At least, this seems to me to be the interpretation he places on the biblical phrase "here I am," a pledge of loyalty in response to the challenge of the Other. This was the same reply given by Abraham when he accepted God's test (Gen. 22.1), and by Joseph when his father sent him back to the brothers who hated him (Gen. 37.13). After all, it is a natural enough interpretation, and one in accordance with the commentary of Rashi: "That is the answer given by pious people. And it also means: I am ready. It is the language of submission and zeal, and prompt obedience. . . ."

By saying "here I am" in the face of other people, the Same takes as its duty the need to bear witness to the Other, and attest with its own mouth what is said about the Other. In Levinas, prophecy acts as a curious paradigm of alterity as it is experienced in everyday life.

This can be taken further. The subject is a *hostage*.[50] A hostage is someone who offers his or her own person as a guarantee of that to which he or she is attesting, a martyr who replaces, by the trials and sacrifices he or she undergoes, the proof he or she is unable to give. The self is condemned to take the place of the other as a hostage in the process of expiation, as it has already done in inspiration. We stand initially as hostages, claims Levinas, when we are responsible for others to the point of being responsible for our responsibility itself. At that point, subjectivity goes so far as to replace the other with itself, and the psychological model that results becomes the other as manifested within sameness. This is the sublime dramatization of a self that is not initially linked to the other; it is its ultimate recourse and compensation in the face of evil. Such drama and compensation enter the philosopher's discourse in stylistic tropes chosen in function of egological premises that are no longer valid.

We should not forget that for Levinas it is the idea of infinity that makes the separation of persons necessary. Between them there is a distance that I see as comparable to that between tall trees in a wood. Once subjectivities have been separated from each other, it remains for Levinas to decide whether this separation is to work to the advantage of the system (in favor of difference), or to the advantage of the self. He reacts as a phenomenologist, choosing the second option. For reasons internal to his own thematics, he therefore ends up corroborating the position to which his premises led him to subscribe.

But what is a self that is totally given over to alterity? I do not discover myself in others by some sort of "movement toward" them and away from the self. The sum of the ego is not really an adsum (here I am, at your disposal). Moreover, what is an Other that is nothing more than a downgraded version of the Same? Yet our philosopher's choice is clear: as happens in the French novel of education (of which the first was Rousseau's *Emile*), the empirical self has experiences; the transcendental self, which (like Rousseau's tutor) is something of a direct descendent of God, looks on most patiently while the first self has its experiences of other people. It is not a question of whether or not this conception is utopian, or whether its ultimate implications are scandalous. it is just that we might think of giving a more nuanced description of personal identity, which would save the self from having to make an all-or-nothing statement and release it from an improbable and exaggerated guilt toward everything and everyone.

Particularly as the self can be much less well-intentioned than the ego as Levinas describes it. Narcissism on the philosophical plane, once it loses the compensation of an admirably demanding moral inspiration, turns into egocentric narcissism on the level of the individual ethos. The other, in his or her original difference, quickly becomes a foreigner or a barbarian. I start to project my own failings onto the other, because I can also use him or her, in a fragile kind of exorcism, as a way of discharging the faults and vices against which I want to protect myself. This is the tactic of using a scapegoat, in which what Levinas sees as a sublime reversal becomes reduced to a cowardly projection. The role of scapegoat can be played by minority or marginal individuals of our choice, all figures of the Same. I fear that the scapegoat and the hostage of which Levinas speaks are the two extremes of a single type.

For the human phenomenon to break through into philosophy does not require such improbable (but, unfortunately, commonplace) strategies as these, but rather, I believe, a rigorous pedagogy of the relation. This being who is human will only need to cast aside his or her ontological condition and reverse the categories of being so that they become spiritual, if they are conceived of as categories of the Same. It is as if Levinas were obliged to compensate for the autological constraints imposed by the idiom of Husserlian egology. As if he were trying to complement them at a late stage in his argument so as to express personal intuitions and convictions of a quite different sort, particularly from biblical sources. This is what leads to a disjointed style made up of apophatic procedures, limited borrowings from Martin Buber, appeals to the prophets, and the reversal of arguments for and against, all of which are evidence of the inadequacy of his initial concepts; this obliges him to "unsay" philosophical language, an obligation that he wrongly takes to be the essence of all philosophy.

In fact, the way Levinas states the problem can be called into question in a number of ways. First of all, we need only to find a way of being "other than being" if we are condemned by the philosopher to a nonrelational alternative of being the same or being something other than the same. More specifically, if we are condemned to a choice between positions in which the Other is either determined by, or on the contrary determines, the Same.

Fortunately, we are not obliged to make the Same adhere by some miraculous coincidence to the Same, or to project the same onto the Other. I certainly agree with Levinas that *respect* is always due to people. But the whole question is: in what way? Respect for others does not necessarily depend on the neutral element of universality, the pure formality of moral law, as Kant believed. But nor is it the immediate respect of the other in his or her originary separation. It is something that is implied in the relational gesture. I respect you enough to speak *with* you, and to enter with you into the game of questioning and dialogue in which the meaning of our words and our reference to the world will be regarded as common property, in accordance with the principle of nonviolence in discourse.

Let me add that my relations with others are not primarily a matter of constitution or theory, nor even of accident. For Levinas, it is necessary to give a deliberate twist to the traditional solipsistic conceptualization (or to erase it) if we are to escape its effects. But the dialectic of Same and Other, the set of concepts that makes my relations with others a matter of constitution or problematic accident, is self-undermining. This is shown simply enough by the fact that I can be in no doubt that another person is in pain— "Just try, in a real case, to doubt the fear or suffering of someone else"[51]— and still less that the other person is really human. To have doubts about somebody you must already be living in that person's presence, in a relationship with him or her, which means accepting him or her as another person.

We cannot understand other people as persons or as faces outside the contexts of living that link us to each other. The question is how other people enter into a whole series of relations with us, with different attitudes and in different contexts. The Cartesian problem of the automaton, or more recently the robot, does not arise. Indeed, let us ask ourselves why the idea that other people are different from robots might pose a problem, and what we might learn from it. It is an idea expressed above all in our relational behavior toward others. Suppose that I am wondering whether or not others are really persons. I would clearly seem to be thinking that they might well be something else. But if you ask me what else, I realize that I was not really thinking of anything precise at all. On the other hand, my lived and active perception of others commits me immediately to recognizing them as persons because it is, or is about to become, an interpersonal relation.

Levinas speaks of a "sincerity of face-to-face confrontation." If this is something real, in what sense? We see the other person standing face to face with us, and placing us under an obligation. Granted. But without any intermediary, any communication? It seems not, for Levinas puts forward the face as a representation of the unity of looking and speaking in a literal, non-metaphorical sense. But once again I would like to ask: in what sense? For this unity is not self-evident. If I stare at you while I am speaking to you, you will say: "stop looking at me like that," although I might only be trying to catch your eye. This shows that looks do not behave in the same way that speech does in a conversation. Nobody could speak freely if his or her gaze could never turn away from the other person's eyes, which in turn were staring back. An insistent, sustained gaze is disturbing and worrying. When someone stops speaking, however, the effect is different from when he or she stops staring. Silence at the end of speech can be frightening, but a gaze averted brings reassurance.

Speaking and Looking

Let us now get down to the fundamental questions. When am I prepared to say that someone else's face disarms me? Less in itself than by what it seems to be communicating to me. For example, by suggesting: "I have not been lying to you." Not because the other person is making some demand on me, or because he or she has rights over me, but because the other person's face confirms the reality of our interlocutive relation.

I admit that ethics is destroying epistemology at this point. But before it can be seen as an epistemological problem—what do we perceive in other people's faces?—it is a logical one: it concerns the logical status of relations, and consequently the way in which we consent to think about them and live them with other people.

Methodologically, I agree with Levinas about one thing: whenever there is a crisis in theory, there should be a return to concrete description. If we now wish to rescue description for the methodological precepts laid down by phenomenology, and Husserlian protocols in particular (which see it in purely intentional terms), the correct question becomes: when are we disposed to say that other people are present to me through their faces? This involves undertaking a thought experiment about a conceptual possibility or impossibility: I would (or would not) say . . . If it were up to me to begin the description again, I should start by saying that this is in no way a self-evident undertaking. We learn the use of a word or expression in appropriate circumstances, but we do not learn at the same time how to describe those circumstances.

Let us therefore ask ourselves seriously when it is that we are able to state (and using what linguistic resources) that the other is present to us in his or her face, or on the contrary, that the face is empty.

Imagine a man in the company of others. The eyes, mouth, chin, and even the angle of the head reflect the position that he has amid this circle of his judges: he is present in his face. As long, that is, as he is in control of his expression; but then, each of us has the expression that we are allowed by others to have. Imagine, on the other hand, someone who does not control her face in reaction to other people, i.e., in function of her relation to them (whether this relation be symmetrical or not is unimportant for the moment): in that case, all expression is lost. For the same reason, it is not surprising that someone absorbed in meditation should have a blank expression.

There is therefore presence and presence. Once speaking and looking cease to happen in an assured, face-to-face manner, there arises a kind of void, an instability that is more subtly perceived when the words spoken contradict the message of the eyes. If the man from the first scenario now leaves the people with whom he was having an animated conversation, his face will continue for a while to display a remanent vivacity which only gradually disappears, and which could easily be rekindled by the arrival of another interlocutor.

By reversing the model, it is easy to see how an expression can seem like a caricature. All that is needed is for it to convey something unilateral, or something unchecked and natural, as happens when an event changes our expression without our realizing it. The face betrays too much emotion whenever it reflects the outside world. For that reason, we should perhaps refrain from scrutinizing people's faces at such moments, when they are most vulnerable to the curiosity of onlookers. Similarly, when someone unilaterally and deliberately adopts a particular expression, that person sends a message without realizing it. Imagine a face that was forever smiling, or always looked intelligent, resolute, commanding, or threatening. These are all promises which cannot be kept, so that we become tired of expressions that we see as violent, even tyrannical. A face that is too expressive is a never-ending source of perplexity. Alain notes that there are some noses, eyes, and mouths that cannot stop being expressive even when buying a newspaper, like those insatiable talkers who just cannot keep quiet.

If one of the first rules of politeness is to maintain a moderately mobile face, it is probably because we have to be careful that our expression fits the relation in which we are involved. This is when the other becomes present to me through his or her face. When the face does not have this presence, let us hope that it has the power to forget, and forget itself. I have noticed that a face is beautiful when it hides within itself, as if it were preparing itself for relational life by standing back for a while, holding itself in reserve for later by initially refusing to express anything at all. A face is beautiful when at first it expresses only indifference. Not emptiness or a complete lack of sparkle, but simply indifference. It is a way of raising the stakes of consent. Afterwards, the face will continue to seem new. It is a precaution: otherwise, what price a smile?

—But the face introduces me in person (as a person); it is the absolutely nonmetaphorical unity of eyes and mouth. How are we to understand it?

—I understand it precisely in the sense that it is impossible to envisage the other independently of the way in which he or she speaks and looks. Our face is indeed that part of our flesh that is continually modeled and remodeled, animated and invigorated, by our relations with our fellow creatures. Whether metaphorically or by transposition, when we perceive animals in turn as having faces it is because we are expecting them to reciprocate: we are "waiting for them to speak." The animals' eyes seem to change the moment we look at them.[52] Other people only appear to me in their singular identity when I perceive them as partners, which perception depends on my entering into a relation with them through looking, or allocutively, by speaking. What animates the face, which is the most fascinating surface on earth, is the scarcely dissociable conjunction of eyes and voice. The more reciprocal the exchange of glances and speech, the more animated it will become.

—Let us ask ourselves for example in what circumstances I might speak the following words: "one glance between us was enough." What does this mean? In the first place, of course, it means that looking is not just about the visible—what I can see—but also about the seer—that other person who can also see. Doubtless our glance moves around from one thing to another in its own imperious, exploratory way, taking views that amount to a sort of prepossession of the visible world, to the extent that we hardly know any more whether it is the person seeing or visible reality itself that is in control of the process. Sometimes a glance will merely register the details of objects, while at others it envelopes them and questions them according to its own lights. But as soon as a seeing other appears before me, everything changes. For one thing, I become visible.

Shall I then claim that I become "a thing among things," as certain existentialists did? Not at all. The look that passes *between* people is not the same as that which they direct *at* things. As we have seen, it is actually the latter that derives from the former: things are offered to our perception in the way that they are determined by discourse, or rather, by the discussions we have about them. The human eye is seen neither as the receiver, nor as the transmitter of its glances. Or, if you like: the eye is that thing which shows me that it can see. We do not continually need to dip into the unique treasure of our vision in order to believe this. When my eyes light up as they meet yours, and our glances cross in the space between us, I say: "we are looking at each other." What, precisely, have I just experienced? It is not that some sort of chiasmus of points of view has occurred, a simultaneous limitation. The poetic image is more accurate:

> Our eye-beams twisted and did thread
> Our eyes, upon one double string.[53]

In fact, what has come about is rather a joint agreement, a process of making similar.

Like a bow bent between them, the look two faces exchange is less something reflected in the eyes of the other, or that goes from one to the other and then shuttles quickly back, than something that happens instantly *between* them, provided, that is, that they grasp it in the full force of its relational present. We can feel mocked by the way someone looks at us, as we can by a smile. And if that is so, I do not want anyone to ask: "But how is it that we manage to look at each other?" The duality into which an exchanged glance is broken down by the needs of analysis in fact cuts straight through to my heart and moves me. This is how a look of desire moves me. We both feel, for a moment, our common relationship to something that we do not have. We can be wounded—that is, changed—by a glance just as easily as by a well-aimed remark. It can also happen that looks take over from words. Paul Valéry puts it very well in his sketch of *Lust:*

LUST: I want to speak to you. But can't you see that I am speaking to you?

FAUST: Your eyes speak. It is true. Your face . . . your hands . . .

LUST: I cannot find the right words. But all of me is speaking to you.

I therefore see immediately that you can see me because I am experiencing a relationship between people who see. Not that this reciprocal exchange of looking will last. It quickly fades away, or otherwise carries on in the same way as has everything else that lasts—i.e., in alternating states of actuality and latency. Why should we find it any easier to face up to this exchange of glances than we do an exchange of words? Why less easy? When the exchange of looking between people disappears, the *you* of the other becomes absent.

Let me stress that the key element here is not latency or the process of folding back, but rather *what* it is that disappears or is folded back. It is significant that if the other person's look transfixes and terrifies me (a tyranny of the eyes), his or her power over me is exactly measured by my degree of consent to this folding back that allows the other to see me.

—But surely you will admit that we can objectivize a person whom we are holding "under our gaze"; and also that one person can "throw a glance" which will be received by another, asymmetrically therefore? For we can sometimes receive a glance like a present, like a smile, something to be taken away and treasured as a gift. . . .

—Certainly, but there is a distinction to be made here. When I receive a glance, it calls upon me to respond. The same is not true when I am subjected to it. Correctly speaking, a voyeur does not *see* me at all. And seeing is nothing if the statue does not know that it is being looked at. Anyway, what is the essential aspect of this? Surely this: that a look that calls for a response depends for its effect on an initial shock, an instant awareness, between two people. Any asymmetry will then lead to a feeling of discomfort, even threat. Sight is a weapon of predation. Piercing, burning, or glacial glances all contribute unilaterally to preparing the other for our attack, as we expose and then take possession of that person. Let us now consider the case of objectivization. Once again, the fundamental fact is not that one person can become visible to the other, like an object caught in his or her gaze, while the other is in a position to receive the first person's image. What counts is the fact that objectivization does not succeed, and above all the reason it does not.

Note what happens: I am in front of you. My privilege is to be able to slip away from your grasp, by objecting: "what do you want from me?" In short, I can stand in the way of my objectivization. Meeting another person means approaching that person as a partner, not as an object. There is no need to bother with the argument about unilateral relations. As with any relation, an interpersonal relation with no converse is not a relation at all.[54] Any more than the fact that A *gives* B to C can be explained by the idea of A throwing B up into the air in the expectation that it will reach C by chance. A glance between two people is a reciprocal glance. It matters little in this context that the reciprocal glance, like speech, is soon over: no structure of relations with other people except reciprocation can be regarded as either the only, or even the most important thing, for they are all only empirical variants in which subsequent analysis will have no difficulty in showing the presence of reciprocity in its canonical form.

I am not trying to force the reciprocity relation into some optimal position at any cost, but simply to establish (or reiterate) its primary character. We know very well that true relations remain fragile and our allocation of them strictly measured. But for the glance to become a threat, and the other person an anonymous obsession, the relation must fall back into asymmetricality, with the self *turning inward* toward its own experience. Asymmetrical relations are only derivative variants, limitations, or distortions of an original form.

Admittedly, when we enter into a relationship, we experience it as a renunciation of our ability to turn in on ourselves. Conversely, once this turning-in behavior begins again, the existence of the other person will no longer be accepted in any other way than as part of my own experience, as one mode of existence of my own *I*. It is clear that without a true conceptual model of relations we are condemned to oscillating between the primacy of the Other and that of the Self. With a sort of fraudulent payoff, as in a court case in which one of the parties is given everything that was taken away from the other. In fact, it is more than possible that a person who believes he or she is introducing the primacy of the Other will in fact end up confirming that of the Self.

—But then, how do you account for the phenomenological correctness of Levinas' conception of the face? Are we not forced to accept that a face in the frankness of its exposure requires something of me directly? Beyond whatever protective composure it may have, it stands before me in its pure alterity. In its passivity which is more ancient than fear, the face makes claims on me as if it really were my business to respond. And it does so before any confrontation with me. By making demands like this, another person becomes that "neighbor" whom I must not abandon to his or her solitude.

I refuse to accept that the face reveals the other to me *first* in its passivity, in its extreme defenselessness, and above all that it calls to me from behind its composure and before any confrontation between us. What is it that disturbs me about this type of phenomenology? Its so-called primitive character. It makes the face more like a mask. A death mask, at once temple and inert mold, still calls for respect. A mind worked there, wore that exterior, long enough to exalt it without measure. Nothing was ever so constantly and intimately modeled as the face. The departed mind used to inhabit these features, used to arrange them to convey an expression. But a face is precisely not a mask. Ultimately, a mask is not that which conceals the face, but instead is at most that which fixes it, as we see in the little livid pictures painted by Goya at the end of his life. Whereas a face is something essentially living, animated by the eyes and the voice. What constitutes it as a face is its aptitude for relational confrontation. From which it follows that any machine with this aptitude will function as a face. So it is only *afterward* that the face calls to me in Levinas' sense, which is consequently a derivative one.

I have explained why I noted a disparity—even a straight contradiction—

in Levinas' work, between his theme of the allegiance to others, on the one hand, and a method and theories that in fact and in principle confirm the primacy of the self, on the other. I am of course in no way quarreling with the correctness of his intentions or the subtlety of his analyses, which I warmly applaud. Equally, one can but welcome the strategic value of his theories against the pointless idealism of Husserl. What is at issue, however, is their centrality and their efficacy. I suspect that phenomenology, even if with Levinas it abandons any explicitly egological premises, is not exactly adequately equipped to absorb the allocentric standpoint that he sets out to derive from the message of the Bible. As he also admits that he has no intention of abandoning a phenomenological perspective elevated to the level of an exemplary method; it is always the experience of an initial self that is presented as canonical. But that presupposes a turning inward, away from an immediate relation of reciprocity which in turn is presupposed by any secondary distortion of it. That relation is experienced through the face, in the processes of both looking and speaking.

It is perfectly clear that the other person is not a simple negation of the self. It is difficult not to agree with Levinas here: other people can neither be constituted in the Husserlian sense, nor conceived of through the category of negativity, by way of a difference which is negation or limitation. But this is where we need to be careful. That does not mean that other people are separated from us. If the other were initially separate, without the mediation of a code or of that third party—the rule of language—to which we always refer (if only in order to transcend it by the novel transgressions we make), the other would represent an absolute threat. Our first thought would be to destroy him or her, as we see in Daniel Defoe's *Robinson Crusoe*. According to the radical view of alterity, those who are not us are not even other people. As long as others remain separated from us by an original difference, communication will continue to be precarious, and dialogue will find it extraordinarily difficult to carve out a path by which to cross the divide of alterity.[55]

Now I would maintain that there is no exceptional transitivity in dialogue. It is the most accurate expression of the dialogism which constitutes all speech, if by that term we mean the distribution of any message between two agencies of utterance which are in a present relation. I therefore find it difficult to conceive of the interpersonal relation in the manner of Levinas, who opposes the asymmetrical dominance of the *you* (*vous*) against the private relationship of reciprocity between an *I* and a *thee* (*tu*). For him, the other person is not my equal, but my superior, which is just another way of confirming the primacy of the intentional ego. On the other hand, I share with Martin Buber the idea that it is the reciprocal (though not necessarily symmetrical) relation between *I* and *thee* (*tu*) which opens up the possibility of subsequent empirical modifications, and even eventually of an asymmetrical relation with the dominance and separateness of the other.

Buber and Levinas do not have the same appreciation of the role of religion, or of the alliance between God and Israel. A part of me is loath to think against Levinas. I have only subjected his ideas to such close scrutiny because I feel close to his position. Particularly as there is no reason why the God of Abraham should have to fit in with the philosopher. The exegete can perfectly well stress the stylistic pre-eminence in the Bible of commandments over narratives, hymns of praise, or writings of wisdom:

> I am but a stranger here on earth,
> Do not hide thy commandments from me.[56]

An interpretation that sees belief as inseparable from obedience is not only perfectly possible; it is indeed a major interpretation. For the highest commandment is obedience to the Law. Israel's absolute privilege, its greatness in the midst of dejection, is to have recognized this fact. Benefits and punishments alike attest its chosen status. Levinas' allocentrism reflects the utterly heteronomous nature of the Law. The primacy of others is modeled on the primacy of an Other whose order is an absolute obligation. Levinas' concept of responsibility reflects the assent of the people who, out in the desert, accepted the Law of the Other. Here, obedience comes first: we shall do and we shall listen. We shall take upon our shoulders the yoke of the heavenly kingdom.

For Buber, God is admittedly the "utterly Other," but he is also "utterly the Same" and "utterly present."[57] If He is the *mysterium tremendum* whose appearances overwhelms us, He is so in the manner of love that breaks the human heart as it enters it, because it makes it respond not according to the law of the Other, but according to the law of love, i.e. according to the paradigm of all relations. Levinas would say that love of God is something that He has *ordered*, and is itself a matter of obedience: "You cannot turn your eyes away from love without immediately becoming idolaters."[58]

And we are made free so as to obey an order that does not come from us. This order brings us neither liberty, which is not the highest good, nor servitude, for obedience does not mean bondage, but service rendered to others. Looked at in this way, it is clear why the self does not draw its legitimacy from itself. As the other person's Other, it dispossesses itself. Its personal identity must therefore be instituted differently, in relation to the other to whom it is obliged. The self is freed so that it may be responsible. It is irreplaceable, noninterchangeable, in certain acts for which it has responsibility.[59]

It can be claimed, as philosophers of religion from Augustine to Levinas have frequently done, that our relation to God is the paradigm for relations between people, and that the latter are a symbol of the former. Indeed, for Martin Buber, the mystery of God is quite clearly closer than that of my subjectivity, because it immediately reminds me of the form of my personal identity.

Therefore, the choice of the relation we regard as canonical is a crucial one. It determines the way we analyze respect, responsibility, looking, and speaking. If responsibility is to be anything other than the arbitrary imputation of certain acts, outside a context of behavior that is experienced as reciprocal; if our meetings with others are not to be a source of surprise and revulsion; if interpellation is to be something other than primitive apostrophe; then all these things will have to be based on an initial relation *with* others. Only, a relation of that sort cannot be conceived as a journey *toward* the other, a process of self-exposure, undertaken by a self that freely agrees, either from the goodness of its heart or out of obedience, to call itself into question. Nor *from* one *to* the other; but both *together*. If my being is—as I believe it to be—relational in essence, I am linked from the start, and even before that, to other people. The most intense form of proximity is that of *relata*.

Even the word "meeting" is unsuitable, in that it implies that there was a time before the meeting with another person when the self was separated from and lacking contact with others. Persons as persons do not meet others; they *are* their meetings. All the figures of an originary asymmetry—the objectivization of the other, but also peremptory interpellation and the idea of allegiance to others—end up reducing the other in his or her alterity, and are therefore ultimately a cause of violence. Only the infinite, which is infinitely other, rescues Levinas' world from being entirely given over to violence. That is a consequence for which the author was not unprepared, because it is a biblical idea. In a country where people do not fear God, it is as well to fear the worst. That was Abraham's reply to Abimelech, when he asked why he was trying to pass his wife off as his sister: "There can be no fear of God in this place, and they will kill me for the sake of my wife." [60]

The Mingled Waters of Discourse

Our conception of the relations between the self and others has for too long been governed by the idea of subjectivity as consciousness. Beginning with the Cogito and the static experience of inner contemplation, philosophy gave up attempting to account for communication between persons, and found it hard to see how to avoid a battle between consciousnesses, with each seeking the death of the others. On the other hand, to start talking about the idea of an interlocutive relation, without trying to measure the extent to which it transforms our conception of the ego and interpersonal relations, would be a very poor introduction to the subject.

The State of the Debate

When they are experienced in an interlocutive mode, interpersonal relations are overdetermined. Each person is both Same and Other, acting in him or herself as a speaker, and as a listener in respect to others. Again it is the relation that makes each in turn alternately into a speaker and an allocutee. The difference is one of function, and it can be reversed at any moment. In fact, the problem is to allow for a minimal asymmetry between the poles of a primary relation, but without that asymmetry ultimately becoming an intrinsic privilege of the self. Each person is an other for others in his or her *positive* difference. For difference only implies negation so long as we insist on regarding it as subordinate to sameness, so that it appears as an opposition or limitation. It is easy enough to get a general idea of what consequences the primacy of relations might have; the difficult thing is to define them accurately, while avoiding the obvious clichés. The first consequence is a need to rethink the notion of alterity as constitutive. The second has to do with the ontological significance of communicative speech.

i. There is no question of attributing to others an essence or a quality that is uniquely theirs, to the exclusion of the self. To do so would be to replace the efficacy of a relationship between them and me with a mystificatory image of alterity. That shows a strange misunderstanding of the true nature of respect, without which there can be no real relationship with the other person. A respectful awareness of an initial distance and separation has nothing to do with the claim that alterity is absolute. On the other hand, the idea of absolute alterity offers a multitude of different alibis. It is a philosophically courageous move to assert the radical heterogeneity and total separation of the other, yet it turns out quite unexpectedly to be another way to establish the primacy of the self. As we have seen, the heterogeneity of others is totally dependent on a first term whose essence is to remain constant.

It is quite another thing to claim that the thoughts of others are truly constitutive of my own. This goes far beyond the observation that I am obliged to take account of the other person's opinion as soon as I see him or her face to face and confront his or her views with my own. The reason is that my beliefs immediately challenge the other person's as soon as I declare them. In semantic terms, this means that the possible worlds that are compatible with my belief conflict with those compatible with the other's, once our first words have been exchanged.[61] The primacy of relations must be taken seriously. It immediately implies that discursive thought is basically dialogical, as C. S. Peirce brilliantly noticed. And that debate, confrontation, and controversy are fundamentally discursive situations, to the extent that they can be regarded as models for reason in its search for truth.[62] As soon as we begin to think, we are in relation with a genuine *you*, and not just our own internalized model of one.

2. In the same way that faces are the reciprocity relation made flesh, so speech is the reciprocity relation made language. What does this mean for speech, if we think about it from start to finish in function of a mutual interlocutive relation? To begin with, it can no longer be considered simply as the tension of a transcendence that directs the self out toward others: speech, much more than an actual meeting, now becomes the way into a relation, which in turn is something symbolized in discourse, something that can bring a new semantic reality into being.

As such, speech is a direct expression of the founding relationship which implants individuals in a discursive context as co-utterers. It is a direct product of the relation which brings meaning about, and simultaneously the effect of a tension that creates the reality of the utterers: an onto-poetic tension that establishes the uttering agencies, of which each is other for the other and not for the same. Looked at in this way, the uttering agencies can be seen as different in a reconcilable and conciliatory way, free from the burden of sameness; their differences are *positive* because the other, who is no longer conditioned by a need to be identical, is no longer qualified negatively. We shall see later how these differences can be established and maintained.

I realize that people might still want to try to account for reciprocal interlocutive relations in terms of an intentional relation. The first step is to assimilate the intentionality of mental states to a relational property. The relation of reciprocity would then be the locus of a double heterogeneity, as Sartre puts it.[63] Apart from the fact that he is here making strange use of words in natural language to solve a problem peculiar to his philosophy, I note that in his description the two projects remain separated; the focus of each perspective stands opposite the other as a vanishing point, an alternative possibility of unification. Each party makes him or herself into a means in the other's project, so that the other will become a means in his or her own. Each person discovers him or herself as an object, and as the instrument of the other's aims, in the very act that constitutes the other as the instrument of his or her own aims. Each foresees the other's next move and integrates it as a transcended means into his or her own, and suddenly moves in such a way as to become integrated as a means into the other's movement. This type of description is exemplary. Far from holding onto the notion of a relation as something fundamental, Sartre reconstructs the relation approximately in terms of relational properties.

Why Grice Fails to Explain the Interlocutive Relation

The same schema can be found in the analyses of all thinkers influenced to a greater or lesser degree by phenomenology. Thus H. P. Grice suggests that it would be possible to do an intentional analysis of the act of linguistic communication that did not make use of the interlocutive relation, or, to put it another way, that reconstructed it. The mechanism Grice proposes defines signification as a process of meaning that can be back-referenced to the ego, insofar as it links the production of an intention by one party with its recognition by the other.

He defines the reciprocal interlocutive relation with the aid of the intentions of the speaker alone. More precisely: The speakers' *third-order* intentions. Take an utterer U. What U means is defined as follows: U means something by saying x if, for speaker A, U states x with the intention

1. that A will give a particular reply r
2. that A will recognize that U intends (1)
3. that A will perform (1) on the basis of his realization that (2).

If, like Grice, we understand by the term *first-order intention* a belief, desire, or meaning, then it is clear that for individual S to believe that another individual T wants p constitutes a *second-order intention*. As a result, (2) attributes to U not just a second-order intention (U intends A to recognize . . .), but a *third*-order intention: U intends A to recognize that U wants A to produce r.

Grice shows that second-order intentions are certainly not enough to express reciprocity. What is needed, he tells us, is an encounter between the speaker and the listener. Maybe. But my question is: is a third-order intention either necessary or sufficient?

It is neither. It is not sufficient: "A wants B to believe that C wishes that p" certainly expresses a third-order intention, but it does not even begin to translate a reciprocal relationship. Nor is it necessary. If I ask the speaker whether he or she intended the listener to recognize his or her intention of making the listener respond in this way, the speaker would probably reply that his or her intention was never as tortuous as that. Neither speaker nor listener need have such complicated intentions in order to communicate. Before Grice, few people knew about this type of third-order intention. If in addition we are completely unaware of having such intentions when we speak, there is no reason to claim that we speak with intentions of that sort.[64]

If we do not take as our starting point the interlocutive relation, which is as irreducible from a logical point of view as it is immediate in our experience, we will not succeed in giving a proper description of speech activity. In the Gricean model, stipulation (3) assumes that A's recognition of U's intention that (1) acts at least in part as a sufficient reason for his reply r. Under what conditions is a reason held to be sufficient? In order to make this clear, Stephen Schiffer introduces a new element that *presupposes* the existence of a *relationship of mutuality*.[65] U signifies p by producing x if U utters x with the intention of bringing about a certain state of affairs E, which is such that the realization of E is a sufficient reason for U and a listener A, in the mutual knowledge that E will come about, and p is a proof that U uttered x with the intention:

1. of producing a response r in A; and
2. that the recognition by A of U's intention (1) should function as A's sufficient reason for his response r; and
3. of bringing about E.

As we have already seen more than once, there is a frequent tendency to break down the relation into its images, representations, or signifying intentions. What we should go so far as to say, on the contrary, is that the personal self will only be found in speech, insofar as it is not just concerned with other people (a point which I regard as insufficient and, in the end, trivial), but is actually reconstituted each time in its living reality by its relations with them. In order to take such an idea to its logical conclusion, we need to listen to what our disappropriated speech tells us in the tense field of questions and answers, without expecting any platonic dominance of answers over questions, or vice versa. More generally, we must listen to this speech which has been cast adrift in a sea of verbal interactions.

The philosophical choice to be made will escape no one. My position on this matter is as follows: verbal interactions are the dynamic result of the interlocutive relation, and not the other way around. If there is indeed an interlocutive relation, it is irreducible. Of course for Sartre, for instance, language is praxis; relations of reciprocity derive from praxis, i.e., from the plurality of social activities within the same practical field.[66] Anyone who wishes to grasp his or her specificity must refer to the social activity from which he or she is derived. And, insists Sartre, in any activity people adapt their own efforts to those of others.

In fact, when two people are engaged in an activity together, I personally do not think that it is because each "adapts" his or her efforts to fit in with those of the other; before each one acts, he or she has *already* integrated the other's action, so that each is moved as a means in the other's movement. For collaborators live in an intimate and dynamic relationship. This sort of mutual integration does not imply that each becomes an object for the other, each reflecting his or her "own" project for the other. As I showed in one of my earlier analyses, projects as such—respected, recognized, and understood by a process of psychological projection—do not exist. The experience of reciprocity cannot occur in separation. Whenever a reciprocal relationship comes into being, it generates its own present terms, so that the existence of each is modified by the other. The same can be said of agencies of utterance. More generally, any joint activity involves an intimate and indivisible relationship which, as in the case of speech, has dynamic effects (transactions, interactions) which are secondary. This is a crucial methodological point.

For Levinas, "telling others" is a precondition of any ontology. I would suggest rather that "saying *with* others" is a precondition of all meaning. The other to whom an utterance is addressed is not an external target, but a kind of co-utterer who is associated with the joint production of the statement. Or else, if by chance the meaning has already been constituted, "saying with others" is the way in which we subject it to dialogical revision and testing. This difference of position is significant. As the reader will have realized, I am unable to accept the whole metaphorical network that Levinas builds up around such commonplace expressions as "openness toward others" and "openness in speech."

When I "address" another person, I am reacting to something he or she has said or might have said, or at least acting in function of an expected reply. It could be shown that a statement can best be explained not by the present state of the speaker, nor even by the present state of the allocutee, but by changes it is expected to bring about—for instance, in the allocutee's state of belief. But it must still be pointed out that the other's state of belief is situated, along with my own, at a particular moment in the dialogical confrontation.[67]

Levinas himself remarks on the degree to which dialogue resists traditional attempts to account for it. But insofar as dialogue is that form of discourse that comes directly out of a dialogical relationship (one in which the discursive agencies are linked by a relation in the present), the reason no logos—as objective and neutral knowledge—can ever "comprehend" dialogue, is not so much that other people are radically different, so that all speech is intended for an other. It is rather that in the dialogism of discourse, the operation by which people understand each other is one that is perpetually beginning again, here and now; and that its result will be new, a newly created meaning. Nor, then, is meaning contained in some prior form of knowledge that is neutral in relation to the dialogue situation—knowledge literally held by neither partner. In the same way, it is hard to understand how, for Buber, a true discussion can require no more than an effort by the self to turn toward the other person and address him or her, accepting him or her as a partner. "Where dialogical speech exists," he says, "everything depends on the legitimacy of what I have to say"; each partner must take care to put into words precisely what *he/she* means to say, but does not yet possess in linguistic form.[68] We have here the same old mythical model, so dear to our inveterate narcissism: our pure thought, which exists before words, and before the others to whom it is to be communicated, is betrayed by the words in which we have to clothe it in order to transmit it to them.

The reader will have realized that I am unable to accept either Buber's expressivist concept of language, or his weak conception of the dialogism of discourse (the two of which are, of course, intimately linked), however innovative they may have been in their day. If we think about what happens in real dialogue as I have defined it, our own speech exists, curiously, only by subtraction. In philosophy, the slight differences are always the important ones. If it is true that I do not just speak to others, but *with* them, then the words (or even word) that I say can no longer express just myself. Precisely because of the singularity of these words, i.e., the fact that the derive from a singular and present relationship. The difference between a handshake and a discourse is not that great. Not a poem, but a discourse; not a sign given to someone else, but a sign discussed with him or her. We only ever speak *through* others, never just *for* them. So that no speech belonging solely to us is ever heard. In the last analysis, as we shall see, that very notion only exists at all on the level of an inference.

Let me now conclude my remarks about solipsism, and look ahead to the argument of Chapter 5. To say that I am the only one who speaks or thinks is not only wrong, but meaningless. How can I wonder whether my present experience is the only reality, as there is no such thing as *my* experience, or even *my* world? The point is not whether or not we should accept the idea of solipsism, and then try (like Husserl) to overcome it, or (like Levinas) to resign ourselves to it, but whether or not we should agree to regard it as a problem. As soon as we accept the idea, it becomes impossible to put forward any serious arguments against it. Therefore, we should refuse to regard it as a problem, because as a problem it is not real. Solipsism is an absurdity that is not even "significant." Speaking and thinking are just not the sort of things we can do on our own.

All that does exist, then, is the concrete interlocutive relation, weaving its strands between you and me, and the mingled waters of full speech. Only then can speech and alterity cease to be alibis for our ethical good conscience. They can no longer be seen simply as external events that offer an optional challenge to the subject, investing it from without (after all, this type of transcendence is terribly condescending), but as signs that the relation has truly come about. The real philosophical experiment lies in redistributing the empirical self of each of the dialogue partners between the discursive agencies, that self which is so often regarded as a simple reflexive reality laid down for all time in the layers of its attributes and possessions. But it lies also in refusing such a redistribution, to show how the death of the mind then follows.

4   The Grand Illusion

The dark-eyed soul descends into the very shadows.
It becomes immense and encounters nothing.
—PAUL VALÉRY
"Fragments du Narcisse," *Charmes*

SOMEONE, SOMEDAY, will have to dare to admit that the emperor has no clothes. We have seen that relationship between the self and the other, as I have just established it, cannot be recuperated within the theoretical framework and premises of phenomenology. Not even by insisting on commitment and being in the world, and with all the corrections and compensations introduced by an ethics based on the idea of a "positive movement" toward the other, who, by an entirely gracious reversal, might even be elevated to the status of a first person. For as we have seen, the self's philosophical revenge is never far away. Therefore, we are obliged to change strategy and begin with the relation between persons, accepting that this roundabout approach will give back to subjectivity a certain consistency. The first step will be to ask ourselves questions not about the fact of subjectivity, but about what I shall call its *effect*. Everything encourages us to do this, for neither the self as consciousness (even if dispossessed by some sublime conversion), nor the self as substance, the holder of qualities, nor the self as structure, can stand as a foundation.

Eurydice, or the Subjectivity Effect

In order to account for the subjectivity effect, it is necessary to start by explaining the empty illusion of a cultivated, protected, and cherished subjectivity. The various different types of discourse on the self have conflicting things to say about this. The self whose intermittent moments of daring and absence Maine de Biran observes from day to day is not the same as Rousseau's guilt-laden self, which recognizes its faults before God while protesting its innocence before men. Nor is it the same as Kierkegaard's subjective existence, which refuses to accept the closure of the system in the name of its concrete singularity. The present chapter will be devoted to the illusion of subjectivity. An illusion whose purpose, in its most philosophical form, is to turn the individual into a subject of knowledge or action, to constitute the subject-self into a *form of being*. An illusion that allows persons to appear to themselves with a feeling of autonomy and permanence, with memories, qualities, and their own baggage of guilt.

What is directly and primitively given to us is our experience of communicational reality, which cannot be defined by reference to two separate terms between which a connection is established. The connection itself, of which the two poles are only differentiable but inseparable aspects, is what is essential. From this there follows my thesis, that:

> Both empirical subjectivity and the status of person are
> derived from communicational reality.

In my view there can be no question of retreating from this principle, even if it does force us to turn our whole outlook upside down and redefine the tasks of analysis. So that, for instance, we now have to understand subjectivity sometimes as an effect, sometimes as an illusion, but never as a basic principle.

In order to do justice to the subjectivity effect, I shall reflect on the implications of the fact that communication originates at a point somewhere back in time. It has always begun already, with others before that other to whom I have now turned. The relationship into which I am now entering with him or her, and which will reconstruct me, can never wipe out my long past of speaking. A past which belongs to me in the sense that in any new communication I can decide either to hold back or, on the contrary, commit myself fully as the person into which all my earlier communications have transformed me: such is the ambiguity of subjectivity, that I am this accretion mixed with pretention which is "neither aware nor ashamed of its subjective illusion."[1]

This is probably the most serious aspect of the subjectivity effect. It may be a residue, but what remains is pure gold. Let us not challenge its importance. It creates the illusion of a private, ineffable interiority. This is of course because subjectivity, which is so loudly rejected on an epistemological level, acquires in our life experience a color, flavor, and tone that are irreducible. Experience, full of trying decisions that we must make as to whether or not to enter into particular relationships, no doubt allows me to separate what is real from what is only a game. But above all, my earlier communications have let me construct a kernel for myself through what is so inaptly named interior monologue, and which in reality is a process of communication of the self with itself. This is most obviously true of exiles or immigrants, who constituted themselves by accretion as members of a homogeneous group that they have now left, and must now integrate with a new group. If the self is able to escape from the impression of being no more than a tactic or a stratagem—of only existing, in short, to the extent that it addresses itself—then it is because of the great communicational inertia that lays down within each of the poles of a relationship a core made up of all the subject's previously acquired *habitus loquendi.*

Moreover, this process of sedimentation is irreversible. A set of positions of utterance are imputed to me which I am not at liberty to change. It is they that contribute to producing me socially as a speaking subject. These positions make up a sort of system, exerting their influence on the conventions of utterance and therefore on the discursive strategies open to me. In each position we tend to strike a pose. Not all types of language are available to me, just as I do not have access to all possible modes of life. All the possibilities I do have characterize *me.* So do *my* states of belief, *my* versions of events. My interior life is to a large extent memory. The vast palaces of memory, so dear to Augustine, cast light on the relative value we should place on the possessive, and the mode of assent we should reserve for our own past. In fact, these "personal beliefs" are the result of numerous implicit and explicit protocols of agreement which we have picked up during earlier conversations and reading. These are the beliefs and versions of events that I bring to today's conversation, and which I aim to make others believe as well.

An illusion lies in wait here that it takes keen eyes to see. We forget that words, and even thoughts, can be kept for ourselves. I am perfectly free to repeat them to myself and use them to my own ends, neglecting my role as a spokesperson and so forgetting the real conditions of their existence. Opinions and interpretations of this sort are indeed "personal," but in three significantly different ways: I can either think about them on my own by entering into communication with myself, or adopt them on the threshold of communication with an other (*alter*), or again I can find myself having to reserve them for a putative interlocutor, a secret sharer, and keep them from anyone else (*alius*). This does not of itself mean that I have hidden motives, but that, as I find myself as a matter of fact in a given interlocutive relation, the selective deafness of my interlocutor gives me what appear to be hidden motives.[2] Our first need is to break out of our isolation. As an *ego loquens* I am no more than a puny spokesman for myself. This is a precarious position, for if no one accepts "my" version of events, or I am no longer able to perceive whether or not it is acceptable, then I am clinically in a state of delirium. Equally, who can withstand a universal curse?

This sedimentation of subjectivity is real enough, even if (and particularly if) it fosters the development of several types of retrospective illusion. Autobiographies, memoirs, intimate journals, and confessions all depend on a narrative art that describes and redescribes the opaque experience of the self and the experience of temporality that seems to be constitutive of it. They all aim to put this experience into words through narration. Narration is probably the best way we have of reflecting on the events of our lives.[3]

Self-Portrait, Autobiography, and the Mirror of Narcissus

Let us reread something written by Montaigne: "For it is myself I paint. My defects are therein to be read to the life, and my imperfections and my natural form, so far as public reverence hath permitted me. . . . Thus, reader, myself am the matter of my book."[4]

Here the illusion is redoubled. First as regards the possibility of objectivizing the self in its qualities and defects, i.e. its images, and putting it to the test as if it were some stranger. But above all because Montaigne rashly confers upon it a genuine philosophical autonomy, and an illusion of fierce self-reliance that makes it capable of behaving in an original way, and concealing as well as expressing what it thinks. His self is able to mean and not say, in a private, interior performance; it has the ability to be without entering into relationships, and is free from the start, with no need to work for its freedom, as we have to for our own dis-alienation.

As we have just seen, the retrospective illusion results from a desire to conceal the origins of the subjectivity effect and prevent analysis of the sedimentation of communicational habits, as well as the formation of propositional attitudes such as beliefs. As the problematical result of a process of reification, the self comes to take on the appearance of a substantive reality. There is a reason why we forget in this way: I never turn toward another person without in some way suppressing the previous occasions when I entered into communication with someone else. The result of this difficulty is that I see myself as if I had been granted some lasting identity. Through this sort of short circuit, the self becomes infatuated with itself, like the madman or the fool of whom Aristotle speaks.[5] Contrary to its experience of constitutive relations, the emphatic, infatuated self begins to think it "really is somebody." It starts to make comparisons and decides it likes itself best; it seeks to project an image, and then to gain the recognition it deserves (what it calls "falling into the social trap"). It is soon distinguishing between self-esteem and a naive love of self, reason, and the baser passions.

We have here a tissue of interwoven illusions, for the retrospective illusion actually seems to derive from a "reflexive" one. This consists in the fact that the subject is only able at first to grasp its experience in the first person. We all have the invincible feeling that our own bodies, actions, and words are the other side of a reality of which we are given an intuition, which is expressible but is not, as such, communicable.[6] Hence the fallacious idea that the ego is an inhabitant of consciousness. This can be very easily demolished, as Daniel Lagache notes, by thinking about our reflexive memories of experiences which in reality were not reflexive, or the conscious experience of subjects in whom a differential consciousness of the self has not yet developed. The reflexive illusion is sometimes strengthened into an egocentric or "Bovary-esque" one, in which the subject becomes totally insular, taking itself for a particular ego in a particular central role, and becoming fixed in a particular objective identity. As this imposter does not lack accomplices, it is able to impress others in its chosen role. Nevertheless, its subjectivity is bewitched and enchanted by the quasi-substantial ego it has constructed. Not that this ego is incapable of entering into relations, but it does so on a secondary level. The relation only occurs after a delay caused by the intervention of a transcendent and transcendental self. Subjectivity is infiltrated by its own creature. And despite the fact that this is an acquired condition, it appears totally natural.

In its nonnarcissistic condition, on the other hand, subjectivity refuses to allow its being to be tied down by appearances. Or at least, its narcissism is minimized. The relationship between subjectivity and the self, instead of tending toward objectivization or a distinction between the transcedent self and consciousness as transcendental ego, initiates a process of identification through communication. This is a free, nonpersonal activity, which is practiced for its own sake and not subordinated to the ego; it is evanescent—an activity that, like Eurydice, vanishes at the first glance. It is not something to be spoken, but to be lived.

I believe that the narcissistic condition survives as a principle within the transcendental ego. That ego still fascinates us. Relations with others only come about through the ego. We oscillate between the negation of alterity and its elevation as an abstract value. The role of philosophical analysis (which here is the same as that of therapeutic analysis) is to allow the self to track down the effects of fascination or alienation through which the imposture of the ego comes about, so that effective communication with the other can be restored. More on this later.

Whatever the psychological mechanism that causes it, the autonomy of the self remains an illusion. But simply denouncing an illusory complex is not an adequate way of explaining the practical, tenacious, and perhaps even vital fiction that is the self. That fiction is doubtless also given further vitality by a final type of illusion that we have already encountered, which I have called the *speculative* illusion.[7] Coming along as it does to reinforce the others, it consists for the speaker in seeing him or herself in the same way that he or she sees the world. This is in fact a particularly unacceptable version of representationalism. First because subjectivity becomes preoccupied by its image and, closed in on itself, quickly turns egotistical. The unreality of its situation is compounded by an interior unreality, as a chosen solitude becomes one to be suffered. This egotistical concern with self-portrayal is, then, the "foolish project" in which Pascal accused Montaigne of being involved. His constant references to pictorial art confirm that we are still locked inside the circle of representation. Knowing oneself, for Montaigne, always means representing oneself—a concern that becomes a fascination. The face is drawn for us line by line, gradually built up feature by feature, so movingly that we almost feel we might die.

Remember Narcissus at his mirror, and his glance that wants to capture itself lovingly in its own eye. What eye can see itself? Narcissus cannot embrace and grasp himself, for there is only his image in the water, surrounded by other insignificant representations of branches and water lilies. Many people have commented on the episode.

"Hail, you child of my soul and of the waters," says Paul Valéry, most evocatively.[8] Notice that there is no event that cannot be reflected in the water, since here the event is the reflection itself. Nevertheless, it needs a very still observer, who takes great care not to disturb a mirror which is more mobile than fragile. The slightest breath would erase the desired and cherished image. An anxious delight for the poet:

> My tenderness comes there to drink
> And is intoxicated to see
> A desire try out its power
> Over myself.[9]

One of the paradoxes expressed in the beautiful fable of Narcissus is that his image is so close, yet it is inaccessible. It is a desperate fiction, and a cunning image. I shall not follow up the commentary by Alain, because what is most relevant here is the attempt itself, and the diversion of purpose it involves.

Narcissus does not look at himself in the mirror simply out of vanity and a desire to please by his appearance. He approaches the mirror in order to draw nearer to himself. His attention is immediately caught by aspects of his appearance, his shape and color, the way he bends forward and straightens up, a quick movement, a threatening glance—all the unchanging signs that individuals are constantly putting out, for others (as well as themselves) to recognize.[10] He is, for once, given over entirely to himself. Normally, I lack what you can see, this body exposed to the gaze of others, just as it appears. In one sense, these appearances are not a concealment. The image is indeed the expression of a similitude. Everything is brought together in the image, that deliciously fragile link between me and myself. It holds out the promise of an absolute singularity. It is the moment of seduction when I am alone with myself, an unhoped-for exception which I can hardly believe. . . . But already this presence to oneself begins to cling to its reflection. Even if it rekindles our fantasies, narcissistic symmetry serves to confirm the self-image.

Narcissus is that person in each of us who wants to see, for whom both himself and the world are representations. The person who loves to bend over this reflection of him or herself, his or her shape and movements, and even every thought, and reflect on them. He loves the living and natural image in which everything might, at last, be made visible. For Narcissus is not simply absorbed in self-contemplation; his image becomes the center of the world. As Gaston Bachelard points out, along with him is reflected the whole forest, and the sky that now becomes aware of its image. The universe is reflected and comes alive in Narcissus' soul; so true is it that for our imagination, nature is an extension of our fundamental narcissism. An image mediates, incarnates, presents reality because it acts as both a metaphor and a substitute for absence, the iconophile might add.[11] The human form, which is beautiful, is also an enigma; but here, draped in a veil of signs, it seems to have some unmistakable significance.

But what? *Quid vidi?* In vain we concentrate our attention on what it might be. Any attempt to know *I* through the self is condemned from the start, retorts the iconoclast. An image might seduce, but it can also turn you to stone. Make no mistake about it. This reflection asks only that you grow sleepy and do nothing. Narcissus is in each of us the person who falls asleep (*narke*). Our image fascinates us but leads us away from reality, precisely because it betrays a presence by taking its place. Narcissus, who delegates to the waters the task of contemplating that which exists, bends forward to see his visions. But his effort to reify the identity of the self can never be success-ful, because it is impossible to love oneself, or in other words, to join with oneself. If it were possible, the moment of embrace would be fatal.

Between death and himself, what gaze is his![12]

Already the image is beginning to turn to ice: the self-portrait is dead, killed by a mere disturbance. On the surface of the water, which is the true mate-rial medium of death,[13] can Narcissus not see what is perishable in him?

Even before the image solidifies, the portrait is also an interminable rep-resentation of a self lost in its own forest, whose meanderings remain in-scrutable. Or if one prefers to avoid spatial metaphors, let us say that the portrait is condemned to failure because it can never act here as a true repre-sentation of the self. The specular illusion is actually such that at the mo-ment when I represent myself as something other than me, in the foreign but proximate image of a reflection, I believe that it is me, myself, that I am seeing. Like the eye, which is foreign to its own gaze that seeks itself in the mirror, I identify myself with what I am not. Here, the eye astounds the gaze. Because by means of the mirror, the whole of seeing and the whole of what is seen can be seen as only a part. Let me give the paradox of Narcissus a fur-ther twist: *cur aliquid vidi* (why did I see something)?

If Narcissus is not permanently neurotic it is because, faced with the water that reflects his image, he "feels that his beauty continues, it is not finished, but needs finishing."[14] After all, even if I can never see myself in definitive form, I can hear myself. The immediate grasp of his being that is denied Nar-cissus might be given to the self which speaks-listens, and to the couple who form, in Valéry's term, a *bouchoreille* ("mouthear").[15] We are absent from everything we see, but do we not have a voice that produces meaning, through which we are not absent from everything we hear? As an elementary form of exchange, the voice that I emit and hear reveals to me that strange and essential property of being two in one. For the voice, which carries the vibrations of an immediately experienced presence, creates its own listener by arousing in us the desire to awaken a similar vibration in others. An inti-mate, a double form of touch.

Once more, how is the personal life of the voice, with its inflections that say so much, its carefully judged intonations, to be saved from the destruc-tive flux of time? Perhaps by fixing it and giving it a visible form. Let us now imagine that Narcissus, who is clearly most interested in himself, looks for another way of forging the mirror in which he has been unable to embrace himself, and decides to turn himself into a *scriptor*, using written words whose graphic characteristics can be worked on like the resonances of the voice. So he takes up his pen. At which point, the myth of Narcissus has returned to its origins as a particular discourse on subjectivity. Like all myths, it only survives because it has speech or writing as its cause. But is narcissistic self-indulgence any less vain for being transferred onto the productions of mind or hand? Montaigne, too, was concerned to do just that: "Finding myself totally unprovided and empty of other matter, I presented myself to myself for argument and subject."[16]

Words on the page have a singular power. On the page also, we can see ourselves, disappointing or more attractive. Thanks to the dual mediation of the voice and its inscription, Narcissus will be able to give himself a stable and simultaneous presence. This time he discovers the visible body, the clearly defined fragment, that he has given himself. What a step forward! Apparently, at least. But must I immediately disappoint biographers by suspecting that, unless they are very careful, this is only a way of combining the aporias of the project of painting oneself with those of the project of expressing oneself. And then redoubling them with a less overt type of defect, utterance in written form. But let us not go too fast.

The myth of Narcissus, like all myths, does not stand up to overprecise analysis. Let us now look into the "narrative" form of the illusion of self that creates autobiography. Imagine an author who takes up the challenge of composing a disturbing decoy-image of him or herself. This sort of experimental writing is now well known. It can easily be decomposed and its semantic mechanisms revealed. Our task is to understand how a fake naturalness can be engendered by a set of false confidences. For philosophical analysis, things are relatively clear. If the attempt to represent oneself is brought back to its first principle, it consists of reflecting speech. Reflecting it by the use of that part of language in action in which the utterer makes back-reference to herself through the fact that she is speaking, in an attempt to provide herself with a self-image. I should like to show that this is a complex and misleading operation. It is complex because, even when reduced to an absolute minimum of stylistic means in the work of an aware author, it requires at least two different things:

1. that she make use of the possibility opened up by different levels of language in order to reflect her being as speech. By which I mean that she will try to establish a theatrical continuity between her impressions, desires as they ebb and flow, love as it flowers, and all the remarkable events of her life as she experiences them in the depths of the self. And to which she will devote a secondary discourse;

2. that the author manipulate the mechanisms of utterance as a means of relating this secondary discourse to the subject of the utterance and her

memory. Even when that subject remains implicit, the reader can never forget it, for it cannot elude an injunction that derives directly from a textual convention. Autobiography depends on a permanent illusion of presence in the text according to which I represent myself by telling my story.

A distinction is normally made between the level of discourse, i.e. any utterance (written or spoken) that presupposes interlocutors, and the level of what Benveniste calls the *history*,[17] i. e. any narrative utterance (nowadays restricted to written language) in which, on the contrary, no one speaks, and the narration of past events is self-sufficient, requiring no narrator. A historian has no need to borrow the formal apparatus of discourse; he or she never says *I* or *you, here* or *now*. As if an event were only given as past by the occlusion of its narrator.

Autobiography is that very special kind of discourse that claims to be at one and the same time a discourse (i.e., a discursive utterance) and a history (i.e., a narrative utterance). Autobiography is a narrative of past events, which are simultaneously presented in themselves and related to a memory that speaks in the first person. Autobiography's founding project (and in a sense its all-or-nothing gamble) is that it will be able to reconcile a narrative text in which remarkable events are normally recounted in the past tense—without any narratorial presence—with a discursive text that makes deliberate use of the apparatus of utterance. Telling one's story means writing one's life. When I write my life, I must manage the feat of linking together the narrated moment, which is in a sense immemorial, and the now of my present memory. I must be able to associate the past time of the man who is the subject of the statement with the present time of utterance. But how can the two be linked without my running into a philosophical impasse? Is it even possible at all?

The autobiographer wants to *remember* himself, as Narcissus wants to *see* himself. One searches for himself in an image like someone who is absent; the other fabricates the fiction of his absence through his attempt to grasp himself by representing things that are absent because they belong to the past. As if he were nothing but memory.

On Self-Knowledge: The Artifact and the Gamble

Let us take one of these mirrors of ink as an example: Jules Vallès' story of his own childhood. It is certainly a narrative. Yet the present tense, the circumstantial adverbs associated with it, and a correlation of persons between *I* and *you* are found throughout. Let us look a little closer. It has been shown that the narrator uses four procedures in different combinations quite systematically.[18] In the first place, he uses the first-person narrative in such a way that the same pronoun *I* designates the adult and the child—in other words the subject of utterance and the subject of the statement—in the same speech segment: "I am six and my behind is all peeling." If we were to put back the adult's voice and restore the sentence to historical time, the result would be: "I was six and my behind was all peeling." Vallès' sentence is literally unsayable, in the same way as "I was born," which is actually an abbreviation of "I am told that I was born," and above all "I died," which is found in some autobiographies and is a sort of logical shortcut for "people will say I am dead. . . ." These are all concealed quotations of what someone else will say. They are an ultimate gamble that ends up revealing the illusion: I borrow the other person's discourse by self-indulgently pretending to be the other person. I see myself being born, and even dying—why not?

The second procedure is the use by the narrator of the narrative present. it allows the moment of utterance and the time of the statement to be superimposed. The third is a use of free indirect speech that organizes the superimposition of two statements by ellipsis. Finally, there are a number of features characteristic of oral language and second-degree narration. Autobiographies with a fictitious or anonymous narrator depend on an even more complicated system. But the convention, which amounts to a pact with the reader, is always that a person is remembering and trying to reconstitute his or her experience as faithfully as possible. A life. "My" history.

Manipulation of the apparatus of utterance implies the manipulation not only of the iterative agency (here is the life of an other who was me, here is me as an other would present me, if the other were me), but also, and often in a very sophisticated way, manipulation of time itself. Montage, ellipsis, suspense: time is always being composed. The finest example of this, a classic of its kind, is certainly Laurence Sterne's *Tristram Shandy.*[19]

From this point of view, autobiographers are like novelists telling stories: they cannot do without time. Temporality is connected to the operation of the narrative in the same way as it is to the structure of a piece of music. This is therefore one of the temporal arts. Time is completely at the disposal of autobiographers, right from the start. It is therefore not surprising that they should think of playing around with it. Sterne is one of the greatest manipulators of time.

Normally, the time attached to a narrative is double: there is one time that belongs to the narrator, the time when he or she writes, and another belonging to the story, the events being told, which are those of the life about which he or she is writing. The reader, and sometimes even the author, can remain unaware of this duality. That is not the case with Sterne, who is very careful to distinguish between the two, the better to mix them up afterward with consummate and pleasing art. We see him systematically organizing the temporal infrastructure of the narration and the temporal structure of the events narrated into a striking and complex pattern. By reference to a master-memory, which is always given in the first person, he brings emphatically together the objective time taken to write the story of his life and the fictional time taken up by the events it contains.

Another layer is immediately added to the fiction once we ask ourselves whether the author (Sterne) is distinct from the narrator (Tristram). Part of the writing process actually consists, on a higher level, in commenting on the operation by which the narrator who says "I" integrates these very structures, setting up the various incidents and digressions by which the narrative moves backward, forward, and sideways, slowly taking a situation and a group of characters through from the beginning to the end. In particular, the author subjects the ambiguity of memory to close scrutiny. Rousseau had already noticed how, by examining both his memory of an earlier impression and his present feelings, he could paint a double picture of his state of mind. The past of a remembered event is actually formed within memory itself. Curiously, its future is therefore formulated in the present of our memory, as we juggle now with past events and rearrange them into a pattern. A memory is in a sense something imminent, a hoped-for and elusive future event.

The humor of Sterne, autobiographer, quickly makes the reader an accomplice in his fiction. Instead of trying to conceal the liberties he is taking, he underlines them. At least the illusionist himself is under no illusions: "My uncle Toby, whom we have left all this while knocking out his pipe." The author deliberately allows the time of the event, which remains static, to get out of step with the time of writing, which moves forward. The utterer, Tristram who says "I," has permanent license to move backward or forward along the line of his story, and to abandon one character in order to go back and look for another. All he has to do is bring event-time to a halt, while diegetic time carries on. Thus Tristam remembers that he has left his mother hanging from some temporal nail, her ear glued to a crack in the door, imagining that her husband and brother-in-law are talking about her. . . . "In this attitude I am determined to let her stand for five minutes: till I bring up the affairs of the kitchen . . . to the same period." [20]

The narrative progresses while the narrator digresses. As the author observes: "My work is digressive and progressive at the same time."

The conventional aspect of the autobiographic pact is even more striking because it is, so to speak, summoned into the writer's present, at the moment when the pen, wet with ink, touches the paper, "this day when I write these lines, which is the ninth of March 1759." A little further on: "a most rainy day, the twenty-sixth of March 1759, between nine and ten in the morning." This insistent present is the point of communication with the reader, when the pact is renewed. For story-telling has an intersubjective dimension. In this imaginary encounter the reader is invited to bring about an imaginative synthesis of such temporal structures as these, in order to follow the story and not be fooled by the fiction. Sterne, by revealing the multiplicity of procedures by which the autobiographer reconstructs a sort of personal identity for himself, institutes the self as a "same as," but also lets the cat out of the bag by the very overabundance of procedures for doing so. Tristram will never have finished being born. We have reached the third book before he comes into the world, and the whole story does not even bring him up to the age of awareness. When it ends, his father is left at the tailor's, choosing his first pair of breeches for him.

The reader is invited to appreciate the humor, to manipulate autobiographical time with the narrator, and, no doubt with the author, to escape for a while from the anxiety of being caught up in time, by artfully recomposing the ruins of time past.

After reading Sterne, the philosopher will have no great merit in filling the gaps in the catalogue of procedures employed in the illusory quest for personal identity. My analysis has allowed the finger of suspicion to be pointed at precisely the place where the first person feels its legitimacy most strongly: at the heart of the autobiographic utterance. This is a privileged place in which to cast doubt on the myth of the full subject. By looking at the way it is formed, we can show that the autobiographic pact is a decidedly self-indulgent one. It gives the author a license by which to make himself exist in a text-narrative—a fiction which, by agreement with the reader, allows the construction of a phantom image.

But the philosopher, who does not necessarily share the author's reasons for agreeing to this pact, can be very much more aware of the artificiality of the process. Then, by denouncing the whole complex of illusions as a double or even triple trap held out for the reader to fall into (with the reader's complicity and assent), he can reveal its formula by analysis. Having pointed out the hidden secret of a fallacious approach, it remains for him to go back over its effects.

The effect achieved by autobiography's apparatus of utterance is clear enough. It matters little here whether the text is constituted simply as a subtle machination of the sort we have just observed—a simulation of utterance, based on temporal manipulation—for in the end the different pretenses accumulate to give us the fiction of a narrated life. This is the price to be paid for inscribing something of the subject into the narrative. Nor does it matter that this is a representation full of interruptions and fragments, whose claim to identity and consistency is indicated solely by the presence of a proper name (Tristram Shandy, Henry Brulard): the result is there all the same. This process of saying is really one of doing, but in such a way that it can be recounted. It is precisely a means of lending credibility to the fiction of a self which is the source of its own activities and the owner of its memories and states of mind—in short, a subject.

We write in order to find out what we are, and in order to write we pretend what we are to be. "Ah!" exclaimed Gide, "if only we could be what we imagine!" Now this fiction, which is beginning to be denounced in our time, was not always recognized as such. What we today can dismantle and regard as a manipulation of writing, motivated by the fantasy of making myself exist, was only yesterday carefully composed and assumed to be valid by the writer, according to a widespread conviction. The same conviction that attaches to philosophies of consciousness when they are incorrectly interpreted, according to which the ego may legitimately stand as both the subject and object of self-consciousness. In the golden age of representation, Pascal and Nicole were already denouncing the trap, and the Church condemned self-portraiture. It obliged the painters of the Renaissance to represent themselves *in figura*, i.e., in the guise of a religious character (for example, Dürer as the taunted Christ).[21]

Does this mean that people can never know themselves? I should not like to go that far. But self-knowledge does not derive from a reflexive turning-inward. That is the point. The self is probably not constituted in such a way that it can see or express itself. What business have I, who am present to myself from the very start, to want to reflect or represent myself, like some new Narcissus, in an image different from myself, as if I were absent from myself? What I need to do is *manifest* myself. This is of course not an auto-manifestation, for people only learn to know themselves after the long detour necessary for interpreting the signs they emit in communicational situations. My understanding of myself is always a mediate one. I can only understand myself through the signs and the works that I produce in the course of my relations with others. They are my real mirror.

But if self-knowledge is from the start an interpretation, it is no easier to achieve (far from it) than knowledge of others. And conversely, we have the same relationship to other people's thoughts as to our own. Since we are immediately in a relationship, the other person's thought and mine can only be grasped by differentiation from within a body of thought that we have worked on together. In a sense, when you have read an author you know everything about him or her. And so does the author. "This uncertain and floating self, this entity whose existence I myself have challenged," agrees Marguerite Yourcenar in her inaugural address to the Académie Française. "I feel that its boundaries are only really delineated by the few works that I have happened to write." Anybody has only to read an author to discover even the slightest tremor of his or her hand.

But the signs and works that I have to read are normally addressed to me in a relational situation by others. Literature *is* communication. It is a contemporaneous way of meeting others. They and I recognize ourselves differentially in it. For each of us it is the means, not of representing ourself, but of differentiating ourself on the basis of the words spoken and work done in the course of our human relationships. Self-knowledge comes only at the end of a wide detour; it is of the order of the interpretation of common signs rather than auto-representation.

This shows how strange it is for an author to decide deliberately to write about himself. For the situation is then quite different: he is giving us an image of himself, which he has deliberately recomposed, despite all the difficulties of such an artificial process. Montaigne was aware of this: "There is no description so difficult to write as one's own . . . ; therefore it is necessary to prepare and arrange oneself before going out: I constantly make myself ready, for I am constantly describing myself." [22]

In principle, this image is similar to one that other witnesses or biographers might give of the author, the only difference being that which separates autobiography from report by a third party or biography. [23] Whatever denials the author may make ("Reader, thou hast here an honest book. . . . I desire therein to be viewed as I appear in mine own genuine, simple and ordinary manner, without study or artifice"), [24] in fact there is always something about discourses on the self that sounds false before it can turn itself into a myth. Why? After all, Goya manages to draw his dreams, and invents both them and reality together. Why should the literary game end up producing only an aesthetic sham, an ascetic's fiction, a mere artifact?

Not that the pleasures of self-awareness are in any sense immoderate. After all, coming to oneself as it were from a distance, one can easily pose as a sage or a moralist. These natural infatuates are no translators of their own inner motives; they do not indiscreetly undress their soul or develop a self-indulgence that could easily turn into stupid sentimentality. No, for others can do that sort of thing with all the success of a good historian. I am writing my life-story, not my defense plea, insists the Gide of *Si le grain ne meurt.* Others again present themselves as lookouts lying in wait for their own thoughts. As Pliny puts it: "Each of us is a very good discipline for himself provided that he has the strength of character to observe himself closely." [25]

But the truth is that a certain discourse confers an ambiguous life on what we call the self. Whether you paint a picture of what you believe you are, without keeping to any logical order, or follow the thread of your experience, it comes down to exactly the same thing. Montaigne, whose work is of course full of contradictions, is the first to admit as much: "If the strangeness and novelty of my subject . . . do not save me, I shall never come off with honor from this foolish attempt."[26]

Subjectivity Made Imaginary: To What Does Sameness Owe Its Prestige?

Let us now consider the literary formula of the intimate journal, and the way in which in it what is true intersects with or covers up what is intimate. The journal is different from autobiography proper, but also from the Augustinian formula of the confession, in which believers constitute themselves before God because they feel that they are living in their creator's gaze: "Why, Lord, should I tell you all the details of these things?"[27]

A confession is also the story of a person, but before God. What, though, about the intimate journal? A few examples have come down to us which were written for public consumption. The main characteristic of the form is that the author uses it as a legitimate reason for doing less composing. This freedom is one of the great advantages of the journal: it legitimizes anecdote and trivial detail, or can at least tolerate them. Next, if some journals do indeed concern the self, the most interesting part (leaving aside the trivia, of which there is an enormous amount) is generally the nonintimate side, the moral pronouncements, sketches for works, chronicles of a particular world or of a few beloved individuals. The same is true of correspondences, though they are already less intimate because they are written with another person in mind. Even in the most famous, which are works in their own right, there are vast tracts of insignificance, of both thought and event: the story of a certain lost pullover in Gide, grog-drinking with the estate manager or the impertinence of a godchild in Amiel. There seem to be only two ways of avoiding this sort of insignificance: either by composing a pseudo-object called *me,* or by thinking about something other than myself, such as torture, the dangers of innovation in the political field, or lack of concern for death, in the case of Montaigne. In short, the insignificant and the intimate seem here to coincide: "If I eat too much, there are things I cannot do. I cover my legs and thighs no more in winter than in summer, I wear only a pair of simple silk stockings."[28]

Nobody is exempt from the risk of writing mere trivia. The unfortunate thing is to do so after much effort. As the years pass, we notice that we have forgotten many things that were unforgettable. We know, or rather feel, that they were sublime or full of charm. The memory of them, at once radiant and indistinct, remains. But what were they? Exactly what was said, accompanied by what gestures, what expressions? At times like that, we would give a lot to be able to say: I was there and such-and-such a thing happened. All we can do is recompose them.

The formulae of classical eloquence, which then passed into Renaissance rhetoric, made a considerable, if unacknowledged, contribution over a long period to discourses on individuality. It was to be expected that a philosophical machine would take over from the rhetorical one and complete the movement, so that it finally fell to the philosopher of consciousness to see the Cogito as the substrate of all objective representation, and to anchor our whole power of reflection in an ego in sole possession of its discourse, the sufficient subject of its own speech.

But even before philosophy made it reflexive, and then began to abuse it, discourse about the self was infinitely complex. Normally, it presents itself at one and the same time as descriptive, explanatory, and narrative. Whether it be autobiographical or learned in origin, the artifact that is the self is based on the same illusory presupposition: that it is possible to constitute a person by speaking about that person in what is ultimately a delocutive way. We think we are observing the workings of the heart, when what we are really doing is reconstructing them in a sophisticated, curious type of secondary discourse which is much less certain than the first.

Once a speaker starts to want to look into her own mind in order to speak about her self, noting its acts of daring, its intermittent absences and reversals, even if she has to test them out as she would an unknown person, she necessarily loses her status as a speaker, which made her somebody. When a speaker attempts to speak reflexively about herself, outside the allocutive register of discourse, she produces the illusion of something quite distinct. This illusion is dissipated when we remember that the self is essentially the inhabitant of its spoken words. That is the only straight recognition that the speaker can have of herself, and even then she risks falling prey to an illusory hegemony.

So the right question to ask is not: "how is it that I can say 'I am me'?" but: "how is it that this 'I' which I make mine when I speak up and say it in an interlocutive situation, can be made into *me* in the sequence of communications in which it claims to inhabit its speech?" We are no longer asking how I am able to establish myself as an operative subject, an autonomous consciousness, without mixing myself up with the different identificational images that others are forever holding up to me. For the subjectivist illusion would persist in such a liberated and pared-down ego. This illusion, which is based on ignorance, must be even more firmly eradicated by pushing our philosophical reflection and asceticism to even greater lengths.

Let me again stress that a speaker only inhabits the words he or she speaks if they are presently being addressed to *and* received by someone else. Forgetting one or both of these conditions will lead to paradoxical results. This limitation is most important. Only once it has been accepted does it become possible to credit the speaker with something like an individual voice. Following from this, certain novelists employed a convention of writing (which is in any case now outdated) to group a set of stylistic traits around a particular character, whom they were supposed to depict more accurately than would a deliberate description. In Dickens there are many examples of emblematic signs of this sort. It is true that every time someone speaks, that person uses language in his or her own way, and this usage can reveal clues about the speaker that are no less certain than his or her fingerprints. However, the theory of *idiolects* should still be reformulated to take adequate account of the convergent or divergent polyphony of intertwined voices that is found in any real speech process.

Self-Confession, and Self-Indulgence as an Art Form

The foolish project of painting one's own portrait, which Pascal denounced, has become a major literary undertaking, and one pursued with not a little ingenuity. It is now a writing performance to be cultivated for its own sake. But when the *I* thinks it can speak *itself* by putting out an image of what it is, when the *I* sees itself in the mirror of the other, the writer's proverbial vanity is redoubled. The writer grants him or herself permission to go straight to what interests him or her most, in the cynical service of self-importance.

What is of more direct interest to us in the present context is the way the balance is tipped in favor of the ego, and the mechanism by which this unjustifiable promotion, this *self-indulgence*, occurs. I choose the term carefully. It seems to me to operate by the patient perversion of the normal, transitive, and relational movement toward others, whose role it is (and not mine) to create for themselves an image of me. In the perspective of the present study, self-indulgence is a trap into which self-love can fall.

This is what it involves: the person preoccupied by appearances (and who is almost passionately committed to making a pleasing impression on others), usurps the point of view of a *him/her* or a *you* while affecting to remain an *I*. A different *I* who nevertheless resembles the real one like a sibling. The self-indulgent person is vain and presumptuous in his or her pretense.

How can we redefine what Valéry called "this self-indulgence in the soul when it loves itself," in terms both of its principles and of the methods it employs? Its mainspring is self-esteem. It attains its goal by manipulating the apparatus of utterance. Thus we find at work in autobiography some of the same procedures as in the ritual of self-confession. They provide indirect confirmation of the relational condition of the self. Self-indulgence too is obliged to bring about a mapping of the three positions in the communicational act. Only in this case the mapping is simulated. The fact that such a simulation can be deliberate, and regarded as a work of art, makes no difference: by submitting to the techniques of self-avowal, the autobiographer adds a fiction to a certain type of communicational distortion. The mapping which he or she achieves as a result is misleading because it is illusory. Must it always be so, in every sort of autobiography? That remains to be seen.

One thing is sure: the project of self-representation by reproducing oneself in a narrative text invites complacency, for that is an easy and readily available solution. An autobiographer cannot grasp his or her own image in the gaze of a real other—for which other should be chosen, and why? Each different person provides me with a different image of myself. One possible solution for the narrator is to stick closely to him or herself and, like Narcissus, look into his or her own reflection. It is a simple strategy, and one which only needed to be thought of to be pursued: the autobiographer will short-circuit the search for an image by offering him or herself as a subject to be read.

Such a person will then take all the things he or she could never confess to anybody and make them into a book. The self as individual will now recognize desires, dreams, thoughts, illnesses, or moments of unhappiness as belonging to it. There is a large measure of playacting in all this. The author will mention the rule that he or she claims to have transgressed, and sometimes even invent it, on the fictitious basis of *confessing* what he or she is and has done, and remembers. He or she will also be guided by an obsession with concealment: how to hide his or her faults, weaknesses, loves, and hates, and the thoughts that go with them, the modulations that have come to inhabit him or her.

But confession implies having someone to whom to confess and expose oneself. Here too there is self-indulgence. First, on the part of the narrator. The moralists have so often stressed our inward duplicity, and even the pleasure we can take in blackening ourselves, that there is no need to go back over the same ground here. Literary confession involves playing one's own part, becoming a little more sensitive to and intimate with oneself, a little more lively than usual, a little blacker or purer. Thus Rousseau, who wants to show to his fellow citizens a man in all the truth of his nature, retouches that truth when he speaks in terms of pure love about a day which was really entirely colored by a rather suspicious sensuality. Second, a complacency is inspired in the reader, who can be flattered, buttered up, made proud of his or her role, by being persuaded that he or she is being let into a secret. At which point, the narrator has achieved his aim: he can now catch the marveling or interested glance of this fictitious other, whom he imagines speaking to or about him, and compose a countenance for himself from that person's point of view. And the reader, who is invited to identify with him, will be seduced, as Narcissus attempts to seduce himself.

Thus the life of the narrator is written with the complicity of the reader. We are led to believe that Tristram's life is that of Sterne, Brulard's that of Beyle. "I seek to relate with clarity and truth what is going on in my heart," writes Stendhal to Balzac. This is sincerity of a kind. An actor's sincerity. There he is, entirely as he would have liked to be, and be seen to be. This is Stendhal liberated, with a Stendhalian lifestyle.

It is clear that this is not the way for subjectivity to authenticate itself. Nothing is more disingenuous than to pretend to be natural and true to reality. The literary confession of one's self is a highly sophisticated discursive technique, which has long been prized as such, for setting up a fiction, not for producing the truth about oneself. We saw a while ago that it requires both the manipulation of time and the control of utterance, by means of which the person becomes a mask and creates a character for him or herself: the *I* becomes a pseudonym. The things to be confessed may be simple, bizarre, exalting, or shameful, but they will always have been selected. It is necessary to constitute for them a conscious subject which, constantly expected, becomes more and more clearly drawn and perfects itself. An invented character suddenly rises up, which we imperceptibly manage to take as a model for ourselves. Is it not amusing to pretend to be "as real as real. and quite original," to pretend to the point of utter naturalness? Nothing is more complicated. It takes all the writer's artistry to substitute what he or she is constructing for what he or she is. And patience, imagination, and insolence too, in order to make oneself that bit more natural than nature.

"Since my face has been turned toward sorrow, for that reason which has led me to it, I spur on my moods from that side, which nourish themselves on it and become exasperated at their own movement."[29] Yet this movement is much more obvious in Gide or Stendhal than in Montaigne. The artist's work feeds directly on self-indulgence, which takes a rather infantile stance. For in the end, I want others to rejoice . . . in me, as the child wants its mother to rejoice in it, in everything that it is and does. So I confess my self-love and I am sincere? Surely not! In the works of those professional sincerity-mongers

Rousseau, Chateaubriand, and Stendhal, it is self-love that complacently confesses itself. Self-love and idolatry are the source of confession, rather than its objects. In the autobiographical attitude in general, there is an overwhelming motive of self-indulgence. It is unavoidable: as if because of a bad conscience, the writer once more must pay homage to his or her own sincerity, and make it into a virtue: "I am setting out on an undertaking the like of which has never been seen before. . . ." Once more, the author is taking center stage and striking a pose, dressed in all his or her ceremonial egotism.

Ultimately, the process of dissimulation ends up becoming quite candid. Rousseau, for instance, affects to ask how, if he were someone else, he might regard a man such as himself. But his gaze would then of course be a complacent one, the twin of that gaze by which he narcissistically constitutes a phantom self. As when one listens to the sound of one's own voice or watches oneself dancing, the writer reads ahead in what he or she is writing, with the delighted or scandalized gaze that he or she ascribes to the reader. What we have here is a multiple illusion, a manipulated, unreal, fantasy self-image.

So it is true that Madame Bovary is Flaubert, and Balzac Madame de Mortsauf? Not exactly. How could we say that both Jacques and Antoine Thibaud are Roger Martin du Gard? Or if not both, which one? We would once more have to ask whether the portrait were a faithful one or not. Apart from the fact that it does not matter whether an illusion is or is not a good likeness, it is clear that this is not what is important in autobiography. It is a process of self-seduction rather than a project for the information of others. Here, self-love is everything that it can be. The really important thing, as can be seen from the etymology of the word, is to write one's own life. That is the true work—the true cunning—of writing.

Could there conceivably be a different sort of autobiography, which would not be tarnished by self-indulgence? Let me lay down a few negative conditions. The whole concept would need to be turned upside down, with a radically different artistic formula and quite different motives. What would abandoning the complacency principle actually mean? It would mean that the reason for self-scrutiny was no longer to edify [30] or justify [31] oneself, nor to linger in the golden rays of childhood or the high-walled enclaves of the past, nor to look back on memories touching or violent, in the fond conviction that one's experiences will be useful to others. [32] Nor would it be sufficient any more to regard autobiography as a means of finding one's direction, with some morose enjoyment, in a confused world, [33] and still less of accumulating credit and reputation for purely commercial ends. Such concerns contain a considerable element of masquerade, for they show us wearing a mask to indicate what we are, so that others will not mistake us. This is perhaps particularly true for those who wish to use writing as a way of constructing themselves, of making self-inscription into a form of being, in order finally to find out what they were.[34]

In all fairness, few major autobiographies are entirely dependent on the complacency principle. There is almost always some humor (as in Sterne) or irony (as in Joyce) that signals the fictitious aspect of the arrangement and distances the author from the conventions. How could it be otherwise? In fact, even a work of fiction cannot be a complete sham. The writer, whether prophet or outcast, often sets out to write a pious work, addressing the reader as someone cut off from society, in order to justify him or herself and plead for reintegration into the community. These are his or her credentials, proof of common humanity, canonical vocation, and exceptional destiny.

It is too soon to explain in detail how a totally different conception of autobiography might come about, and how one's personal identity might be preserved differently. This would no longer be according to a complacency principle elevated to the status of an art form, but in the plenitude of the communicational principle, i.e., with no manipulation or misrepresentation. It would mean taking the longest way around, through encounters and separations, the circuit of effective relations in which it is my lot to become involved, and in respect to which I am anxious to orient myself. It is clear that memoirs of this type would no longer be "inward," that they would be anti-memoirs in a new sense, in which the confession of the *self* would be replaced by that of the *person*. But more of that later.

The Vanity of Absolute Difference

> One's first impulse is to withdraw into oneself, where
> one finds nothing but words.
> —ALAIN

Hegel believed that in each of us there resides some absolute difference, which can be objectivized as such. For my part, I have rejected superficial logic in an attempt to break with the commonly held idea that a person is a pole of individual qualities, or even a unified center of choice and action. This means that the person is no longer a self, the center of whose existence is rooted in a sovereign power of thought. Instead of an *I* that realizes itself through reflection and likes to objectivize its essential difference, what have we found? A writer, a fake Orpheus, erecting an image of him or herself in the mirror of a fictitious other of his or her own invention; an autobiographer prepared to manipulate the apparatus of utterance in an attempt to establish his or her absolute difference.

The idea of an absolute difference of the self, in which the ego shows itself for what it is, does, remembers, etc., is—to say the least—unclear. But it is deeply tempting. Absolute difference, when reflected in all its particularity in a literary work, seduces the reader. By which I mean that it first attracts, then holds spellbound. As in any seduction, it captivates and then captures. How marvelous to be different! This is the whole mechanism of seduction: it makes us attached to what is exceptional, or at least *individual*. For individuality is, in ancient logic, that which differs, that whose essence is to differ, to the point of being refractory as a matter of principle to conceptuality and language. A person who seeks from the start, by inclination or whim, to be "as different from other people as possible," is an egoist. But to seduce is to lead away from the truth. The author calculates that the reader will be dazzled by the unique figure she has erected for him in its absolute difference. And she herself will live with the fond illusion of being someone apart from the rest, someone exceptionally privileged to be who she is, anything but a common being.

Where does this powerful urge to be unique come from? Valéry puts forward the hypothesis that our terror of death produces from within its shadows some frantic wish to be different from everyone else. Perhaps. I note simply that it comes from a disastrous confusion between individual and personal difference. In which case, we refuse to be like others in the same way that we refuse to accept that others are people like ourselves.

We see here the exact opposite of that exaggerated respect for the absolute alterity of others which is found in the work of certain philosophers. For its part, the eros of the Romantics, taking a deliberately wayward view of the relational nature of love, aimed to reach the very center of sameness in its most concrete, immediate, and essential particularity. For the Romantics, to say *you* was therefore to designate the intimate truth of the loved one in his or her absolute difference.

The fictitious, artificial, desperate aspect of the autobiographical gamble no doubt derives from the need to interest the reader. This is something of which the author is not necessarily aware. The condition of many writers is constant loneliness, with the result that they project themselves into all their characters, thereby remaining self-preoccupied the whole time. They can say with Conrad's Marlowe: "Are not our lives too short for that complete formulation which, through all our stammerings, remains no doubt our sole and constant aim? . . . We never have time to speak our last word, the last word of our love, desire, faith, remorse, submission or revolt." [35]

The literary person is likely to claim that he or she is constantly moving outside him or herself. "Through the generous gift of imagination he breaks down the walls of loneliness that surround others on the outside, and separate them on the inside from their deep being." He accepts that he has less made his book than it has made him. But always remaining aware of bearing sympathetic witness and bringing "vicarious self-knowledge to those who have not learned to know themselves."

Such is the fine myth of putting oneself in the other person's place, a myth that can cast its spell over us too. The metaphor is certainly an admirable one. In fact, though, it is impossible to do this: we can only exist in *relations* with others. The paradoxical tragedy of the mirrors of ink about which Borges writes is that there is really nothing for them to reveal or hide, nothing to reflect. "My heart laid bare" (Baudelaire): try living up to the promise of a title like that! Yet the literary reality, the art of intimate evaluation and triumph in defeat, remains, along with the vast range of stylistic formulae for evoking the unrepresentable and the unsayable. Narcissus, unable to seize and embrace himself, bypasses the mirror and tries to "paint his own heart by attributing it to someone else." The pictorial metaphors employed by those gripped by a complacent desire to paint themselves tell the same story: Joyce writes his portrait "as a young man," Dylan Thomas his "as a young dog," and Michel Butor pictures himself as a young monkey.

Does an author who paints him or herself actually want to be seen? In fact, the reader is excluded and simultaneously called upon to act as a witness.[36] When a writer solicits the attention of fellow human beings, he or she does so the better to cultivate his or her absolute difference, the inimitable flavor of what it feels like to be him or herself and nobody else.

Should the writer end up presenting only the writer's procedures or asceticism, he or she will still not have wasted time for all that. The best part in the life of a writer would not be the story of his or her adventures or misadventures, but rather the story of his or her style. After all, the most important thing in *The Man with the Broken Ear* is not what it reveals about Vincent Van Gogh, but what it teaches us about his art. Thus any portrait *by* an artist already bears a likeness to him or her. Indeed, what could his actual self-portrait have to add? Paul Valéry, the most personal of poets, was convinced that inspiration is not the state in which the poet writes, but the state in which he or she hopes to put the reader.

The way in which the autobiographer erects the verbal artifact remains interesting. It is far from being the only conceivable way of weaving the threads of our lives together with certain selected discursive tools. Standing halfway between fiction and history, the author presents him or herself as the chronicler of his or her self, a monadic self that is gradually revealed in its qualitites and "declares itself," like Pierre Corneille's Camille. Our conception of subjectivity no longer needs to conform to any single stage in its long cultural history. But it does seem that subjectivity exists only when inscribed in a certain discourse of the self. Its history merges with the history of such discourses. This history follows the different types of self-confession and literary fashions. Generally, imagination and fantasy are put to work to perform the illusory reification of the self's identity, in the course of which reflections and the subjectivity effect take on an artificial solidity.

Whether it be presented as a desperate gamble or a high moral duty, the negative lesson autobiography teaches us is that a certain form of subjectivity can be constructed artificially in particular ways. Autobiographers think they are recounting a person by reproducing that person in accordance with the fiction that his or hers is a real story, one determined by the archives of the self—whereas the autobiographer's true mode of narrative is that of fiction. In any case, we shall now no longer confuse the identity of the self with personal identity, which is the heart of the subject.

5   The Heart of the Subject

The soul engenders the Word; but mediating love unites
them to each other and joins itself to them as a third.
—SAINT AUGUSTINE
De Trinitate

I HAVE explained the logical reasons why attempts to constitute the self as something fundamental and autonomous can never be
successful. And the linguistic reasons why the fiction of the self's literary
confession cannot be established without manipulating the apparatus of utterance. It is a remarkable fact that it is no more possible to accept a self that
is known as an object in the world than it is a self that sits behind consciousness as a knowing subject. The result is that we have begun to situate the
self, which the whole Cartesian tradition has always regarded as an extralinguistic reality, within discourse. This has led us to reformulate the lessons
of the Cogito, and to reevaluate its certitudes.

Referring to someone in his or her status as a person is quite different
from referring to a thing; the logico-semantic difference is quite irreducible.
Moreover, reference to persons implies a correlative aspect of complementarity and interchangeability between *I* and *you* which does away with the
ego's privileges over the *alter*. Let me repeat that the interlocutive relation is
primary.

Let us therefore accept in principle that it is our response to the interlocutive relation, and to the whole symbolic universe it creates, that gives rise to the effects of subjectivity—effects which will be more weakly or strongly felt according to the vicissitudes of communication. The outcome of the process of personification of the self can even seem quite random. It depends very heavily on our daily interdiscursive praxis, which either does or does not give us an opportunity to close up the cracks in our personal identity and treat the constantly open wound in its side. Nevertheless, it is not exceptional for people to feel a certain inward confidence. It is therefore important to look again at the question of subjectivity and formulate it in a more advanced way: if subjectivity is like this, who and what am I? What might be the origin of my certainty as a subject, and particularly as a subject of discourse?

Reformulating the Lessons of the Cogito

Of course, once my self (and yours) is established by and through our relationship, we immediately lose one useful convenience: there is no longer any question of believing in a self which, like the traditional subject, acts as the conscious medium of its own operations. Equally, we must abandon any idea of a self which—like the phenomenological subject—stands, on the basis of its intentionality, as the source of meaning. This second subject gradually emerged from the first, differentiating itself by a succession of small touches but without calling into question its most fundamental aspect: the ego as an autonomous term, to which relations could be imputed in a secondary manner. To suggest, as I have done, that the self gradually establishes itself through its relationships is to deny that it can ever relate to reality as an isolated subject, or designate reality by means of signs—unless, that is, it is able to communicate, at least with itself. Our problem then consists in understanding how the self comes to acquire an identity as such, through its ability to enter into and maintain relationships with others. As Montaigne said, "The most fruitful and natural exercise of the mind, in my opinion, is conversation; I find the use of it more sweet than that of any other action of life; and for that reason it is that, if I were now compelled to choose, I should sooner, I think, consent to lose my sight, than my hearing and speech."[1]

Descartes read Montaigne. Therefore, it is by returning to the author whom Descartes called "incomparable author of the Art of conversation" that I shall try to define that fundamental ability, which belongs to the true concept of subjectivity rather than to what is generally referred to as the Cartesian tradition. As soon as we admit that the speaking subject owes a debt to the other person, with whom it is in a relationship from the start, it becomes divided in such a way that the ego can no longer be located in a simple act of reflection.

The whole Cartesian tradition sets the stage for the representation of the ego, with its three poles: the self as *res cogitans*, its specular relationship to things, and the idea through which a thing becomes represented in thought. It is impossible to overemphasize the point that the fictitious model that sees thought as something which can be aware of itself contains not one but two extravagant assumptions. The first is that thought could be at once independent, capable of reflecting on itself, and disseminated through all the atoms of consciousness that are our ideas. The second is the notion that these ideas are the bearers both of their content and of the light in which they are seen. Ideas of this sort would be self-sufficient, with words—whether they mark the ideas directly or symbolize them for the secondary purpose of communication—acting only as their external accompaniment. This supposition— that there might be ideas able to maintain themselves in complete isolation, enclosed in their own spiritual substantiality, because they are things themselves insofar as they are present to the mind, things in the interiority of one's thoughts—seems unbelievable to us today.

Such suppositions go hand in hand with the metaphysical myth of the total presence of thought to itself. They stand or fall together. In abandoning the way of ideas for the way of words, I am proposing that we look resolutely in a quite different direction: instead of asking by what ability we are able to act alternately as the subject and the object of discourse, in accordance with the traditional view of self-consciousness, I shall rather be looking at the speaking subject's powerful ability to exchange roles with his or her listener. Now, this ability to take over from one another and so ensure that the message is adequate to its interlocutive context contains an element of that pragmatic competence which is of most immediate interest to us. Because it proves a fundamental indicator of the extent to which the interlocutive relation is rooted in the speaking subject.

At this point, the different personal positions begin to emerge simply as the poles, or agents, of a communicative interaction. Before examining the precise status of this "pragmatic competence," I would like to justify the thesis that pragmatic competence extends beyond self-consciousness, without nullifying it, but preserving and integrating its philosophical virtues.

Let me state quite polemically that, once reduced to itself, the *pour soi* relation is a rather poor one. I suspect that the mind's pure presence for itself is a somewhat fragile by-product of another much more complex activity— in short, it is a secondary abstraction combined with a distortion. How, then, can it be accounted for? In the manner I have just proposed: not by substituting something else for it, but by integrating it. This is by no means an impossibility.

Classically, self-consciousness is able to take itself as its own object. Consciousness is above all awareness of a living self. The life of the self means being originally affected not by something else but by oneself, experiencing oneself speaking, listening to oneself, and throughout this test, being what the self is. The self as living consciousness is monadic as a matter of principle. Everything that is alive has its own ipseity of being, the ipseity of consciousness. And I propose to call autism the state of intoxication into which consciousness can fall when it is bewitched by discovering itself, and still drunk from that recent discovery.

In the classical model of self-consciousness, our self is represented before the *I* as an *it*, with different modes of exposure to consciousness; for there is nothing to prevent that I from reflecting itself in its own pure gaze.[2] There is a striking absence of reciprocity between the I and its object. Even when consciousness is described in terms of an address, e.g., "you tremble, carcass" (Turennes, quoted by Nietzsche),[3] it is seen as a superior subjective agency addressing an inferior objective one. As soon as the first says "you" to the second, this other becomes an object for the "I."

The main thing here is not the confusion between consciousness and reflection—a mistake which, incidentally, Descartes does not make, for he defines thought in terms of immediate consciousness. Thought implies an idea that is not additional to it, but that is one of its forms. Through our immediate perception of that idea, we are made conscious of the thought.[4] Only, when Descartes enumerates the different modes of thinking, he puts doubt at the head of the list. Now it is always possible for doubt to be reflected in immediate consciousness. As the paradigm of all thought, doubt therefore explains the immediate unity of a movement and its reflection, a presentation and its representation for the self.[5] The reflecting and the reflected consciousness are indissolubly linked.

It nevertheless remains true that what I am told by my reflecting consciousness concerns the reflected consciousness, which it takes as its object. The consciousness which declares "I think" is not the one that thinks: what the reflecting consciousness establishes by a thetic act is not exactly *its* thought.[6] In which case, the reflecting consciousness of self remains a relation without reciprocity, a relation with two poles: the meditating subject can never be to the object what the object is to the subject.

Making a Relationship with Oneself

The reason that idea seems to me to be most incomplete is that I believe that this examination of consciousness is just one trope isolated from a much richer spiritual exercise. To be mistaken about oneself is in a sense to know oneself. When I meditate, I enter into communication with myself. On two conditions.

1. First, we cannot think outside language, and the language in which we think is necessarily the language in which we communicate. Thinking alone means speaking to oneself as though to a second self. And thought then becomes both an opening toward the other and a diffusion of the exteriority that constitutes the sign. There is actually a logical relation, and not just a question of habituation, between the ability to think and the ability to speak; and again, there is a logical relation, and not just an empirical link, between the ability to speak and the ability to communicate. At which point, thought can no longer be identified with what is given to an individual consciousness. Thinking is not a question of stringing together representations or ideas present to the consciousness of the individual, nor even of associating words with them. It involves operating in a virtual way within a communicational field. If thinking, understanding, wanting, and saying are mental processes, they are so not in the sense of being occult and private events immediately present to the self's consciousness. As Wittgenstein warned, they all depend much more than we tend to think on mastery of the public language games we play with each other. As soon as consciousness of self turns into the exercise of thought, albeit solitary, it becomes the mode of communication of self with self—then of self with other.

2. Communicating with oneself is not initially a matter of reflecting the self, but of making a relationship with it. A richer relationship, since it involves three poles rather than two: the self constitutes itself as an *it* which can stand before the inward *you*. So that this is genuinely a triadic relation. Let us then see where this leads us. First, the remarkable fact of making a relationship with oneself is enough to endanger the famous subject/object correlation and its unconditional primacy. For the reflexive awareness of self can never be a special mode of relating to it, as if I were in some way an object to myself.

Next, this is not just a conversation with the self, over and over again. It is only possible to communicate with oneself so long as a division—and sometimes a functional opposition—is created, such that a reciprocity arises between the self that has thoughts and a self to which we attribute thoughts: this reciprocity implies, of course, that their roles can also be reversed.

Far from isolating people, what is referred to as consciousness of self in fact marks a return to communication with oneself. Even to the point that there is no longer any dichotomy between relations with oneself and those with others. Quite the reverse. For example, it quite possible to reread the first two *Meditations* of Descartes in such a way as to reestablish a relational structure of this type within the Cogito. People often ask whether the Cogito is intuition or deductive inference. In fact it is utterance first and foremost, dependent on a logic of first-person utterance. And I believe that if Descartes did not cast doubt on language, it was out of neither forgetfulness nor negligence. The Cogito, inseparable from thought, resides in that Archimedean point at which doubt stops. It matters little whether or not Descartes realized the fact: if language cannot be questioned, it is because the Cogito is irremediably bound up with language, and language is present at the heart of the Cogito.

Equally, the mediation process leading to it operates as a sort of dialogue with a character the ego sets up before it, an evil genie, a deceptive partner, a kind of internalized other.[7] "I think" implies an "I say to myself," which in turn implies an "I say to you."

In this respect, it is interesting to note in the Second Meditation the remarkable role played by self-persuasion in actualizing radical doubt, which leads to the first certainty: *ego sum.* "I persuaded myself," writes Descartes, "that there was nothing at all in the world. . . ." *Sibi persuadere* seems to be a privileged option in relation to *aliis persuadere.*

"First of all, in the *Meditations,* I will set out the very thoughts which have enabled me, in my view, to arrive at a certain and evident knowledge of the truth, so that I can find out whether the same arguments which have convinced me will enable me to persuade others. Next, I will reply to the objections of men of outstanding intellect and intelligence. . . ."[8] And when the evil genie makes way for that more consistent other which is positive infinity, the certainty of the Cogito is placed in the consciousness of the ego by God, i.e.—and let me stress this point—by alterity. It is certainly not easy to found a philosophy of human autonomy on the Cartesian Cogito. Descartes is not the heroic defender of solitary thought.

Apart from the fact that the ego arrives at the idea of infinity through the alterity which it accepts into itself, it also depends on others for its concept of affirmation, for it cannot say "yes" without them. For Descartes, the most specific act of my subjectivity is a confession of inadequacy: "yes, I doubt." From it proceeds the "I think," in which I find the revelation of my heterogeneity. The certainty of my own existence only just wins out over my doubts about it. Let me therefore conclude emphatically that the Cartesian movement from doubt to certainty, far from operating simply within the spontaneity of the ego, in fact reveals its underlying heteronymy.

Can we follow the Cartesian model to its ultimate conclusions? Descartes only establishes the constitutive finiteness of the ego by showing that it has dealings with an infinite alterity. Whereas in my own perspective, I prefer to conclude that it is the communicational relationship with the finite alterity of others that must be regarded as absolutely basic. Furthermore, my intention here is to put forward an important generalization. For it is impossible to make self-consciousness into a simple specification for the process of communicating with oneself.

Take Lewis Carroll, for instance, whose Alice is constantly acting as her own interlocutor. As the author explains, she enjoyed "pretending to be two people." One of these two is of course the subject, and the other could, if you like, be the object. But above all, one gives and the other takes orders, one is the aggressor and the other the aggressed; one scolds like an adult, while the other is scolded like a child. We persuade, question, contradict and, of course, deceive ourselves, and these are exactly the same relations that we have with others. In fact, how could we expect to invent others, just for ourselves? If Alice is her own privileged interlocutor, she is not her own first interlocutor. Note that she starts to play at being an adult telling off a child: "Come now, it's no use crying like that, I advise you to stop at once." The same linguistic forms that are used to ask questions allow me to express my deliberations with myself, as well as my momentary objections.

Why the Concepts of Consciousness and Reflection Are Derivative

There is certainly nothing there that stands in the way of the empirical reality of solitary thought. But it does make much less self-evident the principle that there is an irreducible difference between verbally proffered discourse and discourse of the silent mental type. The distinction between thought and language seems quite marginal; in any case, it is no longer the distinction between a private performance and a public one. In my view, it can be subsumed into the pragmatic interplay underlying all effective communication, with oneself or with others, the systole and diastole without which true communication could not continue. Propositions that we keep to ourselves are lost, but equally, those that we do not adopt from others blow away on the breeze. In short, these are two cycles, of which one anticipates or extends the other.

I see these as two tightly interdependent moments in the communicational process. If their solidarity were broken, it would be enough to denature and compromise the whole communication process. No one who shuts him or herself away and communicates only with him or herself can remain sound in mind, or perhaps even survive, for that type of communication is clearly derivative. There can be no effective communication without the presence of at least one other person. Even then, we must be in a relationship with that person, if only so that we can know how our messages are actually received (otherwise we would not even know that they had been received). Madness begins when someone talks to him or herself and excludes the presence of others, or when the only others he or she recognizes are internalized ones. There are many cases in psychopathology in which voices speak and reply to each other without there being any real conversation. It is therefore the participation of two agencies of utterance in the dynamic process of meaning creation that conditions a priori the very possibility of meaning. A discursive agency loses all meaning if the *I* and *you* are not present and speaking together in a relationship. In the absence of the dialogue structure that should characterize any utterance, words cease to be the dynamic environment in which the communal pooling of sense and reference occurs; the words become simply inert. There is some debate about whether pathologies of this sort are monological, or involve sui generis interpersonal procedures. Of one thing I am sure: they all involve a fictive alterity in which the other is no more than an *image* of the other.

From my point of view, if there can be no consciousness of self without communication with oneself, the concepts of consciousness and reflection will have to be defined in a new way. At issue here is the status of reflection: can it in some way be derived from the primacy of relations, or does the notion of a relation presuppose a reflecting ego?[9] In my view, reflection marks a return to communication with the self. It is a momentary return, either between two conversations with others, or between all previous conversations and the one that is about to start, or between an interlocutor who is merely possible and the self whom I presently identify myself to be. This type of reflection which follows communication should not be confused with the pernicious possibility that the centrifugal movement will twist back and reflect on itself before communication takes place. The first type of reflection is doubtless the cause of humankind's greatness, while the second is responsible for its misery. I know well enough that the two themes have often been linked, from Pascal to La Rochefoucauld, but they are in fact quite different. The fact that they are mixed up is the fault of philosophies of consciousness; fortunately, the communicational approach allows them to be dissociated.

Consciousness is not of primary importance for subjectivity. Apart from the fact that subjectivity clearly has an unconscious side,[10] I have shown that consciousness is secondary in relation to communication for two reasons. In the first place, it connotes mental processes likely to lead to verbalization in the process of communication of the self with itself. Next, only certain aspects of human communication are accessible to the consciousness of those involved. Reflection is a sort of re-folding and re-flexion of communication, when an utterer sets out to recycle a moment of conversation into his or her discourse with the self. Therefore, it is not something that isolates people from each other. Quite the opposite; it designates the center in which all the conclusions from past communications can be respoken between the self and itself. Conceived of in this way, there is nothing to prevent the environment in which personal identity is maintained, and in which plural relations with others and the world are integrated, from being called "consciousness."

The Second Experience of the Spirit

The concept of consciousness cannot be reevaluated without our coming to some definite conclusions about the positive significance of solitude. Solitude has its victims, but also its heroes. Robinson Crusoe is both. Solitude can be put to good use. Not the vertiginous depths of solitude, which flourish on the myth of interiority and are given the same privileges, the solitude of Sadian desire which breaks all bounds; for solitude can be a bad counselor; a person alone is not in good company. Nor the solitude which oppresses, kills, or drives people mad, the solitude of the marginal individual or social outcast. Let us also leave aside monadic and prurient isolationism, the appetite for egotistical delectation, which is an existential impasse of the sort that we sense when reading Stendhal. That involves shutting oneself up in the bad solitude of self-identity, a solitude that does not even recognize itself as such.

The case of Henri Frédéric Amiel, who is more subtle, seems to pose a problem. His excellence doubtless derives from his perseverance in articulating the subjective life and formulating its infinite metamorphoses, the long murmur of mental activity which in man goes on ceaselessly right up to death. Montaigne before him had devoted himself to the same task with a delight and application that are well known: "It is a thorny undertaking, to follow such a wayward motion as our mind has, and penetrate the opaque depths of its internal folds, to choose and fix so many small airs from amongst its agitations; it is a new and extraordinary amusement." [11]

Of True Solitude

Amiel is more somber, and doubtless more lucid. The unfortunate thing about this accountant of the self is that he is perpetually holding himself in readiness, in reserve; his life is, in short, nonrelative: "I tried to erase my subjective life from within me, but only succeeded in deceiving myself and repressing it." [12] Particularly as he knows what it is that he is missing. He feels nostalgia for a forgotten life. He is assailed by a sad and painful feeling, a regret that will not go away: "I can only accomplish my vocation through others, I can only be myself through them, and this inevitable dependency which I cannot do without, this invincible need which I cannot satisfy, hold me immobile, neutralize and *annul* me." [13]

He is at an impasse. Any disappointment in relations with others becomes a disappointment about the self. I am not what I ought to be, I am unable to accomplish my destiny. Is this solitude? No, it is a lack of self-accomplishment. This cruel lucidity is what gives Amiel his somber greatness. In his *Journal* he set out to dispel the egotistical illusion that it was possible to explore his own nature in depth on his own: "In short, for months now, and almost for years, I have wanted nothing and been no more than a darkened room, in which I amuse myself by watching what goes on both inside and outside myself." [14] There certainly seems to be a laborious way of being nothing which involves being everything: "I have dissipated my individuality so as to have nothing to defend; I have plunged myself in anonymity so as to have no responsibilities; I have sought my liberty in a state of nullity." [15]

Therefore, the sort of solitude I want to examine is not an index of interiority. It is not the vast territory of the indomitable individual, the lone wolf, nor that of the carefree person who just likes to be alone. For some people have an irresistible demand for solitude, as a child does for sleep. No, the type of solitude that can be put to good use is profoundly implicated in the rhythms of the communicational cycle. The solitude whose praises have been written and sung, from which certain people derive a secret pleasure, acts as a source of inner strength. "Let us bring back our thoughts and intentions to ourselves, at our ease," recommends Montaigne. It means knowing how to give ourselves over to being ourselves, and living at least this little bit of life for us. . . . This is the solitude of the retreat, of reserve, when one collects one's thoughts and lays life's cares aside for a while. The solitude that feeds on silence, and encourages not "interior" growth, but analysis of one's intimate convictions, because it means stripping away what is not essential. Solitude of that sort is an ideal companion which teaches us the value of other company, strengthening all our relations because that is how we learn about them, in communication with ourselves.

There are thus two sorts of solitude, depending on the reality from which we have turned away. The first signifies the absence of any relationship with others. In that case, the solitary person's true punishment is the loss of his or her ipseity. This is what happens when I can no longer explain to anyone else, or even to myself, what I feel, so that I slide gently beneath the waters of fear or anxiety. The second, however, signifies the purification or preparation of the person who is living in communication with others. It is a state into which I withdraw in order to test myself in preparation for what is to come.

The Interlocutive Significance of Silence

Like the solitude it inhabits, silence will often be devalued in relation to communication, which it can either punctuate, take over completely, or prepare.

Winnicott gave a masterly proof of the need, and indeed the right, *not* to communicate, not to be discovered immediately, so that the other person is made to look harder. This right is the most authentic point of contact with my notion of a subjective circuit, which is once again communicational. Let me reserve my explanation of how this is possible for the following section.

In such cases, silence becomes resonant. We all know how advantageously it can replace speech as a means of questioning, forcing, refusing, or giving. In one of the sketches for the fourth act of *Lust*, Paul Valéry makes his heroine say the same thing: "Come. Come nearer still. Listen to me, for I shall say nothing. I shall say nothing with all my heart. (Silence). Can you feel the greatest simplicity of what we are welling up inside us, and the sweetest and most fervent thing we have to give emerging from each of us? You make me produce a flower and I make you send out I know not what radiance from within your being. . . . I am as close as can be to what is arising in you."[16]

Sometimes, as here, silence will replace words, for instance in the disciples' stupefaction at Pentecost, or the reverence of the Pilgrims of Emmaus. It can take the place of a much-anticipated word that someone refrains from speaking out of a sense of delicacy. Sometimes it can reinforce the spoken word by punctuating it, giving it a beat, a particular rhythm. And at the same time emphasizing the illocutionary force of what is being said. Or again—and this third case is more important for my argument—silence is a way of disavowing and rejecting an unacceptable statement or sequence of discourse. Then it takes on a striking metacommunicational value to which the other person is always extremely sensitive.

In that case it is as if silence were a rejection of the whole communicational regime that has come into existence. We remain silent in the face of an order of things to which we have not consented and which would tend (if it were possible) to constitute us as something radically external to it. We remain silent in the face of that most present of verbal modes, the imperative. We do so because of the other person's presumption in laying down all the conditions of discourse as if they were self-evident. It is a kind of protest. But here as always, silence is a way of saying something. It is a sign, for example, of our stupefaction that we will never be recognized in the way we wish, because the other person chooses to deny us in our alterity. We respond with silence when our deepest feelings of justice and injustice are trampled on, or as a protest in the name of the principle of non-violence in discourse. Like a decision not to use violence, silence can sometimes be heroic. Far from being a mere ruse of the weak, it is a weapon, the human weapon par excellence.

The power of taking a firmer grip on ourselves that some silences convey almost tangibly is a vital recourse in assuring our salvation, i.e., safeguarding our integrity. A person has a permanent ability to become aware of any discord between the regulatory ideal of a communicational community and the real situation of discussion, where unjustifiable asymmetries introduce violence into discourse. I am able to break off at any moment the interlocutive relation that just came into being, but that I consider to be inadequate. This is what I call the second experience of the spirit: the power of refusal, withdrawal. It echoes the invitation given to Abraham: "Go toward thyself," which required that he free himself from all bonds, including those of the family, in order to place himself in the presence of God.[17]

We keep silent also as a way of putting ourselves on our guard, when someone says something so pertinent that it has the impertinence to presume what our reply will be.[18] Or, to put it another way, when what is said starts to trespass on our inalienable semantic initiative. Finally, we keep silent as a means of refusal, to indicate that we reject an interlocutive relationship; as a means of escaping from a diffuse feeling of excommunication that we wish to denounce. If I try to describe how this works, I hesitate: does the other person run up against our silence as if it were a cry, or a hostile glance? Or rather, I do not hesitate, for it must be both, as we see with the heroines of Marguerite Duras' novels.

My contention here is that the different ways in which we are able to inhabit silence, some of which I have just described, would be unintelligible unless they had a certain link with the fundamental reality of the interlocutive relation. Even the dumbness that strikes Callicles at the end of Plato's *Gorgias* is a measure of the extent of the disagreement, of the impossibility of pursuing the conversation. Then there is also the silence of the Muse, which causes the poet to speak; it is a language of prior communication, precisely because the relationship between them has already been created. This silence, too, listens, welcomes, nourishes, even if it is something that has to be experienced rather than spoken about. It is no doubt the ultimate language of solitude. For it is the privileged element that allows us to collect ourselves a little on the threshold of the communication in which we are about to engage, and emerge for ourselves as our own colocutors. The public side of speaking has its roots obstinately buried in solitude. It only takes the disruption of the delicate balance, the continual circulation between "interior" speech and public speaking, for our speech to become empty of substance, disappropriated. If that happened, I would be renouncing my share of the semantic initiative.

"Be quiet" would be an excellent subtitle for the essential book of the communicating ego. Speaking seriously also means taking the time to speak to oneself. Indeed, that is our most common (though not our most fundamental) type of everyday conversation.

How is Self-Consciousness Possible?

According to a certain comedian, another reason we always come back to conversing with ourselves is so that we can have an intelligent listener, for once. An excellent reason indeed for being one's own first interlocutor. But whatever strong and noble images we may use to refer to this intercourse with ourselves, there is a danger here of sterility, or at least impoverishment. To what extent is the distance created within the self anything more than a pure trick of the Same? I incorporate what I can of the other's discourse, just enough for it not to threaten my own thoughts. The artifice is obvious. I provide myself with my own resistance and administer my own dose of contradiction, so that, in short, my thought accepts only that which it has created in the first place.

In fact, it quickly becomes clear that the self's isolation is entirely relative. Canonically, the recycling of discourse with the self both precedes and extends any effective communication with others. Which means that all such communication is reflexive. So that when I ask you a question, it is because I have already asked myself the same question and come up with some sort of answer. That is the source of much of the self-assurance and certainty that I feel as a speaking subject. The speaker's *I* is brought to life by this interruption and this distance.

In What Language Do We Speak to Each Other?

I stated earlier that the two moments in the communicational process were so tightly interdependent that there could be no communication with oneself without communication with others. I invoked a functional argument about the conditions that determine the signifying process.

The same state of affairs will be found to apply on the level of conditions of possibility. Let us look at the question of how self-consciousness can be possible. This is a question about communicating with oneself. Now, as I showed in the previous section, communicating with the self means establishing a relationship with it. And there can be no relationship without at least duality and alterity. Self-consciousness must therefore involve the animation of a virtual duality. We tend to say that the ego is in conversation with what we call the self, which is none other than the ego reflected. In order to make the relation of self-consciousness possible, the self is given the same content as the ego, but distinguished from it by its position. In the inner depths of consciousness, rather than being in the interior of myself, I am therefore *mecum*, with myself.

Readers familiar with pragmatic requirements in language theory will perhaps object that the normal usage of the *I* is in allocution to a real *you*.

Interior discourse remains solipsistic. Its use of *I* is a degenerate, fictive one.[19] However, there is assuredly a sense in which monologue exists, and another in which it does not. Seen as the closed world of a consciousness seeking to find expression, monologue is a dead concept. But as an interior discourse, in which the self is simultaneously both Same and Other, monologue exists in a relative and derivative sense.

It exists in a relative sense (which is however adequate for literary analysis), for no discourse can be conceived of as absolutely internal, i.e., as taking place in the absence of any relationship between distinct agencies. And it exists in a derivative sense, because discourse with the self internalizes a more fundamental discourse with others. It is only necessary to think of the discourse of deliberation, or repentance, or resolution. The ego's discourse presupposes (on the transcendental as well as the genetic level) that it belongs to a speaking community. When it speaks to itself, the ego is not a full and complete person. The *I*'s ability to form a relationship with itself depends on its having a prior relationship to a *you*. The *I* is linked to the *you* as someone who in turn is in a relationship with me. The ego comes back to itself through this *you*, it experiences itself as the you's *you*. The silent discourse of self-consciousness can never precede communicative activity. On the contrary, it presupposes it. Relations with others are constitutive both of the interiority of the subject and of the situation of speaking.

I mentioned internal discourse. Let us take this a little further: in what language do we speak? Any communication immediately introduces the problem of symbolism. Not only does internal discourse start by internalizing a more basic relationship with others; that relationship itself already depends on a fund of semic material which is essentially public.[20] The partners in interior discourse are indeed always available. What is known in psychological terms as consciousness is knowledge or actions that turn back on themselves in order to fit their performance to the *I*. The thinker or agent thus undertakes to judge and, as it were, to discuss his or her performance with him or herself. This movement of turning back (or away) is doubtless to be found in all thought and all action. For someone who does not ask him or herself: what should I have said? or: what should I actually have done in that situation? can be considered neither to think nor to act. We say that people who show no signs of this inner debate, who never ask themselves any questions, are unthinking, or unaware.

Descartes' *Meditations* elevate this reflexive movement to the absolute status of a method. Never before had a philosopher so deliberately exposed his person to scrutiny for pages at a time by daring to write *I*, standing up for all to see on the stage of discourse. However, the price of the pragmatic privilege accorded to interior discourse is semantic impoverishment. This becomes easier to see if it is formulated in the extensional language of the logician. There is a limit to the number of possible worlds bound up with the alternating propositional attitudes in a dialogue between the self and itself. The only ones available are those the thinker can imagine. Does that mean, then, that meditation as a whole must be rejected? Rousseau used to joke that a man who meditates is a depraved animal. Is that not to confuse the threat and the risk with the thing itself? It often, but not always, happens that consciousness becomes bogged down in self-indulgence in such cases. But that remains a possibility, not a necessity. I do concede that a meditating ego is tempted to put itself into a comfortable situation where it will not be disturbed as it plays among its own presuppositions. In which case, meditation is indeed poorer than dialogue with a real partner. But in active meditation the dialogue structure is always easy to detect. Any thinker who carries a critique in his or her mind and associates it closely with his or her own work is a meditator: there was a Cartesian in René Descartes.

Let us return to the text of the *Meditations.* They can be read in accordance with a discursive movement broader than that of simple reflection between the self and itself. Without implying any break in continuity, Descartes links the thoughts that he has *secum* (with himself) to others that he will publish in the same volume, in the form of *Objections and Replies.* In fact, he asked le Père Mersenne to collect the objections for him. It is impossible to deny that Descartes' different audiences are inscribed within the pragmatic structure of the text. There is a certain dialogism of the text which is different from the types of intertextual relations that critics ordinarily uncover.[21] The audience to whom Descartes is addressing himself stands as it were on the threshold of the *Meditations,* in the sense that these are open from the start to various specific objections and expectations, in the second phase of a long and balanced process which otherwise could legitimately be regarded as unitary. Whatever else might be said about Descartes' undertaking, it can scarcely be called solipsistic. Is it not surprising that right from his opening address to the reader, Descartes should have anticipated the need to reply to objectors? Particularly as the act of taking up the pen is usually an authoritarian one. The fact that it may be seductively masked makes no difference. It is true that the dialogical principle also operates, to differing degrees, within writing. The author has his or her own audience, and takes it into account. There remains something terribly ambiguous about writing. On the one hand, writers address their messages to unknown readers, exposing themselves and trusting to the readers' discretion. On the other, they close off their messages, determining their form and meaning, with the secret temptation of putting a stop to discussion and drawing the line for everyone, once and for all. In most cases, they will attempt to anticipate the reader's response in advance and incorporate the relationship to their different audiences into their literary message. But authors are always taking away the readers' right to speak, just when they seem to be letting them have the last word. It is not hard to see why, driven by this temptation to dominate their readership, writers should accept the risk of exposure. Most of them dream of a written message that is fixed and unequivocal, one to which no reply is possible, which cannot be transcended and which is, in the end, somewhat terroristic.

In order to attain what is known as self-consciousness, one person needs to communicate with another through language. Psychologists have confirmed over and over again that a person who communicates only with him or herself can never remain sound in mind, or even survive. Which means that even the consciousness people have of themselves depends on their consciousness of the relationships in which they are involved, with signs in the first place, then with other human beings, their interlocutors, and at the same time with things as referents, or rather, co-referents. This is a most important result, however we may subsequently try to reify such a consciousness in the language of psychology, which has remained notoriously monadic.

Let me stress that it is not enough to say that we are conscious of the other person at the same time as (and no doubt before) we are conscious of ourselves, or even that our consciousness is essentially a co-consciousness of the other.[22] Formulations of that sort are not strong enough. They have therefore had only one result, which was to mask the primitive (in the philosophical sense of the word) character of the communication relation. C. S. Peirce puts it in a more effective way: "All thought activity is dialogical in form. Your momentary self calls for the assent of your deeper self."[23]

But the fact is that other people are present so strongly in the very structure of the self that the dialogue form is required by any form of thought. The intermediary between me and myself is another real person. That person may be the target of the communication, but he or she is also its origin, just as much as I am. This must be taken into account when it comes to reformulating the lessons of the Cogito.

Reevaluating the Certitudes of the Cogito

If we are on the right track, the origin of the privileged relationship with the self which was such an important consequence of the Cartesian Cogito, running right through classical humanism and into phenomenology, should shortly become clear. To a logician thinking about personal statements of a particular type, it seems impossible that the pronoun "I" could fail in its mission as an indicator of the person. It is the only signpost that always points in the right direction, for its use presupposes the existence of an *I*. This is corroborated by the fact that if thought is conceived of as interior dialogue, the partners in the act of communication with the self always appear to be available. In fact, if the location of the subject within the Cogito is transposed into linguistic terms, our conception of the subject will undergo a much more profound transformation.

In its original formulation, the Cartesian Cogito succeeded in bringing together the apodictic, the primitive (or foundational), and the immediate (and private) aspects of the "I think" to form the concept of *consciousness.* The foregoing analyses have tended, on the contrary, to dissociate these three aspects. We have just seen in what sense it is the communication relation that is primitive, and we have already noted that privacy is only a pseudo-criterion—a point to which I shall return in the course of the next section. As for the apodictic aspect, I shall try to reformulate the Cogito from my own point of view in such a way as to take it into account, while still reinterpreting it.

As the reader will know, Descartes contends that "I think" is a necessary truth which emerges from universal doubt. His is an enterprise carried out with quite frightening intrepidity. He needed a radical form of doubt in order to create a complete certainty. Whereas the rule of universal doubt applies to every assertion made by the self about things external to itself, the statement "I think" is an exception, for in it the self asserts only itself: first the fact that it is (*sum*), then what it is (a *res cogitans*), with the object of discussion here being none other than the subject. The existence of the subject is posited first as something absolutely certain, before its intellectual essence is grasped in a secondary process of reflection. The thinking ego is the simplest and most general element; it is complete and substantial in itself, the most basic condition of all thought. I can only posit the certainty of my own being insofar as I perceive myself intellectually, i.e. as reason, soul, or thought. Note that the existence of the self here has nothing in common with that of an individual and concrete self, grasped empirically; what Descartes means by the status of person is the purest, least individual manifestation of self, the same in everyone, the universal common denominator.

I shall only examine here the Cartesian dictum: *Cogito, ergo sum.* Let us pause to consider the assertion of existence, "I am." The relation which the particle ergo is being used to express is a peculiar one, something to which my attention was drawn by Martial Guéroult, who pointed out that it does not just express a logical relation between thinking and being, but implies an additional "fact" or "act."

On the one hand, the relation between thought and being acts as an empty principle which has nothing in common with the major premise in a syllogism such that "everything that thinks *is*." For it lacks any sort of existential presupposition. On the other hand, the status of the act—the sudden flash—by which thought knows itself remains quite vague. But if the principle "in order to think, it is necessary to be" conditions the awareness of a necessary link between cogito and sum, does it do so in the same way that "conditions make possible facts, and facts make possible the knowledge of conditions"?[24] It seems possible to give a deeper explanation of the performative aspect of the intellectual act.

Let us turn to some of the results of recent exegesis on Descartes. They confirm the difficulties with the Cartesian mode of reasoning that contemporaries such as Hobbes and Gassendi had already seen. But above all they develop a rival, but at the same time complementary, interpretation in terms of performance.

In the paragraphs that follow, I wish not only to suggest that the problem of the way the subject is established must be reevaluated in this manner, but also to emphasize that this reevaluation needs to be taken seriously. Let me anticipate the argument a little: in my view, the *cogito, ergo sum* is neither a commonplace logical inference, nor a simple performative, but the apprehension of a necessary truth through an inference of a quite new type. This is the pragmatic inference, which is formed by input from the performative aspect of the dictum.

Taking into account Descartes' order of reasons, I would like to reconstruct the Cogito from this point of view, deploying the full resources of a pragmatic interpretation to take the process a stage further.

Question: what happens to the way the subject is established if the establishing is done not outside language, as in Descartes' writings, but within language? Answer: that can indeed be done, but only under certain conditions, and with profoundly different results. Heinrich Scholz was no doubt correct when he said that there are many questions about the Cogito which have not yet been answered, but also many questions which have not yet been asked.[25]

My project has three distinct objectives:

1. to examine as thoroughly as possible the appropriateness of this new interpretation of Descartes' text
2. to expose the pragmatic character of Cartesian inference, and ex-

plain it in terms at once general and precise enough to check its validity

3. to take account of certain parallel expressions of the Cogito, notably the first-person present expressions ego sum and ego existo, and the alternative formation, *quoties a me profertur vel mente concipitur,* which emphasizes the linguistic interpretation that can be applied to the Cogito

Let me start by defining the terms of the problem. Descartes refused to consider the Cogito as a syllogistic inference in the scholastic manner. However, Guéroult points out that on at least three occasions he presents the Cogito as a piece of reasoning, and that he does so whenever he wishes to bring to the fore the necessary nature of the link it contains. If this is an inference, it is not simply a logically valid one, though the time is long past when it would have been possible to reject the Cartesian dictum, as Rudolf Carnap did, simply by saying that it is not transcribable into logical syntax, it is nonsense and therefore its premises collapse. What still remains to be seen is the nature of the link that Descartes presents as necessary between the cogito and the sum. For the objection that the certitude of the Cogito cannot be proved directly without indirectly assuming what one is trying to prove is an objection that must be taken seriously.[26] Let me now attempt to demonstrate that this is the case and show the absurd results to which it leads. I transcribe "I think" by attributing the predicate "think" (B) to an individual, a. As the same individual is said to exist in the expression "I am" and "I exist," let me transcribe the assertion in the manner of Quine: there exists at least one individual identical to a:

$$(Ex)\ (x = a).$$

These transcriptions give the following inference, which translates Descartes' dictum:

$$(i)\ B(a) \supset (Ex)\ (x = a)$$

As Descartes perceives that he thinks, the premise $B(a)$ must be regarded as true, and by *modus ponens* Descartes would be correct to conclude that he exists. Better still, formula (i) is logically provable, because it is derived from:

$$(ii)\ B(a) \supset (Ex)\ [x = a\ .\ B(x)]$$

There is one immediate and obvious objection. An inference such as *ambulo ergo sum* (I walk therefore I am) would be just as valid as cogito ergo sum, even if ambulo is not such an indubitable premise as cogito is supposed to be. A second objection is that Descartes himself denied that sum was derived from cogito in his argument. The third objection is more serious: classically, a formula such as (i) is based on the very general ontological assumption that all singular terms refer to individuals that exist. It follows that the existence of a was already decided when $B(a)$ was written. The inference from (Ex) $(x = a)$ is void and irrelevant, at least in any classical system of predicates.

Let us look at some of Descartes' more careful and explicit formulations in the *Meditations*. From them, it seems that the Cogito is actually supposed to express the fact that we perceive the sum as something evident by intellectual intuition. At the same time, it is also something sufficiently similar to an inference for Descartes to regard his statement as a piece of reasoning (*ratiocinum*). According to this interpretation, the subject's affirmation of existence derives from the impossibility of denying that existence. To do so would involve a contradiction or a certain type of inconsistency. As a result, the phrase "I am" is necessarily true. Moreover, this should make it possible to account for the fact that this result is achieved in a first-person statement, and that this particular sort of inference is linked to the contingent and instantaneous fact of being able to think or utter it. In short: I must necessarily exist if in fact I think. And in that case only, our interpretation might claim to be relatively complete.

Descartes' method for introducing the first truth, the subject's affirmation of existence, clearly starts to take shape as an utterance: "I must finally conclude that the proposition "I am, I exist" is necessarily true whenever it is spoken by me or conceived in my mind." [27] Contemporary commentators are starting to place a certain importance on the *quoties a me profertur* (whenever I speak it), while hesitating over the *vel* (or). How should we treat it? What path shall we follow? The narrowest one.

Quoties a me profertur: A Logical and Pragmatic Contradiction

Now, what is this utterance (*pronunciatum*) to which Descartes refers as an alternative (vel) to the conceptual process that commands access to the Cogito? What advantage might we expect to derive from it that might help to explain what Descartes meant? It is a fact that neither the *Discourse* nor the *Principles* makes use of this *a me profertur* in speaking of the Cogito. It is also the case that the occurrences of the verb *proferre* concern speech true or false, and possibly even magic or deceptive, which animal and artificial machines are capable of proffering, in simulation of human speakers. Descartes asks us to avoid such speech in order to conceive of "simple" things. A proffering made "carelessly" or "from prejudice" might even prevent us from believing in the truth of the proposition ego sum, ego existo. Would a person who gave him or herself over to such speech be anything other than a more sophisticated automaton? Consequently, there is no doubt that this speech needs to be approached with close intellectual attention if the proffering is to be meaningful. Without that, it would not merit a second glance. The type of proffering that Descartes introduces by the term *vel* is performed by the mind more than by the mouth.[28] Which is to say that the vel in no way means that utterance on its own can have the same existential result as conception on its own.

Yet even with these precautions, the utterance *ego sum, ego existo* is not without interest in the sense that it is an accurate reflection of the overall idea. The statement made by the self is stripped of all the words—substance, individuality, and even existence—through which prejudice could creep in, thanks to the repetition of the first person. By this means, Descartes legitimately overcomes Gassendi's objection, that to say "I think, therefore I am" is to leave out the major premise, "he who thinks is." Equally, Descartes vigorously opposed the idea that this argument was an enthymeme. Such a proposition, which the author is careful to avoid, would return the subject to the generic nature of a "he who," a scholastic essence. Descartes refutes this objection through direct recourse to the ego: by conjugating the verb *to be* in the first person rather than, as syllogistics and Gassendi demanded, in the third, he attaches the sign to the self's sudden rise to consciousness, rather than to a general state of things or of people. As it is the same ego which, at one and the same moment, affirms both cogito and sum, it is not possible to object that the repetition of ego juxtaposes a second, different *I* to the first. The objection would be valid if the subject were, so to speak, "substantialized," but not now that it is being "existentialized." As we can see, language here follows intuition as closely as possible, acting as its nearest sign (as André Robinet wrote).

In the wake of recent work in the philosophy of language, I would interpret the vel in a new way, which remains compatible with the lessons drawn from the Cartesian texts. But first, let me sum up the situation so far. We have seen that if the Cogito is not a logical inference, it is nevertheless linked to the logic of a certain form of first-person utterance whose role is to guarantee the necessity of the affirmation of existence. Now we need to understand why that type of logic can guarantee that a truth is both necessary and absolutely certain.

In the first place, what type of necessity is involved here? Notice that the separate intuitions that I have of my thought, on the one hand, and my being, on the other, however certain they may be, are not sufficient to check hyperbolic doubt: I can still regard their negation as true. Such intuitions are relative to the nature of my mind, and to that of mathematical propositions. They are naturally certain and necessary, but have no metaphysical necessity. Now, although the Cogito is a contingent statement, it does have metaphysical necessity. In other words, the question of its status can be reformulated as a question about how it is able to escape from doubt.

One solution involves recognizing that a contingent or synthetic statement can be necessary, in a sui generis way linked to the status of the Cogito as an utterance. Such is the case with the proposition "I think," the negation of a proposition "I do not think," which is false whenever I conceive or proffer (utter) it. The first could be said to be pragmatically contradictory, and its negation necessarily contradictory. For that solution to fit our hypothesis, we would have to explain why this type of necessity, if indeed it exists, proves more resistant to doubt than does the necessity of mathematical propositions.

In the *Second Meditation*, Descartes declares that it is impossible for him to deny his existence: the more I doubt the fact that I am thinking, the more I think that I am not thinking, and the more the falseness of what I am trying to throw into doubt is falsified by the fact that I doubt it. Whether or not the term cogito is mentioned makes no difference as long as I cannot help thinking or saying: "I am, I exist." What is at issue in the Cartesian dictum, and in fact in any argument of a certain type, is the indubitable status of the utterance "I am." Now, Descartes does not prove this indubitability by deducing "I am" from "I think." Moreover, the statement "I am" is not logically true either. The author suggests that its indubitability derives from an act of thought, i.e., his attempt to prove the contrary. The relationship between the two parts of the cogito, ergo sum, and the function of the word cogito now become clear. By this term, Descartes is referring to the act of thought or discourse through which the auto-verifiability of "I exist" becomes manifest. The indubitability of the affirmation of my personal existence results from the fact or the act of thinking it. Properly speaking, it is not something that is thought out in the same way as the indubitability of a demonstrable truth, i.e. by means of thought. The statement "I exist" is indubitable so long as, and whenever, I think actively about it. It is clear that in the argument in question, the relation of cogito to sum is not that of premise to its conclusion, but rather that of a process of thinking or speaking to its product, which is a thought or a statement.

That is not all. Descartes' argument brings to the fore a certain inconsistency that the formula "I think, therefore I am" was only one means of establishing. For the term "I think" actually has a double function. On the one hand, it is part of the proposition whose status of indubitability is in ques-

tion; on the other, the word refers to the performance by which this indubitability is revealed. Why then do I say that the phrase "I do not exist,"
which leads to the necessary pragmatic self-verification of the phrase "I
exist," is pragmatically contradictory?

Let me recapitulate. It is impossible for me to deny my existence. Which is
tantamount to saying that the statement:

(iii) I do not exist

is in a certain way absurd. But what sort of inconsistency is involved here? In
itself, the corresponding phrase is intelligible and consistent. If therefore (iii)
is always false, it cannot be so purely for logical reasons. Statement (iii) is
absurd when somebody proffers it here and now. Then let p be the proposition corresponding to statement (iii). If a proffers p, then p . (Ex) $(x = a)$ is
inconsistent. From this we can see that:

1. the inconsistency is not a property of the sentence, but derives
from a relation between the sentence and a singular term

2. the singular term here designates the speaking subject. In the Cartesian order of reasons, the argument deals with a particular case: that
of the meditating ego. Appreciating this argument requeires an ability
to understand the logic of the first-person pronoun

3. it is not incompatible with Cartesian usage of the word cogito for
the performance by which the phrase "I exist" verifies itself to be also
the act by which the phrase is proffered

The inconsistency of statement (iii) depends on a present performance,
notably the act of proffering a certain phrase. It includes a performative aspect. That is why this type of inconsistency may be termed "pragmatic."

The notion of inconsistency or pragmatic contradiction has a paradoxical
status. A statement such as (iii) is not formally contradictory, and yet in no
circumstances can it ever be true. It is not simply false, as an empirical statement might be. It is therefore neither truly contradictory like an analytical
statement, nor easy to disprove like a synthetic statement. Such a status certainly runs counter to the usual view, according to which a declarative statement must be of either the first type or the second.[29]

Here we have a sui generis contradiction between what is said—the propositional content—and the fact of saying or proffering it. More precisely: the
fact of saying it, insofar as it is indicated in the proposition, and therefore
reflected in the very meaning of the statement. This is indeed what is happening in the statement "I do not exist": its meaning is not limited to its
propositional content, but also includes what the statement indicates by the

fact of its utterance, and which is reflected in it. This includes on the one hand its indicator of illocutionary force, i.e., the assertive form of the statement, and on the other the indicator "I," which is a reflexive token. The fact that an utterance is taking place within the statement thus creates a double reflexivity. By virtue of the usage rules for the indicator of illocutionary force and the personal pronoun, the speaker of the phrase "I do not exist" indicates first that he or she is affirming the fact, and second that he or she exists as a speaking subject. There is an existential presupposition linked to the use of "I." That is why the statement "I do not exist" is not simply rendered false by the contingent fact that the speaker is the utterer of the phrase: the fact of its utterance is reflected in the phrase itself. So that there is a conflict between its propositional content and part of what is signified without being said.

The contradiction in question here remains one internal to meaning, even if it is not a logico-formal one in the usual sense of the term. Whether or not Descartes is thinking is a contingent fact. That contingency is enough to prevent the statement "I do not exist" from being logically contradictory, but it is not sufficient to guarantee the consistency of its meaning. If we did not accept this type of sui generis contradiction, Descartes' argument would lose all of its force as a necessary assertion. It depends on the thesis that the negation of "I exist" is not just false, but contradictory in a particular way, which has the effect of conferring necessity on the assertion "I exist."

A reading of this kind is suggested more or less explicitly by recent exegesis of the Cogito. I would like to take it a little further.

Let us then start with the pragmatic inconsistency that I identified in (iii). How does it normally show itself? The inconsistency of (iii) means that whoever tries to convince anyone (including him or herself) of its truth by proffering it destroys his or her own utterance. Nobody can make an interlocutor believe that he or she does not exist by saying so. It is absurd to proffer a phrase like (iii), because it destroys the function which the assertion of such declarative phrase normally has—that of making the interlocutor believe in what is said. Pragmatic inconsistency is conditional upon the listener's knowing who the speaking subject is, and identifying him or her as the person whom the statement concerns.

Thus Descartes' choice of the word cogito can be justified. Contrary to Gassendi's claim, it cannot be replaced by just any verb. The act or performance which manifests the inconsistency cannot be an action like walking, nor even some kind of mental activity like wanting or feeling. The act in question must be an attempt to think in order to make believe that the speaker does not exist. Incidentally, independently of Descartes' reasons for choosing it, the term cogito is not exactly the most precise way of describing the act through which statement (iii) destroys itself. Descartes may have intended that statement to be considered simply as a possibility, but what he cannot do is persuade anyone, including himself, that he does not exist.

I cannot attempt to utter to others, or to myself of course, the idea that I do not exist, without immediately undoing my own attempt. All the Cartesian texts in which the Cogito is expressed presuppose that one can converse not only with one's fellow human beings, but also, tacitly, with oneself. There are certainly cases in which the uttering of a pragmatically inconsistent statement can occur without a word being spoken. It is enough for me to want to persuade myself, through an effort of my own thought, that I do not exist. That is the absolutely crucial role played by self-persuasion (*mihi persuadere*) in actualizing metaphysical doubt. In this case, a public language act is replaced by an act of thought by the self. That is of course why public language acts are traditionally linked to the notion of self-knowledge. But if we look at it more closely, there is no way in which the move from a public language act to a silent act of thought can affect the *essential logical features* of the statement. This point is vital. The reason Descartes' attempt to think that he does not exist necessarily fails is the same as the reason his attempt to tell one of his contemporaries that he did not exist would also have failed as soon as the interlocutor realized that Descartes was the speaker of the phrase.

Let me summarize my argument so far: the certitude of the Cogito cannot be directly demonstrated in a logico-formal way. As we have seen, the truth of "I exist" cannot be denied without there being a contradiction, nor asserted without the speaker's begging the question. But it is possible to reevaluate the certitude of cogito, ergo sum by linking it to the mode of assent that we reserve for the pragmatic conditions of possibility of a certain type of public language game. Therefore, it is not based initially on the primacy of an "inner experience" and the examination of a process of self-consciousness which is solitary by definition, as is the case in the Cartesian tradition up to Husserl, but rather on the pragmatic a priori situation of that experience itself. Thus Descartes arrives at his first certain intuition by playing for the moment a double role, that of René Descartes—who stands for anyone capable of proffering the statement "I doubt that I exist," or simply "I do not exist"—and that of Cartesius who, as the universal listener, remains to be convinced. The meaning of the Cogito requires its being related to both René Descartes and Cartesius, who conspire together to bring about its proffering.

This is a perfect domonstration of the fact that the ego whose existence is being affirmed is, in the end, in an interlocutive relationship with an other. Effective self-understanding and effective understanding of the other's existence come into being simultaneously, because the ego is involved from the start in relationships. We understand ourselves as an integral part of a virtual public dialogue, or more precisely of a deficient mode of such a dialogue, in which I assume the role of an other in my own eyes. This means that the act of silent thought is actually parasitic on a public language game within which Descartes' intuition is valid as a judgment that is both certain and intersubjectively valid a priori.

In the case of thought as a tacit and interior dialogue, the partners in the communication are always available. However, that privileged relationship with the self can never be taken to its absolute conclusion. Once the relationship with the self in interior dialogue starts to be conceived as something derived from the relation with a real *you* in actual dialogue, the *I* can only appear to itself as something linked from the start to *you*, which in turn is in a relationship with *me*. The ego can only return to itself after a detour via the *you*, by apprehending itself as the other's other. The "I" infallibly designates the person using it, on condition that *I* does not become isolated from its other. Unless it is to become something entirely cut off from reality and for which there is no concept, the ego cannot be defined by the identity of ipseity with itself.

Let us take one last step. I defined utterance as the activity of discourse creation in which the uttering agencies are indissociable from their present relationship—and not as a simple activation of language by an individual act of utterance. It would therefore seem that the assertion "you do not exist" is just as directly refuted by an act of discourse as "I do not exist." Unless of course we accept that the communication act has failed, or not been completed. Even before I could deny the other's existence by saying "you do not exist," I would be undermining the expression by means of which I address him or her.

But in this last case, the sending of a message without a recipient is a type of behavior which, in the context of speaking (unlike singing), is considered pathological and generally discouraged by mockery. Moreover, in such cases of "distracted" proffering, it should be noted that both the "I" and the "you" would have a degenerate function. First the "I." In a universe in which the *I* took over completely, where nothing existed except for me, "I" would only ever be used fictively. Then, if we were not presently in a communication relationship, the other to whom I turn would become no more than a ghostly figment of the imagination.

The certitude of the cogito, ergo sum has nothing to do with a deductive sequence of utterances. Nor is it derived from a simple performance,[30] but rather from a genuine argument which includes a constitutive pragmatic component of performance (by which I mean one that is pragmatically determined). It is founded on the self-reflexivity of an effective act of utterance.

The immediate result is that its certainty does not depend on the primacy of the immediate internal experience of a consciousness which is solitary as a matter of principle: rather, it is conditioned by its reflexive and *communicational* situation. The operation of thinking is just as mediate for the self as it is for others. Thought is never present in its entirety to the ego. We become aware of ourselves by back-reference from our utterances, at the same moment and in the same way that we become aware of the other as the person to whom we are speaking. In this way, the existence of the other person is asserted to the same extent as my own, neither more nor less. This does not of course prevent me from doubting the images or representations of other people, but I can no more doubt the other to whom I am presently speaking than I can doubt myself as the one speaking. A necessary condition of this state of affairs is the declaration I make to the other with whom I find myself in a relationship as soon as I begin to speak to him or her, or rather, we to each other. On every occasion when it is uttered meaningfully, the statement "I doubt that I exist" or "I do not exist" presupposes simultaneously the existence of its pragmatic determinants *I* and *you*, the self and the other. Thus the interlocutive relation does indeed seem to be an event of the spirit as old as the Cogito itself.

Self-Consciousness or Communication with Oneself?

Assuming that we at least accept the dialogical character of thought as inward discourse, how far does that commit us? At this point, it is facility, not difficulty, that our analysis must overcome. Rather than being mental speech, thought is true inner discourse. But here there are two different arguments that need to be distinguished. The first regards this solitary discourse as being addressed to the self, directed toward the speaker by him or herself. In the second, even the most intimate of discourses depends on a virtual allocutee, and is shot through with evaluations and checks deriving from other people. The failure to make this distinction explains why analysis of this question has largely remained on a trivial level.

What about Inner Discourse?

These two arguments commit us to quite different positions.

1. The first, a weaker position, goes back to before Plato. A man who thinks or deliberates is nourishing a form of speech which is expressed in the intimacy of his own mind. In the *Wisdom of Solomon* we read: "They said

within themselves, thinking wrongly" (Sap. II.1). Saint Augustine compares this to a similar text in the Gospel of Luke: "The scribes began to think, saying to themselves: who is he who is uttering blasphemy?" Is this thought as speech, or speech as thought? Augustine concludes: a man speaks to himself in the depths of his heart, or in other words, he *speaks when he thinks*, even if his words are not sounded.[31]

Let us avoid the notion of mental speech, which is both discursive and inadequately articulated, and which is no doubt a pure illusion. Inward discourse can then be seen in the form of a question-and-answer discussion. Or it can be analyzed as a series of assertions followed by objections, of replies in dialogue form. An idea that was not accompanied by the slightest intention of exchange, either with others or with oneself, would subside into incoherence. Ideas that we keep to ourselves are lost. There are, of course, days for having ideas, as Valéry noted: "Ideas are suddenly born on the slightest of pretexts, in other words, out of *Nothing*. They are preceded, foretold, demanded by nothing. . . . As far as their production is concerned, they are perhaps no more than 'local' incidents which quickly disappear, leaving no more trace of their passage than a fleck of foam on the sea. . . ."[32]

What is there to say, according to our principles, about these ideas that seem to belong to us, without being formulated, that are born out of nothing and that can be disturbed by the slightest thing? It is important to avoid making the obvious but trivial points, for it is superficial appearances that need to be overcome.

We can bet that the days when we have ideas are simply those when we are most full of available energy, the sort that has not yet been assigned to any particular activity. Moreover, however new and unexpected they may be, such ideas are basically foreign to us in at least two ways. First, they shoot through us like a pain; then, they are essentially indeterminate, changeable, and they tend to dissolve into something else. In no case can they stand as evidence against what I have been saying.

There are some strong prejudices afoot concerning our inner life. People imagine that thoughts, memories, and feelings are all ineffable, and that they develop without any input from the senses, without being given expression in words. What misleads us into believing that thought can exist prior to the attempt to express it is the existence of ready-constituted (but, therefore, already expressed) thoughts which we are able tacitly to remember. They are what gives us the illusion of our inner life, which is really a discourse, or rather a dialogue between self and self. I have no knowledge of the ideas that hover on the fringes of consciousness until such time as I have formulated them for myself. An idea that was happy with existing for itself, without any attempt to move toward a formulation that would mark its completion, would fall back into my unconscious—in other words, it would have no existence at all for me. Do we in fact "experience" ideas? Yes, in the sense that we give ourselves ideas by communicating with ourselves. Being alone involves at least being with oneself, and therefore being two: "Without this 'inward' difference or division, we would never be able to get on with other people, for that involves substituting a foreign voice or audience for the other voice or audience which is inside us, forming the second branch of each thought."[33]

In any case, thought is not something inward; it cannot exist outside words (words that might at least potentially be spoken), or outside an interlocutive relationship that is at least possible; it does not exist outside the world. Thought is of the order of meaning. It is what a person says to him or herself, and it must not be confused with the ability to conjure up an idea or representation in the mind.

2. We need to see in what sense "inward" language creates an Other within the Same. Far from communication with oneself being explained by the simple "redoubled self-consciousness" of thought,[34] we are in a relationship with an authentic *you*. This must not be misunderstood: the intimate to-and-fro dialectic that the philosophical tradition has passed down to us is not real dialogue. It is only a dramatized version of the fictitious dialogue in which the soul engages with itself in order to pick up the thread of its thoughts. As long as thought continues to interrupt its spontaneous progression so as to reflect, question, and reply to itself, it can still be seen as deriving from the apparent autarchy of the Cogito. At the most, it might be split between the different accomplices or supporting roles that belong to the Same. Real dialogue is not about making others see reason—a single, common reason whose unity has simply been lost, and to which everyone should submit by renouncing his or her alterity. It is about the very intelligibility of the intelligible: in dialogue, meaning is established anew through the joint semantic activity of different interlocutors, by their responsible participation and willing renunciation of any rights of ownership over the truth.

I shall therefore adopt a much stronger, and doubtless more accurate, line of argument. Far from "inner" dialogue conditioning the possibility of effective dialogue with others—as if it were possible in some way to accommodate within inner discourse the discourse that goes out toward all others[35]—it is, on the contrary, the logical space of interlocution that becomes my inner milieu. As long as we are not deceived by the spatial imagery. This space is a logical, interdiscursive one.

In my strong thesis, communication with oneself is limited either to recycling an earlier act of communication with somebody else, or to anticipating a later one, using a putative or simulated interlocutor. The inward discourse of the Cogito appears as a derivative of conversations with other people. When it interrupts its spontaneous forward flow in order to reflect on itself, thought is simply attesting an older interlocutionary relation. Why else should I suspend my spontaneous thinking experience?

People only know how to communicate with themselves insofar as they know how to do so with others, and using the same means. The symbolism used by the soul as it converses with itself presupposes interlocution. It is a fact that we learn to speak to ourselves only after speaking to a real other. That is the beginning of thought, of that conversation which is at once real and "inward," which lasts our entire life and makes us believe that there is *someone* there, a personal self.

It is not really that we are split in two by others, haunted or inhabited by them. These are all metaphors. But that we are involved in relations from the start. Hence the idea philosophers have been putting forward for some time now, that the other is already present in both the genesis and the structure of the self. And that, as a result, the other's voice is always mingled in with mine, expressing the viewpoint of the person I want to persuade, or, as Mikhaïl Bakhtin would have it, the social class to which we both belong.[36] Descartes' language only really becomes intelligible if we remember that for him, the inner interlocutor is a theologian or a geometer, or even simply an *honnête homme.* In other cases, it could be a real objector, a tenacious and precious opponent, such as Niels Bohr and Max Born were for Albert Einstein.[37]

In one sense, only the strong thesis gives explicit recognition to the primitve nature of the communicative relation. This recognition is essential, if only for a logical reason. Self-consciousness can always be reconstructed from the interlocutive relation. And in a much more authentic way: consciousness is no longer the architect of the communication relation, but its inhabitant. It realizes and accomplishes itself using the semic building blocks available for communication within an organized community. From the point of view of the social and interpersonal network, it is words that constitute me. It is through speech that I establish myself as one of the more or less stable nodes of the communicational circuit.

But the converse is not true: the communication relation can never be explained on the basis of the "relation" by which self-consciousness is achieved. The polarity of the intentional act *ego cogito cogitatum* is not reversible. Moreover, it is a fact that however our consciousnesses might try to put together a common project, that project will not be seen in the same way by each of us. Which is a major weakness, for everyone makes projections from deep down in his or her own subjectivity. The forcible reduction of the communicational alliance to a specular relation within consciousness is an undertaking that cannot possibly succeed. Particularly as only some aspects of the human communicational process are consciously accessible to the participants.

It is easy to show that this is true by examining the difficulties encountered by Husserl. The aporia in which he found himself was that the consciousness of the ego can in no way be used to found a genuine intersubjectivity. In me, and therefore relative to me, it takes the form of a plurality of egos. The other can only become accessible to me as another constitutive subjectivity, because it is unthinkable for the ego to explore operations specific to others on anything but its own terms. Ultimately, incommunicability is the ego's right, and communication is infinitely precarious. Stated in egological terms, the question of how it is that people can reveal themselves while keeping their minds secret is one that cannot be answered.

There is therefore a characteristic tendency for philosophies of consciousness to pass over the theoretical problem posed by linguistic communication. The two in fact go together. Admittedly, Husserl's theory of meaning does give some consideration to signs, which are to some extent recuperated by his meditation on the relationship of objects of thought to the signifying acts of the ego. The intentional relation is thus invested in linguistic expressions, but only in a secondary way. The ideal meaning intended by the ego still has the last word. The identity of the same meaning, which is the one the ego means, is what allows signs to signify. So that the logic of meaning regulates the use of signs.[38] If the primordial philosophical act by which consciousness splits itself off from the world and constitutes itself as an absolute is called reduction, then phenomenological reduction is what makes all forms of being have a meaning for consciousness. Reduction is the condition of possibility of the symbolic function. It is the transcendent value behind language, conditioning the ego's ability to relate to reality by designating it through signs.

The same characteristic exclusion of language is found in the logic of Port-Royal, where, as is well known, the problem of signs comes in only via an analysis of ideas. "If our reflections on our thoughts had only ever concerned ourselves, it would have been sufficient to consider them in themselves, without attributing to them any other sign."[39]

There is never any attempt to raise the problem on a fundamental level— where its existence, the way it operates, its conditions of possibility would be tackled directly. This is because the subject's act of thought can be an act independent of any communication with others. The link between words and thought is not one of reciprocal implication: "When we think on our own, things only present themselves to our mind with the words in which we customarily clothe them when speaking to others."[40]

Customarily clothe. . . . How striking is this translation of a simple relation of habituation into a clothing metaphor! How effective, also, as a way of stretching apart the link between language and thought, and making it contingent. There is absolutely no question that this verbal "covering," as something external to the idea, might have the slightest claim to condition thought. There is of course a pressing reason for this illusion, for the rationalist "Cartesian" approach prevents the authors from envisaging any rational approach to the specificity of linguistic reality.

The Subjectivist Argument

One possible objection to this interpretation might be that linguistic mediation is not present in all cases. As evidence of this, there is the short circuit of immediate experience, the so-called intimate evidence of the senses. Is there not a particular certainty attached to subjective events such as: "I am in pain," "I am depressed," "I am bored," and equally: "I am disappointed," "I am confident," "I love"? All these are things about which I am sure. By which I mean that this local pain, this peculiar sensation, this fleeting but obsessive image, are things that I *have*. In a sense, it is *my* pain; and I am the only one able to know whether I am really in pain.

At the root of this objection I once again find the indivisibly cultural and linguistic fact of the centrality of the self. A critique and analysis of this position would need to show that it is based simply on a superficial grammatical privilege which can be contradicted by an examination of the actual circumstances in which such expressions are used.

Let me start by conceding that these are indeed intimate sensations. When I express a sensation that I have, there is certainly a recurrent experience which corresponds to the word I speak. But the point is, in what sense does it correspond? This whole subject is extremely difficult, because it is cluttered by inaccurate accounts. Much is at stake, however, particularly as far as a communicational approach to persons is concerned. Fortunately, we are not condemned to following the traditional subjectivist interpretation of these so-called intimate sensations.

This is a discourse that has been heard on many occasions throughout the history of philosophy. It sees the invisibility and secrecy of Gyges as the constitutive features of the psyche, and even the essence of our human condition. It states that intimate sensations are the immediate data of subjective experience. I am the only one who knows what is going on inside me, as the mind possesses a sort of inward sense by means of which it is able to converse with its own contents, operations, and products, in a relationship of the same type as the one by which it is linked to the world outside through its external senses. Such knowledge is regarded as having a private justification. Moreover, the experience is mine and I could never make anyone else have it: it too is private.

The same is true for perceptual events. On the basis of my own experience, I alone can know what it is to have a visual image of the color red, and therefore, by stages, what it means to see, think, or understand. At which point, the descriptive terms I apply to the external world would have a private meaning in addition to their public one. Their sense would be so directly linked to subjective experiences that saying that they designate subjective experiences would be deemed an adequate account of their usage. Of course, they do relate to the world according to a system of common criteria, but always through my subjective apprehension of them. A subjectivist therefore believes that it is correct to conclude that the meaning of an expression I use is determined by things of which I have immediate individual experience. With the help of private definitions intended for public use, names could be given to subjective experiences (pains, visual data, etc.), which could then serve as criteria for the correct application of such terms. But this quickly leads to the extreme case of a language which itself would be private: aporia is not far away. Subjectivist discourse is happy to burden us with three rather bad questions, which are both typical and insoluble:

1. How, on the basis of subjective experience, can the divided world of external objects be brought back together again?

2. How can I communicate the content of my subjective experiences, which are my exclusive property, to other people?

3. How can common meanings be guaranteed, when verbal exchange about intimate sensations is subject to so many reservations?

A communicational approach to persons is perhaps nowhere more fruitful than here. It allows us to overcome the impasse into which the three questions above inevitably lead. But first, it provides the means of refuting subjectivist discourse almost term by term. In what follows, I shall not point out when my arguments run parallel to those of Wittgenstein and when they are purely my own. Nevertheless, concepts such as "privileged knowledge," "private" objects and language, and "mental vision," which are now dead and increasingly difficult to understand, could be reduced one after the other to absurdity.

A Critique of Subjectivist Discourse, and the Incommunicable

Let me sum up the argument so far. Subjective thought, with each one of us thinking his or her own thoughts in watertight isolation from others, is a bad starting point. The whole idea is suspect: that sort of thought would only ever *appear* to be communicable. Understanding would only touch on desperately external signs, and never have any hold over thoughts, which would be subjective, belonging to me alone. I would know, through familiarity with my own case, what it is to have a sensation of redness. But what does it mean to say: "red is something singular"? The same things as: "This is something singular that I call red." Now, for that to be intelligible, it already needs to signify our concept, "red." We are thus faced with a conceptual problem.

Let me formulate it: what are our concepts of "red," of "pain"? How did we acquire them? How do we give life to the signs corresponding to them? In order to examine this problem, I shall ask how it is that we can attribute a sensation of color or pain to a person (myself or someone else). We must be able to perform this attribution through a linguistic game we play with each other. In this game, the behavior patterns of the perceiver or the sufferer, and those of other people toward the person who is said to perceive or suffer, have an essential role to play. At which point, what I can utter and know about my subjective life is not independent of what others have to say about it on the basis of their observations, nor of the manner in which they react to what I say about it.

I am not, of course, asking whether the fact of feeling something subjectively presupposes the possession of a common linguistic criteriology, or whether such a thing ever occurs in reality. I do not wish to challenge either the reality or the specificity of subjective experiences.[41] I am simply asking whether the predicates in our psychological vocabulary that are applicable to "what happens inside us" really do designate subjective experiences that relate to a self which is supposed to "have" them, or whether they are actually used in a different way. In particular, it may well be that it is only within a certain type of language game, which itself is brought imperatively into play in an explicitly interlocutive situation, that a person will say of him or herself, or of someone else, that he or she is having a particular experience—sensation, image, or idea—and in so doing, apply the corresponding concepts.

As can be seen, this is solely a problem of concepts. The question is whether we can or cannot say such and such a thing (i.e., apply one particular concept or another) meaningfully. Now, only if someone has learned to master a particular language game does it make sense to say that he or she has experienced this or that.

The idea that what gives life to signs or meaning to the things we say is some sort of occult presence which makes the use of signs possible seems a highly unlikely idea. A much better explanation is that there is a certain interdiscursive practice which includes the expressions "I see a patch of red" or "I have a toothache." This conceptual problem can be examined by distinguishing between cases where we assert these things and those where we do not. The best reply to the (misguided) questions raised by subjectivist discourse is:

First, to ask a better question, while pointing out that the burden of proof lies with the supporters of subjectivism. Is it certain that our expressions do designate private experiences? The notion of a sign that is independently introduced, and that could then be used equally independently, is a dangerous one. Its correct usage would no longer depend on agreement with others, but on the acceptance of some mystical mental link between the sign and the thing. This would prepare the ground for the recognition of private languages and meanings—fertile ground on which all sorts of aporias, and particularly the insoluble "problem" of other minds, could flourish. It is very much to be doubted that the meanings of our expressions derive from private experiences rather than from public interdiscursive practice. Even supposing that I apply words to my experiences, someone must have taught them to me. The process of assigning meaning to signs is already problematic enough when we know the language available to us and can draw on its supply of ready-made semantic categories, but private designation for public use becomes an extremely perilous performance if we wish to attribute it to someone who is acquiring language for the first time. We should try to establish some rule, but that is typically something for which there is no basis of agreement with each other. Nothing that I can do on my own, whether it be paying attention to my subjective experience, addressing myself to it, imagining future experiences, or whatever, is sufficient to allow me to do this.

Next, we should ask ourselves directly what we actually mean by using expressions that concern subjective or private experiences, such as "I am bored," or "I am depressed." When somebody says that something is "getting on his or her nerves," we certainly do not ask that person to prove it. Equally, when we make such statements, we are not claiming to describe observable phenomena. We admit that we are depressed in an already depressed tone of voice.[42] Saying and doing are one and the same thing; we are here doing something that is part of our mood of depression. It does not have to be true or false, just sincere.

As for saying we are depressed, how do we in fact find out that we are? A depressed person discovers that he or she is depressed in the course of conversations with other people, and in the same way other people find out, just as we discover that we are sleepy when we yawn. It is therefore not the case that I am the only one who can know these things. On this point, let me acknowledge a debt to the author of the *Philosophical Investigations*. The claim that I am the only one to know must either be false—because other people can also know—or absurd, because it is not possible to say, in real usage: "I know that I am suffering," but only: "I am suffering now," which is all that the expression means.

—But at least my pain, my feeling of shame, are things I *have?*

—Do not be fooled by a superficial grammatical analogy. Consider the phrase "I have a feeling of shame," leaving aside, for the moment, the fact that it only has meaning in an interlocutive situation, and conceding to the subjectivist, for the sake of simplicity, that it can be considered on its own. Compare:

(i) I have put on weight, and
(ii) I have a watch on my wrist,

with:

(iii) I have a feeling of shame, and
(iv) I have a toothache.

In (i) and (ii), "I" is used in a way that does not exclude empirical error. In my judgment, a particular individual has put on weight. I could replace the pronoun "I" with the proper name *F. J.* as the subject of statement (i), at least—which immediately introduces the possibility of error. On the other hand, (iii) is comparable to (iv), where the use of "I" excludes the possibility of error from the start. For:

(v) I do not know whether I have a toothache

is just as absurd as saying: "I feel really happy, but I may not be," unlike:

(vi) I do not know whether X has a toothache,

which is not absurd.[43] Consequently, (iii) and (iv) are no more statements relating to a particular individual than, for example, moaning would be,[44] so that shame cannot here be given the predicate "possessed by X." Having a feeling of shame is not defined by a relation of belonging between shame and myself, at one time, and somebody else, at another. From which we must conclude that impressions and sensations, such as shame or pain, are not my experience of an individual called me having something.

Statements (i) and (ii) are empirical propositions. Statements (iii) and (iv) function as grammatical propositions, in the sense that it is grammatically impossible for someone else to have my shame or my pain. The utterance

(vii) You have a toothache

is strange. Note that to restore it to an iteratively correct form and so achieve an acceptable utterance, at least two operations are necessary, as in:

(viii) You do have a toothache, don't you?

By using a stressed form of "you," I both detach the allocutee and restore the interlocutive situation, while by adding a so-called "confirmatory" question, I further situate the utterance in relation to the allocutee.

Utterance (iv): "I have a toothache," functions in part as a grammatical proposition. Wittgenstein would add that to say that I am the only one to have a pain is almost a tautology. "If as a matter of logic you exclude other people's having something, it no longer makes sense to say that you have it." [45]

I have the experience that I have, and not some other, and particularly not someone else's. It is nonsensical to suppose that more than one sentient being could have exactly the same sensation. That is a grammatical reality. If we remember that, it will help us to avoid succumbing to the grammatical fiction that the names of sensations, such as pain, are private and incommunicable, because they are attached to inner processes of which only the sentient subject is aware. It is marvelous how such an apparently harmless grammatical fact seems to go right to the heart of things and express the essentially subjective and private character of the experience. But that is just not the case. What is actually happening is that a strange collusion has come about between a natural reality (a standard human reaction) and a grammatical fact (the elimination of doubt and error by the form of this type of statement).

From the fact that a person may be mistaken in asserting "he is in pain," but not in asserting, "I am in pain," it is often fallaciously inferred that the evidence available in the first case (groaning and grimacing, injuries, words spoken) is inadequate, and that it is only in the second case that we have access to truly conclusive evidence, i.e. the pain itself. But that leaves out the possibility of error and doubt being eliminated by the type of utterance, rather than by the nature of the evidence. The opposition between "I am in pain" and "he is in pain" is not one between two accounts, one of which depends on external and fallible evidence while the other is founded on evidence internal and infallible, but between an "account" and what some philosophers have called an "avowal." Once again, to suppose that a person is wrong when he or she claims to feel a particular sensation is simply nonsense.

—Still, you must accept that there is a way in which the self understands itself directly, a form of tacit and privileged knowledge, free of any linguistic mediation, and therefore of any interlocutive mediation. You are then forced to admit that what we communicate to others is the form, not the content, of our subjective experiences.

—I do not see why *having* a subjective experience should put us in any position to *know* it. It is true that nobody knows whether others also have that experience or a different one, but that is another question altogether.

—Does not our real life experience form its own sequence, adding itself to the same series, in the same sphere, and contributing to the same closure of the self? Is there not a nonintentional part of life that is also noncommunicable?

This question seems pertinent. In fact, though, its terms are not properly defined, because it is hard to understand what an incommunicability that is prior in principle to any communication might be. Something that has not really been thought or said is neither communicable nor incommunicable. On the other hand, incommunicability can be related to the radical limits of both language and thought, for they are coextensive. My answer to the above question, which leads nowhere, is therefore to ask another, along with Wittgenstein:

—Does this mean to say that there is something unique to be known about these contents, which would correspond to an experience that is mine? In that case, how can the sceptic or the subjectivist bring in experience in this sense, which is something that cannot in any way be tested? How do we learn to distinguish between the expressions "my experience," "your experience," and "his (or her) experience"? Unless we play around with the word "private" as a solipsist would do, like a child referring to things "on top" of the globe, for our experience is no more "private" than we are "on top" of the earth in relation to the peoples of the Antipodes.[46] Moreover, you claim that it is impossible to pass on to someone else the content of our subjective experiences. Does that mean that we talk to ourselves about them? If so, how do words relate to this content of which I am conscious? Or, to put it another way, how do we communicate our own experience of ourselves to ourselves? What language do we use?

Unless we are going to claim that it is a private language, the very notion of which is demonstrably absurd,[47] a "speaker" can only understand what she is saying to herself if other people can also understand it, i.e., if the language she uses is a public one.

A sceptic with more than one string to his bow would doubtless raise a further objection:

—You have inherited from Wittgenstein an analogy between subjective experiences as the property of a self which "has" its experiences, and private property. The private/public opposition is a specifically late category taken over from the history of law. It cannot be used to invalidate a classical tradition of inward meditation.

—No, not on its own. However, it should be noted that the term "private" characterizes the content of immediate experience quite well. Behind (and before) its legal sense, the word "private" derives etymologically from *privatus*, meaning "apart from the State and its public rules," which in turn is derived from *privare*, to deprive someone of something by violence. What began as a privation was then seen as a separation from the State, and finally as a right of being left alone.

—The fact remains that raw experience is individual and subjective by its nature.

—Who would disagree? That is virtually a tautological statement, though a fairly harmless one too, as we saw earlier. But when it comes to knowing or referring to our experience, we can only do so within a whole framework of concepts. Just because we are looking at a colored object does not mean to say that we have the concept of color *in* us. Concepts point immediately to a mastery of public language use, and the underlying behavioral and linguistic patterns it serves to express.

—And yet, does not common language use leave out something singular and individual, by not acknowledging the unique position of the self?

—You are going back there to the whole question begged by subjectivist discourse, which is precisely whether or not it is legitimate to demand such a privilege, or whether it is anything more than a figment of the imagination. Once it is defined in this way as that which escapes the understanding of others, and by which they also remain forever foreign to it, this self is also quite unable to understand itself.

If there is an experience of self for the self, we can only communicate it to ourselves in terms whose usage obeys the rules of a common criteriology, even if the context in which they are used and the mode of access to this type of so-called "subjective" event were both singular.

—But must we not at least identify the mental with that which is given to a consciousness as primary or primitive? Descartes' attempt to find a radical starting point in something that is evident for the subject was a move in this direction.

—Properly speaking, turning to the Cogito as a short circuit in the search for a reflexive-type radical starting point would also imply that we suspend our naive attitude to language. By which I mean the attitude we adopt when we spontaneously say: "I am disappointed," "I am confident," etc. Descartes does not consider doing this for one moment. He devotes a few lines of the *First Meditation* to throwing out foolishness and exaggeration, but not a word to exclude language from (or on the contrary, to include it in) the circle of philosophical investigation.

Let us be clear about this: according to Noam Chomsky, Descartes' conception of language has it that we think in a certain way outside language, before we come to externalize our ideas. In fact, let me say again, Descartes does seem to recognize that the language in which we communicate is also the one in which we think and make judgments. The only thing is (and this has considerable methodological implications), he does not subject language to hyperbolic doubt. It is as if language remained at the disposal of the meditating ego. For anyone bringing a radically critical approach to bear, expressions such as "I think," "I doubt," and "I know" only have meaning, like the ones cited earlier, in function of certain public language conventions. The remarkable thing about these conventions is the way they lead us to forget their existence.

In fact, of course, Descartes begins to meditate in an already speaking universe: he doubts, he thinks, he grasps his existence through language. And it is precisely language that instills in us the certainty of our existence. There is no tacit Cogito, and therefore no pure ego cogito, in the sense that it must necessarily be declared in a language others can also understand. That is the nature of the "I think" for a divided self. Or rather, a self which is initially in a relation, as it encounters the prior reality of the linguistic institution. Equally, it is not enough for the speaker to be certain that he or she means something by the words "I doubt that p," for the expression really to have meaning. This requires more than a private experience. It is necessary for the interlocutor to be able to know or doubt whether the speaker does doubt.[48] And again, is "I believe that p" the description of a state of mind? No, any more than it is an external experience. Whatever they may say to themselves to achieve self-understanding, people also need to be understood by others. And in order to be understood by others, they must begin by understanding these others. A last example: "I know that p" does not mean that p is true unconditionally and that I am the absolute bearer of that knowledge. To speak of knowing it is meaningless, just as doubt is meaningless in the context of what goes on inside us. Still less meaningful is the idea that we know it through some privileged process which may stand as exemplary of the way we know everything else. I cannot transfer to you my subjective experiences as such, for the sufficient reason that they are not things about which it is in any way meaningful to speak of "transferring" them. But I can inform you about them, and indeed I regularly do. I produce statements about them which you are all able to understand. As for whether or not we are better placed to test some statements than others, that remains an open question. From what I have said, however, it is clear that the solipsistic answer, that there is a form of access which is privileged as a matter of principle, can no longer be taken for granted.

To return to "I know that p", the only real usage of this phrase is in a pragmatically determined interlocutive context. Thus it will have equivalents. "I know" is always a bit like: "I am telling you that I know," and consequently: "I am passing on my knowledge to you," "you can rely on what I am telling you."

In my view, this type of criticism is fair. We must not accept the identification of the mental with what is immediately given to a subjective consciousness, seen as something private, primary, or primitive. The mental as it appears in the concepts of "thinking," "knowing," and "doubting" is much more dependent than is generally believed on the mastery of an interlocutive activity. It nevertheless remains true that an accurate reading would take care to distinguish between Descartes' concept of the inner self and the inner meaning of the Aristotelians, which are too often confused in English-language philosophical polemic. The inner self of which Descartes speaks is of course the direct knowledge the soul has of itself, as pure understanding. It has nothing to do, either, with the intimate self which Maine de Biran entrusts to his *Journal.* As for the reflection that gives this direct knowledge as much rigor and impersonality as mathematics, it must obviously not be confused with the observation of inner states, nor with any simple confidences of a personal nature. Rightly or wrongly, Descartes intended it as a critical analysis of intellectual activity.

A Second Approach: The Impasse of Negative Difference

A self possessed of an exclusive subjectivity may satisfy the subjectivist's definition of the subjective, but it is not the subject for which we are looking. If I were this subjective self, I would neither think nor speak. Thinking and speaking—including about oneself—are operations which always require our individual, purely negative difference to be put aside.

We are looking for a way of reformulating subjectivity on the basis of the interlocutive relation. Once this is discovered, everything changes. The subject/object relation is subverted by the way in which our critical discourse itself proceeds. Suddenly, self-consciousness conceived of as an "inner transcendental experience" is put firmly back in its place. It is now transcended in turn by the interdiscursive praxis which both provides its origin and allows it to function. Transcended and integrated. For I would not maintain, as did Freud and Claude Lévi-Strauss, that the operation of consciousness is itself a problem. Nor do I believe, as did Jacques Lacan, that the subject is occluded in consciousness, or, as did Karl Jaspers, that the Cartesian "I" is existentially too lightweight. I am inclined to believe that it is not radical enough.

Rather than trying to define the limits of a philosophy of consciousness, as Maurice Merleau-Ponty made a desperate attempt to do, my aim is to see self-consciousness as the product of the self's own labors, as it seeks to overflow its own boundaries. Philosophies of the subject rightly stressed the importance of the fact that man is born into a world of meaning and symbolic thought. But the price they paid was undoubtedly too high: they cut out any reflection on the system of signs and rules of discourse, to get straight to the source of the significational power. This also meant abandoning linguistic expression to its contingency and falsifying the description of speech activity, or rather, interaction. If we want to describe the speaking subject's true interactional and relational function, it is crucial that we make the long detour of looking at the signs that are actually exchanged in the common work of discourse. This will allow us to integrate the relationship between person and object with that between person and person, and bring out the real importance of each. A pragmatic and semantic approach should allow the articulation of two types of relationships: those linking human beings with each other, and those linking them with things. An individual standing before someone else becomes a person when the two of them form a dyad of interlocutors who are agents in a process of co-reference.

An undertaking such as this presupposes an epistemological decision about language, a foundational gesture. This will allow us to treat language not in a rationalistic way, in an attempt to answer the question of what a language must be like if it is to fulfill its instrumental function of communicating thought,[49] but in a rational way—which is something quite different. How can language be treated as an autonomous, positively valued object? The logicians of Port-Royal had much to say on matters related to language, but very little about language itself. The deliberate refusal to see language as a problem must now stop. It was tied to philosophies of the subject which privileged the Cartesian model of thought reflecting on itself, a thought disseminated into those atoms of consciousness which are ideas, the bearers both of their own content and of the light by which they are illuminated.

What will most significantly mark the contemporary period is the reintegration into linguistic discussion of things as referents. For the grammar of Port-Royal, things did not count; all that mattered was the relationship between thought and language. The problem of language's relationship to the world lay outside grammar. After all, when we speak, we never do so in order to say *nothing*. How, then, to describe patterns of verbal behavior without taking account of their nonverbal environment, and to analyze linguistic competence without reference to the conceptual competence on which it depended? How could a message be reconstructed indepenently of its context? Grammarians always remained blind to the fact that language is made for speaking, and that speech occurs between people in an interlocutive situation.

Nowadays the immanence postulate, according to which language should be studied in itself, by excluding the extralinguistic context, is being challenged from all sides, while the pragmatic approach seems to be gaining dominance. A fruitful exchange of hypotheses is now coming about between logic and linguistics. It is becoming more and more clearly recognized that real thought has a dual relationship with signs and with things, and that the reality of signs is itself an intersubjective one. Instead of relating signs to ideas, as in the classical model of analysis, sign theory is now relating signs to objects and to interlocutors. Objective reality is not a given, something incommunicable, but is rather always a communicated construction, and one indeed constructed, in part at least, by communication.

Third Experience of the Spirit

This decision about language is not without its consequences for the way in which the problem of persons is stated. There is now room to give the person a properly linguistic—i.e. communicational—status. Once the concept of language is seen as part of a wider concept of communication, *homo loquens* becomes *homo communicans*.[50]

We all participate in communication, rather than being its origin or its goal. Which means that it is our entry into the universe of canonical communication that gives us access to the function of utterer, and therefore to our status as persons.

Pragmatic Competence and Status as a Person

All in all, this principle has already provided us with quite a good understanding of the notions of subjectivity and the person. Admittedly, the primary character of the interlocutive relation means that subjectivity too will be fundamentally relational. Note, though, that I as a person am not just a point of random accumulation, an irreversible accretion of protocols of belief.[51] Once a distinction is made between two problems that are generally confused in discussions of the subject—the role in principle of subjectivity as the basis of personhood, and the entirely positive question of the subjectivity effect—then my earlier analysis can be extended by the following proposition:

> *Thesis:* I am that pragmatic competence which makes of me
> a subject capable of intercepting and interfering discursively
> with what goes on in the network of ideal communication.

To the concept of linguistic competence it is necessary to add at least that of communicative competence. For several reasons. First, speech performance is as much the product of rules as is language itself. The rules are partly social and cultural, and therefore of interest to sociolinguistics, and partly universal, thus falling in the domain of pragmatics in the true sense of the term—i.e., having to do with communicability in general, for performance in general involves competence.

Next, linguistic competence, as Chomsky for instance understands it, accounts for the possibility of proffering an infinite number of sentences. It does not explain our ability to form new utterances, to fit new situations. Consequently, what differentiates people as speaking persons from the machines that imitate them is not so much their linguistic competence, but its use in concrete situations. It is the person, not the machine, who makes real (i.e. communicational) use of language. Let us agree to call this form of linguistic competence *communicative competence.*[52]

It still remains for me to actualize the knowledge represented by this disposition, or competence, establishing my presence as a person by actually communicating. Here, and here alone, is where the ethical moment is located. For knowing is not wanting, nor does it help us to want. We sometimes do not wish to do everything that we can, although wanting is something anyone can do. When intentions are put into action, the result can be terrifying. Consequently, the question is whether or not to exercise our communicative competence. Will you accept this "responsibility," which constitutes your being (your act) as a person, and which no one can take over from you? However, this responsibility does not emanate or derive from subjectivity. It is the mark made on subjectivity by its fundamentally relational constitution. To be or not to be in a relation with another person—the choice is ours. Whether we accept or refuse is not a matter of indifference. It is the all-or-nothing ultimatum, the sudden mutation dear to the Stoics. The responsible exercise of this pragmatic competence, our responsibility for a responsibility, has an immediate value. Here lies the one essential asymmetry; it is impossible for the subject to discharge onto others its responsibility for the exercise of its communicative competence.

Now, from where does this power of mine derive? We must necessarily receive communicative competence into ourselves before we can exercise it. Like any other competence-based knowledge, it is not properly something that can be learned. We are coming close here to the essence of the human. If I were to describe (rather than explain) what happens, I would say that it is something that we are graciously and gratuitously given. The gift of communicative competence instills in us an urge to communicate which engenders the very possibility of community. Wherever there is the spirit of communication, there is community. Whenever a community is gathered together in the expectation and acceptance of communication, the creation of meaning is possible.

Here we have a new experience of the spirit. Like the two earlier ones, it depends on a power that only human beings possess.

Let me recapitulate: the first experience of the spirit was the possibility for the individual to aspire to the singular identification of his or her personal self. This was, as we saw, the legacy of a Cartesian problem reevaluated in other terms: instead of the center of personal existence being rooted in reflection, the person identifies itself as the other person's other (*you* and *he/she*, and *he/she* no less than *you*). The ego is no longer the product of a process of conscious self-realization, but a differential pole which retains its permanence during and through its interpersonal relationships.

The second experience of the spirit is, as we saw, the ability to call the relation of communicative mutuality into question in certain crisis situations. The speaking subject shows itself able to appeal against an instituted, official communication regime within which it regards itself as partially (or totally) alienated, in the name of a different regime in which speech would be full, rather than curtailed, and communication free, complete, and direct. To gain access to this canonical regime requires that a practical or a pragmatic break be made. The spirit always remains that part of us which only becomes something definite by its refusal to be anything in particular.

As for the third experience of the spirit, it involves the way in which we receive a communicative competence into ourselves. In a sense, it is something that we obtain simply by asking for it. Like grace. Is it an experience? Yes, metaphorically speaking. This "experience," to which analysis is now beginning to give us access, is an ontologically original one. Our ability to receive such a competence is neither simply anecdotal, nor mythical. It does however take us beyond the ordinary life of the individual; it gives us an opportunity of gaining access to the relation of personhood. The ability to receive something in itself implies a certain acceptance because it derives from an act of confidence.

This makes me unique and irreplaceable because I am the only one in a position to respond to, or slip away from, the challenge. With this new experience, the status of the person comes to include something like a gift: "And I shall give you a new spirit. . . ." Here, the personal self is clothed in a strength from above, something indivisibly given, like being, like relations in general; because of that, it is quite unlike the individual self, which is received as a possession in the midst of an egocentric environment. The gift of personhood is also the gift of the spirit. It is equally free. The spirit is therefore not just the power of grasping oneself as identical in one's relational life, as the first experience suggested; nor is it simply, as in the second experience, that ability to make a radical break with the communicational regime that makes us "inaccessible and impossible to grasp," an ability some philosophers have seen as the power of infinite doubt, questioning, or reserve. The spirit is above all a capacity for being and maintaining oneself in, and entering into, relations, as the third experience implies. It constitutes the beneficiary in the uniqueness of his or her existence, which is no longer that of a given biological or social individual. It constitutes him or her virtually in his or her essence, i.e. in his or her personal identity.[53]

We are now in a position to interpret Gen. I.26: "Then God said: 'Let us make man in our image and likeness to rule the fish in the sea, the birds of heaven, the cattle, all wild animals on earth. . . .'"

The proximity of man to the divine is not of the same order as the degree of resemblance of an image. By which I mean that man will share the same capacity for speech: he will name things in the same way that God does. God created the world through the Word. Man, created as male and female, will have dominion over animals by imposing his names on them. If he does not share in the creation of beings, he at least shares in the creativity of meaning. It is the sin of disobedience that takes away from Adam the ability for direct communication,[54] and loses him the benefits brought by a similarity of competence.

The call to live according to the gift of the Spirit is transmitted by the Holy One sent by God: "He taught them with a note of authority" (Mark I.22). He Himself already lives in that way, and commits Himself as He speaks. How could people not listen to His word? Authority in speech is the prerogative of Him, He who pays with His person.

There is certainly no question of our being foolish enough to want to explain the divine mysteries, when we cannot even count the grains of sand in the desert, the drops of rain that fall, or the days of all the centuries. But that does not mean that any possibility of making a critical appreciation of the religious experience is closed to the philosopher: first because human experience, taken in its constitutive dimension, is the only place where people can ask authentic questions about the absolute. Second, because the religious relation itself can only take place in the context of human relations. Kant accepted as much: "Between philosophical reason and Scripture, there can be not only compatibility, but harmony, so that a person who conforms to one will not fail to live in accordance with the other."[55]

The Trinitary Paradigm Again

At this point, I ask the reader to allow me a critical digression on theology. However we may interpret the harmony between Reason and Revelation, it is clear that the latter may include a pure religion of reason, while, on the other hand, the historical element of Revelation escapes the bounds of reason.

However, it seems to me that philosophy can lead us, *motu proprio* (by its own motion), to a different idea of Revelation, and in particular to the notion that it is a hopeful message about sincere communication between human beings as something conditioned by a true interpersonal relation.

In this perspective we should again recognize that the trinitary paradigm has something both powerful and illuminating to say. The Absolute is not a substance, nor a state or a system; it is, in its entirety, a living relationship with otherness. This invites a commentary on the splendor of the formula: God is love.[56] The divine essence is entirely to love. It may be that anything that cannot be loved is vain. It is also love that makes goodwill good. A pure intention itself is none other than an intention to love. The true God is then He in whom the relation produces Being,[57] in whom love is incarnate, in whom logos, the relation, is made flesh. It must be said that this God in whom love produces the body meshes admirably with the doctrine of the Incarnation.

From this point, the status and destiny of human persons are revealed to us at the same time that they are accomplished by the action of the Son as he comes to constitute and grasp the person so as to introduce it into the glory of the Father. In him God is made manifest no less as paradox than as light, and as provocation rather than explanation. His ministry accompanies his effort to realize what in Kant's Dialectic of Practical Reason is called "the entire object of will". Before I can produce it by my own effort, I find in me, thanks to Christ, the image of man which is pleasing to God.

But the real reason that it is not possible to make messiahship into a privilege of the Self[58]—a self universally responsible and called to bear the suffering of all—lies elsewhere. It is not so much that it would be an anthropologization of the Mystery, but because such a return to the self, though for a perfectly admirable reason of ethical probity, in fact conceals and compromises the primacy of the Relation, in both the life of the divinity and in messianic reality. In Christ, God becomes visible, restoring the Alliance through mercy. He not only speaks of it, like the prophet Hosea, but he is also its incarnation. He is himself the proposition mercy, and in him God becomes visible as the Father rich in mercy.

The difficulty in sustaining a relational version of biblical Revelation, and particularly the messiahship of Christ, to the limit of its possibilities, lies in keeping everything in proportion. Christ's messiahship is not just an unexpected event in a drama of salvation played out before one's birth, nor does it represent the ethical responsibility of the self, but it is a true figuration of deliverance and return: in this sense it is crucial for the messiah to be given and not simply promised. In my view, it is harder to give than to offer oneself.

The treatise on the Sanhedrin in the *Talmud* states that the Messiah is everyone, here and now, who obeys the Law. The Messiah thus becomes simply an ethical category, a "beggar at the gates of Rome," any man from among the damned of the earth. Whereas Isaiah sees the messianic gathering in terms of a banquet to which all will be freely invited and where each will be satisfied.[59] There is no doubt that the Cross adds to the meaning of the word *God* the notion of His relation to man as something freely given, that of a sacrificial love which is stronger than death, and finally that of our relationship as concerned people with Him. It seems that the human person has the vocation of sharing in the very life of the Trinity. We learn that the recognition and acceptance of this offer by an individual in fact involves ratifying a personal reality which cannot be obtained from him or herself alone. Thus the Revelation of the Son completes the neutralization of the heteronymy introduced into human history, and the asymmetry brought into the Alliance, by the Revelation of the Father. The Son reveals not only the nature of God's self-communication in the Trinity, but also man's admirable vocation in God's plan, which is to gain access to the life of the divinity.

We have rightly been warned, it seems to me, against a regrettable conception of messiahship: the objectivization in a Messiah of a salvation that precedes us, and above all the temptation to shrug off responsibility for the Passion onto someone else.[60] We are told that it is essential for the Messiah, if he does not want to alienate man, to be promised but never given. It seems to me on the contrary that the messiahship of the Son, duly coordinated with the dogma of the Trinity, loses any sense of redemption by extrinsic means. It is no longer a saving operation which would alienate man's autonomy. Now the Incarnation of the Son is thinkable as a figure of humility rather than an objectivizing fixation on a tangible presence. Instead of seeing it as a saving deliverance which takes away man's responsibility and conditions him in an external way, we should read it as the most effective emblem of the destiny of the person.

Kant gives an admirable description of the idea of Christ and his function as a figure of hope. Independently of the event itself (which is not Kant's concern as a philosopher), his idea of Christ and his reading of the Incarnation in relation to the dogma of the Trinity are quite different. Both can be illuminated by reference to the theology of divine missions and energies. Is this something we can accept?

According to the theology of divine missions, we can only meet God from within Him and through Him.[61] In the theology of the Holy Spirit, the Holy Spirit is the *semen Dei*. Proceeding from the Father,[62] he is God himself as eschatological, ultimate and absolute gift. As for the ministry of the Son, it expresses the action of the Spirit:[63] if the Son is entirely turned toward the Father,[64] it is because the Spirit himself is the breath of the return to the Father. Christ is the Son made man, and the Son is turned entirely toward his Father. This concerns us because we are children and Christ, who deigned to allow himself to be counted among creatures, is our universal brother.[65]

I know of nothing so sublime (and unbelievable) as this assignation to man of the formal model of trinitariness. The human condition is a filial one. To which we must immediately add (rather than separating it, which would make Freud's critique pertinent) the offer of assimilating the human to the divine condition through sacrifice. A God who (like Abraham) does not refuse His own Son, a Son subjected to the trial of death so as to allow us access to the plenitude of life: this shows us the secret way to lay down our life as individuals, by accompanying the Son into the battle in which He has preceded us. Secret, because the heart of man is not yet deep enough to contain the plenitude that God reveals in His Son. In Him, God gives us His own life, introducing man to the life of the trinity and in that sense making him divine. The Son, the One to whom we must listen, lets us into the secret. "God sent His own Son, born of a woman. . . . in order that we might attain the status of sons. To prove that you are sons, God has sent into our hearts the Spirit of His Son, crying: Abba! Father!"[66] We can only return to the Father by accepting the gift which He makes to us of the Son and the Holy Spirit.

To complete this admirably coherent design, let me add something about the Holy Spirit. It acts in us as we listen to the Word, so that after the Son has ministered, His work may be accomplished and men may have an opening into the Trinity. For the Spirit, there are neither Greeks nor Jews, men nor women. Equally, the Son was that being linked both to God and to all people. What did His ministry announce? It announced a relationship contained in Being, at the heart of the absolute, capable of being extended to men as a fundamental competence. So that they may share in plenitude.[67] They shall be sons grafted onto the life of the Trinity. The effect of this extension is to promote men into persons. I ask again: how are we to understand this?

First, the new Law is such that to say "God is light," "God is love," or "God is spirit" has little to do with the essence of God. These attributes bear on the relations between God and man. They are terms of Alliance.[68] As love is the preeminent form of the relation, including that from God to man, this involves what in Revelation is termed the love of God (by and for man). Its presence can only be seen negatively, when it is deliberately destroyed. It is not an object for our consciousness. Is it not significant that transcendence cannot be experienced here in a positive mode? In us, it is God that loves God, and He is not an object.[69]

We observe that once it is interpreted in this way, religious experience no longer poses a problem of religious psychology. Moreover, this use of the term *experience* is also recent, superficial, and dated: William James, for instance, speaks of mystical states of consciousness as so many religious experiences. In the first place, *experience* must be taken in its pragmatic, relational sense. Next, it is neither alienating (Marx), paradoxical (Kierkegaard), nor a matter of exploiting resentment (Nietzsche). Religious experience is only human experience in its constitutive dimension. It teaches us that the status and vocation of personhood comes to humans from the fact that they are linked together, in that this relation is also absolutely present in the life of the divinity. The human person then has the unique experience of existing not through him or herself, nor through someone else (not even God Himself, the Totally Other, as is sometimes believed), but through the very relationship that unites us and precedes us only by its free nature.

It is sometimes said that this is the experience of the power of the Word. Yes and no. I would concede that proclamations and parables, psalms and prophetic discourses, teach us that we have a particular dependency on speech. It is true that they are where our real relationship with language is most effectively manifested, where it is revealed to us by a sort of inversion of our ordinary discursive practice. Instead of saying something on which we agree about beings and things, we have the experience of being created, reborn through language (this is in general the poetic experience), and giving ourselves up to language rather than using it.

But what exactly is the act of speech? It is not so much a question of submitting to the meaning of words we have heard spoken and then interpreted, or to that of a text we have deciphered. The heart of the operation, its key, remains hidden so long as the efficacy of the speech is not related to the Relation that sustains it. A believer experiences a speech even when he or she tries out an interlocutive relation, a situation in which the mere fact that a relationship exists obliges him or her to respond as a person. Which means that he or she is effectively being summoned, called forth anew as something irreplaceable. To submit oneself to the experience of the spirit is to give oneself over to actively experiencing the plenitude of communicative competence.

Is the term "interpellative discourse" (*An-rede*), which has so often been put forward to characterize the function of the Old Testament,[70] preferable to that of interlocutive relation? Not at all. Yes, speech does make a call upon me, but only thanks to the Relation that carries it and which it presupposes. This means that the believer enters into a relationship with God. Man has relations with men, but with God also, and indeed it is through the way he accepts communication with God (for he does have this communicative ability) that he acquires his own relational being, his complete being as a person, his act of being.[71]

Let us then see where this leads us. However we read the text of Genesis on evil, it is clear that relations between people depend on the relationship each of them has with God. Thus the evil of Cain's verbal, then murderous, violence toward Abel is presented in the Bible as a failure of human relations, accentuated in surprising fashion by fraternity. Cain and Abel fight because they are close, not distant. Now this profound misfortune, this relational transformation, is preceded by a dialogue between Cain and the Eternal about a sacrifice of which God did not approve. Abel's offerings, on the other hand, were acceptable. Should this be seen as a test? On the contrary, it is a sanction, the just returns of an ungracious sacrifice in which the elder brother had not offered himself at the same time as what he was offering. According to the interpretation in the Midrash:

> Abel offered the first-born of his flock,
> Cain offered just any fruit,
> And Abel *brought himself* as well.

Abel implicated himself, invested himself, in the sacrificial gesture; Cain did not. The one agreed to make the ultimate religious gesture of giving by giving himself, materializing the gift of his being through the gift of what he had. The other held himself back, slipped away. Their two responses were unequal.

The fact that God loved us first is enough to reestablish the disproportion between Him and His creatures. Abel accepted the correct relationship of which God is the canonical principle. He called for it in prayer, and received it as good news, as a competence to be exercised. But Cain, who was no less *capax Dei* than his brother Abel, chose not to exercise that competence.

Breakdown and Betrayal of the Relation

The story of Genesis is a rapid sequence of relational events. If violence breaks out and disintegrates a fraternal relationship, it is because it was itself the result of a disintegration already under way, an effect of entropy that had built up over time. One day, the dissymmetry of the relationship between Cain and Abel becomes apparent. It is significant that the event comes after the story of the relationships, themselves asymmetrical, that each has with God. What a difference in the way they receive the divine gift! Compared to Abel, Cain's attitude was mediocre. The Bible presents him as the firstborn, his mother's favorite. He appears rather unfraternal, nonrelational. Abel, on the other hand, is from the start a relational being who is called "the brother."

The most striking thing here is the intrusion of temporality. Time intervenes at the heart of the microsystem of relations between God and Cain, God and Abel, Abel and Cain—to say nothing of the relations between each of the brothers and his parents. Time derives from sin—a fall that happened further back, at the instigation of the serpent, the transgressor of the absolute. Time follows from moral breakdown as its punishment; it does not precede it; it is a breach opened up by that breakdown, but one that can be repaired by a possible restoration of integrity. What has happened is that a relational system has become unbalanced and threatens to disintegrate. Evil has "entered the system," and time has clothed us and everything else in its unreal veil, and hidden things from us.

Evil enters the system as a moral weakness which opens up a crack in our relations and causes their breakdown. But how can a relation that, ontologically, has the guarantee of being itself, become changed? This question, which I ask in connection with the relationship between Cain and the Eternal, is a difficult one. How is it possible for a relationship to be degraded? This is the form in which I see the classic problem of the irruption of evil into the world.

I have given much thought to this question. This is where, I believe, human fallibility, man's essential finitude, comes in. Rather than being an absence of the absolute in us which deepens our feeling of imperfection, rather than being an inherent weakness of our subjectivity, this finitude manifests itself as a tendency to renounce relational plenitude. Instead of being the trace of an absolute of which we have been deprived, it is a deficiency caused by withdrawal and betrayal, a pit within us that we dig deeper from one breakdown of a relationship to the next.

How Is It Possible for Relations to Break Down?

There is an order in the manifestation of evil which goes from deficiency, to breakdown, to betrayal. The first step is a deficiency of simple omission. For human beings, this means not actualizing one's status as a person. Conversely, the full exercise of that competence implies implementing the relation in a manner which conforms to one's being. Translated into theological language, this means that grace will be there so long as I am willing to accept it. Faith here means refusing to interrupt the relation, and hope is not accepting catastrophe. I no longer need a psychological act of will which proceeds from an individual decision. The only clear decision here is a negative one, occurring out of weakness on my part. It is also a misfortune, the suspension of something viable.

Some would wish to relate the breakdown of relations to an extrinsic temptation. Is that a reasonable thing to do? At least my weaknesses belong to me. But how can I take them back to the depths of myself, if they are nothing? Valéry tried to do this in his poem "L'Insinuant" (which is probably a first sketch for his *Serpent*) by describing a movement which is the speaker's but seems foreign to him:

> O you Curves, you meander,
> Secrets of the liar,
> Is there any art more tender
> Than this slowness? [72]

The temptation to lie seems like nothing at all. Yet, says Valéry, its almost nonexistent possibility lays seige to us. Furtively, the serpent begs us to be weak, undermining us and mocking our weakness. Diabolically, he divides us; he is the separator. All his art is in a gentle whisper. Therefore the poet describes in him negative terms:

> My evil design
> Is not to do you harm. [73]

There is in this extrinsic temptation a double perversity. But the fascination it exerts over us is not really very significant. It is like a moment of suspicion in love, when the lover's feeling turns back on itself and decides to keep its own company. To say that I am tempted is to say that my resolve is shaken. Alain comments, more accurately: the deceiver's ruse is abstract. His aim is to "shake by not touching." The idea that evil is exogenous, that it comes from somewhere else, is the comforting fable of persuasive perversion. I search all around me for the corruptor. I name him. I make him responsible for all the coincidences that are the reward for my cowardice, and that gratify the individual in each of us.

It is clear, of course, that the weakness is really ours. We are our own serpent. Let me quote Shakespeare here to extend what Valéry has to say. Troilus is a Trojan warrior who is returning to battle. His tearful wife swears to remain faithful to him. No, no, do not swear, Troilus replies to Cressida; it may happen that we become devils to ourselves. Such is the weakness of man. Here is the dialogue:

TRO.   There lurks a still and dumb-discursive devil
       That tempts most cunningly, but be not tempted.
CRES. Do you think I will?
TRO.   No,
       But something may be done that we will not. [74]

Yes, we are sometimes demons for ourselves. Along the poet's road, I point out this idea in passing. We may, with the agnostic, call the devil that which in each of us aspires to destroy us. But a relational definition is also possible that calls the devil that which aspires to break the link between us and destroy us in that way instead.

Do not be deceived by the license I have allowed myself in describing the breakdown of the relation. The fact that its failure may be experienced by one of its terms must not be allowed to mask the relational character of the phenomenon. Properly speaking, to say that a relationship is broken means that the notion of being-as-relation has been lost or is in decline. Don D. Jackson recently confirmed this intuition: clinicians, he tells us, are increasingly in agreement that conjugal relations never become unbalanced as a result of the actions of just one of the partners. It remains the case, however, that one of them may decide to suspend the exercise of his or her communicative competence, or not to accept it. The first moment of breakdown is one of withdrawal from the demands of the relationship, which cease to be taken into consideration.[75] It is therefore not in itself a positive and unilateral act, imputable to a subject, but rather it is an evasion, a stepping back (or sometimes a stepping aside). We first drift, or atrophy, into evil. Every day I become more separated from others, and from myself.

However, there is sometimes a second moment when this absence is used. At that point it becomes a true privation, an ill deliberately done to the other person, whom I have betrayed. It can happen that I accept and declare my betrayal, in an act of real ontological mendacity; then, the relationship to which I have been unfaithful declines and becomes deficient. It matters little here whether the dissociation of what had been tightly associated comes about through indolence, instability, weakness, or a suicidal impulse; the fact remains that I turn in on myself and the other person correspondingly backs away from me. This attack on the relationship is a sin against the spirit, or against love, whichever you prefer. If I do still accept the existence of the other as a person, it is at most only as a mode of existence of my ego. Is this egotism? It is at least a turning-inward of the self, which is depersonalizing in its nonrelational nature. The person in me strays and becomes lost. What began as a deficit in our relationship becomes an attitude of hostility toward the other person which is not a relation at all. And there is no way of propping up Satan's kingdom, whose decline is irreversible.

Let us return to empirical matters. For an individual engaged in a communication situation within a speaking community, there is a question about his or her concrete self. Let me reformulate it in terms of personal status. For nobody says *I* in the same way that his or her neighbor does. Do we ever know who is speaking? How, then, am I different from you, as a person?

Personal Status and Proper Names: From Individual to Person

From the start, I shall be careful to avoid exaggeration: when I refer to the speaking community, I do not wish to give absolute priority to the circulation of meaning, and reduce persons to being merely poles of communication. Let me dispatch one false idea straight away: I have not privileged man-as-link over man-as-node in order to reduce his status as a person to zero. We shall see in the two following sections how the self may be given back its personal status and singularity.

"Who are you?" Our first response is generally to give our name and a few socioprofessional details. It is always an embarrassing question. We reply by offering our individual visiting card. Here, according to Hervé Bazin, is Madame le Conidée's: "Black hair, round face, straight nose, olive complexion. Born of a long-haul sea-captain father and Brazilian half-caste mother. And, I would add: former medical student. . . ."[76]

Let us now examine the same question on the basis of my own premises. We see that the content and identification of our empirical subjectivity are given by personal predicates, some of which qualify and describe our particular status as persons, while others situate persons in their personal status within the community ("son of," "sister of"). There are also our beliefs and, more generally, propositional attitudes about states of affairs, on which we are constantly taking up positions interlocutively.

Let us think about what happens during a fully developed discussion. The need for mutual understanding forces each interlocutor to assume all the propositional attitudes adopted by everyone else. Which requires a communicative ability to listen in turn to what is said. But one person cannot occupy all these different positions without the various possible worlds that they imply coming into conflict. Yet what happens? Each person's personal subjectivity reveals itself formally as such. Any successfully formulated language act gives us information about its utterer and his or her particular preferences for the realization of certain possible states of affairs over others. If u_1 tells u_2 that he or she believes p, he or she is revealing his or her own belief—i.e., belief in a situation where, in the perspective of all the possible worlds compatible with his or her other beliefs, p would be true. This is precisely how subjectivity becomes differentially perceivable, in an interlocutive context: by means of the possible worlds, variants of the real world, which are enveloped in the propositional attitudes formulated at any given point in a dialogical confrontation.[77]

Whatever theoretical model may be chosen to explain propositional attitudes, its aim will be to allow us to understand the fact that in a certain way I *am* that concretion of beliefs that have been engendered little by little in the course of my active communication with all the different human beings I have met. While this may not establish the permanence of the subject (something ultimately impossible), it at least implies the constant renewal of certain states that combine to form a series or system. The attempt to find out how the successive beliefs of a personal self organize themselves in a more or less stable way would be a rich field of investigation.

On the other hand, the very possibility of personhood implies that an individual can take his or her place within a communicational universe, with the opportunity of exercising his or her pragmatic competence. This is the condition sine qua non of his or her recognition there as a particular person. The individual then establishes him or herself in a network of interpersonal, and not just interindividual, relationships. Whereas the subjective self is properly unnameable, and the individual is a purely referential reality, part of being a person is having a name.

Let me stress the importance among proper nouns of names for people, which act to support our personal status. Some names are full of warmth, others frigid. Some are highly unfortunate: "My surname: offended; my first name: humiliated; my state: in revolt; my age: the age of stone," says Aimé Césaire's rebel.[78] Some remain unspoken because they are too common or because people do not want to say them, while others diffuse through the speaking community in a haze of notoriety. This is because they do not indicate the person as would some kind of pointer, as a serial number that denotes the individual without saying anything more about him or her; for in my view, their role is to evoke the self in its personal status, by conferring on it a social existence. I should add that they are also multifunctional.

First, of course, they are singular terms like those of common language. According to one still quite widespread view, they are a particular segment of the vocabulary: without any meaning of their own, they are seen as serving a merely denotational function, and as having no role in human communication. Like deictic expressions such as demonstratives, they are supposed to represent direct associations between segments of meaning and fragments of the world. This is a highly approximate characterization. Proper names have both a denotative referential function (they designate) and an identifying function (they describe). But the semantic value of a unique designation needs to be actualized in an utterance.

The linguist adds further requirements, particularly pragmatic ones, to those of the logician; these combine to give three types of singular terms: indicators, descriptions, and proper names. Indicators relate the object to the present circumstances of utterance; descriptive expressions treat singular objects as specimens of a class which could contain other objects (e.g. the firstborn of Abraham). As for proper names, they establish the object's full importance, its positive difference. They are what makes ordinary language able to emphasize the contours of the universe, and particularly to give those who are close to us, and whom we are eager to single out by naming them, a definite place within it.

As a means of designating persons, the specificity of proper names is a pragmatic one; my name only denotes me in so far as it carries the memory of the different self-presentations by which I have already declared myself as a speaking subject in a communicational universe. Nor can it denote me without reminding others of the different ways in which they have addressed me, so that it also carries the memory of what they have said to me. That is why proper names are so much at home in questions and supplications in the second person: "O Rome, O Bérénice, O unfortunate Prince!" exclaims Racine's Titus. In this irreducible and no doubt primary function, proper names are used in speech to make invocations, or their counterparts, vows and prayers. When turned toward God as a person, this is the language of the Psalms. Turned toward people, it is the language of exclamation. More than their indexical value (which I do not need to go into here), the interpellative function of proper names manifests the relationship between a speaker and a named person in a specific language act. This function is difficult for logicians to analyze, because they cannot account for it by extensional means. Grammarians themselves are unable to assimilate the vocative case to the nominative, or to any of the oblique cases.

In the third place, a proper name does not designate a person without describing that person's place as a *him/her* within the speaking community, as the center of a criss-crossing network of interwoven communicational relationships. The marginal individual is anonymous, or ill-named.[79] Note that once named, a person can be described in terms of his or her own actions or statutory titles, as well as characterized by reference to the empirical traits that derive from their individuality. The sort of description that derives from the giving of names is pragmatic. There is nothing to stop this description from diffusing through the community, at the same time as the noun to which it is attached, the proper name that inhabits people's memories, the support and vessel of a person's reputation:

> I give you these lines so that, if my name
> Should chance to reach the shore of times far off,
> And cause some eve the brains of men to dream,
> A vessel favored by a great North wind. . . .

Now, the three pragmatic functions of proper names—self-presentation, apostrophe, and intracommunitary delocution—derive, as the reader will have realized, from the three positions in the communicational act.[80] It is remarkable that, among singular terms, only proper names can fill all three; if they assume one rather than the others it is only a matter of emphasis, the other two remaining virtual. For example, in the case of the speaker's self-presentation, what do we find? He or she has only to say "I" to designate him or herself as a speaking subject, without needing to add his or her name. When a speaker does so, it is not as a way of designating him or herself in individual uniqueness, but so as to situate him or herself in a certain social grouping. A proper name is only *I* to the extent that I am part of a universe of communication. It accompanies the pronoun *I* not so as to specify my personal identity—we do not give a full account of our identity by giving our name—but as the abbreviated vehicle of a presumptive identity. Taking or giving one's name is still a major commitment.

A breach opens up in the objective fabric of things. Anything that possesses a proper name can no longer be an object, or belong to anyone as does a thing; nor can it belong, like an individual, to a species or genus. Nor does it have its place like an object in the objective world, or like an individual at the center of its biological environment. Anyone who possesses a name has a place at the nexus where certain possible relations meet within the speaking community. By actualizing them, such a person realizes a potential fragment of the communicational universe, transporting his or her *here* and *now* along with him or her. This person is not, however, the center of that universe—and still less its origin—otherwise there would be as many communicational universes as there are speakers.

All this means that a proper name is much more than an index for localizing an individual, an abbreviated form of a definite description, or a more or less limited set of such descriptions. We can use a proper name correctly without being ready to provide on demand the description of what it is supposed to abbreviate in our minds. People are sometimes extremely reticent about committing themselves to giving a particular description. On the other hand, we cannot entirely do without descriptions relating to persons. But such descriptions as we may impute, just like the personal predicates we attribute, are properly subject to the approval or recognition of the person concerned. Even if none of the three pragmatic functions is particularly stressed, any proper name is virtually multifunctional. Which is precisely what makes it able to act as the support for our personal status.

It will now be clear why our status as persons is more fundamental than our personal status. Logico-linguistic analysis of the process of reference to someone has already shown the central (and utterly irreducible) role played in it by back-reference. Naming by the use of proper nouns, and the descriptions that serve to specify what I have called our personal status, are necessarily secondary in relation to reference by means of personal pronouns. This last occurs as soon as the message is communicated, for it brings its own agencies of utterance into existence.

I am linked to others by obligations in respect to their status as persons. A network of such obligations links each of us to all the others. It is always the person as such that is the bearer of these obligations. When they come down into the factual domain, they show themselves as (positive) rights belonging to individuals. These depend on the conditions under which people belong to the group that conditions them. In contrast, the obligation of respect that we owe to all human beings as persons is an unconditional one. Each person therefore sees that his or her communicative competence, which allows him or her to work at personal integration and thereby build his or her own destiny, is recognized by everyone else.

As a result, this obligation does not depend on any factual situation, whether it be a certain balance of forces, a heritage from the past, a supposed future orientation, or even a social structure. The respect owed to an empirical community depends on that community's ability to organize, here and now, respect for communicative competence. As for individuals in the group, the inevitable differences between them must never lead to different degrees of respect for their status as persons. But this obligation does not relate directly to the possibility of each individual having a personal destiny, which remains his or her own affair. So how can this obligation be fulfilled, i.e., how can this respect for persons be expressed? No doubt, as Simone Weil suggests, by way of people's physical and moral needs (hunger, freedom, responsibility, security, etc.).[81] These are the needs of individuals whose vocation is to achieve the status of persons.

Let us take the analysis a little further. From the functional point of view I have adopted here, it is a good idea to consider on the one hand communications induced, with more or less distortion, by the knowledge associated with competence, and, on the other, the decision whether or not this knowledge should be actualized. As we shall see, the consequences are not without interest.

In the first place, linguistic acts and communicational behavior in general represent the present exercise of a pragmatic competence. I agree that this process is empirically conditioned, subject to constraints that restrict free and open human exchange. But in itself, it derives from a disposition specific to personhood.

I am deliberately adopting Kantian terminology[82] to bring out a displacement that has occurred in such classical and controversial distinctions as that between the theoretical and practical interests of reason. Once the prog-

245

ress of the rational discourse of science, particularly on a metatheoretical level,[83] comes to depend on our obligation to actualize our pragmatic competence in our interpersonal relations, it is the person as a being at once reasonable and rational who must oblige him or herself to respect the nonconditioned nature of that competence. The ability to perform correct linguistic acts is present from the start, in that it is a necessary part of the very possibility of personhood.

Second, there is the decision whether or not to actualize my pragmatic competence, a decision which falls within my own responsibility. This is where it is open to me to exercise my freedom, a freedom that extends exactly as far as my willingness to respond to the gift of competence made to me, and to make of it the motive for my symbolic behavior. Here again we see the spectre of evil and its cause, the failing of simple withdrawal which I referred to as a moral weakness, or breakdown.

Different individuals are more or less strongly predisposed toward personhood. I am forced to define it by an ability to feel respect for communicational legality, in so far as respect is a sufficient motive for my action and speech. Some people are more easily able to overcome the individual in themselves than are others. It is a fragile aptitude. It can easily be undermined by an acquired propensity to mix in purely empirical motives, and even to prefer them out of a sort of perversion of the heart.

It is clear why this should be. Is not the first law of all beings self-preservation? Individuality is constantly working in living beings against their disposition toward personhood, through two of its commonly recognized characteristics: the feeling that we are absolutely singular, and that we cannot be divided without deterioration. We tend constantly toward the idea that we are a self-sufficient organism. As in our societies the class of persons is co-extensive with the class of individuals, the personal self is constantly at the mercy of its finiteness and its fleshly limitations. It is threatened by ways of thinking that resolve around the frontiers of the body and which, when they try to justify themselves, take on every appearance of the most spontaneous egotism. Because he or she is also a psychosomatic being, each person-being has a partial, spontaneously egocentric perspective. The individual can easily have second thoughts, start to make its own demands, and see itself as non-relative; its disposition to personhood is then short-circuited. There also arises, beyond any demands for physical self-preservation, an unjustifiable egotistical preference whereby each living individual tends asymmetrically to acquire a superiority over others. Thus passions of envy, rivalry, and ingratitude are born, which devour personal being. The individual will sometimes give up and accept them. The cynic will even go further and treat others in an utterly insolent way.

To return as an individual to a state of substantive nondividedness from oneself simply means being subject to the empirical and contingent conditions of life, which are a constant threat to the exercise of our pragmatic competence. Our fallibility lies in the fact that we are tempted to prefer individual to personal identification. There are two strong cases in which an individual will decline to see him or herself as a person: such an individual can refuse to put his or her identity at stake in the universe of canonical communication, by shutting him or herself off and taking refuge in self-sufficiency; or he or she can live out in mechanical fashion the communication relations contained in the established system, without making any effort to invest him or herself in them and change them. Of course, these resurgences of the individual are not to be confused with the entirely legitimate process by which the person in us reaffirms itself, at a moment when the established communicational regime does not allow it to actualize its pragmatic competence without unacceptable distortions.

We commonly oscillate between deciding to give ourselves over to our pragmatic competence or, on the contrary, to postpone its actualization. Individuals tend to want to delay the moment of full acceptance of their pragmatic competence and are often prepared to allow the exercise of straight communication to be influenced in other ways, by their organic needs or the suggestions, latent or violent, of collective conformism. The mystical expression of these flights from the true path is well known: God has hidden Himself from man; because of his "disobedience," His creature has lost the similarity with his creator that his capacity for speech gave him. On the other hand, whenever man acts upon the joyful Annunciation of the metacommunicational message, he chooses himself in conformity with this personal being.

Whether or not to exercise one's pragmatic competence, whether or not to actualize it: these two sets of contrary options bring about a duality in us. It is no longer the duality of mind and body, or of empirical and transcendental selves. Nor that of the two interests of reason; still less of two distinct faculties. This duality is now the division that forms between two relational entities, who stand one with another in the relationship of a producer to his or her product. And we again find in the person the opposition between active and passive which marks his or her destiny. This is a considerable simplification. Kant discerned three elements in an individual's destiny: his or her disposition as a living being; his or her disposition to humanity as a living, rational being (a disposition conditionally governed by theoretical or technical reason, but subordinated to subjective motivations of self-love); and finally, his or her disposition to personhood—in other words, to practical reason which legislates unconditionally. In my analysis, as we have seen, the second of these dispositions disappears. Indeed, in my view communicational rationality presides over the search for theoretical truth through the exchange of meaning, no less than it does over relationships between persons. It is not divisible:[84] its significance is indivisibly ethical and theoretical.

Everything here depends on the technical notion of communicative or pragmatic competence,[85] a notion which has some crucial implications, as I have pointed out, for a transcendental philosophy.

We must first accept that the ability to produce recursively an unlimited number of well-formed sentences does not exhaust the productivity of discourse. In particular, we must recognize the pertinence of pragmatic parameters in determining the illocutionary force or actional value of such sentences within an interlocutive context.[86] The notion of pragmatic competence is now taking its proper place in the analytic study of the discursive communication of speaking subjects. We may assume that the pragmatic dimension of discourse analysis has been recognized. Next, however, this notion has a key philosophical significance: just as a pragmatics can have a transcendental value, as a means of discovering the conditions of possibility of discursive activity, so what I have called pragmatic competence can be seen as the acceptance by the utterer of the formal a priori principle that constitutes communicative interaction.

It then becomes unnecessary to wonder about exactly where this competence is embodied. It is superfluous to embody it in any particular reality, any psychobiological entity. It consists in the mastery of the pragmatic rules that determine the conditions under which a sentence will succeed in a given interlocutive context. We no longer need to invoke the mind as its support. Linguistic competence means internalizing the conditions of possibility governing the construction of well-formed sentences and the assignment to them of a semantic interpretation. It must be accompanied by an ability to fix the meaning communicated by discursive activity. All these conditions together constitute a formal a priori. There is indeed no point in regarding this a priori as something substantial, as Chomsky does. It is an a priori that governs the production of communicated discourse. In my view, it relates directly to a transcendental agency which is the interlocutive relation. But this is too sweeping a contention to be defended in detail here. Let us pass on to something else.

6　Difference and Differentiation

・　・　・　・　・

I express things asymmetrically and I could express
them symmetrically; only then would we see what it
is that pushes us toward asymmetrical expression.
—WITTGENSTEIN

THE CONDITIONS under which our pragmatic competence is
exercised are enlightening, in a number of ways. They allow us to understand why personal identification—my own as well as other people's—is an
ongoing process. Persons are continually in the process of construction, without repeating themselves. We can also see why this construction does not exclude the maintenance and preservation of a certain sense of self, nor even
the creation of differences: being oneself and being different are virtually
synonymous in everyday language, a relationship it is not impossible to justify. We tend to regard difference as a characteristic trait of persons, and
even as a value in itself. But what sort of difference?

In fact, as we have already seen, the search for absolute difference, separation for its own sake, is only a by-product of egotism. An original person is
supposed to have a strong personality. We feel that the person is threatened
by the increased uniformity of patterns of behavior, and that people no
longer know how to tell their own story. But what we perceive at any given
moment is not someone's individuality, but only that person's difference from
other individuals, and this difference is relative. Moreover, it derives from

the fact that persons are relational entities. Now, curiously, this also allows us to conceive of difference as something positive, without its being originary. The present chapter will be devoted to showing how this may be done, and to completing my analysis of the person.

All about Difference

People often say that all you have to do to avoid seeing others as rivals and trying to dominate them is to look into yourself, and this will fill you with concern, even tenderness, toward them. This is the experience of the sojourn in the desert, a period of reordering which purges us of our enmities. But there is also another way, less uncertain and erratic (and less well known): it is a way that is already there in the relation, and that allows us to see difference in relational terms.

This raises the opposite problem to the one facing philosophers of consciousness. Instead of a way for the transcendental ego to break out of its desperate solitude, what is needed now is a method by which, starting from the interpersonal relation and its explicit manifestation, the interlocutive relation, a person can awaken to his or her own difference. It is a question of his or her making and maintaining a place within the relation, without demanding any excessive privilege, but in such a way that his or her difference will be assured. For a long time, the generous moralist had been recommending to us that we love other people so that they may awaken to themselves.

A New Strategic Attack on the Question

Philosophically, this turns our whole way of looking at things upside down. We can no longer start out from the primitive exteriority of persons constituted in their respective interiority. We must even reject the more subtle theme of the essential alterity of the other, according to which isolation is a direct function of being: to claim that relations with others happen contemporaneously with the process by which each person is constituted as self-sufficient would again amount to saying that the self is an absolute point of departure. According to this view, I set off to discover the other person, that other *I*, much like Columbus crossing the Atlantic to discover an other as far away and foreign, on a cultural and historical level, as we may choose to imagine, an other who is perceived in abstract and negative difference, because he or she belongs to a group to which I do not belong. . . . But that would be another individual, not another person.

It is clear that in order to exist as a personal self I must necessarily find another person. For each of us, other people become agents in the formation of our person. In this sense, it takes two selves to make one. Let me stress the words *find* and *I*. But here a new objection arises: if it is I who do this, is what I actually find another person? Is it not rather, once more (though more subtly), the Other as negative image of the Same, and the Same as negative of the Other?

> Who can be the shadow
> Of each of them
> At the same time as
> His image of the other.[1]

These pairs of oppositions conceal from each of the parties the essential relation that gives them their being.

To defend the ontological priority of the relation, it is necessary to fight and argue on two fronts: this priority must be established both in relation to difference and with regard to the system. Methodologically, the systemic approach must be seen as relative to the relational one, and the reasons for the latter's priority explained.

The first difficulty is one of description. If we are not able to describe each person as the other's other, without privileging either one, it is because we are used to observing relational processes using the language of the individual. This is easier, and fits in better with the (now largely defunct) substantialist schemata to which we are accustomed. It is important, however, for our description to counteract the spontaneous tendency for the observation of relational phenomena to stray into using the inadequate language of individual roles. A number of theorists in the human sciences have begun to resist. Among them is Don D. Jackson, a collaborator of Gregory Bateson, who succeeded in altering his conceptual frame of reference in his study of a family in such a way that he was able to explain in particular the psychiatric symptoms exhibited by one of its members.[2] He regarded the various transactions between individuals in the family as atomic, and therefore primordial, data.

Examining the conceptual problem from our point of view, what we have to understand is above all why it is that individual differences, on the one hand, and systematic integration, on the other, are secondary to relations.

Let us look at the favorable case, for my argument, of a continuous, long-term family relationship which is important to its members. It is possible to show that a conjugal relationship, for instance, can be described in itself, and not just by reference to the respective roles of the man and woman. Apart from the sex of the individuals involved and their different roles, marriage has a number of obvious characteristics: it is normally a voluntary, permanent, long-term relationship. It is even the only type of relationship that is

meant to be for life. At the same time it is exclusive, and supposed to be sufficient to allow the partners to integrate a large number of different sectors of
their activity. When we add to this, as Jackson does, that it is a relationship
with wide-ranging and complex objectives, many connected with life itself, it
can be seen as a set of quite specific characteristics which (and this is the
point) suffice to distinguish it from other relationships. Both ontologically
and methodologically, it deserves to be considered in its own right, before
individual factors are taken into account.

A description of this sort reverses the traditional attitude which, on the
contrary, stresses sexual difference, further accentuated by social experience, problems of compatibility, and the fact that the ability to assume the
male or female role is seen as decisive for the success of the marriage. This
reversal of perspective is striking because, in the end, we are perfectly well
able to define the conjugal relationship in terms of an original dyadic relation.

Individual Difference and Personal Difference

What about sexual characteristics? They can be regarded as a form of differentiation, a way of helping to "make the difference," as people say. Imagine
the absurd case of two identical individuals who found themselves living together. They would now have to work out differences between themselves on
the level of their structural coupling and context of collaboration, differences
that did not exist before. If only to decide who should go through a door first,
or who should have the last word in an argument. But as soon as they declare
that one should, rather than the other, they cease to be identical. It matters
little here whether the relationship in question is symmetrical or complementary. Individual differences are used as one means of solving a relational
problem. They can be treated as the products of an active process of relational construction, rather than as its first cause, and seen, in short, largely
as an effect.

Not that genuinely individual differences do not exist. They are indubita-
bly present in a marriage. But there again, they are certainly less important
than the relational problem that is to be solved, which makes it necessary to
define differences in order to determine, regulate, and stabilize the relationship. I call differences of this new type *personal* ones. Of course such differences, which are worked out on the relational level of the couple, rather than
at some earlier point, are inevitable. Particularly in a relationship as difficult
to master as the conjugal one. As for sexual differences, we should not over-
estimate their theoretical importance. Their prominence doubtless derives
from the fact that they are always available, and can therefore form the basis
for, or at least one of the supports on which the interpersonal relation is con-

structed. The right question to ask is what their function is in the establishment and organization of a given relationship.

A Methodological Choice: A Systemic or Relational Perspective?

As we shall gradually observe, difference in such cases can be explained in terms of differentiation. Let me reiterate the principle: in the beginning is the relation, out of which there emerge terms, or rather poles, which diverge and de-center themselves in their positive difference. How does the ontological primacy of the relation manifest itself on the methodological level?

Of central importance is the fact that it is possible to show that human relations possess a general specificity, together with individual characteristics that suffice to distinguish them one from another, without our needing to refer in advance to the reality of the individuals involved.

As can be seen, then, it is the relation that resolves or stabilizes through compromise interactional problems that have nothing to do with individual differences.[3] Conversely, these problems are solved, thanks to the active elaboration of differences, by the persons involved: these differences are then personal ones. In the example discussed above, we are no longer talking in terms of roles or abstract models of an individual's status that can be attributed to members of the real family. Rather, we are talking in terms of the relations that exist between them. As a result, individual differences are no longer seen as the cause of relational phenomena. On the contrary, both conceptually and in reality, they are derivative: thus any complementary relationship will engender concordant differences between its poles. The same is true, of course, in the particularly significant case of the interlocutive relation, when partners in a discussion give up certain individual differences in order to build a common language. By showing that they are prepared to speak together, they discover that they are different from one another. This is a point to which I shall return.

The Two Dimensions of the Social

Ultimately, relations are the elementary links that condition all the different ways in which groups are structured. From them we can move on to look at the relative positions and rule-governed behavior patterns that stabilize relations, and in so doing we might choose to adopt a systemic approach. Let me explain. Take the same example of a family group. Each particular relationship is determined within a system of other relationships that are normally compatible with it. In that system it acquires its own stability and even identity. That is undeniable.

Yet we would be wrong to conclude that the systemic point of view takes priority here. It certainly allows us to understand certain structuring effects, particularly the collective dimension of the social phenomenon. But this is not the only dimension that characterizes members of society. In most communities, there is also an interpersonal dimension.

We can say that we are looking at an essentially collective phenomenon whenever the coexistence of people is systematized by an organizational and communicational model that is established institutionally. Then the links between people are the source of common actions. Incidentally, this state of organizational linkage (specialized and coordinated tasks, differentiated roles) is induced by the fact of living within a communicational community. Its power is that of its institutions, and of the strength of the constraints it can exert on individuals.

In its collective dimension, society demands conformity and detests independence, whether it be in educating children, driving cars, or caring for the injured. Any attempt to separate circulating information from the system of communicational relations and the decision-making authorities in the real collectivity is a highly abstract undertaking. The different layers intermingle with each other. Power relations are not external to them, like a kind of superstructure, but immanent in them. A given community may indeed be oppressed, but where shall we say the oppressor is to be found? *Power*, impossible to call to account or even locate, without a center or seat of its own, is in fact everywhere. Let us be nominalistic about this: power is the name we give to a complex communicational system and its set of overlapping hierarchies. For power relations to appear, it is generally enough for the communicational regime to be institutionalized and to channel the circulation of information in a preferential way. Between secrecy (of state, clan, or clique) and power, there is a relationship of reciprocal implication. I am not saying that this is the ultimate reason for power, merely indicating one of its most revealing signs.

Power only appears to be something that an individual can take for him or herself; something that can be monopolized or hijacked, or that can slip away. Still less is it something that derives from the choice of a prince or the decision of an individual subject; for it emanates from the communicational fabric woven by all the social actors. The Prince is only another name for restricted communication. For better or for worse—because when that happens, individuals are either carried by the collectivity or destroyed by it.

This state of collective linkage does not yet mean that person-to-person relations exist between two individuals. The fact of both belonging to the same whole, with the same collective dimension, neither encourages nor hinders the development of such relations. But it is certain that only the sort of communication instituted by the system is compatible with the fact of belonging to a group, and it must not be confused with interpersonal relations. Of course, many groups try to eliminate such relations in favor of the purely collective element.

Note that individual behavior is programmed and learned by the community's members, just as they learn its ideology. Such is the hold the social fabric has over individual beings that they each become capable of maintaining their place in a system of places. It is easy to understand why a systemic approach is possible, and even necessary, in anthropology. The fact that it gives only a partial view is another matter, which I shall consider in due course. It is thanks to the system that people have a specific relationship of belonging with their community. In contrast, it is impossible for one person to belong to another: their relationship is one of reciprocity, not possession.

I remind the reader of my decision to distinguish between the individual and the person. It is the individual that might be defined on the basis of the self's position in the social "space." The notion of individual identity to which the systemic approach gives access is undoubtedly at once objective, synchronic, and collective. Objective, because the individual's place within society can always be determined; collective, because his or her identity is such that the group can delegate to the individual; synchronic, because we are not in the least concerned with how his or her identity came to be formed in the course of his or her existence. In a more elaborate way we might say that an individual in the collective space is a living system of social relations between behavior patterns. Historical and social forms of individuality are objective matrices of activity for individuals.

Let me emphasize that those relational conventions which we call social rules prescribe patterns of individual behavior by organizing them into a viable system. Collective organization appears as the fruit of the interaction of various subprograms. This explains why it can contain a considerable degree of inertia, and therefore why it has a homeostatic function. The degree of inertia will vary according to context, from the primitive societies studied by Claude Lévi-Strauss, to family groups, to bureaucratic or military regimes. But the homeostatic function is essential in explaining how social relations stabilize. And how individuals integrate their existence into them. Thus, for instance, the regime of the exchange of women (as goods) studied by Lévi-Strauss belongs, in one sense, to a system for the transcendence of individuality, but in another it is a general condition of the individual existence of women. But what if women exchange words? This is crucial, for it is a direct manifestation of the transcendental aspect of their personhood, i.e., a general condition of the personal existence of women. An awkward question: what if women exchange words about the collective regime of exchanging women?

While the systemic approach is indeed relevant, it cannot therefore be seen as the only one, nor be given epistemological priority. It is not the only one because the collective dimension of the social is not the only one, as we have already said—even if, unfortunately, relations between persons tend to be hidden by collective imperatives in the majority of known societies, so that instead of turning toward each other, the individual members of the group all turn toward the collective task at hand, and meet to exercise only those types of personal relations permitted by the system. Furthermore, the systemic approach has no epistemological priority because human systems are essentially (to say the least) open systems,[4] in which relations should be able to change in a reciprocal way. It is therefore impossible to overemphasize the fact that the system which integrates relations between persons in a dynamic—i.e., interactional—way cannot be closed in on itself.

Let us move on to the truly relational approach, which has two key advantages from a philosophical point of view.

1. It shows the irreducibility, alongside the relation of belonging that characterizes the collective dimension of the social, of the no less specific relation of reciprocity that characterizes its interpersonal dimension. While the fact of belonging to a group provides the individual with an identificational predicate (I am a Bororo. . . .), it is other human beings, through the reciprocity relation, and not the group, with its relation of belonging, who are constitutive of my personal identity.

2. It establishes its fundamental role within the system by defining it precisely as an "open" one. For if each person is linked, by work or interest, love or family, to a number of others, the result is not a fixed set of definite values, but rather a shifting, widely dispersed set of reciprocal relations.

Note that as a social phenomenon even the smallest language act stands at the crossroads of a double determination. Its value is defined on two different relational registers: on an interactional level, it involves interlocutive reciprocity, while in its institutional aspect it derives from the speaker's belonging to a community. This is something that should be remembered when the illocutionary force of discourse is being analyzed.

It is when the system is closed that relations are compatible, but also then that they start to degenerate into relations of power, oppression, or parasitism. The price we pay for these is alienation from ourselves and from those on whom we impose them. But such relations have instilled in many intellectuals a fascination with the negative.

It is true that reciprocity or mutuality does not protect human beings against reification: relationships that were originally reciprocal are often covered over by others, which they support, and which can be oppressive or reified. Pathologically constituted families form a rigid system with its own closure and homeostasis; lacking as they do any metacommunicational ability, they do not have true relationships either. More generally, pathological systems seem to lack any usable metarules, i.e. rules which, among other things, offer the possibility of changing the rules of the system.[5] Consequently, what makes a system appear primary is the fact that it is closed.

This is a point that cannot be overemphasized. Human systems are open, living systems—so long, that is, as the relations within them continue to change. I concede that human beings do not only have reciprocal relations as persons, but also as individuals, institutional relations of belonging to an instituted community. Only the conditions under which they belong are modifiable in function of interpersonal relations of reciprocity, at least in historical societies, so that they can be made compatible with them. As a person, a human being is no more than a structural integration of such relations. In exactly the same way people have a hold over the system, which they can always modify. Metacommunicational discourse provides for a certain freedom in the social contract. An essential aspect of our freedom is the ability to switch out of our place in an instituted communicational community, into the position of an ideal speaker-listener in a canonical communication regime.

It is indeed to relations, and the constant modifications brought about in them by the activity of communication, that we should look for the source of change and progress. In particular, there is much to be said about the process by which members of a speaking community communicate about communication itself, in order to shift or alter its rules. Systems evolve through intercommunicational relations. The metacommunicational ability of persons is the determining factor here. It involves not only speaking about, or commenting on, interpersonal relations, but also changing them. It is a commonplace experience to find that we can now communicate with someone on a different footing altogether; when we speak to each other, it must now be in the context of a new relationship. Among all the unpredictable ways in which human relations are formed and reformed, all the vicissitudes of their negotiation and renegotiation, "the most interesting process is perhaps the one by which subjects set up between themselves common rules for the creation and mutual comprehension of messages."[6] These common rules are the framework in which their new relationships can be deployed.

In *Who's Afraid of Virginia Woolf?* Edward Albee illustrates what a vital resource this metalinguistic ability can be. The bankrupt couple, Martha and

George, hope that their relationship will survive as a creative one. We see them make a series of attempts to break out of the rigid game, almost the ritual, which masks their sterility and failure: their shared fantasy of an imaginary son, a fantasy by which they are imprisoned. They are finally able to destroy this fantasy after they have taken refuge in a new series of games whose rules they can recognize and comment on, and ultimately challenge and replace. Without starting from an interlocutive and interpersonal relationship, they could never have played this sequence of games leading to the rediscovery of an authentically preserved primordial link between them.

This is indication enough of the decisive importance of the metacommunicational ability, without which this type of complex evolution would be impossible. We already knew that the interlocutive relation, as embodied in dialogue, works for the creation of personal identity, as it is indispensable in conferring personhood on its actors. Now we find that it also has another property in relation to the various systems of social integration. Admittedly, it can only achieve stability and identity within a system of compatible and properly articulated relations, combined into a formal structure. But when it comes to counteracting the closure of the system, or making conflicting relations compatible, the interlocutive relation regains its initiative.

Consider a verbal compromise arranged by a diplomat who has managed to establish viable relationships with two countries at war with each other. The metacommunicational ability allows the interlocutors to discuss their relationship, either directly or by commenting on a particular relational event. This involves a whole linguistic process in which the interlocutive relation is both the cause and the effect of change, the more so the more exclusive it is. Not that a relation is exclusive in the sense of excluding other relations. Molière's Alceste is an excellent example of this error, for he wants to concentrate all possible relationships on himself:

> Yes, I could wish that no one found you charming
> That your predicament was quite alarming. . . .
> So that my heart, a gleaming sacrifice,
> Might compensate and might alone suffice.[7]

Alceste, or the pseudoexclusive relationship. A dead end:

> Since this is something that you cannot do—
> Find all in me, as I find all in you—
> Go, I refuse you.[8]

Célimène is not taken in:

> No, you don't love me in the proper fashion.[9]

A relation can only be exclusive in respect to other relations in the sense that, by including them, it acts as the only way of making them compatible, because it ensures both their integration and their mobility. It is then the only source of metacommunication about those other relations, the means by which they may be ordered and hierarchized.

In the flexibility of its semantic transactions, a privileged interpersonal relationship is quite opposed to the exclusivism of those dangerous liaisons out of which relational schizophrenia can so easily irrupt. The more extensive a relationship, the more privileged it is.[10] Once again, therefore, it is the relation that retains the initiative. Far from remaining insensitive to the priority it has, philosophers would do well to emphasize it, as I shall continue to do in what follows.

Again: How May We Speak of the Other?

By making the personal self the seat of a pragmatic competence, I have sought to delineate a free, pure, and positive type of difference, and also to show how that self is defined in return by all the singular relations in which it becomes involved, and in which it can also see its own image. Thus the self is born to itself. Far from alienating the other from itself, the self now stands as the other's other. This time, we can truly say: "I is another." Without going that far, however, my claim is that the real difference of other human beings has until now been misunderstood.

Indeed, several things have now become clear. First, the other only has to be designated or described delocutively by the speaker for him or her to become something known, predictable in his or her qualities and reactions. It is clear that in this case, difference is represented by sameness. What form could it take, if not that of a negation or a limitation? Conceived of and objectivized in this way, difference soon becomes indifference and frustration, when it is not actual hostility, for the ego.

It is not necessary to speak a language that others do not know, or simply to pronounce one's own language badly, to be regarded by the other as a barbarian. Where there is no positive relation, any sort of strangeness arising from distance is sufficient. A few superficial resemblances or points of partial identification will not change matters. In all such cases, the other person's meaning, or lack of it, will be directly related to myself: it is the reverse or negative image of a relationship that has been curtailed and will shortly reify, supported by the prestige of a myth or the stabilized violence of an institution.

Ontological, transcendental, and affective errors are linked here. On an ethical level, their signs are wrongdoing and guilt. A person who designates himself as a white, civilized adult is manifestly someone for whom the Other is very hard to untangle from the Same. For him, children, primitive peoples, the insane, and animals are all Other, all some kind of complementary or repressed aspect of his Same. Even the poet Pierre Emmanuel, the very Catholic author of *L'Autre* (*The Other*), closes his trilogy by reactivating this mutilated form of the relation, in a final gesture of avarice.[11] Apparently, then, even the religious conscience of a poet is incapable on its own of guaranteeing the progress of consciousness.

For the real subject of *L'Autre* is as always the Same, in its struggle against the centrifugal forces that threaten it. Whatever the poet's scruples (and in fact he finishes by catapulting them off into the distance, as far away as possible), it is impossible not to read his book as if it were only *man*, the male of the species, who is speaking. The poet is convinced that he has attempted something that few have succeeded in doing, which is to expand his consciousness of others; he therefore accepts the need to become slightly "other" himself, as an inevitable risk in the process of encountering other people. Passion, experienced within the self, has led him to aspire to a twin-like fusion,[12] an identification with the original couple, in which he could be one and the other at the same time. But this nostalgia for a mythical unity, which he wishes to restore in all its mysterious androgyny, is ultimately an expression of the primacy of a self that makes its own salvation, on its own. The experience that he relates fails in its aim of being the story of a relational maturation. In the end, the being referred to as feminine is never anything more than a repressed aspect of the male, which is used in the service of the man's autoerotic economy: "The lover wants the woman he loves to be his matter-mother, while she draws her form and breath from him."[13]

Philosophers of alterity could hardly regard it as satisfactory for the poet to give the masculine and feminine principles as the paradigm of relations between the Same and the Other, before finally recasting them in the mold of the old Aristotelian distinction between form and matter. Even when consolidated by "the primordial dreams which stabilize the unconscious experience of humanity," propped up by Christian symbolism and further complicated by the Jungian complementarity of *Animus* and *Anima*, the poet's initiating story stops far short of explaining the mystery of the sexes.

The Christian poet's work will no doubt arouse protest in feminist circles, which in fact seems quite justified. For a number of years now there has been a vigorous denunciation of the inveterate attitude by which women are seen as things to be used and exchanged by men, when the male's imperious right to choose does not put women in the position of competing merchandise. It is possible to predict that part at least of the reaction to this protest will be hostile. When the other protests, even in a legitimate attempt to recover a lost identity, he or she becomes an adversary. Other people are objectively a danger to me, as I am to them. My concrete existence is threatened by theirs. Yet the intention of giving back to the female other her sex, and the language of her desire and imagination, is a salutary one.[14] But if the ambition of feminist protests were simply to reverse the order of things, like turning a glove inside out, the result would only be a return to the same ruinously nonrelational situation. It is no doubt too early to say whether feminist rivalry and protest is just a sign of specific unease, or a dialectical moment on the road to the double and indissociable liberation of men and women, restored to their positive difference by a viable relationship. The difficulty as I see it is as follows: when women form themselves into closed communicational communities in order to confront the supposedly closed ones of men and thereby rediscover themselves, they are not merely postponing the moment when communication with men might be resumed, but actually starting it off in a conflictual mode which merely confirms their own closure. It is relations between men and women that need to be regenerated as a matter of priority.

However this may be, a general strategy that seeks to proceed by making gradual improvements would be totally inadequate. The other is neither another self that I could know and grasp by identifying or assimilating it, nor someone quite different from me whose own solitude, stature, and transcendence I need to respect. What is needed is for me to make a relationship with him or her. If philosophers really want to detach the other from being the Other of the Same, they must follow a longer path. That is why I, for my part, have changed strategy. Only a notion of differences that is genuinely not based on identity—a positive difference—seems to me capable of overcoming the alternative, or the rivalry, between the Same and an Other defined by opposition to the Same. Difference would then no longer be seen as a matter of subordination, hierarchy, or annexation. The subjective experience of the strangeness of others would remain just what it is—subjective.

From Joint Action to Differentiation

I shall not try to answer the question of where our desire to reduce difference comes from. It is a paradigm lost in the mists of time. In Aristotle, difference was seen as the negation of what is identical. All difference has an appropriateness that was explained by reference to something else—the species for individuals, the genus for species—it marked a characteristic, but in a negative way. Thus in relation to genus, difference serves to constitute the species to which it is attributed. Made into a medium by the Same, by some concept of common identity, it becomes a tool of classification. It provides an analytical way of moving up from the individual to the species and from the species to the identity of the genus.

I have begun here with a negative conception of difference. We can consider the individual in his intrinsic singularity by indexing him according to his last difference. Or situate his singularity at the nodal point where his various differences intersect. According to this traditional logic, we can then define the single human subject that all individuals have in common, as the basis for their diversity. Negative difference of this sort is however neither true alterity, nor just diversity. It can never be a suitable way of defining subjectivity in terms of the person.

Making a Difference

It is still significant that Aristotle's system allows diversity to remain among the categories of Being, when Being itself is not a genus. For my part, my aim is to conceive of an individuating form of difference that arises out of the relation. It would not itself be a relation, but rather a de-relation, by which I mean that it would be obtained by differentiation on the basis of a relation, like a differential characteristic. This type of free difference is difference per se. Anyone who does not accept this can only fall back on an oppositional relation that is itself subject to the identity principle.

What is involved here is a difference that must be made, and that is an object of affirmation, not negation. In that light, the individual ceases to be a reservoir of absolute singularities or purely negative differences. Individuation is not an extension of specification, but it works by differentiation.

Making a difference means differing, after an initial meeting. The verb *to differ* in the sense signifies a relational act in the process of self-innovation. Its product is a divergence, occurring not before speech, as a result of something present in the code, but *after speech together*, during which one of the protagonists in the communication process grasps his or her identity. Let me suggest, strictly programmatically for the moment, that difference of this sort can only be adequately accounted for by a semantics of action, combined with a pragmatics of speech acts.

Let me explain. Positivists are convinced that assertions that can be verified by independent states of affairs are the only sort of propositions. But action precisely destroys this imperialism. By doing, I make the proposition that observes the result true; it is not a state of affairs about which I have been informed. *Making true* is here the result of doing. The difference between the Same and the Other comes about in a language that makes sense, without observing or verifying. The mistake made here by logical positivism is to have identified the meaning content of a proposition with one of the illocutionary figures, that of factual assertion in the delocutive register.

Differentiation is not the same as simple distinction. Difference loses its specific reality once it loses its positiveness. Particularly in the personal sphere, there could be no positive difference if Same and Other were happy to alternate indefinitely by simple inversion. For they would then remain in an imaginary mirror-relationship with each other, in which the pleasure of the one would find its image in the pleasure of the other, sometimes seen as resistance and sometimes credited with a pleasant complementarity. No true reciprocity, no positive difference between persons can be born out of a philosophy of representation.

Consequently, the problem is not so much how to find the correct interpersonal relation as how to break the vicious circle, the sterile opposition of complementary forces or the mirror-identity of symmetrical images, whose archaic figure is the fantasy of mother-child body contact. Opposition refers back to identity. It is not the greatest difference, only the greatest negative difference. It also presupposes a set of different underlying positive differences.[15]

In order to explain how it is that relations between persons can generate positive differences, I adopted a genetic and a structural point of view by turns. We discovered in the genesis of the child's self a first necessary, though far from sufficient, condition: the appearance of a symbolic function, represented by the father figure. This is how the self-devouring oscillation between the terms of an imaginary relation, and the corresponding attraction and enchantment, are broken. By giving each person a differential status, the father imposes an impersonal rule of communication which is at the same time a recognition rule.

There is a second condition that must be fulfilled if Same and Other are to be engendered without the one being privileged over the other: the third party represented by the communicational code or rule must not be absolutely fixed, but must serve at most as a point of departure for its possible transgression. What is there to be said about this transgression which is so essential for the differentiation of persons? That it is limited but effective. Everyone has the power to actualize the virtual meanings deposited in the common code, and therefore the right to share in the semantic initiative. When an interlocutive relation becomes a relation of reciprocity, it becomes possible to reestablish a positive difference between persons as utterers. What needs to be understood is that the progressive conquest of difference here corresponds to the transgression of meaning. In this respect, it should be remembered that actions and personal presence are equivalent in discourse conducted on dialogical principles. But it is also important to pick up certain asymmetries that allow the utterers to be differentiated.

Before setting out to show that the asymmetries in discourse can be either normal or reduced, clumsily imposed or self-proclaimed, minimal or marginal, let me first of all establish that, whether for a general theory of action or for a particular theory of speech acts, certain consequences hold true. That is the case, for instance, with verbal cooperation.

If we are to redefine the discursive agency to take account of the fact that *I* and *you* are cooperating to produce discourse, we must go beyond the classical definition given by utterance theory, to define the discursive agency in function of the primum relationis principle.

Let us consider the nature of a cooperative action. Suppose, by analogy, that three lumberjacks, A, B, and C, jointly cut down a tree. The analogy is a weak one because cutting down a tree is something that one man can do on his own, with more or less effort and time, whereas speaking is not something that can be done on one's own, any more than obeying a rule or agreeing to something. Let us also ignore the doubtless unequal energy and efficiency that each man brings to the task. To whom can we then impute a joint action? Not to a particular individual, without committing a sophism of the *trahere commune ad proprium* type, in which something common to several people is attributed to one as his or her property.[16]

On what conditions may we affirm that the definite description "the man who performed action x" is appropriate to lumberjack A? It is not sufficient to say, like certain medieval logicians, that an appropriate predicate is half-way between a common and a proper predicate. The problem is complicated here by the fact that we cannot say of each lumberjack that he has performed the same action, which is to cut down a particular tree, for that would not be correct. We can however say that:

1. They all cut it down.
2. What A did is not the same as what B did: A cut down a tree with the help of B and C, whereas B did it with the help of A and C

Let us return to our act of discourse. In a similar way, to say of two individuals u_1 and u_2 that they are in communicative interaction is, in particular, to assert that their linguistic activity is a joint activity. This pragmatic thesis about their utterance has an immediate semantic implication: as they are engaged inseparably in the activity of verbal cooperation, u_1 and u_2 share in one way or another in the establishment of the utterance's meaning. Let us see where this leads us.

First of all, a joint activity is not the same as a common one. Otherwise, the attribution of the referent, and the evaluation of the statement's truth-value, would not remain suspended between the interlocutors, as is the case with any referential dialogue. The reference would be known immediately. Nor is a joint activity simply a set of coordinated individual acts. Otherwise, it would be possible to relate an utterance q, proffered at some point in a conversation, directly to one of the interlocutors. But no utterance p that has truly been proffered in the logical space of interlocution may be back-referenced to either u_1 or u_2. It must be taken back to both of them together, because they are in an interlocutive relation. Can we not at least say of u_1 and u_2 that they have performed the same verbal action, utterance p? This is no more accurate than what we said earlier. They actually uttered p together. The verbal activity of each consisted in participating in the construction of the meaning of p. So there is indeed something that each has done, which is to utter p with the other's help, and in relation with the other.

Other things being equal (and whatever the communicational history of each, and however unequal a share of the semantic initiative they may take), the speech activity which consists in having uttered p with the other's help is already a first step in differentiating the speakers. The important thing is that their speech act should no longer be imputed to them individually, as in classical theory. It is certainly true of u_1, but not of u_2, that he uttered p with the help of u_2. And the definite description "the person who uttered p with the help of u_2" can legitimately be applied to him, a description which individualizes him all the better because a sequence of such utterances p can be related back to him. Equally, it is quite true of u_2, though not of u_1, that she uttered p with the help of u_1.

As this suggests, my contention is that the occurrence of p here is indeed particular, and contributes to individuating u_1, without its referring back in any way to a speaking subject who would be its (sole) originator. All that can be said is that in his or her role as a co-utterer, the speaking subject exercizes his or her particular power of proposal in the joint process of meaning construction. Or on the contrary, the subject might decide not to play his or her part in the verbal interaction, choosing not to keep the rally going, to borrow a phrase from tennis. This gives us an asymmetry by default.

Asymmetries in Discourse

The question of discursive asymmetry was waiting around the corner. I have attributed so many things to the primum relationis, the interlocutive relation that is both initial and initiatory, that I must now answer the objections of common sense, and those raised by the first results of conversational analysis. Asymmetries do remain in all discourse, creating a gap that subjectivity can fill, as it declares its identity by saying "I." How can this situation be reinterpreted in the light of my chosen premises?

Language provides us with a system of nonnatural rules by which to govern our collaborative symbolic activity. Like any institution, its intersubjective coordination has a certain effectiveness, without however swamping the contribution of individuals. Successful language acts have both a semantic value (a meaning) and a thetic one (a reference or truth-value). In particular, assertions convey a certain type of information about the speaker, i.e. about the uttering agency which is currently in a position to take the speaking role. They make us aware of his or her particular preference for the realization of certain possible states of affairs over others. If u_1 asks u_2 to pour him a cup of tea, he reveals among other things his preference for any situation in which he would be given a cup of tea, as against those in which he would not. He reveals something about his particular aims. In order to accomplish those aims, the speaker will employ linguistic means that he adjusts to fit in with the aims and means of others.

These aims and means are, however, still defined derivatively by reference to a present interlocutive relation, without which the meaning of assertions is properly unintelligible. In accordance with the primum relationis principle, they are differential and relative. To that extent, we can talk about discourse being asymmetrical. But this is a quite marginal extent, by which I mean that it lies at the furthest edge of the process, but within its overall continuity. For we must accept several things together:

1. The speaker assumes an institutional role that he or she shares with all the members of the speaking community

2. He or she participates in communication as an uttering agency in a present interlocutive relation

3. He or she manifests a marginal preference relation in an asymmetrical manner

This is a long way from the original asymmetry between the self and the other, in which the former grabbed the speaking role as a matter of principle and appropriated the meaning of what was said. The most extreme version of this sort of linguistic subjectivism would be to say that words mean what I choose—a position taken to its absurd conclusion by Humpty–Dumpty in *Through the Looking Glass.* If this type of asymmetry did exist, it would do violence to discourse and be utterly unjust.

We have also moved away from asymmetry by discourse appropriation, as when someone claims the right to question another person in order to make the person confess something about him or herself, or say the things about the world that the questioner wishes to hear. There is really nothing exceptional about this sort of asymmetry. It commonly occurs in discussions that have nothing about them of dialogue beyond its rhetorical (i.e. crudest) form. Things begin very badly for Alice. Lewis Carroll, already a pragmatist, shows her trying in vain to attract the rabbit's attention (*Alice in Wonderland*). "If you please, Sir!" Of course, the rabbit slips away. When it does consent to speak to her, it demands to be treated with respect, though it never treats others the same way. Then the speaker goes on the attack, and his interlocutor is rendered speechless. In this way, Alice's conversations are dominated in turn by the points of view of the rabbit, then the duck, then the flower, then the gnat, then the caterpillar. . . . The gnat: "What sort of insects do you rejoice in, where *you* come from?" Being human, Alice is puzzled. What will happen to her? As we might guess, a sequence of mutations, in the course of which she timidly defends her personal identity. The caterpillar: "Who are you?" Alice admits her confusion, then remarks: "I think you ought to tell me who *you* are, first." We are told that humorists enjoy creating a topsy-turvy world. But is this really a topsy-turvy world, or an exact description of our normal conversations? You only have to try introducing yourself to a ministerial usher. . . . These anti-dialogues are simply dishonest dialogues, and are extremely common. Are these discourses, written by a logician, themselves logical? The use he makes of different forms of reasoning is certainly cheeky at times. There are some bare-faced paralogisms, in which syntax and semantics break down in turn under the strain. Sometimes Humpty–Dumpty observes the rules of both, but then gaily suspends all pragmatic rules. "How these creatures do argue!" sighs Alice in distress. In fact, what they leave out of their discourse is the pragmatic dimension, which is also part of the logic of communication. The rabbit and the gnat introduce a systematic asymmetry which negates any possibility of communication. I offer this idea in passing: it might inspire someone to produce a genuinely new commentary on Lewis Carroll.

The type of asymmetry that I want to explore is simply a feature of our discursive mode of expression as such, in normal use; it is marginal, in the sense referred to above, but more or less marked.

Some time ago I examined the mechanism of certain asymmetries that remain, even in authentic dialogue, when the states of belief of two interlocutors are contrasted.[17] This asymmetry is stronger if the interlocutors happen to belong to two different speech communities. The same is true of conversations in which the protagonists do not share identical criteria of pertinence. One may intend to address the other in accordance with a totally open communicational regime, while the other wants the first to respect certain well-defined positions of utterance within the group. Or they may both belong to different established communicational regimes, with quite dissimilar language-games. This is what happens in the absence of any basis of prior understanding between them, such as would be provided by the sort of register of the habits and customs of everyday existence which is produced by long centuries of communal life, with its different conventions, compromises, and strategies. For that there is a whole folklore concealed within language, which is extremely useful in preventing misunderstandings.

There are certainly deeper asymmetries than these, and ones which are more stable. I shall show in a later work that these too are interpretable within my theory. At first sight, speaking subjects, as changed by all their previous communicational experience, exhibit an original difference. Their discourse moves on a plane that is distinctively theirs. Thoughts corresponding to someone else's discourse do not come into our minds. Charles Peake, a colleague from London, tells me that as somebody born on the south bank of the Thames, in an area where dockers live, he can chat quite happily with them, knowing exactly how far to put up with their jokes and how much he can get away with in return, without verging on insult. But he only needs to cross the water to have a drink with the railwaymen on the other side for there to be an immediate risk of misunderstandings and disputes. In reality, therefore, interlocutors belong to communities which are just too different for the interlocutors not to be themselves separated by a fundamental difference, not as something inherent in them, but simply as a result of the fact that they belong to different communicational groups, with their particular sociolects and language acts governed by different pragmatic rules. The same state of affairs is found in certain paradoxical controversies, in which arguments that are conclusive for one interlocutor are not seen to be so by the other, and in which it is therefore impossible for one to convince, or even contradict, the other. Each speaker in turn feels let down by his or her normal discursive technique, while the other feels he is "banging his head against the brick wall of language."

Suppose there are two people, one of whom believes in God and regards suffering and illness as a sign that one has been chosen (or, on the contrary, as a punishment), while the other regards it as pure folly to even think such a thing. Can we say that they do not understand each other? Is it even meaningful to compare their beliefs, and find that these are contradictory? We know Wittgenstein's answer: "'Do you believe in this?' I'd say: 'No.' 'Do you contradict the man?' I'd say: 'No.'"[18]

Discursive asymmetry appears in the general category of "evaluatives," whether they be axiological (splendid, excellent) or not (large, hot). Such expressions are in fact said to be subjective. Their usage depends on the speaker's view of the evaluative norm as it relates to a certain class of objects. This norm exists in any speaking community, where it can be more or less stable. In fact, it is easy to see that evaluatives themselves anticipate and explain the reactions of interlocutors. The speaker puts forward his or her evaluation in differential relation to that of his or her partner. The greatest degree of asymmetry is reached when each makes an extraordinary use of certain words like "believe," "God," "last judgment," etc., reflecting certain peculiarities of their cultural and ideological competence. But even in this last case, the speaking subjects are only involved in an asymmetry by way of the communities they represent.

These asymmetries are all normal, inevitable, and accepted. Others are more deliberately created. During verbal interactions, power relations are often negotiated and renegotiated. A particular interlocutor, who may have a powerful position of utterance within the institutional system of communication (i.e. strong personal status), begins a language act designed to close down the range of possible answers available to her interlocutor, whom she regards as an adversary. In this case asymmetry is part of a deliberate discursive strategy, its main offensive weapon.

Another example is polemic. Two interlocutors differentiate their positions by increasing their doctrinal content, and even by deliberately seeking to provoke dissension. Both exaggerate, and insist on maintaining their own codification of the problem to the bitter end. Let us imagine a discussion between two theologians about the procession of the Holy Spirit. They are living in the fourth century and speak Greek and Latin respectively. Exaggeration becomes possible once an original difference in codification hardens into doctrine, without there being any will to go beyond it. Thus the first theologian could quite easily use the meaning of the Greek preposition ἐκ to claim that the Father is the only supreme principle. The second, for his part, might refer to the meaning of the Latin preposition *ab* and regard God as being the Trinity, rather than just the Father. This is because the derivation of Latin *ab* is an accidental one, whereas Greek ἐκ has an essential and absolute derivation. For the Greek theologian, led on by the suggestions of his own language, to say that the Holy Spirit proceeds ἐκ τοῦ υἱοῦ would be to insinuate that the Son is the ultimate and original root of the Spirit, something that, according to Catholic doctrine, is actually the prerogative of the Father. Each will refuse to budge from his position. The fact that this is an unnecessary exaggeration is however confirmed by the fact that other Greeks, such as Cyril of Alexandria, were perfectly well able to do without such arguments.

Asymmetries occur naturally in any discussion that goes beyond conversation of the insipid sort where the words spoken could equally well be put in the other person's mouth. They occur naturally, because each speaker brings to the threshold of the discussion, as so many personal differences, the presuppositions which are a heritage of all of his or her earlier communicational experience; it is then up to him or her either to make the other person share them, or to call them into question, depending on how his or her present interlocutive relationship develops. This can be quite a difficult thing to do. We sometimes avoid certain topics, and end up having a merely reasonable conversation, because we have realized the immensity of the task involved in bringing about such a sharing process. On the other hand, discursive asymmetries are inevitably exaggerated in discussions in which each party is presented from the start as a spokesperson for a particular doctrinal viewpoint, and constantly feels obliged to return as far as possible to "its" position. Finally, asymmetry is often deliberately and illegitimately cultivated by peremptory[19] or indiscreet individuals. Illegitimately, because such pragmatic infringements are quite unnecessary.

A Pragmatic Approach to Secrecy and Indiscretion

By way of illustration I would like to add a few traits to La Bruyère's character "portrait" of Nicander.[20] For me, the indiscreet person, rather than being just an irritating "character" or a distressing moral *habitus*, exhibits a specific defect in his or her personal relations. As something which is felt quite strongly by everyone, this defect can in turn be interpreted as a particular sort of pragmatic violation. More important, indiscretion can be used as a test case for the type of analysis I am pursuing.

Nicander listens in on everything around him that is not his business, and passes on to others anything he has been told in confidence (the ordinary confidence of friendship). Not that he thinks for one moment of deliberately telling; it is just that he drops hints in what he says, whatever the consequences may be. When he himself has a confidence to tell (or when he wants to hear someone else's), he does not realize that this presupposes a mutual agreement:

—I should like to tell you something in confidence.

—You can trust me, whatever it is will remain between us.

In other circumstances, Nicander is surprised to hear the reply:

—I don't want to know (implying: as I am not prepared to help you or become your accomplice).

Disconcerted and hurt, the indiscreet fellow goes off to peddle his secret elsewhere. He has learned nothing. Indiscretion is therefore also a form of inattention to what other people are saying, complicated by indifference as to whether or not they are listening to what we have to say. Nicander declares as much:

—Me, I say whatever is on my mind.

Would he start pouring his heart out before making sure that the other person is ready to listen? I fear so. People like him are quite capable of affecting an intimate complicity with the first person they meet, and always have something important to whisper in your ear:

> A wonder they make of a trivial thing
> And whisper good day in your ear.

Just as the same sun both melts wax and dries roofs, the same structure of pragmatic violation can account for apparently contradictory forms of indiscretion. It would however be quite difficult to explain them simply by reference to a monadic and substantialist conception of secrecy, in a spirit of separation and singularity. In that view, a secret is a thing or a substance to be wrung out of the person who possesses it. Or locked up inside a house with a solid padlock. And I might add, like the twelfth-century Arab philosopher Averroes: the key to the padlock might as well be thrown away and the door sealed up, if the possessor of the secret really knows how to keep it, and holds his tongue. A typical form of secret would be that which is intrinsically hidden in the psyche: there is something hidden, secret, in the sense that something sayable is held to be unsayable. To penetrate this secret is to be accursed; it is to steal something unilaterally. Something has been shut away, concealed, by virtue of some essential limitation coming either from me or from the other. Because it is assumed, once again, that the Same and the Other are separate.

I shall not dwell on the taste for secrecy that is so widespread among those who lack the strength to exist as persons, who use it simply as a way of asserting their existence. We must not be duped into taking this intimate weakness of nature for a superiority of spirit. People hide even their most insignificant actions for the pleasure of having a life to themselves. Not a solitary life, which is a utopia (Rousseau is persecuted even in Ermenonville), but a secret one. It is possible to hide oneself even without having anything to hide. And the "simple and permanent state" that Jean-Jacques believes himself to have found, like a secret happiness, on a favored island of the Lac de Bienne, can no doubt be seen as merely a retreat into lethargy.

People tend to have a novelistic view of secrets. They regard them as something specifically concerning themselves, something private, like a tragic affair, a cruel misfortune, or some traumatic and now buried event.

There is no shortage of suitable metaphors. A secret is something unsayable as far as another is concerned. Sometimes I tell it to myself and hide it from you, sometimes I do not even tell it to myself.[21] We suppose that the other either is unable to hear it by nature, or should be prevented from hearing it by his or her situation. It will therefore be "well guarded," and I will prevent others from "discovering" it. These are all rationalizations, substantializing metaphors.

How can we steer a course between Charybdis and Scylla? Fortunately, there is no question of doing so. The reason for secrecy is neither in you nor in me. It is between us. We need to repudiate these incomplete definitions of a substantial secret, which make it into completely formed but silenced, repressed speech, which it would be a curse to reveal. As if the self always had the power to tell, and the reason for keeping quiet always came from the other person. A secret is neither something that must remain hidden in me, nor something that the other cannot hear because of his or her inadequacy. Something sayable that is unsayable is nothing at all, or nothing more than a laughable contradiction.

Therefore, I shall use the term "sayable" to refer to what can be said in accordance with a certain interlocutive relation. This, like any other relation, has its own domain. Unless it is in some way unusual, it will immediately divide individuals up into those who are able to enter into speaking relations with me—those for whom there are no secrets—and the rest. Now, what is secret is only relatively unsayable: certain things, which are not yet formed into words, would never come to my lips with you. Relative to what? Be they state, business, or personal secrets, they remain hidden from some people only to be shared with others who have been let into the secret, meaning that they are in the circle or clan, i.e. the domain of the interlocutive relation. Secrecy is not just about what is said, but what is said in relation to the way it is said and to the determining (and restrictive) conditions under which it is said.

Let us return to indiscretion. In the three cases I have distinguished, a remark that is hypothetically attached to a particular interlocutive relationship cannot satisfactorily be detached from it. Who am I to ask for someone's confidences? Who is he or she to invite me to divulge mine? In other words, anything that is addressable to another person is so only according to particular relational rules, on which its semantic content will depend.

Sometimes I might fail to ensure that my relationship with my interlocutor is well established; sometimes I will unilaterally ask for his or her confidences or confession, and sometimes I will simply repeat something I have been told in the course of another relationship. Even if such a transfer takes place in the presence of my original informant, it remains highly indiscreet. In all three cases I am proffering something that has no place being said here and now: indiscretion ignores this fact. It is not that everything we say has its place of utterance, outside which it is intrinsically unsayable. Unless we are clear that its place is not a point, but a certain space in which people have things to say to each other. It cannot be said, not from a particular place of utterance, but according to a particular relation underlying the logical space of the interlocution.

There is nothing more false than finishing something you began to say to one interlocutor in front of someone else who has taken his or her place. Indeed, it is actually a good question: under what conditions can there be a pragmatic transfer of something said from one interlocutive relationship to another? I shall not try to answer it in any detail here. However, it seems that this is neither utterly impossible, nor certain to succeed in every case. But is it enough for the substitution of interlocutors to occur between analogous positions or places?

Pragmatic tact, which in matters such as this is always decisive, is not shared equally. Perhaps only those people who have the same degree of discretion and the same sense of what not to say can ever really be intimate with each other. Only a perfect education can make human beings capable of complete intimacy. Hence the fact that we only seek regular contact with people in whom we are prepared to confide to the same extent as they do in us. There is something of the barbarian in the indiscreet person who tramples all such rules of tact underfoot. Nicander, who is peremptory in this way, never doubts that his confidences will be accepted. He prejudges—and even worse, makes use of—the reactions of his listeners. He is astonished that you would always (or almost always) betray the secret that he has confided in you.

There are of course other types of peremptory behavior than Nicander's indiscretion. And it is not sufficient to appropriate the semantic initiative for oneself, unilaterally, to become indiscreet. Indiscretion always manages to divert confidences. But what exactly is it that is confided? Let me try to define it from the semantic and pragmatic point of view I have adopted. Classically, our intimate concerns are defined as being those which belong to us in a direct, personal way.

Let us look at this more closely. Nicander discusses with the first person he meets the delightful life he lived with his wife from the day he chose her to the day of her death. He has already said that she has left him without a child, and this he now repeats. . . . In indiscretion, as the world itself suggests, there is a considerable lack of discernment and a certain lack of measure. Something goes wrong in the interplay between the allocutive and the delocutive registers.

A fortiori, if what there is to say concerns *me* in my own individuality, for me to tell it to *you* it must also concern *us* in some way, because we are linked. An exclusive human relationship precisely allows the communication of things concerning each party in his or her individual difference. That difference thereby takes on a new quality; it may now become part of the individual's personal status. The language of predilection and happy love is full of such confidences; it is indeed the language of confidence itself.

The existence of secrets is a pragmatic phenomenon in any discourse: as a matter of fact (though not necessarily by rights), some things cannot be said to certain people—sometimes, even, to most people—a fact that provides some justification for the esoteric. That is also a procedure, or an excuse, commonly used by castes of all sorts: x is confidential, they say, reserved for a narrow class of trusted people.

Superficial relations are easy to engage in as long as they remain conventional: it is enough to know the code. Intimate relationships, those to which people commit themselves more deeply, are much more difficult. They are "deeper," not in the sense of some abyss, but because they are productive and semantically innovative. As we might guess, intimacy makes the slightest unilateral deviation or pointless asymmetry really stand out. I do not believe that intimacy is a state in which indiscretion is allowed, offered, or invited. It rather requires considerable pragmatic tact if it is to be exercised without damage or unforeseen consequences. From dawn to dusk there is a voice continually warning us: be careful, friends!

If true dialogue can be defined as discourse made subject to the principle of pragmatic pertinence,[22] discursive asymmetries within it will theoretically be largely reducible. All types of pragmatic violation—from incongruity to insolence, verbal blunders, and of course indiscretion—could then be avoided, and it would also be possible for initial asymmetries between the participants' different codes to be overcome at the same time.

How Can a Marginal Asymmetry Engender Personal Differences?

This is not the place to examine the limits of the reduction of discursive asymmetries. Notice, however, that if they were to disappear altogether, we would soon be condemned to inept conversation or simple tautology (anything that has already been heard and understood *goes without saying*), or indeed to some pathological form of language. Thus it is a characteristic of hysterical discourse that what one person says is completely modeled on an anticipation of what the other will say; nonpertinence here is, then, the paradoxical result of hyper-pertinence.[23]

The idea that the self is the chronological point of departure in the speaking process is apparently a truism: who, indeed, would deny it? Its priority is only chronological, however, and certainly not semantic, whatever Humpty–Dumpty might say: "When *I* use a word . . . it means just what I choose it to mean—neither more nor less. . . . The question is which is to be Master—that's all." [24]

Alice's oft-quoted reply is that his mastery of words could never go that far, freeing him entirely from the common usage that regulates all initial exchanges between speakers. On your own, you can never make the same words mean different things. Which is to say that all words begin by having a meaning in the language: they mean what they mean. Only later can speakers bend their semantic value a little, in the course of their conversation, using them jointly to refer to what *they* (the speakers) mean.

In what sense is the self primary in the order of speech? Not because it is in any way sufficient, but simply by the fact that it initiates speech. Let me explain. The self obviously has no priority in relation to the concepts signified, such as God or the world, which belong to the order of language. It is rather the contrary that is true, the speaker's identity being guaranteed by the permanence of certain signifieds. Nor does the self have any priority in relation to the process of designation. The essential key to all referential expressions and indicators is I-you. As for referring the meaning of words back to the beliefs or desires of the person using them, we should not even think of doing so, for it is in fact those beliefs and desires that depend on the conceptual implications of meaning.

Alice is right: if we must give up the idea that the ego has the initiative in the process of saying, we may in this case still allow it the initiative in speaking. "If you only spoke when you were spoken to, no one would ever say anything." In this nonsensical or blocked situation, nobody would ever agree to speak first. The priority of doing so would, however, be entirely provisional, because everyone must speak in turn. Time can sometimes create more marked asymmetries. It is because of time that interactions between persons are sequential, never simultaneous. The inexorable nature of time determines the discursive features of dialogue, as a result of which it becomes a powerful factor in communicational differentiation between persons.

As I have already pointed out, any complementary relation sets up differences between its poles, differences that are concordant. The interlocutive relation is constitutive of personal identity in a number of ways: it creates asymmetries in discourse, and therefore differential traits that can be grasped by both parties. Thinking means being in a thinking relationship, then judging "by surprise," as Goethe puts it, secretly, differentially, between oneself and oneself. In this way, the individual is able to annex for him or herself some of the contrasting propositional attitudes that have occurred in the course of dialogue, and which he or she has either expressed or come to agree with. Moreover, the interlocutive relation makes the positions of speaker, allocutee, and delocuted third party, which are variously assumed during communication, available for the identificatory mapping of the persons involved.

Whether they lead to agreement or confirm a disagreement, discussions, controversies, and debates all restore positive and relative differences between speaking persons, at the same time obliging them to participate in continual semantic transactions. It is well known that understanding a sentence is something we all do in the past conditional tense: we could have uttered it in the form in which we understand it. But when we are actually uttering it, we do so in the present conditional: moment by moment, we must judge whether or not it would be acceptable to say such a thing by listening to our partner's reactions.

This once more shows the philosophical importance of communication. It is not simply an extremely delicate undertaking pursued by joint action; it is also a continuous process of verbal interaction, and a constantly renewed attempt to institute semantic transactions. These three dimensions are in any case inseparable: verbal action only becomes communicative if it takes place in the context of other joint actions directed toward an agreed goal. The conjunction of speakers, for its part, creates interactional effects that condition any transaction about meaning. We now also have a result to add to this description. Thanks to communication, interlocutors do not remain confined to their individual contexts and their own code, which is at least partly private: communication is also a means of exchange. Insofar as partners in a dialogue are willing to give up some of their individual differences in order to build a common language, they are able to return to construct other differences of the type that I have called *personal*.

Other People's Discourse

However precarious or personal they may be, interpersonal relations as we see them being created in the here and now of human interactions are clearly fundamental. The pedagogical relationship, for instance, is just as constitutive of the teacher as of the pupil, to the point where the teacher finds that she is also being taught by the person whom she is teaching. Although this situation is often regarded as one that will inevitably remain asymmetrical, its relational aspect is in fact decisive, giving rise to a semantic richness which has often been noted. Equally, instead of searching at all costs for whatever it is that is passed down unilaterally from father to son, we would do better to think about the parental relation as something that constitutes the father as well as his son. The father is engendered as a father by the son whom he has engendered as a son.

Shall we then say that individuality is created by the diversity of our human relations, until the point when we finally discover our own voice? There is an ambiguity here: does this voice belong to the person who is speaking? But the speaking subject always shares the semantic initiative to some extent with his or her partner, and can never appropriate for him or herself the meaning of what is said. This means that the person who speaks is not really the one who actually *says*.[25] Yet we do normally impute an intention of meaning to the ego when we say such things as "I mean that." Let us look at this again.

Own Voice, Private Voice, Tacit Language

Can a person ever really be accurately said to speak for him or herself? When we search for words, we are also searching for a listener. Whenever words have a meaning, it is because they are addressed at least to a possible interlocutor, who makes their meaning with or against us (against also being with, in a different way). Such a line of argument seems utterly paradoxical, because it runs counter to two well established conventions: man is given speech to express his thoughts (unless it be to conceal them); each person has his or her own voice, as a bird has its song. In this way, everything I say puts into words what I mean. My words are the bearers of a message, like Noah's dove.

We can reject this argument in its absolute form straight away: a voice does not express only one individual. Speech does not originate solely in the self, nor in the other. As a consequence of the premises we have adopted, what seems plausible to philosophers of consciousness (who always argue in the first person) has become problematical for us: a voice that belonged absolutely to one person could never make itself understood. And if it is true that my original condition is to be in a relation, and that language is specifically a mode of verbal interaction, a medium of joint actions and semantic transactions which brings at least two parties into play, then there can never be, at least in any nontrivial sense, such a thing as a private voice.[26]

If language is a way of being in a relation, a person's own voice cannot be regarded as a private one. Even if an isolated individual wanted to express her inward subjectivity, she would need to have at her disposal expressions other than those she might invent arbitrarily, otherwise she herself would be unable to understand the signs she was using. Hence the fact that the small child rapidly gives up using the language he has invented for himself. How would he ever understand his own language when his mother does not speak it to him? Instead, he learns his mother's language in return: his every word gradually starts to drift toward real words in a slow process of interlocutive transformation.

Those who, like James Joyce, have spoken up for the right of poets to resist the speech of others in their work, have always dreamed of a secret, expressive language that would be fully appropriate to speaking subjects freed from the yoke of the social. Remember Stephen Daedalus' highly individual meditation as he walks along the beach in Dublin bay, narrated as a soliloquy. It is certainly true that interior monologue, which is regarded as one of modern literature's most important inventions, distinguishes individuals by the content and form of what they say. But the "interior" monologue that begins in the second chapter of *Ulysses* actually has nothing to do with the private use of language. Indeed, even the voices we hear in *Finnegan's Wake*, each with its own rhythm, timbre, and style, and which we can only understand after a massive effort of interpretation, are a highly sophisticated linguistic creation that nonetheless remains within the bounds of language. The book is a prodigious poem, created at the moment that the sun was going down on a whole culture—a culture, however, which it presupposes in its parodies. Its hermeticism makes no difference to this fact. Using the fiction that Finnegan is a dreamer who is all the people whom he meets, Joyce reworked his text to the point where it became impossible to decode. His aim of using language to transcend the human condition marks the limit of what can be done, rather than being a counterexample to my line of argument.

Wittgenstein, for his part, demonstrated the absurdity of the concept of a private language by analyzing the very notion of a linguistic rule. Even supposing that an isolated individual so wished, he or she could never produce utterances that depended on the construction of his or her own language. As a matter of principle, it is impossible for an individual to introduce or obey rules that do not resemble those of the linguistic community, whose use he or she alone would be able to verify.[27] Consequently, I shall rule out from the start the fiction of a logically private voice, which would be incomprehensible to anyone but its owner.

Another fiction pure and simple is the idea that I could say things in accordance with a public criteriology, but addressed in fact to nobody, or on the contrary to everybody. We know very well that a voice such as this would be empty. There is nothing more difficult than speaking to a completely invisible, faceless audience, or to someone you do not know, particularly at the beginning. As long as you do not know to whom you are talking, no bivocality is possible, no dual understanding, and therefore no quest for mutual comprehension. As you are unable to anticipate clearly what the response might be, you are quickly reduced to exchanging previously agreed signs in the hope of reactivating the code or establishing some phatic contact.

Unlike the experience of the hero of Malraux's *La Condition humaine*, who does not recognize a recording of his own voice? Our own experience of telephone answering machines is instructive, and certainly much more subtle. We are surprised when the suddenly distanced voice of our absent correspondent asks us to speak after the tone. Do we leave the same message that we were preparing to compose with him or her, interlocutively? The fact is that we find it difficult to reply, and we hesitate to obey the injunction. We realize that we are in an artificial, semantically false situation. As far as my semantic initiative is concerned, the message I had mentally prepared contained a deliberate degree of indetermination that I intended my interlocutor to resolve, in a present interlocutive context. When, having recovered my composure, I do decide to record it, it is only after I have carefully decontextualized it and taken the risk of making it specific. My hesitation comes from the fact that I was expecting to have to adapt my voice to my interlocutor's; I was not prepared, on the other hand, to have to adapt it to an uncertain and delayed response. I therefore speak hesitantly and with embarrassment, while what I am saying starts to sound like a monologue, because one's own voice interweaves with that of a future response very differently from the way it does with the present voice that was actually expected.

The Paradox of the Psychiatrist's Couch

It is becoming clear that if our *own* voices do exist, they do so of necessity within communication. Whether that communication be real or curtailed, whether it take place between a person and him or herself or with someone else, it is only in an interlocutive context that people's own voices have any pragmatic reality. In what sense can I then still make the assertion: "I say that"? Imagine the absurd situation in which a man says something while he is on his own, then repeats it in front of his double in the mirror. What I call *Narcissus' paradox* is that the more he repeats it, the more senseless it becomes.[28]

What is missing from the speech of Narcissus? First, it needs to be addressed to someone, virtually or actually. Then, it needs to elicit a response. We can imagine a situation in which the voice would be correctly addressed and listened to, but without there being any response. This is typically what happens in psychoanalysis, in which the other remains silent. A systematic silence which frustrates the subject, depriving him or her of an answer, so that the subject will often have the experience of his or her words losing all their meaning. He or she must make a great effort just to keep on speaking.

However trivial this experience may be, it runs counter to received opinion, the *doxa*. I shall therefore call it the paradox of the psychiatrist's couch. It differs in an interesting way from Narcissus' paradox. I am speaking of someone intelligent, patient, well-meaning, and extremely sensitive, and yet my speech can only maintain itself with great effort, and soon begins to crumble and fall to pieces, progressively losing all meaning. It is a strange pact that links the analyst to her subject. One undertakes to put into words his suffering, his body, and his whole world, while the other agrees to be present and listen to whatever may be said. Then the analyst projects herself into the position of one who is supposed to know what forms of desire are at work in the speech being proffered to her. While the subject is supposed to change into speech acts those thoughts that he considered impossible to communicate to other people. Overall, someone is being paid for listening to me confiding details of my sexual life; she devotes a little over half an hour of her time to me, and yet my speech still falls apart again; any sentence or word that is spoken without being addressed to someone becomes a thing.

Let us look more closely at what is going on here. The paradox is correct. The analyst may be listening to me, but she is not, properly speaking, my allocutee. Her ears are hired, as it were, and insulated. It is not that she is listening to her own unconscious at the same time. Just that she does not have to reply. She plays dead, and seemingly regards the patient's words as a dead letter, too. My speech can only maintain itself with difficulty, and only if I continue to expect a reply. Once I am convinced that there will be no reply, the tension is at its height. As everyone knows, the effort required for the subject to project himself into the normative place of one who essentially proffers is extremely difficult to bear throughout the whole experience. It is quite different from the well-known anxiety caused by the basic rule that he should tell everything.

One's own voice must therefore exist within a full-fledged communicational context, from which its reality is derived. In that case, one of two things must be true. Either we are in a communicative situation with someone else, and the voice that we proffer is necessarily interwoven, almost plaited, with theirs.[29] However unequal the two voices may be, I cannot negate that of the other person: there exists no zero degree of his or her participation. Discourse is unavoidably codetermined by the identity of the two uttering agencies. When I compose a piece of discourse, however small, I anticipate the other's voice because I want what I say to be addressed to and exchanged with someone. A voice for you. . . . I shall come back to this point. Or else the voice in question is once again the voice in which the speaker addresses him or herself in self-to-self communication. For we do not think outside language. And the language in which we think is also the language in which we communicate with other people. Thus I use the common language for my solitary discourse. If my own voice cannot be a private one, it can still quite well be "inward." It then becomes a strictly personal use of a public language. This inward voice can also sometimes be proffered. It does not go unnoticed, as in the following dialogue from Dostoyevsky's *The Idiot*; it takes place between the general's wife and Prince Mychkine.

Having examined the portrait of Nastassia Philippovna in silence, she said at last:

"Yes, she is a beautiful woman, very beautiful, even. I have seen her twice, but only from a distance. So hers is the type of beauty that you prize?" she added, suddenly turning toward the Prince.

"Yes," replied the Prince, with an effort.

"That beauty, exactly?"

"Exactly."

"Why?"

"In the face . . . there is much suffering. . . ." said the Prince mechanically, *as if*, instead of answering a question, *he were speaking to himself*.

"I wonder whether you are not dreaming," declared the General's wife.[30]

Our own voice can also, in this sense, be a tacit one, hardly a voice at all. In Descartes' *Second Meditation*, we read: "Quamvis haec apud me tacitus et sine voce considerem. . . ."[31]

What follows indicates that this tacit language is of course not a private one. For immediately afterward, Descartes sees the trap of vulgar language, which was anyway developed with a view to ordinary life and conversations:[32] "Nonetheless, the actual words bring me up short, and I am almost tricked by ordinary ways of talking. We say that we see the wax itself, if it is there before us, not that we judge it to be there from its color and shape."[33]

My own, tacit, voice is privileged in that I am always listening for it, whether I am questioning myself or calling on myself as a witness, attempting to persuade myself of something or raising an objection. Its pragmatic situation is a significant one, for the speaker can adopt at will an ideal speaker-listener regime. It is indeed by way of this tacit voice that I "meditate," in the Cartesian sense of an inner, private dialogue that may involve objections and replies, and that prepares me for public dialogue. I also use my tacit voice to go back over what I have understood from my earlier communications, to prolong and reflect their effects. Nevertheless, it is still very clear that just because I am anticipating or going back over things in this way, this does not make the process in any way monovocal.

In the end, why should I declare this tacit voice to be *mine* at all? No doubt because, from a pragmatic point of view, I listen to it myself in the same way as would an ideal allocutee who can deliberately adopt a free position. I am my own guaranteed listener, who will never be absent. From a semantic point of view as well, this tacit voice functions in a peculiar way: there is necessarily an upper limit to the set of possible worlds to which what is said could refer; this limit is given by the set of assumptions I have currently adopted. In particular, it can never extend to cover the possible worlds corresponding to the assumptions made by another real person.[34] It is certainly true that when we think on our own, reference does not remain invariable in our dialogue of self with self. But it cannot be supplemented in any unexpected way by the alternation of language acts. This is a crucial point whose implications there is no space to follow up here. On a communicational level, our own voice in its tacit mode remains privileged by the availability of an intimate interlocutor, and by our very familiarity with it. Privileged, but also to some extent impoverished. Take care, I would say to the egotist, for the one who speaks in your heart knows no more than you do.

Critique of Bakhtin: The Dialogical Principle

Normally, our own voice, which creates a communicational path for itself between self and self, is a prolegomenon to communication with others. Real communication is like Janus, turned toward both oneself and the other person. It is born of the interplay between self-to-self and self-to-other communication, without the former having any harmful effects on the latter. Speech speaks to me and to you. Suppose that a discourse is explicitly addressed: what happens to my own voice? It intertwines bivocally with the voice of someone else.

The conventional view does not take into account the fact that when I address another person, my voice integrates and includes his or hers, or rather, becomes entwined with it. Ordinarily, only two forms of alterity are recognized in discourse: on the one hand, people agree that language does indeed only exist through the other person, for the trivial reason that we must after all be speaking to someone. On the other hand, they know that language allows others to be alluded to in the third person, i.e., as absent third parties.[35] Unlike the animals, man is able to quote the words of someone who is not there, and incorporate them into his own discourse.

The other person's discourse, it might be said, is present in various forms, slight or substantial, diffuse or manifest, in my own. Moreover, its presence is not always interpreted by linguistic description in the same way. It makes a considerable difference whether the description speaks of the composition, the conflict, or simply the mixing of voices; and whether it emphasizes the interpenetration, impregnation, or close combination that appears in the production of the message. Mikhaïl Bakhtin cannot be praised too highly for having been the first to establish the dialogical principle. If since 1977 I have been putting forward a radicalization of his viewpoint, which I am pursuing in the present study, the reader will see that it is in no way foreign to the spirit of his work.

The most obvious form of the presence of the other person's discourse is found in reported speech. This can be analyzed by stipulating that the act of utterance, characterized by a statement m and a speaker s (who is the other person), in a situation containing at least a time t, can be represented within the verbal string of the statement M, produced by a different act of utterance U, by a speaker S in temporal context T

either as indirect speech: He says that he will come;

or as direct speech: He says, "I will come."

Let us first consider the case of direct speech, in which the other's message is supposedly reconstituted without any deterioration. Let s be the speaker of the reported words and S the person reporting them. This gives $L \neq l$, $T \neq t$. The words of s appear like an isolated own voice within the message of S, who effaces himself as a speaker in order to give a verbatim report of s's discourse. In a more or less ostentatious way, S does not intervene, as if the other person's discourse had to be preserved like a massive, inert block, a foreign body with an independent existence of its own.

Notice first of all that even in this most favorable case, S's self-effacement does not guarantee the transparency of the direct speech and the objectivity with which the words are reported.[36] Indeed, the string reported in quotation marks as being the very words of s only acquires linguistic existence through the message of S. However much its autonomy is delimited, it is only simulated. Discourse reported as direct speech in fact lays a trap of fiction for us. Whereas the linguistic fragments of S's message are inserted into an interlocutive context within which they can be interpreted, s's message depends for its interpretation on its own context, and consequently on the indications that S agrees to give in order to help reconstitute it. These indications are left to the relative discretion of S.

But there are other signs of the presence of other people's discourse. First, certain clues from earlier discourses, toward or against which what the utterer says is directed. Among these clues, the use of quotation marks indicates that I am distancing myself from the words that I am using. Thus, for instance, in an interview Paul Feyerabend gave on the subject of contemporary physics, he stated: "The principal contribution made by 'dissipatory structures' is to be found outside physics, in chemistry and biology."[37] The quotation marks he used signal a local metalinguistic operation in which the speaker partially suspends his responsibility for what is said, while leaving implicit a critical commentary. Whereas in indirect speech the other person's words are mentioned and possess the status of antonyms marked by a break in the syntax and by the presence of a verb of speaking—here a group of words are signaled as *inappropriate* to the discourse of the speaker alone. And while indirect speech openly juxtaposes usage and mere mention in the same verbal string, in the present case, a group of words belongs both to my discourse and to that of the other person, by a sort of double appropriation. The words "dissipatory structures" are not proffered like the other words, but referred back to another discourse, that of the physicist Prigogine. Here, the quotation marks indicate that someone else has already used the words uttered by the speaker: the usage has been doubled, while still being accompanied by a form of mention.[38]

The status of this double appropriation is therefore complex and personal. First, because certain words are signaled as inappropriate to the discourse of the speaker alone. He indicates that he wishes to differentiate and distance himself: the quotation marks therefore function as "distance signals." So much so that the dual appropriation in fact weakens the attribution to the speaker. But at the same time (and this should be emphasized) they also suggest that the other words are fully appropriate, and that the speaker takes full responsibility for their use and recognizes that they are his. They are, then, a way of insisting on a complete, but illusory, division between words that are fully the speaker's and an exterior linguistic domain made up of the words of others. Thus the subject of the utterance dispossesses himself of certain words in a defensive and ascetic gesture, as if trying to resist their pressure, and rejects their usage as something for which he cannot be, or is not allowed to be, responsible. At the same time, words spoken at a distance appear on the fringes of the speaker's discourse as the limit case of genuinely appropriate speech. In short, this procedure relies on a conviction that there are two specific discourses at work—which is an illusion.

Let us look again, for there is actually more to the problem than this. A certain amount of convention and practical necessity always enters into the exclusive appropriation of a discourse, which can be revealed by analysis. In fact, speech from a distance is an echo in discourse of my encounter with the words proffered by the other person. This encounter does not take place along a line of juxtaposition, but in a zone of interaction with no fixed boundary, where the ties of belonging are weakened. This effect is confirmed in an explicitly interlocutive situation. Ultimately, in dialogue there is not one word that I can seize on as my own. I must renounce my claim to an illusory mastery. Not that I then become the victim of words, possessed by them in the way that poets sometimes are, by their homophonies and poly-semies, and their probability of occurring together, so that I could hand over the initiative to them. No, it is simply that words are simultaneously appro-priate to both the speaker and her interlocutor, without the need for any con-descension, distancing, or reticence by one in relation to the other. If the speaking subject must give up any claim to control her words on her own, this does not mean that they are suddenly cast adrift, but that they in fact have two masters. Or rather: the utterer's voice becomes involved in an inter-action with that of the other person, to whom she addresses herself in an interlocutionary context. Is this because the utterer has some mental image or representation of the other? Not at all: it is simply the result of the fact that she is in an effective relationship with him or her. In this particularly radical sense, even an apparently monological discourse is heterogeneous. We also need to go beyond the simplified notion of spoken dialogue having two masters. In reality there is only one, which is neither of the speakers, but the interlocutive relation linking one with the other.

That is the last of the forms of the other's presence that I would like to emphasize here. According to Bakhtin, no individual voice could make itself understood without integrating itself into the complex chorus of the other voices that are already present, in relation to which it must situate itself. This idea is a rich and suggestive one. Contemporary criticism still has some way to go before it will have fully understood and applied it. Bakhtin uses it very successfully in interpreting Dostoyevsky's text.

Yet this is still, I fear, an inadequate conception of the dialogical principle. If the most important characteristic of utterances is that they are dialogical, if the dialogue structure really is constitutive of their pragmatic and seman-tic operation, then we must go so far as to say that the discourse of the Same is never understood as such. What it designates, in short, is a principle of differentiation: whether it is mine or the other person's, an own voice is not a simple given; it is only accessible by subtraction, once it has been dis-implicated from the compromise in which it is involved with other people's voices. Difference is still distance. Whether it be dominant or dominated matters little; for the analyst, the own voice is still a component that can only be inferred. But it is also a measure of my contribution to the message, the motive force that I put into the discursive situation, and to that extent its reality is unquestionable. Dialogue is only fruitful and creative (of informa-tion or meaning) if my own voice manages to achieve implicit recognition; if it is able to be disentangled at any moment by the interlocutor, but at the same time allows itself to be integrated into the progress of the conversation. As a differential reality, however, it is not heard. On this point I diverge from

Bakhtin: in my view, my own voice is precisely, and only, a prerequisite of meaning and the communal pooling of meaning, a pragmatic prerequisite.

It is not saying much to suggest that the ego only appears in dialogue by a process of turning back on the self, and that this process in turn depends on a detour through the dual alterity of the world and other people: in a correctly exchanged utterance, meaning, in its pragmatic and semantic reality, exists not only for others, but through them. Particularly as the *we* is the only point of equilibrium in the couple formed by the uttering agencies. How could the ego seize the semantic initiative for itself? Let me repeat, "I" can indeed be said by the person who *speaks*, but it can never designate the one who *says*.[39]

My own voice, which must be reconstructed differentially, as we shall shortly see, is therefore more or less accessible. In principle, it needs to be discovered in and dis-implicated from the individual utterances in which I am involved, all of which have a dialogue structure. But because many pragmatic situations have an even more complex structure than this, the first step is often to identify the uttering agencies.

This is the case, for example, with interviews, in which journalists rarely speak in their own names, although they never disappear from the discussion altogether. Journalists' questions correspond to the presuppositions and expectations of the reader. Through the vocabulary they employ, they establish the language level and lexical framework which the interviewee should use, even though neither they themselves nor the interviewee might share the corresponding conceptual habits. In reality it is the newspaper's readership that forms one of the uttering agencies, the other being the interviewee.

Where does this leave us? The agency really responsible for the question that has been asked no longer coincides with the speaking subject—here, the journalist. He or she warns us that this is so: "I must ask you whether . . ." Normally, the reference of "I" is formed the moment the questioner appropriates for him or herself the general meaning of "I," which is: "the person who is speaking," to designate him or herself. But the situation is complicated by two things. We have just seen that the person who is speaking, as speaking subject, is not the same as the one who says, as saying subject, because in a very general way it is not possible for only one person to be responsible for a communicated meaning. In the particular context of an interview, I must now add that the speaking subject hardly coincides at all with the speaker, or with any of the other uttering agencies. In this case, the real originator of what is said is essentially a certain conjunction between the expected audience and the person being interviewed, who are the two uttering agencies present. As for the speaking subject that is the journalist, he or she is deliberately acting mainly as a spokesperson, fulfilling his or her own role in the interview in a marginal manner. Consequently, the difficulty in reconstructing his or her own voice is caused by the complicating factor that the real pragmatic structure of the interview is different from its surface structure, which is apparently that of a dialogue. The interviewee knows this but normally plays along with it anyway. But it can happen that he or she forgets for a moment, or pretends to be surprised at the way the interview is being conducted. A discussion in 1981 between a special correspondent and Lech Walesa contained an almost perfect example:

> "The noise of marching boots is getting louder. Are we seeing preparations for a military intervention?"
>
> "I am starting to get fed up with this question. I must have told you at least a dozen times already that I don't believe there will be any intervention. Do you block up your ears when I am talking to you, or what?"[40]

Differential and Integrated Components of Discourse

It remains for me to dispel the illusion that has been exposed in this way, that the own voice is the same as that of the speaking subject seen as the originator of what is said. Admittedly, this voice is no longer being seen as a private one, but it is at least individual. Does not the legend of the ego begin with a voice?[41] That most beautiful human voice, taken back as near as possible to its source. It is a tenacious illusion that feeds on the conviction that in the voice there vibrates a presence, and that a voice properly tuned is the closest contact possible with our immediate experience. In it, meaning becomes flesh. "The inflexion, the fullness, the priceless timbre . . . the giant tree of the voice, a sacred tree, growing out of our flesh."[42]

Equally, does not the speaker sometimes insist that he is the originator of what he is saying? This is the last bastion of subjectivity. Its last retreat, once the rampart of absolute subjectivity has been demolished. This will be our final battle.

I have consistently tried to show the nonvalidity in principle of the untenable idea that, in order to construct his message, a speaker will freely select a particular lexical item or syntactic structure, with no other constraint than what he himself has to say. We have seen that speaking is not a matter of telling someone what we mean, as in the traditional view of communication, which uses an unacceptable utilitarian and instrumental definition of language. The subject is master neither of the meaning nor of the pertinence of the utterance.

Nevertheless there are many cases, people will insist, in which an individual seems to be expressing himself directly and in his name alone, to the point where he seems to insist on taking full responsibility for the utterance himself. Are these not counter-examples which call into question the dialogical structure of the utterance? Conversely, if the dialogical principle is applied to all utterances, does that mean that we have to give up any idea that persons are original and that what they say can have expressive value? In short, it remains for us to understand how the singularity of speech is possible if we accept a communicational paradigm.

Originality means something different from personal identity. "But my dear fellow," André Gide would ask, "do you never feel that you are singular?" Let us take this remark seriously. A person may have good reasons for proffering the things that he or she seems to be saying. We regularly hear people say things that imply that the speaking subject is the originator of what is said: "You won't make me say what I don't mean!" Or, to defend themselves against ill-considered imputations: "That's not what I'm saying!" Others have taken exactly the same view. In *The Idiot*, for example, Lisaveta Prokofievna comments thus on the attitude of the prince: "Very probably, his words did not always express what he wanted to say." [43]

Within the dialogue form itself, it can happen that the speaking subject declares explicitly: "I mean," or, in a peremptory way: "what I am saying is . . .", emphasizing the illocutionary force of her words. She seems to be not only saying what she thinks, but thinking what she says. Which would mean that she is taking responsibility for what she says, showing that she is speaking seriously and that the meaning of her utterance is indeed what she meant to say.

In a philosophy of representation, it is easy (and usual) to describe this experience as an attempt to match language to one's own thoughts, and what is said to what is in one's mind. Since Locke, the commonly held view has of course been that "I mean" signifies "I have it in mind that," or: "I am the seat of a mental process which I can translate into words thus." To the point where if I did not know what ideas the words I speak arouse in your mind, I would not be sure that you understood what I was saying. Correlatively, your words would mean nothing to me if I did not have an idea of what you meant by them.

"Between Us, I Mean . . ."

From our point of view, we need a quite different description of the discursive situation if we wish to turn to the advantage of the dialogical principle the very facts that seem to shake its foundations. Asking someone what he or she means by an expression or a word does not mean inquiring what is in his or her mind, but asking what he or she is prepared to say—to him or herself or to me—in connection with his or her use of the word. If we take this a little further, we find that we need to know what effective transactions the idiom "I mean" allows us to perform. At the risk of going back over old ground, and being content with less radical results than those already obtained in the course of the present study, I propose to subject the two traditional hypotheses to the test of concrete description. These are

1. That saying and meaning are two parallel activities, the first of which (language) is articulated and public, while the second (thought) is ineffable and private, and

2. That the process we call saying works in the service of the free expression of the linguistic subject's ideas, by expressing secondarily his or her own intention of meaning.

The first hypothesis is extremely widespread. In it, we convince ourselves that what we perceive of a written or verbal sign is only the external face of an intimate subjectivity, inside which the authentic operations of signification are going on. A brief account of the reasons often given for pursuing such a hypothesis, which were discussed by Wittgenstein, should suffice.

If we are inclined to make the process of meaning an internal one that is synchronized with speech, it is because we believe we need it if we are to make an utterance something more than just an assemblage of lifeless signs. But let us think about the following statement: "The occult element to which we attribute the power of bringing signs to life can itself only be a sign, in relation to which the same problem arises again."[44]

At that point, what interest do we have in introducing any sort of mental discourse, i.e. internalized speech in the manner of Hobbes, if its relation to reality raises a problem similar to the one that its own invention was supposed to solve? It is not that subjective processes are simply a myth; there is no question of denying their existence. But what would be the point of arguing that understanding what someone means involves gaining access through his or her discourse to the representations that are going on in his or her mind, because these representations would in turn need to be read and understood? As such, they would be something else that, like signs, only had meaning by virtue of belonging to a certain system, and also of a certain type of use to which we put them.

Perhaps we are now ready to describe what really does happen when we use the expression "I mean."

—Yes, you might say, how indeed can we account for turns of phrase such as "expressing a thought that is at the back of one's mind," or "his words betrayed his thoughts"? They suggest very strongly that there is some process of translation of the ideas we have in us, as if we could see an expression in our mind's eye, or better, as if what we were trying to express in words were already expressed, but in some kind of mental language, and all we were doing was translating it into words.

—In fact, if we examine the real circumstances in which we are prepared to use these expressions, we will see that their value is simply metaphorical.

This is how Wittgenstein, for his part, disproves the second hypothesis: "In most cases of what we call 'expressing an idea,' what actually happens is something quite different. Imagine what happens in cases when, for instance, I have to cast about for a word. Several words are suggested and I reject them. Finally one is proposed and I say: 'That is what I wanted to say!'"[45]

This reply is satisfactory in part: the expression "I mean x by y" does not behave in the same way as: "I have mental representation x when I say y." But does it follow that it always behaves like: "I intend x by y"?

For my part, I consider that the expression "I mean," at least when it is employed in a normal way in language, behaves as a sort of metalinguistic operator. I pause to give an opinion on what has been said. In such cases, the word has in fact preceded the idea, since thought is accessible through meaning, and meaning through saying. It does not yet follow that I am, properly speaking, the originator of the saying process.

Let us try to tie down the exact function of the expression "I mean," so as to extend the therapeutic process of counter-exemplification begun by Wittgenstein in a slightly different direction. First, there are contexts in which the expression serves to put right a mistake, with emphasis on the corrected element:

—I mean, *Paul* came.

Elsewhere, it allows an ambiguity that may have been my fault to be cleared up. Or the speaker may be interrupted so that an additional referential detail can be introduced, in function of the information available to someone else:

—He means the president of the *university*.

Unless it is a matter of specifying a meaning more closely, salva veritate:

—I mean, *weird*.

In this case the expression is being introduced simply to ensure that the speaker has been understood. Such interventions by the speaking subject do not constitute an attempt by subjectivity to appropriate the discourse. By claiming that the expression always has a metalinguistic function, I mean that it serves to call attention to what is most important to the speaker in what is being said. More decisive still for our purposes, however, are the ways in which it is used in explicitly interlocutive contexts.

Normally, the speaking subject has no intention of seeking recognition as the sole originator of the ideas which he or she has translated into words. The lexical element "to say," which is often regarded as the archi-lexeme of all verbs of communication, can be used in two types of nominal phrases. They are grouped either around the form of the words spoken, as in:

"He has said the forbidden word"; or around their semantic content, as in: "He has said stupid things." In this second case, it is the meanings of the words themselves that are significant. If, in the first case, "say" is equivalent to "proffer" and does not commit us to regarding the speaking subject as the originator of what he or she has said, then what about the second? And in fact, who exactly has said stupid things?

In an explicitly interlocutive situation, it is understood that each party will make his or her own contribution—no more, no less—to the semantic initiative, which is a joint activity. This explains why we always seem to resent it when an interlocutor has contributed to the stupid things that have appeared in the conversation, forgetting that we have contributed to them as well. It is a commonplace experience that the need to coproduce the meaning of what is said leads us to remove certain rules of self-censorship from our discourse. This also explains why it is that we should dislike attempts to dominate a conversation, just as much as when someone refuses to talk to us. If someone appropriates for him or herself something that is said during a conversation ("That's just what I was saying to you") the breach of etiquette, however slight, does not pass unnoticed. This is because it is almost impossible legitimately to appropriate meanings. Conversely, an insistence on staying out of a conversation is felt as a weakness, or even a refusal to participate semantically: "I don't know anything about that. What does it mean?"

As soon as the context becomes that of a conversation, it is not up to *I* or *you* to impose on it a content of meaning, or to determine the identity of the referent (or a given class of referents). The resulting conversation will rarely turn out as any of the participants imagined it would. Semanticists have not yet realized the full importance of this experience: the most that one person can do is influence slightly the direction in which a conversation goes, but often we are simply swept along by it.

Let us look closely at what happens when we take two extracts from the same conversation. How do we recognize that they come from the same speaking subject? In a rule-governed dialogue, the slightest utterance will be genuinely pooled.[46] An utterance is defined by its insertion in a certain communicational regime that determines its pertinence. Words are not chosen and put together by the speaker alone.

Conversely, communication with others cannot be derived from the coincidence of each speaker with him or herself. Communication would never be possible if it relied on an absolute initiative by the speaker to get it going. The best, and most absurd, proof of this is provided once again by the anti-dialogues of Lewis Carroll. He confronts Alice with a series of delightfully closed subjectivities. The externally dialogical form certainly does not prevent them from revealing everything about themselves, but the absolute difference between them makes any meeting impossible. With a very English type of humor, Carroll has actually applied Sterne's paradox of "the impossible usage of words"[47] in certain dialogues, when words come straight from each speaker's arbitrary individual interests, and everybody imagines that he or she only has to be the master of words to become the master of pertinence, and ultimately of the whole verbal exchange. Beneath their conventional appearance, words will always reveal themselves to be outrageously impregnated with subjectivity. What, then, is to be done? Should we look for other, doubtless even more unpredictable forms of communication? The solution, which is one of principle, lies elsewhere.

Once dialogism enters discourse, the subjectivity of the protagonists ceases to be eccentric. Contemporary logicians of epistemic modalities, doubtless more sophisticated and learned than Charles Dodgson, suggest that subjectivity is made alternatively perceptible through the "possible worlds" implied by the propositional attitudes (believing, knowing, doubting) that are brought face to face in the course of communication.

Alice's impossible dialogues with the Cheshire Cat, the March Hare, and the Caterpillar work, in my view, as a proof and an absurd illustration of the necessary conditions governing the process of "meaning" in an interlocutive situation. Instead of bringing it about, such dialogues destroy any chance of communication between the two participants: "Then you should say what you mean," says the March Hare pompously to Alice, who humorously agrees with him: "I do. . . . at least—at least, I mean what I say—that's the same thing, you know."[48]

A logic without any pragmatic dimension becomes simply a way of ensuring one's own ascendancy over others, and satisfying an empty need to assert one's subjectivity. Such anti-dialogues show how a false apprehension of the real world and the reality of others goes hand in hand with a false presentation of oneself. Faced with such companions, Alice begins to have serious doubts about her own identity. We have seen how often she is asked the question: "Who are you?" In the end she is forced to admit that after so many changes, she no longer knows the answer, to this or any other questions.

The Dialogue-Structure of Saying

We keep coming back to the same conclusion: anyone who wishes to get away from expressivist subjectivism must find a different way of looking at subjectivity. Such a person will also need to try to dispel the hegemony of the illusion according to which "I" is the sole subject of the saying and meaning process. After looking at Carroll's absurd refutation of this idea, I will now make a few remarks toward a direct demonstration.

To argue that saying has the structure of a dialogue is really to assert that at the moment when language enters the communicational field, it is transformed into discursive agencies characterized by a set of internal references whose key is *I/you*, and not *I*. The case of a discourse that is reported as being that of an uttering collectivity, *we* or *you*, of which *I* and *you* stand as spokespersons, is no exception to this rule. Such cases are derivative. In itself, language is only an ability to say which must be reinvested and actualized in a new "meaning to say." Only, this new process of meaning must not be taken back to an "I" in possession of its own discourse, and able on its own to appropriate the inventory of linguistic forms for itself; instead, it must be conceived in a way that takes fully into account the consequences of the fact that discourse has a communicational structure. Meaning will then appear as something virtually interactional and transactional. When "I" begin to speak, that does not mean that I take over the function of saying, for I can never take the semantic initiative on my own. If a human experience is contained in language, it does not refer back by some original asymmetry to the proffering by an "I," but to an initiative of saying that is in some way necessarily shared.

The simplest cases of meaning, explains John Searle, are those in which a speaker utters a sentence and *means*, exactly and literally, what he says. In such cases, Searle adds, the speaker has the intention of producing a certain effect on the listener, by making her recognize his intention of producing it, thanks to the rules governing the utterance of the sentence. Notice, however, that the author is soon forced to supplement his body of hypotheses to take account of indirect phenomena: "In direct speech acts the speaker communicates to the hearer more than what he says, by way of relying on their mutually shared background information."[49]

That is not all: the explanatory apparatus must include "certain principles of conversational cooperation." These new hypotheses are obviously of a quite different kind, because they tend to reinterpret the illocutionary force of a sentence as a communicative force, and speech acts as true linguistic interactions. Searle admits not having properly proved his thesis, and that his mode of analysis, which leans on certain Gricean concepts, leaves a good number of questions unanswered.

For his part, Emile Benveniste realized that by attributing a dialogue structure to *all* utterances, he was breaking new ground.[50] Yet he has also made a major contribution to the acceptance of the idea that every speaker, at the moment he or she takes up the speaking role, may legitimately consider language from his or her personal point of view. According to Benveniste, the speaker's privilege is also that of regarding him or herself as the originator of what he or she means, the center or source of a system of pragmatic coordinates. The person who occupies the role of speaker at a given moment is also, in his view, the one who has the semantic initiative. Now, and let me stress this point, the first-person pronoun certainly gives the speaker a convenient means of designating him or herself. But no less significant is the fact that the word "I" obliges the speaker to do so using the same sign that the other person will use to designate him or herself.

Can we even say that the subject of the utterance is identified in the speaker's self-designation? Things are not so simple. In the to-and-fro of questions and answers, who actually is the utterer? In the course of a real debate, people on all sides take turns to examine, and in a sense safeguard, the question under discussion, independently of who happened to ask it in the first place. The utterance is set adrift, in a power vacuum, between the voice that has asked the question and those which respond to it. The question anxiously awaits a reply, and the reply is directed toward the questioner, if only to deceive or elude his or her expectations. We know that symmetry is a property of the relation of verbal communication: a message generally calls for a response, and the allocutee functions as a potential speaker.

Any utterance that seeks to enter an interlocutive framework will be presumed to act both as the reply to a virtual question from the interlocutor, and as a tacit question addressed, or "suggested," to him or her. The result is that any utterance, however small, that fits into such a framework must be able to be located simultaneously from the standpoint of two interlocutors, who are to some extent its co-utterers.[51]

Let us take this a little further. Until now, we have assumed that the two utterers have been playing the roles of speaker and allocutee in turn. The study of paraverbal behavior in fact shows that the allocutee is quite likely to react with gesture or mimicry during the speaker's utterance. What is more, we have assumed that the reply would make use of the same code. In fact, the utterers will not have exactly the same competence in the language. A certain consensus does exist about lexical meanings, which makes possible the first mutual understanding between them. But each will have a slightly different code, and such idiolectal divergences mean that they will have to use their initial intercomprehension as a basis for understanding each other afterward.

Imagine now that instead of two speakers replying to each other in sequence, their words are mixed up into a single utterance: this overlap gives rise to an intrinsic bivocality. For good measure, to impute a dialogue structure to an utterance is to see it as if it were spoken by two voices, constructed by their convergence or undermined by their internal divergence.

Any utterance made by the speaking subject must fulfill certain very strict conditions before it can be said to belong to the logical space of interlocution. It must be part of the thread of the discourse. First, in that it accepts the presuppositions common to the partners; then, by helping to advance the sequence along the lines of an agreed discursive strategy—for example, toward an answer to the question that opened the discussion.

I have had occasion to analyze these conditions in detail for a type of dialogue in which information is being sought.[52] The partners open up a logical space of interlocution in which their utterances will be located in a tightly controlled way by an initial question of the type "will it be this or that?" This question defines the object of the discussion simply by imposing its presuppositions on it. From that point, a semantic framework is set in place to which all the participants consent, and which is gradually enriched as the interlocutors build up a set of shared new presuppositions in the background. This case, which was almost too perfect, allowed me to demonstrate two things:

1. the total misguidedness of the common methodological postulate (at least until the last few years) which defines the largest unit of linguistic analysis as the sentence: there clearly must exist trans-sentence combinatory rules to account for the logical coherence of utterances, anaphora, presuppositional isotopies, and the construction of common semantic frameworks;

2. the extent to which interlocutors are associated with each other in the initiation of meaning. Even the slightest utterance in the sequence is a message suspended between them. The utterance in a sense has two focal points; it is bifocal, or bivocal. What each one says is designed not only to convey his or her intention, but also to take account of the way the other will hear it. As he or she produces an utterance, the speaker is also obliged to take the partner's part. It must be assumed that the allocutee might have said the same thing him or herself, or at least have incorporated the idea into another statement of his or her own designed to complement or challenge it.

As we can see, the diction of the speaking subject can never exhaust what can be said. No amount of self-sufficiency or interiority can suffice to inscribe the "I mean" within the "I." The ego can no more be a fixed reference than a point of origin. It only arises against the background of the interlocutive relation, of which it is no more than a secondary requirement, constituted by a process of withdrawal, turning inward, or return to the self.

This implies that we now need to refine further our description of "I mean," and redescribe its linguistic function in the real circumstances of its use. In an explicitly interlocutive context, metalinguistic intervention occurs not unilaterally, but bilaterally, operating on the utterances produced during the discussion. The utterance in relation to which "I mean" introduces a modification is largely detached from any particular speaker. That is not all. The other person has asked me to rephrase, or simply repeat, what I have just said, with a "you mean . . ." A harmless question, but it takes away from me any naive possession of the meaning of what there is to be said. In reply, the expression "I mean . . ." invites the other in turn to agree to the statement, to which I am presuming that I have now given an acceptable linguistic form. Here, for example, is a reformulated question that resembles a request for confirmation:

—He's killing himself with work.

—You mean they are making him do too much?

—I mean (i.e., let us say) that it's destroyed his health.

This sequence is typical. The speaker finds herself being asked to approve and accept an earlier utterance which her interlocutor believes can be imputed specifically to her; she is invited to specify its meaning or provide additional referential details. In a variant of the same scenario, the speaker does not wait for any invitation, but uses the expression "I mean" as soon as she realizes that the words she is speaking (to which she listens as the other person would) might be understood in a relatively different way:

—When I say that the working day should be shortened, I don't mean we should reduce output.

For my partner to understand the message as I would wish him or her to do, I have to formulate it differently. So "I mean" signifies "you can understand me as saying," directed toward the other person, which is proof of the dual way in which we listen to what is said.

Other uses of the phrase are designed to circumvent the dialogical principle, and show a desire to monopolize the speaking role asymmetrically, or to prevent it from being captured by the other person. In such cases, "I mean" is a sign that self-to-self communication has come back into the picture, as one of the participants jumps in to negate by force what the other is saying. I believe that violence in whatever form, including in discourse, should be shown up for what it is. It is cheating.

We tend also to use the expression to present what we say as the considered and delayed result of our inward deliberations:

—We need a fairer tax system; I mean, it is important to overhaul the system as a whole.

It is still necessary to distinguish between cases in which we want to claim responsibility for an argument, when "I mean" is close to "I argue that," and those in which we intend to reserve for ourselves the initiative of stating the problem, when "I mean" stands for: "This is the point, and I am the one who is supposed to make the semantic choice of terms."

Of course, such an appropriation of the semantic initiative, which is ultimately impossible anyway, should not be confused with the various efforts we might make to influence the communal goal of the discussion to our own advantage, or to protest against too rapid or too unilateral a change of direction in the conversation. Some people spend their whole time trying to break down the discourse that is being constructed and correct what has been said. We might also, however, be concerned to prevent the other person from going off on the wrong track, leaving us to carry on alone:

—I reject socialism with a stony face, by which, and let us be clear about this, I mean the perversion of socialism.

Polemical discussion or disputation in which each partner tries to achieve dominance of the exchange, and anti-dialogue as imagined by Lewis Carroll, can be seen as extreme cases of dialogue. Such extreme limits can never be reached without marking the pragmatic end of the conversation, because the linguistic fragments produced lack all pertinence, and even meaning, once the essential condition of communicability has been flaunted in this way.

The illusion that hegemony is possible in discourse is undoubtedly a tenacious one. Is the fact that it seems to survive so well explained by discourse's ability to tolerate asymmetries of utterance? Another limit case is a reply given by Jacques Chirac, the mayor of Paris, to the journalist A. Fernbach: "You can understand whatever you like, *I* know what I mean."

Either this same illusion, or the speaker's situation, seems to make him want to regard something that he is proffering communicatively as an absolute expression of himself, and somehow to antedate its meaning so that he can think of it as autonomous. We wish to regard ourselves as the owners of meaning, in the same way that we are responsible for truth—as if the one derived legitimately from the other.

Let us therefore remember the dialogical principle: an utterance is produced in a community of meaning, in some way bilaterally, between utterers who interact bivocally, through dual listening and meaning. As I demonstrated above, saying has its origin in an interlocutive relation that exceeds even the reflexive resources of the thinking ego. It follows that no one can actually take the speaker's role in such a way as to *have* it, as others claim to "have the right" or "have the responsibility" to do something. No one can have speech to him or herself, as a jealous husband ensures that he has his wife to himself; no one can make him or herself its master or its owner, and take sovereign control over the institution of meaning. There is little doubt that votive or imprecatory formulae, and, in a more unilateral way, numerous conflictual strategies, do come close to this situation. In front of a microphone, some people will apparently ignore their audience on purpose. The inscription of the allocutee in the utterance can, therefore, sometimes be whittled down to nothing, as the speaker grabs the semantic initiative to an absurd degree, demanding the "right" to take no account of the other's existence. The sanction for this sort of behavior is that such speech is immediately curtailed, and meaning crumbles. These are, then, at most exceptions which confirm the rule that when I speak, it is actually *we* who say. Otherwise, leaving aside humor, verbal interaction ceases to be communicative.

—You haven't read much!

—You mean to say I am uncultured?

Beyond this point lie invective and vociferation, and at one further remove, vituperation, threats of war and cries of pain (our demand to be heard by our body, which is deaf).

Normally, the originator of what is said is "split" in two, because he is also concerned with his other. In fact, this expression is still metaphorical, in the same way that speech might be described as "two-pronged," etc. Let us say more prosaically, but more rigorously too, that both speakers are linked in an interlocutive relation, which is what constitutes them in their duality and forms them into a dyad. Not only because we all need to see how our messages are received in order to know that they were, but, more radically, because as a consequence of the primum relationis principle, what is said cannot have meaning for the other (the weak thesis), if it did not first mean *through* him or her (the strong thesis). Now that there is no unified and fixed subject to carry the fixity of meaning, discourse will only signify to the extent that it loses any fixed meaning.

We can now return at our leisure to the old conviction that, as a speaking subject, I am also the subject of the saying process. And that subjectivity itself is the hegemonic subject of the process by which meaning is established.

In the first place, as we have seen, the speaker may have lost her exclusive right to the semantic initiative, but she still has the possibility of intercepting, intervening in, and interrupting the construction of what is being said for her own advantage, by in a sense recycling it into her own self-to-self communication.

Typically, this would be the moment when I sound out my own mind before answering a question. I am, then, my own first interlocutor. And the expression "I mean" is a way of bringing the product of these prolegomena forward onto the threshold of my communication with the other. It also marks the moment when, by a process of turning away and withdrawal, the speaker grasps her own identity within the interlocutive relation, at the same time appropriating her own contribution to it. But she of course will draw on the same virtual meanings of words in the language to communicate with herself and with others, but contextualizing them in a different way. Next, the speaker is not absolved from all responsibility for the words spoken. It is up to her to actualize her communicative competence. She is also committed to supporting whatever her words may say, to maintaining her assertions, replying to contradiction from others, and respecting the pragmatic rules that govern linguistic interaction. Consequently, it should again be stressed that even though her own voice never exists in a free state on its own, but only appears interwoven with other people's, it still represents her driving contribution to the discursive process.

Moreover, her own voice can always be reconstructed in its relative difference, which forms a positively valued gap. We saw earlier that there is a limit to the reduction of asymmetries in discourse. At any moment, our referential activities remain distinct within the interaction itself. The words that we each speak are not subject to exactly the same context. It is revealing that an interlocutor will sometimes say "you mean . . ." when all I was doing was fictively adopting what I took to be *her* context, and effectively saying: "*you* yourself mean this, but let us be clear that I do not want to share what I infer to be your belief." By going back over the context which he has imputed to his partner, the speaker hopes that he might be able to induce her to modify her background assumptions.

Even in this case, however, the speaker's autonomy is only relative. For communicational interaction implies that both speaker and interpreter pay close attention to the dual movement of contextualization and its chances of advancing toward a consensus. As in the case of the speaker's own voice, which is never heard by itself, his own context is also an inferred entity, which is derived by abstraction from the communicational process. Even when the pragmatic search for consensus has a positive outcome, the coincidence between contexts has a limit. It is unstable. This is no doubt why, however marginal the distinction between speaker and allocutee may be for the theory of meaning, it remains indispensable on the level of discourse analysis.

It is difficult to put forward a unified linguistic description of what is happening here. However, the particular sensitivity of expressions such as "I mean . . ." and "you mean" to their interdiscursive context is obvious, and far from random. The metalinguistic function that we can agree to grant to such expressions operates despite the more or less marked disappropriation of earlier utterances from the speaking subject. As a general rule, the meaning communicated has the form "let us be clear that what I mean is . . .".

My aim has also been to show what the notion of pragmatic intelligibility

299

can contribute to philosophical analysis, in that it allows philosophers to reflect on a different class of examples, and so make their thinking more flexible. It is generally held that "I mean" expresses the speaker's intended meaning. What I say is then simply what differentiates my utterances from what someone else might say about the same referent. A more accurate description shows however that what I say is really:

1. That which differentiates the things I am about to announce from what you expect me to say, or were going to let me say. Our own voice is a differential component. Normally, I expect the other to concede my share in the semantic initiative to me. This concessive structure is an essential part of the dialogical ability.

2. That which, at the moment when we are talking together, I want to say, over and above what I surmise that you expect me to say. Each time, I am striving to make a difference between us. This can be a complex operation. Suppose that I want to convey the singularity of my point of view: of course, this does not release me from the obligation of choosing the linguistic form of what I say in function of the fact that we are both listening to it. But I shall choose precisely the words that you would never dream of uttering. Our own voice is always differential. As such, who can hear it directly? But it can be reconstructed. Its difference, even its discordance, stands out against the background of convergent bivocality which forms what I shall call the integrated component, as opposed to the differential one.

3. That which I would utter to a putative or ideal interlocutor. Or one who is absent, as distinct from all the present allocutees who are listening to me from within a system of sociologically marked positions of utterance. Note that innovative individuals, or those who claim to be "original," will often declare themselves to be strangers to the language that is spoken here, loudly announcing their refusal to occupy the position the institution requires them to adopt. As can be seen in the scientific conversation that Berthold Brecht stages between Galileo and Cardinals Bellarmin and Barberini, originality in such cases consists in proclaiming that one belongs to a different communicational community where speech is supposed to be free, i.e. one in which all language acts are canonically regulated.

The Three Meanings of the Subject

As we have seen, the differential and integrated components are found in varying proportions in most concrete forms of speech. By directing the analysis of subjectivity in discourse, these two notions should prevent it from straying into either of two opposing blind alleys. In the first, saying is defined exclusively in relation to the speaker's intention of meaning, while in the second it is defined, more subtly, as an effort to bring about the convergence, then the coincidence, of two intentions of meaning.[53] Rather than demanding an effort to recognize the other's intention, discussions with him or her require an effort by both interlocutors in a present relation to project their words, at least partially, into a common interlocutive space. Whatever their initial individual differences—and their final personal differences—may be.

In accordance with these definitions, I shall end my discussion of this point by selecting three definitions of the term "subject."

In its strong sense, which I have deliberately excluded from this section, the subject is regarded as the true discourse-producing agency, and the resulting discourse is considered to be its particular production. This is the solitary, superb voice of the ego. We were forced to abandon the assumptions underlying this strong definition, in which the subject says the utterance, and what is said is a function of what the ego means. I have argued forcefully that this is not *saying* at all. If the thinking *I* simply had something to say, it would not need saying at all: thinking it would be enough. Always supposing, of course, that thinking were possible without saying to oneself.

We have also looked at two other possible meanings. According to the first, the speaking subject is able (in a weaker sense) to take responsibility for the meaning of its own words, and discourse relates back to it as an admittedly common production, but one which it could appropriate in the first person. In that case, the subject remains the speaker. I concluded, on the basis of psychoanalytic practice and the existence of the phenomenon of pragmatic prematuration, that this assumption—that the subject is always in a position to listen to what it is saying and therefore to recover its full meaning—was also unrealistic and had to be abandoned.

As a result, I am led to put forward a definition of the ego that is weaker still, in which the speaker is a speaking subject to the extent that he is able to take charge not of the meaning of his words, as before, but of the meaning of the words exchanged in the course of a discussion, as long as he is engaged in fulfilling the conditions of a genuine act of communication. The subject "holds" the speaking role in the sense that he does not abandon words to their own devices, but he can never appropriate their meanings for himself. As we have seen at some length, discourse is, by its pragmatic and semantic constitution, a joint linguistic production which cannot be taken back to one or the other of the interlocutors in particular. This does not mean that the speaking subject is not able, in a later conversation, to go back over the meaning of the words spoken and give his opinion about them, comment critically on them, etc. The subject is really a speaker in this third sense. He thus takes on something of the identity of a personal self.

Avowal of the Person

Others talk about me, but we speak to each other: the partners in a situation of reciprocity are in part established through this relation. Not because I become "I" simply by virtue of saying "you," thereby acquiring the status of a person, and one who is originarily in a relation, but because, in part at least, I am the person that I am, equipped with certain propositional attitudes, only by virtue of the present interlocutive relation, in which my attitudes are continually being compared and contrasted with those of other people.

Difference becomes inveterate through the suppression or immobilization of the communicational movement, or the petrification or freezing of dialogue. Once one of the parties deliberately proclaims his or her difference, a lasting asymmetry is created. This is admittedly not an originary asymmetry, but it will often tend to acquire the importance of one. It comes from a narcissistic inertia that is always potentially there: we all have a constant tendency to assert ourselves as the center and anchor point of centrifugal patterns of behavior and speech, because we all see ourselves as available for this sort of role. This possibility is directly present in the communicational movement, which can always fold back on itself. Self-to-self communication of this sort marks a departure from dialogue and a return to a less rich model, one of mediation or even of storytelling.

Difference Is Not Just Positive; It Is Relative

This sort of self-proclaimed difference quickly becomes absolute, as the self seizes on it and imputes it to itself as one of its qualities, in its attempt to achieve its own self-representation. Many and varied are the strategies used by self-esteem. I have examined those of the autobiographical narrative, which works by manipulating the communicational movement so as to close it back on itself. It is also possible to do the opposite, and exploit the communicational movement to construct the image of oneself that one wishes to give.

We would really need to add to this dossier all the different ways in which the speaker can interrupt or distort the communication process. If it is indeed true that people need to communicate with others in order to constitute their personal identity, it seems likely that we will all be tempted at some time or other to interrupt the process in order to put forward definitions of ourselves for our own ratification.

In such cases, the speaking subject wishes to turn communication to his own advantage in an attempt to accomplish his self-identity with and through the other. In so doing, he uses the other for his own purposes, which is, as we know, an insult. He uses her as a means to an end, and communication as a place in which to achieve his fantasy goals. As in the autobiographical fiction, the subject intends to represent himself to others as he would like to see himself, and calls on them to ratify this self-image.

But this time the whole operation takes place within communication itself, which now takes a decidedly metacommunicational turn. There are innumerable examples in which speakers stop discussing external matters and turn to the interlocutive relation itself as the subject of conversation. Discourse can then become a vehement appeal to, or a unilateral solicitation of, the other person—a desperate attempt to establish oneself in one's personal difference. Each party has recourse to the other solely as external confirmation of his own definition of himself. Here we see the grand maneuvers of seduction, when the encounter is nothing more than derisive narcissism. At the same time, one speaker generally seeks to elude the definition of himself that the other is trying to give. In short, each seeks to individualize himself in his own eyes and establish himself just as he aspires to be, with his own self-image, caught fleetingly but complacently in the narcissistic mirror, as proof of success. Man is a being who discovers in himself a singular and dubious ability to prefer individual to personal identification.

It is perfectly clear that the desire to *individualize* oneself by representing oneself to others through a partial and often mendacious story cannot be confused with the legitimate attempt to *differentiate* oneself by grasping one's identity through and in a current interlocutive relation. I defined self-indulgence of this type as the manipulation of the self by individualization, a process by which it becomes the owner of its appurtenances and qualities, and appears to have memories, initiatives, and feelings—in short, to have individuality.

It certainly seems impossible to confuse the type of pseudopersonal identification that operates by individualization with the real thing, which works by differentiation within pairs of speakers, taking due account of the stock of earlier communications and the respective sets of relations in which each individual has already been involved.

It is not a matter of chance that the discovery of differential identification should have been made in all its freshness in the same Greek tragic tradition which was also able to paint such a gloomy picture of solitude. Whether the hero be Prometheus or Ajax, Philoctetes or Oedipus, the tragic event always leads the hero to a position of solitude from which to look back at himself. Some of them accept heroically, taking the first step toward self-reidentification, in what I have called the second experience of the spirit. They identify themselves by making a break, often at a point of crisis. Thus Antigone loudly proclaims in the face of her family that the behavior they call an "impious piety" is in fact a "pious piety," and the Chorus eventually decides that she is right. But there are also those who go through life clothed

in solitude, and whom only death seems able to free from an earlier alienation. Thus Oedipus learns that he grew up in Corinth without being the son
of the man whom he took to be his father, and that his reign in Thebes was
similarly solitary. Oedipus finally rediscovers himself in his retreat, a process
of identification upon which beneficent death sets its seal. Then again there
are those who, like Creon, pass through solitude only to drown themselves in
it, for whom it is only a foretaste of worse anguish to come.

Sophocles' genius lies in his ability to explore personal differences within
tragedy. The identification between Antigone and her sister Ismene, for instance, only comes about through the double relationship in which he shows
them both to be involved. They gradually establish themselves as what they
are when the conflict between their respective relations with their uncle and
dead brother begins to unfold. Thus Sophocles is able to set the docility of
the one against the other's revolt, at the same time that he places the rebellious daughter in the context of a family dynasty. On this point, the progress
made since Aeschylus is clear. In the work of the earlier author, the pairs of
brothers and sisters were still made up of more or less interchangeable
individuals (see Agamemnon and Menelaus, Orestes and Electra in the
Oresteia). Always the same throne, the same scepter and the same rule: in
other words, the same place in communication.

> Menelaus, with lord Agamemnon, his peer
> Twin-sceptred in sovranty ordered of Zeus
> Children of Atreus, strong brace of command . . .[54]

Seen in this way, differentiation is a reflexive operation entirely compatible with the notion of personal identity that I have constructed. It is in no
way constrained by the illusory norms of self-esteem—which is a self-
indulgent love of the ego. It derives from what Rousseau, and Augustine
before him,[55] called love of self. The distinction, which is a classical one in
philosophy, can now be redefined as follows: love of self in fact defines the
essence of the self as a person, but in such a way that the self cannot claim
that definition entirely for itself and sustain it absolutely by a whim of its
own. Love must be something other than love for oneself; it is a relation between people who love each other, and, in relation to oneself, it creates
ipseity.

During each present interlocutive relation, *I* and *you* are specified together, though at the same time they also both attempt to reintroduce their
own differentiation, as derived from the earlier relations in which each has
been involved. During their conversation, the singular and positive difference of both self and other is constantly in the process of emerging. In particular, it is up to the personal self of each interlocutor to grasp differentially

his or her own propositional attitudes (e.g., states of belief). But it should be noted that this operation can only be performed within the canonical process of communication in which the propositional attitudes of each interlocutor are constructed relative to one another: the ego must not intervene unilaterally to influence the direction of the conversation for its own advantage. Which means that singular difference is not only positive, as we saw earlier, but also *relative*. On this point I am forced to differ, once again, from Martin Buber. For him, the I–you relation ultimately always involves an encounter with someone external to oneself, who is radically other. Like Levinas, Buber attempts to maintain the absolute heterogeneity of the you, by considering the personal terms as independent in spite of the relation in which they are involved. But once the primum relationis principle is applied, personal difference must necessarily derive from relative differentiation.

In every kind of autobiography, the author is attempting to express in language the history of what shaped him or her: to that extent, this subspecies of narrative art which redescribes the human past operates on both the fictional and the historical levels. It is accepted that the author is not writing to pass on information, but for him or herself, so that he or she can be his or her own creator. The aim is always to construct and preserve one's identity by instituting oneself through writing as "the same as X." But is there perhaps a different sort of autobiography, which would not depend on complacent self-individualization at the cost of a whole series of illusions? One that did not seek simply to fix the formless wanderings of existence and attach them to a self as if they belonged to it, and did not always relate memories and states of mind to an autonomous organizing center, like so many possessions?

In Support of a Just Autobiography

The question, then, is how the personal self might authenticate itself. We have already ruled out the type of self-avowal in which one attempts to construct a truthful discourse about oneself, according to the very threadbare convention that we bring up "from the depths of ourselves" a most secret truth that was only asking to be brought to light, and which a confession of this sort releases. Autobiographies are most commonly of this type. They take as their model the attribution of qualities in monadic psychology, supplemented by the legal notion of the imputation of actions and the moral notion of responsibility. Thou shalt be consistent in thy actions and thoughts. Being consistent with oneself. . . . Does that mean I expect myself to be nothing but a sequence of events? Thou shalt confess thy thoughts, dreams, and desires, as well as thy misfortunes and crimes. And thou shalt be accurate, please, in saying what is hardest to say.

Autobiography of this primary sort is written using a very special confessional technique that has been stripped of its old ritual localization, combined with a gratuitous narrative about the self, and a pragmatically amputated form of discourse. It has become evident to me that we need to reverse the way in which relations between subjectivity and its discourse are represented: instead of anchoring it in a specific agency whose story is to be told, in the belief that this will in some way liberate us, we can understand the first type of autobiography as a specific technique related to the procedure of avowal. As we have seen, both are associated with an ecological way of doing philosophy, whose aim is to define the ego's relations with meaning and truth on the basis of the certainties of consciousness.

Can we imagine a second type of autobiography which would no longer depend on a manipulation of the apparatus of utterance, and which would be founded on the process of relational self-differentiation, rather than individualization? It would be based on a quite different principle. There would also be a different cross between historical and fictive narrative modes, according to suitable criteria of reference to and predication of persons. I ended my earlier analysis of autobiography with the hope that there might indeed be a different way of writing the self. I stated some negative conditions for it above. It would no longer depend on the complacency that I have defined as a characteristic of self-esteem, but on the full communicational principle which is compatible with a love of self. Now it is time to give a positive account of the style, the object, and the positive meaning of this new way of writing the self.

I have just indicated the main principle. The new autobiographer would renounce the idea of self-avowal, in which the ego as individual is supposed to confess its thoughts, intentions, and acts. She would no longer aspire to express the singularity of the self and its absolute difference, which are both illusions, or even the "history of a mind." There would be no question of her telling the "truth about the self." The technique of avowal has become extremely commonplace; we should not be fooled by style. Before we encounter it in autobiographical narratives, we find it in a whole series of relationships—between parents and children, pupils and teachers, patients and psychiatrists, delinquents and social workers—it is found in interrogations, questionnaires, and medical visits.

In fact, such new autobiography would be a matter of telling something quite different, the truth and the avowal of the person, in a discourse not couched in terms of temporality. This would also be the normal form of avowal, one no longer concerned with the qualities of the self or with individual differences, but with personal predicates, and no longer based on a category error. Reference to persons would only occur through the communicational experience that constitutes them; "personal" predicates—beliefs, feelings of relative integrity or alienation, various relations of reciprocity (whether fictive or real), etc.—would only be attributed against the background of a communicational act and the various functions such an act involves. The aim would no longer be to establish an artificial continuity between the different experiences of the self, by linking them together in a secondary discourse, but rather to use the various levels of discourse to describe the real difficulties, uncertainties, and errors of personal identity and its long-deferred identificational mapping, so precarious and often so recalcitrant.

Let us take the case of intellectual autobiography, and compare the life of Giambattista Vico by himself with the *Discourse* of Descartes. The latter is the story of the achievements and advances of a mind in search of theoretical self-justification. It tells less the history than the genesis of the thinking subject in general, through the "I" of René Descartes, a gentleman from the region of Poitiers whose studies were undertaken at La Flèche. That is because, for Descartes, truth has no history. The progress of an intellect owes nothing to the ancient masters; it finds its sovereign path marked out for it across the virgin territory of autonomous reflection. Vico, too, writes about his own studies and his works, but his project is quite different. His aim is to stress fortune's causes and the opportunities, the favorable circumstances, and the obstacles he has encountered along the way. It is true that at the beginning of the eighteenth century the European Republic of Letters was eager to display its institutional foundations, and that the collective dimension in intellectual activity was coming strongly to the fore. This development reached its peak in the twentieth century in the autobiographies[56] of contemporary thinkers collected by P. A. Schilpp, which were written to be read aloud and discussed in the presence of colleagues who would hardly be likely to tolerate any distortion of the network of intellectual relations.

The fictive nature of the *Bildungsroman* has now become obvious.[57] The formation of a mind by the individual's encounters, trials, and experiences is a procedure clearly designed to serve the establishment of an absolute difference. This is an illusory aim. A just autobiography would tell how it was that a person came to awaken to him or herself, including in an intellectual sense. It would retain those aspects of the past which can be identified differentially. Those memorabilia, definitely cleansed of any trace of egotism or romanticism, would be selected as worthy of preservation from among the communicative values of the past that have on occasion presided over our lives. No attempt would be made to exclude diversity, i.e. the variations in the ways in which our identity is maintained. This would give back its full meaning to the term "confession." To confess oneself in this sense is to admit one's weaknesses and idolatrous tendencies, but in a spirit of integrity, regarding them as failures of personal integration, and ultimately, of the relational behavior that makes integration possible.

Self-avowal of this sort includes telling of the role which one has agreed to allow joint action to play, by narrating one's links with others. An avowal (*aveu*) was originally a written declaration certifying that one man owed loyalty to another in exchange for what he had been given. Those people who are linked to nobody, who have no links to call upon, have little indeed to avow in this respect. The aveu was above all a guarantee of status, value, and identity granted to one person by another. I imagine true autobiography as a discourse about one's relations with others, and how they have been ordered (and integrated) into a series that has helped to constitute one's identity, while their failures are responsible for the fractures in one's history. A personal self can only be consolidated, including in its differences, by borrowings from other people and even from those whom it does not know. Thus the person is authenticated by reference to others, and by constantly manifesting its links with them. Should we lack such relations, our existence would be no more than a rhapsody of individual acts, a mere plurality of states of mind.

Of Sincerity

Autobiography in good faith involves an evident change of style: now that its art does not have to reproduce or represent anything, it no longer needs to pretend. The wide range of human actions will now no longer be imputed to a self whose role was to be the indisputable cause of the events which it set in motion; instead, as far as possible, it will be seen in terms of interpersonal relations, interactional strategies, transactions, and compromises. Autobiography of this sort will be resolved to say less about the shadowy depths of self, and more about the individual's efforts to enter into and sustain him or herself in relationships. Nor will it forget to account for periods when the communicational regime was suspended, and its latent or blatant distortions, at times when the subject felt itself to be excluded and found the experience painful, withdrawing into itself, or on the contrary, decided to make a break and excommunicate itself in order to recover and start again. The just autobiographer knows, as Aristotle would have said, *quid decet, cui et quando.* But his or her business is above all to be scrupulous in identifying relationships that are pure fantasy, resulting from our all-too-common tendency to confuse a real relation with its image. Sincerity would then consist in telling of all the weaknesses that led us to back away from a relationship, recounting love's allegations and all the reservations bred by avarice of the heart.

If it is true that being sincere means refusing to believe in our own lies about ourselves, the sort of self-impersonation which is a lie perpetrated against being itself, we can see more clearly the direction in which autobiography might go. This would also allow us to answer, without any excessive anxiety, the question asked by Rousseau, Stendhal, and Amiel: can one put oneself into words, and if so, for what purpose? Can one ever be one's own memorialist? The attempt would have one clear purpose: to collect together the deep problems and decisive changes that have occurred along the road of our quest for personal identity. It would be wrong to take this quest for a conservative enterprise. The aim is not to preserve intact some kernel of the self, but to record a laborious process of continued identification through the most varied types of communication. An identification whose incompleteness is essential, synonymous with life itself. An equitable identification, that prevents our personal life from becoming locked into a narrow range of weak-willed mutual dependencies in which we surrender ourselves to just a few others. The broadest possible identification: we are not faithful to ourselves when we take a wide and honest detour via all those whom we have actually been fortunate enough to meet in our lives. In this sense, the personal self that such a process gradually constructs can be seen as the highest common factor of the most extensive group possible.

Genuine sincerity is a virtue of the intelligence, as courage is of the will. It is at once a virtue and a commitment, a literary application of integrity. This is where it is to be found, rather than in an impossible exactness of facts, or in the writer's deeply held convictions. Sincerity lays bare and simplifies, taking ipseity back to its essence. Its role is to integrate, but also to reintegrate: the true autobiographer tries to restore what is constantly breaking down and disintegrating in our relational life, but can yet be reconstructed. He is the anti–Narcissus, tearing himself away from the fascination of the mirror.

A concern with the construction of our personal self may well be something that comes to us at a time when we are no longer sufficiently loved to be diverted from the task of finally giving some shape to our destiny as persons. This way of writing the self would be no different from the adult's way of living. It would first be a matter of bearing witness to ourselves through all the different ways in which we have participated in human life. But collecting these events together and narrating them in the lofty perspective of communication demands an equal and opposite caution to that of Narcissus. It also requires a different type of meditation. If the narrator wants to relate a life like his own, he must reconstruct its constants and its particular profile; then, like any life, it will be both dynamic and open. His is then a dynamic art in the service of a personal self, a self ceaselessly pursuing its own identification as its most fundamental potentiality.

If there is one thing in which I cannot avoid believing, it is that in my existence I can never fail to recognize the existence of others, because my relational condition as a human being envelopes both them and me. The personal self has no other ontological concern than to become that which it has begun to be, but is not yet. This is essentially a concern for our personal destiny, a poignant but vague notion to which my analysis has now given a precise content. An individual has a destiny to the extent that he or she is in a position to pursue the structural and dynamic integration of his or her personal self. The price of a personal life is precisely that the identificational mapping of the three communicational agencies will remain incomplete. Necessarily, because I am open in principle to what anyone may say. And fortunately, too. Completeness here would mean monadic closure, a personal catastrophe, for it is the mortal enemy of the person; but it would also be a mistake and a moral fault. The project of completing oneself is a stupid one indeed! This is because the human person is by nature *futuritive*—an ugly word suggesting that it is not yet, but can become. The concern generated by this incompleteness has the dynamic effect of projecting us into the future. In us it is memory that desires—memory, and what we call hope. Therefore, we can never find happiness at the end of a solitary journey of the soul. Happiness, that fine flower of an old nostalgia, remains suspended like a promise that will be not the completeness, but the accomplishment of the person, finally in tune with itself because it is in tune with all others. Such an accomplishment will obviously always be deferred, for the task is ultimately interminable.

There is nothing to stop autobiographical narration from having a privileged center. But it will be different from the constant fantasies, fascinations, and traumatic fears of a self condemned to immaturity by an unfortunate childhood. Where will this dynamic heart of the narrated life be located? Perhaps at that distinguished point when one became an adult. Or at least, came near to being one; for there are really no grown-ups.

Can we say what it would be like for a person to put into language her quest for identity, her will toward greater identification, in short, the whole history of her formation as a person? Yes and no. In a sense, everything I have already said is summed up in this formula. In fact, the extreme sensitivity of subjectivity to the discursive forms that take it over and, properly speaking, invent it, demands a reversal of perspective: we can definitely no longer construct a history of the different forms of subjectivity by reference to an agency called the self. On the other hand, it was important to show, as I have tried to do, that the various avatars of subjectivity are historically dependent on a certain discourse that always subjects it to the harsh violence of interpretation.

There has gradually emerged a powerful parallelism between the forms of subjectivity, the forms of discourse on subjectivity, and the different forms of self-avowal. This must not be misunderstood: I have set out to suggest that these discursive figures of the self are very real in that they have definable pragmatic conditions, while the ego may also be allowed a certain role in discourse. But I have argued that it is these figures, and nothing else, which create the self, the individual, or the person, as speculative elements necessary for them to function.

We can always find an assumption that will give meaning even to the most incoherent statement. But it is clear that not all discourses about subjectivity are of equal value, just as not all the myths of philosophers are equally viable. Those of Narcissus kneeling before the water that reflects his image and the universe around him, and of Robinson Crusoe on his island, ruling over the monkeys and parrots of his mind, are not the least improbable of such myths.

People will always accept the form of such improbable illusions. But it is another matter when in addition they expect them to be true and viable. As the competition between these different discourses, in their simultaneous diversity, could not fail to create worse illusions of its own, I decided to order the various discursive figures on subjectivity into a hierarchy. I have taken as my reference the one which, in itself and for its object, most closely respects the complete communicational regime: this was the self-avowal of the person, at the moment when the self comes to the full acceptance of its relational condition, and sets out to construct a personal identity for itself. By thus replacing the fictitious anchor point of a self in possession of its qualities with that of a person without qualities, whose integration and relations are its only riches, I have substituted for the fiction of a permanently guilty self the communicational activity of the person, regulated by its own categories. In this way, a more legitimate discourse can make possible both an acceptable form of personal self-avowal in autobiography, and the pertinent attribution of genuinely personal predicates to others.

This therefore fulfills the broadest aim of the present study, which was to demonstrate once and for all the solidarity that exists between the spectrum of possible forms of subjectivity and the register of its discursive forms, in the hope of discovering the criteriology for a legitimate discourse that would give to subjectivity a consistency of the only acceptable kind, one linked to a particular function: that of playing the most complete and responsible role imaginable in communication.

Conclusion

I had become a great question to myself.
—SAINT AUGUSTINE

CONTEMPORARY CULTURE is hesitating over the correct path to follow: whether to reestablish the traditional humanistic subject, or destroy it once and for all by returning it to insignificance. This hesitation is only an extreme expression of the dual movement that was already to be seen in the metaphysics of subjectivity, toward the expansion of its role on the one hand, and an increasing limitation on the other.

Expansion?

A profound change had come about, which was manifested in the Cartesian Cogito. This change marked a move from being to thought, from substance to subject, from a philosophy of the world to one centered on subjectivity. It was now thought possible to look at everything from the point of view of pure subjectivity. Even God could be seen as a moment of the ego's reflection, allowing the supreme Being to be integrated into the circuit of meditation. Heidegger saw clearly that by positing a transcendent God as the foundation of its Being, the subject also posits itself as that which creates a link with the infinite, and so is able to confront the mystery of its Other.

Limitation?

The history of subjectivity, in parallel with that of the discursive forms that constitute it, shows at the same time that there has been a gradual growth of awareness of its finiteness. After all, it is also in Cartesian doubt that the ego finds the revelation of its lack of autonomy, as if subjectivity were being given a central role only in order to demonstrate the existence of a higher subjectivity which radically constrains it.

Beginning from my mind alone, I might be able to discover the foundation of truth, but it is not my mind that constitutes that foundation; it is God, my mind's other. After the infinite and perfect alterity of God, I soon come to realize that there is also an alterity of other people, which is inseparable from my own finiteness. The end of German idealism is eloquent in this respect: the very fact that reason understands becomes incomprehensible if reason alone must posit itself and its ideal structures. These categories have their own historicity, a transcendental progression from one to the next.

Above all, recent analysis by epistemologists and historians of science of the contexts in which discoveries are made has demonstrated the importance of scientific controversy. Innovation occurs thanks to the comparison and confrontation of ideas in the interdiscursive community of experts. The outlines of a communicational conception of knowledge are now emerging; it is a conception in which inventiveness has an essential part to play in the progression and constant structural reworking of theory. We are beginning to see that rational reflection could never be founded by an infinite alterity, absolutely different from human reason, but must rather be established jointly by working with beings who are only relatively other.

Who indeed decides what makes a statement scientific? In other words, who establishes the rules of the scientific game at a given point in its development? The community of experts does. Such discourse on the conditions of theoretical discourse can only take place deliberatively, by metatheoretical debate. Which makes the object of science, the thing itself, a kind of ultimate *causa*, in a sense close to the old legal meaning: its case is debated, for and against, in a supreme communicational act. It is understandable that progress should be the essence of science. The attempt to found the referential value of our statements on deliberative reason has therefore replaced the old subjectivist problematic of knowledge. We are no longer interested in a correspondence between our clear and distinct ideas and things which exist in themselves, as guaranteed by divine truth (Descartes). Nor in seeking the foundations of objectivity through an analysis of the internal mechanism of our knowledge of the object (Kant). But rather, we are interested in understanding how decisions concerning the category of any possible theory are made, at a given moment in the evolution of science. Such decisions are reached after discussion between experts on the principles involved. The role of the epistemological history of science is to reconstruct that discussion from the traces it has left behind.

It is not hard to see how far we have come: in a reflexive view of knowledge such as Descartes proposed, I could only have certainty if the necessity I discovered in myself revealed itself to me as something utterly evident, imposed by an Other than myself—God—who exercised over my finite subjectivity the control of an infinite and personal nonself. In a communicational view, reason is rather the product of joint work with another person who is in a relation to me. It is a means of preventing the erosion of truth. We realize retrospectively that the recognition accorded to God by the metaphysics of subjectivity did no more than shift onto the speculative plane the monadic impotence which lies at the heart of the human power of knowing and meaning.

Consequently, far from our being able to treat everything from the point of view of pure subjectivity, it is intersubjective communication that forms the original medium of our understanding of the world, and therefore of our scientific progress. It is, then, up to us to rethink the status of the ego from top to bottom. Anyone who wishes to make a systematic study of the dialogical structure of signification, or to put forward a communicational approach to knowledge, will sooner or later need to redefine subjectivity, which refers back to the self as well as to the other (that indispensable partner in communication), in relation to both the self and the other as possible interlocutors. I have explained above why this means making the subject into a *personal* self.

My aim has been both to give consistency to subjectivity as personal self and to define the criteria of a legitimate discourse about subjectivity. Why both together? Because I was led to posit the principle that discourse about the self is subject to the same conditions as the presence of the self in discourse. The result was that the two sets of conditions were either canonically fulfilled, or seriously infringed, together. A legitimate form of discourse on subjectivity would therefore be one which, while respecting the canonical conditions of communication, also imputed to the self in general the conditions of insertion into discourse which it has by virtue of being a person.

The results of my analysis have been to provide a way of avoiding two ruinous gestures of rejection that dominate and compromise our modernity.

On the one hand, we have seen a rejection of relations, caused by the passion for being one's own master that characterizes the bourgeois and working-class subject. We want nothing so much as to owe what we have to ourselves alone. We persist in taking the achievements of the human spirit back to our own minuscule individuality. The ideology of individualism, which confirms the individual in his state of isolation, is one of the poorest that humanity has ever known. Emmanuel Mounier was right: it is still in its death throes today.

Then, on the other hand, we have seen an equally insistent but opposite rejection of the subject by the system thinkers and certain French structuralists, whose subversion of the concept was almost too efficient. Once it had been assimilated to the monadic self, the subject could be shown up as a fiction as easy to disprove as that of the ether, though no doubt less useful. Here was a systematic attempt to repudiate the person altogether, after seriously challenging its claims not only to be the source of meaning, but also to have privileged access to the private sphere. Any consistency was denied to the subject and to consciousness itself: if *I* could be said at all, it was only as a manner of speaking, a sort of language-game.

My whole intention and argumentative strategy have been to play these two extreme attitudes off against each other, by demonstrating their secret complicity in the confusions they make. The introduction of structures decenters subjects and shows them to be regulated by processes of which they are in fact the nodal products. It confirms the desolation of Narcissus by teaching him, if he did not already know it, that he is nothing at all except that image woven out of absence which autobiography seeks to stabilize. In this replacement of the defunct autonomy of the subject by the sorts of effects that constitute the signifier within the system of its differences, we see a move toward the second ideology of the industrial world—the ideology of the system.

But it is not enough to bring these related contraries face to face. For my part, if I agreed to write "I" in quotation marks, it would only be as an indication that its meaning remains in suspension, that it is a word for whose meaning we need to search. Far from refusing to grant the subject any consistency, I have regarded it as the sign of a problem. In order to solve it I had to develop a new theoretical approach: in my opinion, an anthropology constructed from a relational point of view can provide modern people with a rigorously coherent way of interpreting their experience. The challenge I faced was to illustrate the fundamental nature of the relational idea in anthropology, measure the full extent of the conceptual restructuring that it would entail, and progress as far as possible down the road that it opened up. For this is not an easy approach to interpreting our experience: the relational mode of thought is often extremely difficult to grasp, and description constantly betrays one's intended meaning.

The Pragmatic Test

Those whose aim is to bring back subjectivity must be prepared to alter their view of it radically if they wish to take account of the successive waves which, in the wake of the crisis in contemporary science, have led to the abandonment of the concept of self: structuralism, the system thinkers, and above all the last and tallest wave which I have called the communicational one.

It is clear to us today that the first step is to show that subjectivity is a derivative problem. Let us remind ourselves of its origin. Freud taught us by his merciless critique of the immediate Cogito that consciousness is above all false consciousness. We can have secrets from ourselves: subjectivity is divided between those who think and know they are doing so and those who think without knowing it, and again between those who think without knowing it and those who do not know what they think.

It has become commonplace to say that philosophers of reflection, having scarcely gotten over this first hurdle, must also come to terms with Marx's critique of ideologies and Nietzsche's interpretation of values. In other words, it now seems that the speaking subject cannot always say what he or she means. Consciousness, which had learned with Descartes to doubt the world, has now itself become several times doubtful. Doubtful as a pole around which our states and actions spontaneously unify, a center from which proceed the qualities we appear to ourselves to have; doubtful too as inwardness, for which being and knowing are the same thing. A fortiori, it is doubtful that the meaning of discourse could be immediately present to consciousness. We have realized that mastery of utterance is no longer the same thing as mastery of meaning, with freedom to say or not to say, for there are things that our individual situation seems to prevent us from communicating.

The pragmatic test (in the technical sense of the word) is the most recent to have been inflected on the ego. It is one thing to know whether the speaking subject can communicate with other people or turn inward in solitary meditation, as it chooses, but it is quite another to decide whether it can be defined as an agent of communication. I have argued at length that the pragmatic analysis of utterance has the effect of invalidating the communicational autonomy of the speaking subject in respect to the meanings themselves that are being communicated. Meaning is no longer that which the ego wishes to say. As a matter of principle, the notion of meaning is located in a different field entirely from the ego's intentional aims. The conviction that there is a subjective support in a present, central position in all discourse has been overturned by pragmatic analysis. In a weaker sense, the speaker is the speaking subject insofar as he or she is able to take responsibility not for the meaning of his or her own words, but for the meaning of all the words exchanged in the course of a conversation. Despite what the axioms and clichés produced by certain interpretations of French-style personalism may imply, it is certainly not conscious subjectivity that it is now urgent (or indeed possible) to establish as the focus of a theory of meaning. Nor, incidentally, can straightforward empirical communication, or the different varieties of *ars communicandi*, be used as a foundation. I have explained why my own choice was to turn to an original form of transcendental intersubjectivity founded on the relation.

I have devoted this book to establishing such a conception. It could not satisfactorily be fitted into any existing philosophical tradition, and particularly not traditional philosophies of consciousness, which have extended rather than abandoned their egological premises. If consciousness considers others at all, it sees their existence and their individual differences as nothing more than a negation of itself; its temporality and theirs are mutually exclusive. I therefore set out to rethink transcendental intersubjectivity, and with it the very opposition between Same and Other, in an entirely new way, fully aware of the size of the task I was setting myself, and particularly of the complete redrawing of perspectives and the radical reconstruction that it would involve.

The negative or deconstructive part was as always the easiest, once I had formulated an effective hypothesis: the primacy of the relation, and especially of the interlocutive relation. Through Pascal's paradox, the paradox of Narcissus, and what I have called the paradox of the psychiatrist's couch, I was able to expose several varieties (particularly the retrospective and speculative ones) of the *illusion of the self*, and trace it back to its origin in a manipulation of the apparatus of utterance. I found the same thing among writers of the type of autobiography I qualified as primary, each of whom is perhaps no more than a false Orpheus. We at last had a precise idea of what the illusions of subjectivity were. The self definitely no longer existed as a substantial and transcendental principle: it was no longer that full kernel, the master of words and of meaning, standing on the threshold of future sentences, able to decide on their semantic pertinence and controlling them from its lofty and external position. Nor was it any longer the speaking subject, capable of identifying itself when it spoke by saying, or making others say, who it was.

The subject is not condemned to being that empirical self which can be forced to confess what it is, what it has done, and what its plans, its faults, its sex may be. A particular discursive form may sometimes encourage it to present itself as the possessor of qualities, the seat of ideas and memories, the legitimate owner of a character. We may accept that the characters created by Dickens are like this, all composed of traits in a certain configuration. But what about the characters in Kafka? And Dostoyevsky? Prince Mychkine is a man without qualities, who does not possess his experiences. Their content could have been different, but he would still have been the same person.

When the illusion is helped along by a suggestive discursive form, it is at its most tenacious. All in vain, however; "the Holy Empire of clouds has lasted too long."

This type of identification of the self remains that of the Same, defined by its possessions and an entirely relative negativity. Defoe's Robinson Crusoe teaches Friday that he has a soul, before standing on his neck and reducing him to slavery. The Other's difference is, then, a subtractive one, in which both parties fall back on their own territory. I showed that the avowal of a self in its own insular space of separation can never be confused with personal identity. The self can only avow itself as a person, and before that, identify itself through communication. We saw that difference in that case is something positive and free, and is established by differentiation and a compensatory divergence. In such cases, the self is the person engaged in a primary relation with others, even if on occasion it later presents itself as the spokesperson of the *we* that was formed as a result. This type of reappropriation of the self as a figurehead is a secondary process, and should not be allowed to confuse matters.

Along the way, I systematically reminded the reader of the reasons that when I address myself to you and recognize what others say about me as a *he*, I am able to identify myself as *I*. And the same is true for the other person: when she addresses me and recognizes what I am saying about her, she has an opportunity to identify herself as a personal self. We are linked by our tripersonal identification structure in a relationship of solidarity.

This brought me to the positive part of the demonstration. It is at the moment when I speak to *you* that we simultaneously institute ourselves in our status as persons and construct our personal status; there is an immediate consequence that linguists will have to meditate on (and which they will doubtless challenge): that the speaking subject is ultimately not the subject of the process of saying, nor the self-sufficient subject of the utterance, but that which is finally constructed in the course of the interlocution.

Methodologically, I wanted to present my way of proceeding as an attempt to distinguish on grounds of principle between the *person* and the *individual.* I attempted to define the identity of persons on the basis of the communication relation, in contrast to the identity of individuals, which act as supports for the relation, rather than forming its poles. If we are able to maintain several personal relationships and more than one friendship at a time, it is because of the plurality of such individual supports. In a communicational universe in which the relation of reciprocity (or better, of mutuality) sets the norm, the person is not constituted by the organism in its environment, nor the social individual in the collective milieu to which he or she belongs. The idea of the person breaks apart the closed sphere centered on the organism and the individual. Therefore, I also ruled out from a very early stage the two traditional criteria of subjective memory and the permanence of our bodies, at least as possible criteria of personal identity. I explained why, although they represent necessary conditions, they were not an adequate basis on which to construct a coherent concept of person. The first is derivative, while the second concerns the individual, not the person. As far as possible, my arguments were illustrated throughout by logical and linguistic analysis. Technically, this means that I have subordinated a systemic approach to a relational one.

Not Much of a Self?

The reader will doubtless have realized that I have here been confronted by a major problem of philosophy. I am not leaving it as I found it. The categories of Same and Other as they are traditionally used predetermine a certain number of verbal games which are disappointing, though not entirely meaningless. There seem from the start to be two formal possibilities. In the first, the self remains trapped in the circle of the Same; this is the problematic of the self at the center of its appurtenances, at the heart of its qualities. It is often shown fully occupied with its task of self-identification, able to modify itself in calculated but limited ways that do not compromise its essence. What we have here is identification with the Same, which condemns the Other to being no more than a mere negation of the Same. In the second possibility, however, instead of presenting itself as the Same, the self chooses to expose itself to risk. From the depths of its solitude there arises an asymmetrical relation to the Other. This is still the Other in relation to me, my image: whether I set off in search of the other person, or encounter the person in his or her original irreducibility. A distance is maintained within proximity, without the contradiction being overcome.

These choices are mutually ruinous. Therefore, I set out to show that the first option was absurd. In its search for the Other, subjectivity can never find anything but more figures of the Same. The Other can never be realized in subjectivity without there being an asymmetry with the Same; as the Other of the Same, an afterthought, he will always be as Abel was for Cain, surplus to requirements, an evanescent haze.[1] If, however, we grant the person the structure of a trifunctional mapping, the very movement by which it identifies itself immediately establishes it in a relation with the Other. Now the Same and the Other have only a differential meaning, as they constantly identify themselves as poles in a primary relation. No need now to search for the Other. We have both already found each other in the relation we are experiencing together. The self as a person is no more the Same than others as persons are members of the species of Others. But do we want to detach the Other from what I have called the Other of the Same? This is an audacious question.

It was necessary to make a clear break, once and for all, with narcissism, particularly philosophical narcissism (the very worst sort), however much it may be compensated for—and even overcompensated for—by an absolute emphasis on the absolute difference of the Other. For that was merely a way of eluding the relation and secretly restoring the primacy of the self. Subjectivity is neither for itself nor for the other person; it is a differential reality, in me as in the other person, which is to be conquered in the context of the relation. Unless we give up the secret idea that the world and other people are constituted in an original manner for the ego—the ego as the only being for itself, the absolute being[2]—the Other is condemned to being nothing but a moment of my transcendental being, my own intentional product.

Note, therefore, the limits within which we can still talk of the Same and the Other. Certainly not in the sense of a principle according to which others would have a privileged relation to me, I who have them present in my consciousness and attribute to their being a meaning which is appropriate to me, for this would be to find the Same in the Other. Certainly not either in the sense that the other person whose body and life stand opposite me and who refers to my body and my life as foreign to him, for this would be to find the Other in the Same.[3] However sophisticated such a formula may be, it is much too roundabout; we are very close to the view of the other given in the *Nicomachean Ethics*, as something that we can never apprehend except in relation to ourselves.

Does this mean that it is sufficient simply to take the opposite stance? We saw why this is not the case: by leaving the speaking role to the other person—considered as infinitely other in his or her stature and separation—I become embroiled in impossible contradictions, the underlying principles of which I have analyzed. An other of this type may no longer be me, but he or she retains the transcendental character of a *self* which is modeled on mine; while the absolute mystery of a plurality of others quickly leads to a very crowded world. For these reasons, it is very difficult to leave the relation with the other in a state of originary asymmetry.

I therefore argued that only a mode of thought based on relations will be able to reveal both the being of the self and that of the other. One based, more particularly, on a relation of reciprocity, before any of its empirical modifications have occurred. This is not merely a preference, but an a priori principle.

I believe that the primum relationis is something philosophically primary, as I have tried to show through the convergence of different indicators. Logically, the relation is irreducible to any interpretation in terms of properties, images, or signifying intentions. For its part, transcendental analysis of the conditions of possibility of meaning also leads back to the interlocutive relation. Finally, a certain number of our experiences—love and the glances we exchange, silence, our projects, indiscretion, and even secrecy—which until now have been given an egological treatment by phenomenologists, can be described more adequately as relational phenomena. Even the will is powerless in the face of relational spontaneity: just try *wanting* to enter into a relationship with someone. There are also some relationships which just cannot be improved, whatever efforts the individual may make.

The primum relationis allows us to play off two conceptions from the same source against each other. According to the first, the *I* has the task of establishing itself in its autonomy and its "logical egotism," to use Kant's expression.[4] It is a being in charge of and belonging to itself. According to the second, the self has the task of graciously coming out of itself to meet the other person, to whom it turns with a delighted fascination. The application of the relational principle immediately removes the possibility of the self's establishing itself in either of these ways, destroying both the philosophical narcissism of which they are a sign, and the self's fascination for an other which is ultimately being seen as another me. The primal experience of being a person is no more the experience of the *you* than of the *I*. It is in fact not an experience at all in the agreed sense of the word, but rather the precarious activity of mapping one of the poles of identity in our relational life. The same is true of those simplest and most fundamental things in life which are love and death. My aim has been to show why a philosophy of the relation has a universal validity, and how it can give meaning to the universe.

It can hardly be objected that this does not leave us with much of a self. No doubt the self is no longer the holder of being. But nor is it just a phenomenon. For as the seat of a communicative competence, it has a function that we cannot ignore: the speaking subject can decide whether or not to actualize its competence, and it remains responsible for its decision. It will be called upon by others to act as an agent in real communication, but it may also decide to refuse. On the one hand, the empirical self is constructed as the irreversible result of all the earlier communicational acts in which it was able and in which it agreed to take part, of which it preserves as far as possible the cumulative and integrated effect. On the other hand, it is the source of a constant synthesizing activity of integration, sometimes grasping its identity positively, sometimes negatively, by taking the initiative that belongs to it as a person and breaking off relations.

This rather extraordinary process of positive identification, which I see as one of the true experiences of the spirit, is still dependent on communication: the sort that occurs between self and self, in an "inner" discourse that is pragmatically (if not semantically) privileged, and whose norms of coherence, continuity, and even creativity are its own responsibility. On the condition, that is, that it is not given any priority, or self-sufficiency, on the level of principle. This is where we find the heart of the subject.

The Relational Condition of the Spirit

I needed to find a way of explaining the structural presence of the other at the heart of the self. Most of the formulas already available in philosophy were either too partial, too simplistic, or excessive. An author, discovering the importance of interpellation by the *you* or the address to the allocutee, would give that aspect such a high emotional charge as to obliterate the rest of the interpersonal structure; while even in the best case, I found the logical complexity of that structure obscured by stylistic effects. In the first place, the other which is present at the heart of my self is not only the person whom I address as *you*, still less his or her mere image. It is also the absent third party, about whom I speak with you as *he/she*. The touchstone of alterity is as much the absent *he/she* as the present and proximate *you*.

I therefore needed to be quite clear abut the role of these three agencies—I, you, and he/she—their mutual dependency and their mode of articulation within the person (that of the other as well as my own). The interlocutive communication relation has the effect of establishing a tripersonal structure. In my view, this gives us the means to describe the difficulties and crises that occur in the identification process, and no doubt also lead to the birth of neuroses. There is something very logically complex about this mode of integration which has never been properly accounted for by the contemporary commonplace view of alterity. Commentators who realize that this complexity is there prefer to enclose the "I" in quotation marks, to show that they do not really know what it is. That is probably the honest thing to do.

The Spaniards had quite a good understanding of the Aztecs. What is more, they admired them. And yet they exterminated them. Why, asks Tzvetan Todorov?[5] Yes, why such intolerance? It is important to try to understand. A misunderstanding of alterity (that of the *you* but also of the

322

he/she) and an incorrect view of personal identity go together and encourage each other. I might add that if the Aztecs and Mayans were unable to combat the conquest in any new way, it was because their civilizations, trapped in their dependency on the cosmic order, could do no more in the face of others than reenact their absolute difference. Both victims and conquerors were symmetrically allergic to alterity. We can say about the person what was originally said about God: it is dangerous to get the person wrong, for it is man who has to pay the price.

Even in the egotistical writings of Paul Valéry, we find quite lucid statements such as: "to become ourselves, we need other people" and "we can only reach the summit of ourselves by taking a detour by way of other people, and accepting their help." The context of such remarks shows however that such views can perfectly well be reconciled with the jealous sovereignty of the Same. They fail to conceal the fact that the self, with its divine right to create intelligibility and value, has nothing but inveterate jealousy for this other who is its rival. Should we then accept that we can "discover others" in ourselves, and "realize that we are not a homogeneous substance?"

Yes and no. That is certainly one of the first meanings of the aphorism "I is another," but this kind of statement is only partial, and it conceals the derivative character of the phenomenon it is describing. For this split within the Same is only the side effect of a primary relation in which each person is the other's other. If the third person is included with the other two in the movement of mutual identification, we will be able to do away with a double exaggeration: on the one hand, treating the Same on the basis of the Other (Husserl), and, on the other, taking the interlocutive relation to absolute extremes (Buber). That is why I argued in favor of the strong thesis, which reverses the priorities: human beings only communicate with themselves insofar as they know how to do so with others, and using the same means. It is not that others are constantly being created out of our refusal of the Same. There can be no philosophy of communication in which the other does not play an equal role with the self. In other words, the identification of the *I* is constantly at stake in the communicational process. Unless this fact is appreciated, it is impossible to understand how it is that dialogue as a communicational interaction can be fruitful and creative. A concerted discussion or a polemical controversy only brings out something new if it comes from persons in a relation, who continue to retain their intimate convictions and maintain their positive difference.

The relational principle has allowed me to develop some new theses, most notably the idea that personal reality is the highest form of existence. The plenitude of the person necessarily follows from the plenitude of the relation. Some of these theses are paradoxical, particularly the idea that the person is that which, in human beings, can be treated neither as an object to be separated and defined, nor as a subject which centers the objective universe on itself. The person is not the object of a delocutive discourse; but nor is it the sufficient subject of such a discourse.

It was no doubt already difficult enough to derive a philosophy of human autonomy from the Cartesian Cogito. Descartes had a vertiginous experience of the fragility of metaphysics. His version of the ontological proof is well known: subjectivity cannot derive the idea of a more perfect being from within itself. But the ego, for Descartes, still seems to have the power to generate within itself the idea of any finite substance at all.

Let us not go back over the essential finiteness of subjectivity, which has come down to us over the years from Kant's *Anthropology*. The subject has to deal no longer with an infinite alterity, but with an other which is inseparable from its own finiteness. Kierkegaard gives finiteness a (theological) foundation: "It is sin that makes me understand why I do not have the right of access to transcendence." I have tried to give it an anthropological foundation, by reinstating the interlocutive relation at the center of human communication, and by making it the source of meaning.

Today, the interlocutive relation is the great element missing from the dominant theoretical model of communication, from Roman Jakobson to H. P. Grice. Even Grice disguises communication as a unilateral manipulation of an audience by the speaker, although he is soon forced to concede that some spirit of collaboration is required from the listener.

A correct view of human communication allows the subjective condition to be defined. It is in communication that the subject will find the right conditions for its self-construction, as well as the danger of being led astray by a desire to achieve dominance over others. It is in communication, rather than consciousness, that I become a great question for myself. For traditional philosophy, consciousness was a synthetic and individual totality entirely insulated from other totalities of the same type. Its inwardness made it incommunicable in principle. In relation to consciousness, the ego defined its intimacy. I gave up the idea of looking for the person in this type of primary subjectivity. Self-awareness may be implied in personal development, but it does not follow that it is its essence. Just like my ability to think, my consciousness of myself is a late product, a derivative reality which I have set out here to reconstruct from the basic idea of communication with the self. In this sense, I cannot help but agree with the verdict reached—for different reasons—by Nietzsche, Freud, and Marx of course, but also Etienne Gilson and Jacques Maritain. These authors did not angrily strike out the very notion of person, but simply warned us that western philosophy had danced for far too long to the tune of subjectivity.

324

The reader will have realized that the question of the subject, which is so easy to misunderstand, is not to be confused with the question of the person. The person transcends the traditional subject. Both the disappropriation of the subject and the reevaluation of subjectivity are processes that serve to reinforce the notion of an interactional cooperation between persons. I believed that I had realized something important here, which was that the question of the subject could only be examined freely once it had been freed from the question of subjectivity. But the problem of subjectivity could only be dealt with accurately once it had been seen to depend on the more fundamental problem of the person.

One thing is immediately clear about the person: in its construction, in its intimate structure, it cannot simply derive from itself. *Person* is perhaps the name for what we had been seeking through all the apparently disparate histories of communication. In the beginning is the relation, on the basis of which there emerge alternating and cooperating persons who become decentered and divergent in their difference. There is no absolute presence or back-reference to oneself, no primordial glance turned inward to the depths of our being. The person only becomes self-conscious in its act of interdiscursive confrontation with others, as a result of experience. It is therefore impossible to find any first moment when the person exists in its solitude and autonomy, forerunner of a second, optional moment when it chooses to "enter into relations" with others. One face of man has faded away, but it was his detestable face. For the person, existing—i.e., being a reality—can only mean grasping our identity in a nonpossessive way within all of the different relations that have ever been present and real to us. Thinking can only mean entering for a time, and with a degree of seriousness that not all human beings share, into the provisional loop of discourse with oneself.

The personal self to which my analysis has led is in no way a derisory entity. Its power of thought will admittedly no longer be anchored in an ego which is the possessor of its discourse and which remains identical to itself. The mind does not develop solely of its own accord, unfolding an intentionality whose structure is preestablished. As a result, the whole image of what thought is has been transformed. Thinking is now not mainly a matter of constructing (on the mathematical model) or reading (on the hermeneutic model), but of being able to enter into a relationship and sustain it against all the odds. In the opposite case, I asked how it is possible for relations to break down. When the relation is an authentic one, the idea is scarcely bearable. The decision to break it off appears as an indivisible mixture of murderous and suicidal impulses; to do such a thing is undoubtedly a sin against the spirit. To make the Cogito a production of the *I* would be to make thought into an object, a state, something entirely passive. The ego undoubtedly does play a role, but only a marginal one. It will define its positive difference by contact with relational events. Following its different interactions (some of them verbal), it will be able to reabsorb its share in them without ever putting itself forward as an object. The communicational mapping of the ego is constantly in progress.

The relational condition of the spirit does not mean that it has to dissolve away into nothing, but rather that it needs to create itself by integrating the different agencies of the tripersonal structure. Nothing preexists the relational condition from which it emerges, except its own vertiginous possibility. A personal self possesses nothing by birthright, but has a great yearning to be and to love, and a great communicative competence. Loving others means saying to them not "you exist" but: "*we* exist."

As far as a speaking subjectivity is concerned, we can never take away from it the power to indicate itself as an *I* by back-reference, at the moment when a present utterance designates the *you* (singular or plural) of allocution. The same back-reference will designate the ego, neither more nor less strongly than its allocutee. It is through the communicational quality of their mode of insertion into discourse that the self and the other ensure their recognition as persons. With the exception of a few asymmetries that I have endeavored to show are marginal, the problem of the self and the problem of other people are essentially the same. Both derive from the question of the person as an agent in the transactional activity of communication.

All of this having been understood (and it will take some time to be properly understood), we realize yet again that the ego can never occupy the throne. The self is a differential reality. How could it then be constitutive of meanings, or of objectivity? It can actually do no more than rebuild itself on the basis of a relational reality. I have shown that the ipseity of the self was not the identity of myself as an individual, but the identity of the person. The first confuses the self with the Same; the second is in an originary relation to the Other (you, him/her). In the same way that there are two types of solitude—the bad one, a feeling of identity with oneself and the real one, which is implicated in the communicational cycle—here are at least two types of identity for the self. The traditional solution mixed them up, by wanting to make the self-sufficient establishment of persons contemporaneous with the moment in which they enter precariously into relationships with each other.

A Return to Transcendence

In traditional conceptions of the subject, communication was always blocked by the subject's need to assert itself, possess its qualities, and subjugate the other. Sartre explored the philosophical consequences of this state of affairs. Because of it, relations with others were formed within a structure that was too weak to support them—the structure linking a possessor to his or her possession. Now, it is becoming more and more clear that most mental processes, including scientific and philosophical thought, cannot be controlled by consciousness. Therefore, what seemed to me to require an explanation was *consciousness*. I have attempted to account for it in terms of an integrated segment of communication from self to self. If the self is still required in a communicational approach to the person, it is as the seat of a communicative competence that makes it into a diligent worker in the cause of cosignification. If the other is also still required, it is because I can only exercise that competence with you, or with him/her. How can the other be a limitation for me, since I depend on him/her for my being? The experience of true communication is always the emergence of a meaning that is both new and communicable.

This competence gives to the self, in addition to its inalienable role in semantic innovation, a fundamentally relational character. The primacy of the interlocutive relation, which I illustrated in a number of detailed ways, acts as a kind of super-maxim, a theory of the use of language, and controls the analysis of linguistic fragments in context. Any analysis of discourse that stays wedded to a single source of utterance must expect to suffer from the assumption that the other agency remains in a stable state. Words are not neutral, but are inhabited by two interlinked voices. The other toward whom my speech is directed is not an external target, but is associated with the joint production of meaning. In fact, the sources of utterance are linked from the start, and this relation has dynamic effects on the process of signification. This consequence, which is not directly relevant here, is the central subject of another book.[6]

A solution in which utterance has a single source seems to me to be definitively ruled out by the foregoing analyses. And, more radically, by the new way of stating the problem of transcendence. I have shown elsewhere that the interlocutive relation co-originates the relation of reference to the world. The ego cogito cannot take the principle of communicative interaction back to its own intentions, nor can the Wittgensteinian ego, which is merely a point of view and has nothing else to do except ensure that the world is *my* world; neither can language dictate its own version of truth in the absence of people, as a whole generation of structuralists argued. None of these things can take on the role of a transcendental value.

French structuralists will be surprised that the disinvestiture of the ego can be used in this way for the furtherance of a notion such as that of the person. And particularly that it is being brought about by a transcendental-style philosophy. But the paradox is well founded. By enquiring into the conditions of possibility of any communication by signs about the world, my critique divests subjectivity of all its prerogatives in the same gesture with which it accredits the interlocutive relation.

Among all the implications I have drawn from my analysis of the mind's relational condition, this is perhaps the most crucial. Intersubjective communication is the originary milieu of our understanding of the world. It comes from the application of our communicative competence, which is an ethical as well as a theoretical requirement. Its power of induction is considerable, without being in any way mysterious: it induces persons (those of others as well as my own) into the cooperative path of integral speech. Here lies its first virtue, which is *integrity*. The exercise of our communicative competence is just another name for our essential responsibility, while it also conditions the progress of the symbolic function and of knowledge in general. This therefore allows us to overcome the old oppositions between fact and value, the reasonable and the rational, and—the split that deeply divides the work of Kant—between the critique of theoretical reason and the critique of practical reason. It reduces the gap between a concern for people and a discourse about things. It also brings out the ethical essence of rationality.

Controversy between experts provides singularly eloquent epistemological confirmation of this point. It brings about a pronounced externalization of knowledge in relation to the knower. Our contemporaries are less and less willing to accept the private and subjective contents of consciousness as suitable data for scientific study. Confrontation of views within the learned community seems indispensable if there is to be any possibility of progressing toward new categories, so that the foundational crisis can be exposed and the development of new theories envisaged.

It is important to understand what progress means in science. It is a deceptive term. There is no progressive enrichment of a body of true propositions bringing us ever nearer to a single satisfactory theory. A certain number of rival theories are constructed. Those whose research programs are less productive, or who are forced onto the defensive and exhaust themselves in producing ad hoc explanations for all the new data generated by their competitors, are soon eliminated. This is even truer when what is involved is the critical restructuring of the whole field of knowledge itself.

The plurality and relative discontinuity of theories can only be overcome if the experts are in communicational relations with each other; even if they disagree, the important thing is that a more or less explicit confrontation occur between their ideas. Rationality is deliberative before it is constitutive,

328

and *in order* that it may be so. Only mathematics can claim to be to a certain extent a subject about which there is universal agreement. In the sciences of reality this is just not the case. Knowledge is something that is indefinitely challenged, corrected, and restructured. The greater the differences between languages, the wider the separation between different fields of knowledge, the greater are the effects of oppression by the proprietors of the code in the encyclopedias. As we have seen, the movement by which communication is broken off restores the need for it elsewhere. This is undoubtedly true on the level of philosophical discourse, and on the metatheoretical level of science itself, whenever discussion about the scientificity of a given discourse is used as a means of freeing it from the dominance of false paradigms.

But if controversy is responsible for progress in science, a deliberative structure is essential to all scientific operations.[7] Today there is no longer any epistemologically responsible subject of knowledge capable of playing the role of a reciter of truth. A philosophy of consciousness no more allows us to account for advances in the category structure of political economics or quantum mechanics than to explain the theory of real variable functions.[8]

The disinvestiture of subjectivity to the advantage of the person has also been the prelude to a movement to reappropriate the identity of the knower. The I-as-person which is bringing this about has ceased to be the *I* of the individual's thought or consciousness. Its transcendental function must be sought elsewhere than in the subjective domain. The subject of science has now become partly an interceptor of the messages that circulate around the scientific community, and partly a subject divided according to a principle of duality: once it becomes involved in controversy, its role is to integrate the uttering agencies formed by the protagonists into the relation that constitutes them. The result is to strip the ego of its transcendental function in favor of an ultimate relational agency: the interlocutive relation that I have identified as the foundation of meaning. The individual remains the seat of a communicative capability that confers on him or her the status of a person, but whose a priori structures have ceased to belong to him or her. The individual is therefore no longer an ego in the sense that the word has in philosophies of the subject. The a priori structures are first and foremost communicational in nature. They immediately presuppose the relation with others and its dynamic effects of semantic cooperation and transaction.

Let me repeat: this disinvestiture of the self in favor of communication (based on a pooling of meaning and reference) poses serious difficulties for all philosophies of reflection. For this is a much more radical disappropriation of the speaking subject than those previously brought about by the Freudian unconscious or the structural unconscious of language. However we may choose to extend the detour of reflection, the notion of meaning now exceeds the intentional aims of the subject. For the good reason that meaning is not something that can be appropriated or reappropriated, except in a trivial way, by a subject that is simply the spokesperson, a pseudonym, for an earlier communication: meaning is, in a fundamental way, inseparable from the logical space of interlocution.

In that case, what significance can we still grant to the process of subjective *appropriation?* It has been possible until now for a hermeneutic type of approach to discover the full meaning of reflection, and account for my effort toward being through the signs that formed the objectivized and materialized image of the ego. The disappropriation that we are now witnessing is more radical than anything that has gone before. Its consequence is a definite *Selbstlosigkeit,* a loss of any reference to the self. This time, it is no longer possible for the self to begin by surrendering itself to a set of signs burdened with history, reserving any intentional reappropriation for a second act of reflection by some resultant *I.* It is no longer possible to re-launch the philosophy of the Cogito on another level of reflection, whose task would be to reiterate the "I think, therefore I am," and actualize meanings through the mediation of cultural signs. The ego that is no longer the starting point is no longer the result either, except as the purely empirical self which steps in to interrupt the communicational movement for its own momentary advantage. Such an appropriation by the ego has an empirical rather than a transcendental value. If by chance it manages to confirm its own image in self-to-self communication, it does so thanks to a deliberate and functional break in relations that is only the prelude to new interactions. Of course, knowledge remains the domain among all the communicative interactions in which a personal ego can participate without any loss of identity. Such an ego is a living self, and cognitive systems in this sense can be called living systems. But, as we have seen, communication carries with it obligations more radical than the structural ones revealed by general linguistics.

We are now seeing the full philosophical implications of the idea of communication. Structuralism had already sent a considerable shock wave through philosophies of consciousness. It introduced difference without a subject, as the condition of possibility of the system of differences that appear in language. But in the final analysis, the thinking subject could still claim to analyze the system of differences, then appropriate it for itself in the first person and put it to work in its own discourse. We have seen, however, through the convergence of a number of analyses on the relational condition of the spirit, that communication has an even more powerful effect, which is definitively to detach meaning from the conscious metaphysical subject. The subject needs to be inscribed as a person within a true communicational universe before it is able not simply to mobilize the language to its own advantage, but to take an active part in the pooling of sense and reference. It can participate in the process of semantic construction without ever making any claim to be its origin.[9]

The "I think" can certainly accompany all our meanings, but it can no longer be their origin. This dissociates two of the theses that Kant left linked together, but which we no longer need to regard as interdependent. There is indeed a foundational agency, but it is the interlocutive relation, not the "I think." This marks the end of a certain tradition of reflexive philosophy, though not of foundationalism as such: on condition that we now see the founding agency as relational, the paradigm of a constituting activity is not yet dead, although the hubris of a transcendental subject is clear. Unlike Wittgenstein, I do not regard solipsism as a significational absurdity, but rather as the sign of a mistaken view of the transcendental agency.

Man exists transcendentally, but also anthropologically, not in the isolation of a subjective self, but in the completeness of relations between one person and another. If we now return to our personal mode of being, we notice that persons must be part of a communicational universe before they can be recognized as persons; only afterward do they acquire an empirical content.

On the Categories of the Person

"What is the person?" and "what is man?" are questions that go together. If we want man to exist, if only so that we can argue that he has class-consciousness, or is capable of prayer, or love, then he must exist together with the person. Now, my argument is that it is precisely because man is caught up in a network of interlocutive and cooperative relations that he becomes effectively capable of taking his inalienable share of the semantic initiative, i.e., constantly intervening in the constitution of sense and reference. The marvel is that an utterly singular faculty of speech can be actively pooled as a communal property. It is in a sense a child that we have all made together, just as we wanted it to be, less mortal perhaps than a child of perishable flesh.

We have broken with the Cartesian conception of the person as the conscious and detached observer of an impersonal cosmos. Man is a pilgrim invited to take part in the game of life. The process-based nature of this theory corresponds to the incomplete character of the world of our co-references. Both require the commitment of the person.

Subjectivity takes shape when we acquire our status as persons by observing the canonical usage of the different personal indicators. Only then is the person who says "ego" truly an ego. But subjectivity only exists empirically when it acquires a personal status. This is carried by the proper names that are conferred on it, as well as by the titles of social recognition guaranteed by law. And so long as it is attached to the person, subjectivity is slowly formed in the course of its communications by the interplay of epistemic operators. If its form is determined by personal indicators, it becomes alternatively perceptible through the possible worlds implied by the propositional attitudes it expresses during its communications.

But in both cases this usage works in a relational and interactional manner. This in my view is what is meant by saying that the reality of the person is irreducibly intersubjective. In fact, the person is a structural and dynamic integration of relations. A science of the person cannot be the science of any separate thing—be it substance, individual, or character—for it must be a science of relations: not the type of social relations that are established around the production or exchange of things, but interpersonal relations which sustain social relations and keep their system open, maintaining our co-referential relationship to things.

What I have called the subject's personal status, which is nominal and qualified, is conditioned by its status as a person, which is something beyond nomination and is not qualified, just as the result of an identificational activity is conditioned by the very way in which that activity is exercised. On this condition, the person can perfectly well be named and later described in the delocutive register of language, without thereby being denatured by objectivization. Many intuitive and partial oppositions noted by Martin Buber and Gabriel Marcel can be integrated at this point into my conceptual framework.

Far from status as a person and personal status dissolving in the network of real and possible relations, against all expectations that network turns out to be the only context in which man can effectively be a speaking subject, or rather a speaking person. We have therefore seen that the philosophical notion of the person is diachronic, communicational, and intersubjective, overflowing all the old psychosociological categories.

A mistaken, *sociological* interpretation of the process of entering into relations would assimilate it to the formation of a collective whole composed of linked individuals. It seems to me that the systemic approach in anthropology will sooner or later have to make way for a relational and interactional view of the human phenomenon.[10] If there is now no question of accepting the closure of our inward experience, or the intentional primacy of subjectivity, it is still less possible to deny the existence of persons to the exclusive advantage of the power of the system, as the ideology of industrialized societies invites us to do. Interhuman relations constitute the citizen as much as the city. The aim of the social contract is to guarantee their quality. Citizens must make sure of that quality if they want the terms these relations bring into being to remain faithful to their reality as persons. Therefore, the program of tomorrow is to create not the individualistic and monological city of goals, but the city of dialogue. Or if that fails, then the significational neutralization or symbolic execution of its witnesses.

This emphasis on relations is a way of stressing the interdependence not only of the whole and its parts, but also of the relation and its terms. The result is that the self, considered in itself as a psychic phenomenon, is truly an abstraction. A fortiori, it would be incorrect to take relational phenomena for nothing but subjective dispositions. That would be to shut relations up in natures, as in little boxes. Human relations are interpersonal structures whose most explicit locus is language. In particular, during a conversation, what goes on in the mind of the two participants is certainly a concomitant phenomenon, but this experience can never be confused with the meaning of what is said. The process by which meaning emerges is far more complex than ordinary semantic theories would lead us to believe. Lexical signifiers and syntactic structures obviously have their role to play, but so does the speaker's relationship to the reference as something that comes about interlocutively. We have known since Frege that the meaning of an expression must be distinguished from its representation (*Vorstellung*), which is something mental. Now we find that the meaning of an expression is to be found neither in the speaking partners, nor in the couple that they form together. It necessarily proceeds from the interlocutive relation between them.

At the same time, the true concept of subjectivity now includes not the ego's ability to stand alternately as the subject and the object of discourse, but man's quite remarkable faculty of rising up and intervening as an agency of utterance in a relational context. This faculty has nothing of a soporific virtue about it; it is the product of a pragmatic competence, which is none other than the relational principle applied to discourse. By accepting it fearlessly, and reactivating it and taking responsibility for its exercise, man acquires the power to challenge the communicational regime, always more or less curtailed or violent, in which he finds himself living here and now.

This power of grasping one's own identity is not just of theoretical importance, as if my or other people's being were measured by the knowledge that we all have of it for ourselves; it also has ethical significance. It is up to all persons to recreate themselves for the best, i.e., for the preservation of their integrity. They thereby test and prove their communicative competence. Thus there is still a sense in which we can speak of the *I* in philosophy. A sense which is no longer the traditional psychological or transcendental one: the *I* is what exercises in a responsible manner the competence of which it is a priori the seat. Of course, we should not confuse this power with its opposite—the ability to withdraw oneself from communication for the worst, having broken down and betrayed our relationship, or even simply retreated into a state where the self listens to its own processes and ruminates on its states of mind. The ability to break up a relation derives from the person's power to hold itself in reserve in order to grasp its identity. To this marginal though decisive extent, the person too can be said to exist for itself. I have referred to this competence as the "third experience of the spirit," the one that orders and recapitulates all the others. Theologians can translate this into other terms if they wish: it is through this experience that people can be elevated to an I–you relationship with the divine persons and achieve fulfillment.

The aptitude must be seen as one of the three defining categories of the person, along with the ability to enter into and remain in communicational relations, and the marginal ability to grasp itself by breaking off relations or turning in on itself. This condition poses the problem of the person's self-sustaining nature. All men and women should learn to look out for and recognize in themselves the moment of daring. Everyone's heart vibrates with this same string of iron. With the feeling of our own power, advancing through decisions made by, and permission granted to, ourselves, but without solitary action or thought. At such moments, each person should be, to use Ralph Waldo Emerson's term, utterly self-reliant. That is why the person in its own particular identity is in the end formed as much from a relationship with itself as from one with other people. It is essential for it to maintain for itself, independently of its ability to turn to others, the set of operations that define it as free.

I propose to show in another book, in accordance with this relational approach to the person, that the three categories I have just delineated correspond, by a sort of logical duality, to the categories of communication itself, provided that we change radically our notion of what communication is. The person does not lack the power, nor indeed the duty (in the sense that its very identity is involved), to displace the messages that pass through it. This is its way of guaranteeing its own positive difference, as well as its particular responsibility and destiny.

But I must finish by returning to the self. To begin with, it is the major philosophical mistake and indiscretion, one that leads to multifarious illusions. It is taking things back to front, like going the wrong way up a one-way street. But can we ever do away with the self? The unity of the person is neither initial nor initiatory, final nor conclusive. It proceeds from a daring demand for unification, which is part of human life. We are never out of the game. If the person within us is forever being called into question, it is because it cannot isolate itself. Straining toward the totality of communications still to come, it is made of futurity as bodies are made of the void. It is an arrow and not a target, the beautiful mirage of a great labor. Age modifies the balance between external communication and the self's discussions with itself, until the day when death, the black depths and the incurable night, do us the violence of shutting us off forever from the words of all men.

· · · · · ·

NOTES

Full bibliographic information is provided in the Bibliography.

Preface to the First Edition

1. Nora and Minc, *L'Informatisation de la société*.

2. See Husserl's *Sinngebung:* consciousness is the source of units of meaning, which in the final analysis are immanent to consciousness. *Ideen zu einer reinen Phänomenologie*.

3. Bell, *The Coming of Post-Industrial Society;* Lyotard, *La Condition post-moderne;* Touraine, *La Société post-industrielle*.

4. See my contribution to *Dialogue pour l'identité culturelle*, 293–305.

5. *Dialogiques 1: Recherches logiques sur le dialogue*.

6. *Dialogiques 2: L'Espace logique de l'interlocution*.

7. Russell, *My Philosophical Development*.

8. As can be seen in Catherine Kerbrat-Orecchioni's *L'Enonciation de la subjectivité dans le langage*. For the author's reservations, to which I also subscribe, see 6–8.

9. In the technical sense: the pragmatic approach puts forward a theory of language in context, or language as usage. In the history of the language sciences, this

337

point of view follows from the historical and structural schools. Making language a communicational phenomenon involves going beyond the straightforward opposition between syntax and semantics. Depending on the context, the word "pragmatic" refers either to the analysis of the discursive competence of speaking subjects, or simply to a mode of discourse analysis. Logicians, linguists, psycholinguists and others have yet to agree on a standard meaning. Cf. Grunig, "Plusieurs pragmatiques," 107–118.

Introduction: A Communicational Approach to the Person

1. See, e.g., Culioli and Desclés, "Systèmes de représentation linguistiques et métalinguistiques," 71: "the basic situation underlying the production of any statement is described by Sit (So, To). It is defined by the action of binary operator Sit on the pair So, the speaking subject, and To, a spatiotemporal reference point."

2. Descombes has devoted a book to this problem (*L'Inconscient malgré lui*). But as my approach treats the subconscious as a possible interlocutor, and the ego as a dialogue partner, I cannot make the straightforward link proposed by Descombes between the unconscious and the subject of the utterance.

3. Malinowski, "The Problems of Meaning in Primitive Languages."

4. See, e.g., *Philosophica* 27, "Pragmatics and Philosophy," ed. L. Apostel and A. Kasher (1981).

5. A full bibliography can be found at the end of Kerbrat-Orecchioni, *L'Enonciation de la subjectivité dans le language*. A historical overview of the origins of the notion of *énonciation* (utterance) is given by Fuchs in "Les Problématiques énonciatives."

6. Benveniste, "L'Appareil formel de l'énonciation" in *Problèmes de linguistique générale 2*, 79.

7. *Ibid.*

8. I have attempted to provide such definitions in *Dialogiques 2: L'Espace logique de l'interlocution*, chap. 8.

9. Anscombe and Ducrot, "L'Argumentation dans la langue," 5–27.

10. See the useful article by Fraser and Joly, "Le système de la déixis," 125.

11. The term used here is not simply a metaphorical approximation; it has a precise theoretical status. See, e.g., my *Dialogiques 1*, second and third investigations.

12. In fact, although Benveniste first used the term, he did not invent the concept of *énonciation* (can we indeed speak of it as a concept at all?). The word as it is used today involves a number of different ideas, from Louis Hjelmslev's "presupposition" (any statement presupposes an utterance), to "engagement" in the Jakobsonian sense (a statement is "shifted in or out" in relation to the subject of the speech process), and the concept of a generative path up toward the surface from a primitive mode of existence, which goes back well beyond Benveniste, to Zelig Harris and even Leonard Bloomfield. In any case, the concept of utterance remains a problematic one: we still feel that we do not yet have the right predicates with which to talk about it, and that the very ideas it brings precariously together are individually doubtful: what if utterance were not presupposed by statements but reconstituted from linguistic units

338

larger than statements? What if the utterance-process did not "engage" with the speaker alone, or even with the interlocutors, but with the interlocutive relation? This composite concept nevertheless remains fundamental: utterance has implications first and foremost for the conditions of possibility of meaning and, correlatively, for the linked problems of subjectivity and communication. There is obviously something amiss in Benveniste's account.

13. On the mechanism of this illusory hegemony, see *L'Espace logique de l'interlocution*, chap. 6, sec. 4; or below, chap. 6.

14. This approach becomes central when the paradigm of communicability is substituted for that of expressivity in the metatheoretical language debate. This replacement depends on certain epistemological decisions, whether taken consciously (Irving Cresswell, Clarence Lewis, Robert Stalnaker) or unconsciously (Morris and Rudolf Carnap). Ideas that were previously lacking—such as *act, context, performance*, and, I would add, *interlocutive relation*, are now appearing in the theory. The pragmatic approach has implications for philosophers for several reasons. First, it is still not established on an adequate footing, and its field of application needs to be delineated by interdisciplinary exchange between linguists, logicians, semioticians, communication specialists, psycholinguists, and others. Second, it allows philosophers to become actively involved in the metatheoretical debate about language. Third, this approach implies new ways of looking at certain philosophical problems, such as the status of the Cogito, some concepts in the philosophy of science (what does it mean to accept a theory as true?), subjectivity, alterity, and personal identity.

15. Grunig, "Pièges et illusions," 28.

16. Shannon and Weaver, *The Mathematical Theory of Communication*.

17. Lyons, *Semantics I*.

Chapter 1. Num Quid et Tu?

1. Mounoud and Winter admit as much in *Le Reconnaissance de son image chez l'enfant et l'animal*, 8. A basic bibliography of the contribution of French-language psychology can be found at 17−20.

2. See the overview and conclusion of Penelhum, "Personal Identity," 95−107.

3. Paillard, "Le Corps situé et le corps identifié," 123−131.

4. Wallon, "Syndrome d'insuffisance psycho-motrice."

5. Vigarello, "Le Laboratoire des sciences humaines," 90.

6. Lagache, "Modèle psychanalytique de la personnalité."

7. Amélie Rorty gives a historical and literary account of the problem in "A Literary Postscriptum," 302.

8. *Ibid.*

9. Further literary examples will be found in Rorty, "A Literary Postscriptum."

10. Butler, "Of Personal Identity," 263−270.

11. "Loose and popular, not strict and philosophical," comments Chisholm in *Perception and Personal Identity*, 82−106; 128−139.

12. Kenny, *The Five Ways*, 65.

13. Locke, *An Essay Concerning Human Understanding*, book 2, chap. 27. Because Locke in fact remains attached to the concept of substance, which however he had already shown to be unusable, his analysis makes little progress.

14. Paul Valéry, *La Jeune parque, Oeuvres* 1, 105.

15. Paul Valéry, *Cahiers* 1 (Paris: Gallimard, 1973–1974), 809.

16. Kant, *Critique de la raison pure*, book 1, chap. 2, sec. 2, par. 16.

17. Husserl, *Ideen* 1, sec. 2, chap. 4, par. 56ff.

18. Sartre, *La Transcendance de l'ego*, 19–23.

19. *Ibid.*, 27.

20. Kant, *Anthropologie in pragmatischer Hinsicht*, book 1, sec. 1.

21. Alexandre, *En souvenir de Michel Alexandre.*

22. Mounier, *Le Personalisme.*

23. Simone Weil, *Attente de dieu.*

24. See Canguilhem, "La Théorie cellulaire."

25. Lagache, "La Fascination de la conscience par le moi," 41.

26. Levinas, *Totalité et infini*, sec. 1. On Levinas' paradoxical approach to the problem, see chap. 3, below.

27. Nicole, *Traité de la connaissance de soi-même.*

28. The juxtaposition of the self's and the other's discourses, and the attempt to make them interlock, are again ways of avoiding having to think about relations. Cf. chap. 6, below.

29. For instance, Melanie Klien, *Envy and Gratitude.* We should not confuse this feeling with the decision often made by innovators to look only inward, toward a small group of specialists, or to appeal to an ideal community in which the Word would circulate more easily than it does here in the real world.

30. See also Desclés, "Recherche sur les opérations constitutives du langage."

31. See, e.g., Benveniste, *Problèmes de linguistique générale 1*, 225–236.

32. *Ibid.*, 256.

33. Tarski, "On the Calculus of Relations," 74.

34. Peirce, Ms. 1903, *Collected Papers*, 1: 343; 345–347.

35. Russell, "The Philosophy of Logical Atomism" in *Logic and Knowledge*, 206.

36. See Torris, *L'Acte médical et le caractère du malade.*

37. La Bruyère, *Les Caractères de Théophraste traduits en français.*

38. Watzlawick and Weakland, *Sur l'interaction.*

39. Aulagnier, *La Violence de l'interprétation*, 35. See also, by the same author, "A propos du transfert: Le Risque d'excès et l'illusion mortifère" in *Savoir, faire, espérer: Les Limites de la raison*, 421.

40. Maxim Gorky, *My Childhood* (London: Laurie, 1915), chap. 1.

41. *Ibid.*

42. Milan Kundera, *Life Is Elsewhere* (London: Faber and Faber, 1986).

43. On the concept of back-reference (*rétro-référence*), which I introduced in 1977, see my "Les Conditions dialogiques de la référence," *Etudes philosophiques* 3 (1977).

44. Fernandez-Zoïla, "Présence à soi et espace sémantique." And see especially Ortigues, "Quelqu'un, identité et personnalité," 605–628.

45. Geach, *God and the Soul.*

46. For Rudolf Carnap, the phrase *ego sum* was not even transcribable into the logical syntax of language.

47. Thus, Descartes said: "We are setting about discussing these things in the wrong way. Just let each of us look down into the depths of himself." Descartes, *Entretien avec Burman.*

48. Plato, "Alcibiades," in *Complete Works.*

Chapter 2. Man without Qualities

1. Montaigne, *Essais,* 2, chap. 6.

2. Laing, *Self and Others,* 81.

3. Levinas, *Totalité et infini,* 3.

4. Aulagnier, "Remarques sur la fémininité et ses avatars" in *Le Désir et la perversion,* 55−79.

5. Aimé Césaire, *Les Armes miraculeuses* (Paris: Gallimard, 1970).

6. Dostoyevsky, *Le Sous-sol* [*Notes from Underground*] (Paris: Gallimard, Folio), 122.

7. Inscription on the great obelisk in the Circus Maximus, Rome.

8. Gregory of Nazianzus, *Five Theological Orations.*

9. Saint Augustine, *De Trinitate,* book 1:4, 7 and book 5:8.

10. *Ibid.* 1:5, 8. For my analysis of the notion of joint action, see chap. 6, below.

11. Tertullianus or Clement of Alexandria thought that it was not the Father, considered to be truly God, but only the Son, considered to be subordinate to the Father, who had made himself visibly manifest to men. Even Ireneus accepted the possibility of activities specific to each of the Persons within the works of God. On the long struggle over the Trinity, which concerned the most fundamental mystery of the Revelation, compare E. Hendrikx, introduction to the Benedictine edition of the *Works* of St. Augustine.

12. Augustine, *De Trinitate,* chap. 7, secs. 4, 7.

13. Among these heresies were Subordinationism, Ditheism, and Modalism.

14. See *De Trinitate,* chap. 5, secs. 13−15.

15. I am combining here the terminologies of Gregory of Nazianzus and Basil.

16. *De Trinitate.*

17. Aquinas, *Summa Theologiae* vol. 1, quest. 3, art. 4; see also vol. 1, quest. 29, art. 4, and *Summa Contra Gentiles* vol. 4, chap. 14.

18. Tertullian, *Adversus Praxean,* 7.

19. The term was only really adopted into official doctrine in 554, at the General Council of Constantinople.

20. Augustine, *De Trinitate* 7:6, 11 and 5:9−10.

21. Gregory of Nazianzus, *Theological Discourses.*

22. Augustine, *De Trinitate* 4:9.

23. *Ibid.* 15:7, 11.

24. See Augustine, sermon 71:12, 18 in *Patrologia.*

25. Books 8 to 15 and 1 to 7, respectively.

26. *Ibid.*, first sect., 2 : 2.

27. Hegel credits Kant with this idea in his *Encyclopädie*, sec. 47 : remark.

28. *Dialogiques I*, 110.

29. See *Dialogiques 2: L'Espace logique de l'interlocution.*

30. N.B.: Manifesting, not revealing or representing itself. On this subject see below, chap. 4.

31. Aquinas, *Summa Theologiae*, quest. 37, art. 2.

32. On God as a person in religious statements, see my "L'Analyse des énoncés théologiques."

33. Pascal, *Pensées*, frag. 688 (323).

34. Compare, e.g., Husserl, *Cartesianische Meditationen*, sec. 11.

35. Leaving aside the metalinguistic level, which will be dealt with later.

36. Montaigne, *Essais*, 1 : 27.

37. Dostoyevsky, "The Gambler," in *The Gambler and Other Stories* (London: Heinemann, 1914).

38. Jankélévitch, *Traité des vertus*, chap. 11, sec. 3, 445 : "Un 'autre moi-même?.'"

39. Saint Bernard, fifth sermon on the *Song of Solomon.*

40. Saint Bernard, *De Diligendo Dei*, 7 : 52.

41. Jankélévitch, *Le Paradoxe de la morale*, 170.

42. Compare Saint Bernard, *De Diligendo Dei*, 7 : 53.

43. Aquinas, *Summa Theologiae*, quest. 28, art. 2.

44. Aquinas, *Summa Contra Gentiles*, book 5, chap. 19; also *Compendium Theologiae*, chap. 45–50. But this is because of the unity of the divine essence, and nothing to do with friendship as such. For Aquinas, that oneness which unites two human persons is not given by the real experience of their act of loving; each of them continues to experience his or her own act, which gives us two loves and two acts of loving. The most they can do is to fit their two hearts to the same object. It is this object—the desire of doing good and the substantive persons to whom they wish to do good—that unites them. For persons, mutual relations operate along the subject-object axis.

45. Plato, *Phaedrus.*

46. Stendhal, *De l'amour* (Paris: Editions de Cluny, 1938), chaps. 39b and 34c.

47. Marcel Proust, "Un Amour de Swann" in *Du côté de chez Swann* (Paris: Gallimard, 1980).

48. Dostoyevsky "The Gambler," 54.

49. Proust, *Albertine disparue.*

50. Proust, "Un Amour de Swann."

51. Interview with Catherine Clément, *Le Matin* (12 November 1981), 18.

52. Jean Clavreul, "Le Couple pervers," 94.

53. Aristotle, Nicomachean Ethics, 9 : 10, 6.

54. Racine, *Phèdre*, (Paris: Larousse, 1965), ll. 1220–1224.

55. Louis Aragon, *Le Roman inachevé* (Paris: Gallimard, 1967).

56. Russell and Whitehead, *Principia Mathematica*, para. 31 : 13. Every relation

has a converse. See also the commentary by J. Vuillemin, *Leçons sur la première philosophie de Russell* (Paris: A. Colin, 1968).

57. Genesis 29:28–30.

58. Montaigne, *Essais*, 2:8.

59. *Essais*, book 3, chap. 1.

60. *Ibid.*

61. Psalm 23.

62. On this point, see Watzlawick, "Patterns of Psychotic Communication," 44–53.

63. See, e.g., Jankélévitch, *Le Paradoxe de la morale*, 176; for the true personal significance of obligations, see below, chap. 6.

64. Canguilhem, *Essai sur quelques problèmes concernant le normal et le pathologique;* see also Valabrega, *La Relation thérapeutique.*

65. The term *ascription*, and the basic concept it conveys, are borrowed from Hart, "Are There Any Natural Rights?", 175–191.

66. On this point, see my "L'Explication dans les sciences humaines," 77–109.

67. Sartre, *Critique de la raison dialectique*, 182.

68. Locke, *Essay Concerning Human Understanding*, sec. 13. This passage is discussed in detail by Anthony Flew in *Philosophy* 26 (1951), 53, and by Bernard Williams in his *Problems of the Self* (Cambridge: Cambridge University Press, 1973), 4.

69. Gen. 8.21. Also 1 Sam. 1.13; Dan. 1.8.

70. Psalms 10.3–4; See also Gen. 27.41; Esther 6.6.

71. In *Studies in Bereshit* (Genesis, 1972). I would like to thank Françoise Armengaud for pointing this out to me.

72. A different objection to this dichotomy will be found in Williams, *Problems of the Self*, chap. 5.

73. Locke, *Essay*, sec. 10.

74. See Jacques, *Dialogiques I*, 106.

75. *Ibid.*, second investigation.

76. Hofstadter, *Gödel, Escher, Bach*, 385.

77. For this notion, see *Dialogiques I*, 222, and chap. 5, below.

78. See *Dialogiques I*, and especially the fourth investigation. It is based on the principle that all statements provide a self-reflexive commentary on the act performed by their utterance. However, I explain why this principle, first stated by J. L. Austin, is inadequate to account for the verbal interaction between persons, whose presence is also indicated in the utterance.

79. Molière, *Le Misanthrope*, trans. D. M. Frame (New York: Signet, 1968), 1:1.

80. Foucault, *La Volonté de savoir*, 75.

81. *Ibid.*, 81.

82. I am most grateful to him for passing on this information to me.

83. Between 18% and 23% from 1750 to 1780 (*Ibid.*).

84. On this crucial point, see *Dialogiques I*, 110ff.

85. As writers from Jacques Lacan to Michel Foucault have done.

86. *Dialogiques I*, second investigation.

Chapter 3. Primum Relationis

1. Wittgenstein, *Philosophical Investigations*, sec. 540.
2. *Ibid.*, sec. 25.
3. As will be seen below, the two things are confused by Martin Buber.
4. Russell, *Problems of Philosophy*.
5. *Ibid.* I shall return to this below.
6. Alexius Meinong, "Relationtheorie," *Gesammelte Abhandlungen* 2, 44.
7. See chap. 3. On these *modo intelligentiae* relations and their heterogeneity, compare the different points of view of Vuillemin, *De la logique à la théologie* (Paris: Flammarion, 1967), 153–163, and Gilles-Gaston Granger, *La Théorie aristotélicienne de la science* (Paris: Aubier, 1976), 291.
8. Russell, *My Philosophical Development*, 54–55. See also his *Principles of Mathematics*, chap. 26.
9. Russell, "The Philosophy of Logical Atomism," 497.
10. *Ibid.*
11. *Ibid.*, 498.
12. Russell, *Principles of Mathematics*, part 2, chap. 11.
13. Classically, an extensional relation is known if its sets E and F, and its graph G, are known. Getting a relation means getting a subset G of the Cartesian product E × F. Remember that given a relation R ⊂ E × F, a reciprocal relation (R-1) is defined by $R^{-1} = (y, x) \; \varepsilon F) \times E / (x, y) \; \varepsilon R$
14. W. V. O. Quine, "New Foundations for Mathematical Logic," in *From a Logical Point of View*, 87.
15. Kuratowski, "Sur la notion d'ordre dans la théorie des ensembles," 161–171.
16. Kurt Gödel, "Uber formal unentscheidbare Sätze der Principia Mathematica und verwandter Systeme," 173–198.
17. Church, "A Note on the Entscheidungsproblem," 40–41.
18. The term "agency of utterance" is a technical one with no psychologizing implications. Even as used by authors who identify it with the speaking subject, it cannot be assimilated to the ego or the psychoanalytic subject. It is a metalinguistic parameter that is independent of real speakers.
19. By individuality, I mean that which maintains an individual's identity; by personality, I mean that which maintains the identity of the person. On personal status, and the distinction between individuals and persons, see chaps. 5 and 6.
20. For a more thorough analysis, see Conclusion. See also *Dialogiques 2: L'Espace logique de l'interlocution*, chap. 8.
21. Hegel, *La Phénoménologie de l'esprit* (Paris: Aubier, 1939—41), 151.
22. *Ibid.*
23. *Ibid.*
24. *Ibid.*, 157.
25. *Ibid.*, 297, 302.
26. See Martin Buber, "Education," in *Between Man and Man* (London: Collins, 1966).

27. Buber, "Distance and Relation." See also Rotenstreich, *The Philosophy of Martin Buber*, 97.

28. According to Todorov (in *Mikhaïl Bakhtin*, 151–152), they can be found in Humboldt (1827), Fichte (1837), Feuerbach (1843), and above all in the writings of Existentialists such as Sartre and Levinas. Heidegger is also quoted by Bakhtin, who seems to belong to this intellectual family rather than to Marxism.

29. Merleau-Ponty, *Phénoménologie de la perception*.

30. See Husserl, *Formale und transcendentale Logik*, sec. 96.

31. *Ibid.*, sec. 103 ff.

32. Jacques, *Dialogiques 1*, and also *Dialogiques 2, L'Espace logique de l'interlocution*.

33. Sartre, *L'Être et le Néant*.

34. *Ibid.*

35. Sartre, *Critique de la raison dialectique*, 181, 186, 192.

36. Levinas, *Autrement qu'être*.

37. *Ibid.*

38. See *Quatre lectures talmudiques* (Paris: Minuit, 1968), 61.

39. Levinas, *Totalité et infini*.

40. Husserl, *Ideen I*, 144.

41. Levinas, "Le Temps et l'autre," in *Le Choix, le monde, l'existence* (Cahiers du Collège philosophique, Arthaud, 1949).

42. Levinas, *Les Noms propres*, 107.

43. Levinas, *Totalité et infini*, For counter-arguments to Levinas' solipsism, see my *L'Espace logique de l'interlocution*, chap. 8.

44. Levinas, *Totalité et infini*.

45. E.g., R. Blum, "*La Perception d'autrui.*"

46. Levinas, *Totalité et infini*.

47. Levinas, *Autrement qu'être*.

48. Brentano, "Die psychische Beziehung in Unterschied von der Relation im eigentlichen Sinne." For Husserl it is noesis that is real, while the noeme remains unreal.

49. Levinas, *Ethique et infini*.

50. Levinas, *Autrement qu'être*.

51. Wittgenstein, *Philosophical Investigations*, sec. 103.

52. Compare Henri Bosco, *Hyacinthe;* quoted in Françoise Armengaud, "Le Visage animal."

53. John Donne, "The Ecstasy" in *The Complete Poems of John Donne* (New York: New York University Press, 1967).

54. Remember the axiom of 31.13 of the *Principia Mathematica*, in which Russell states that every relation has a converse.

55. For Levinas, dialogue seems first to open up "an absolute distance between the *I* and the *you*, separated by the inexpressible secret of their interiority. Then the "extraordinary and immediate relation of the dia-logue" is deployed and interposes itself so as to "transcend and negate that distance." See *Du Dieu qui vient à l'idée*, 221.

56. Ps. 119.19.

57. Buber, *Je et tu,* 60.

58. Neh. 10.33.

59. Levinas, "La Croyance."

60. Gen. 20.11.

61. A demonstration of this can be found in *Dialogiques 1,* fourth investigation.

62. See the proof by Nicholas Rescher, *Dialectica* (Albany: State University of N.Y. Press, 1976), 178ff. The basic idea is that innovators should be regarded ex officio as proposers or defenders of certain theses. Instead of approaching nature in the manner of impartial and detached researchers, they confront it, and their adversaries, in rational discussion, as committed supporters of a particular point of view. After all, is not the aim of research to lead to defensible results, i.e. ones that can be proposed, defended, and attacked in rational discussion? This disputational approach to research (on the theoretical and, above all, metatheoretical level) is based on the remarkable principle of equality of testing. It will doubtless have been noticed that this conception of research methodology makes quite irrelevant the opposition between those who insist on inductive confirmation of hypotheses and those who, on the contrary, regard the essence of the critical scientific approach to be the ability to refute or invalidate hypotheses; this saves us a quarrel.

63. Sartre, *Critique de la raison dialectique,* 195.

64. See the critique by Dennett, "Conditions of Personhood," 175–194. Grice's definition can be found in "Utterer's Meaning and Intentions," 151.

65. Schiffer, *Meaning,* chap. 4.

66. Sartre, *Critique de la raison dialectique.*

67. Jacques, *Dialogiques 2, L'Espace logique de l'interlocution,* chap. 2.

68. Buber, "Eléments de l'inter-humain," in *La Vie en dialogue.*

Chapter 4. The Grand Illusion

1. Amiel, *Journal intime* 2, 32. It is ironic that a denunciation of the subjective illusion should come from his pen.

2. This is a common experience in psychoanalysis, with its resistances, transferences, and counter-transferences.

3. Mink, "Philosophical Analysis and Historical Understanding," 667–698.

4. Montaigne, *Essais,* "To the Reader."

5. Aristotle, *Poetics* 4:10. Aristotle quotes Homer's *Margites,* the earliest known example of the comic genre. I might also mention the *fabliau* tradition of the Middle Ages, and the comedies of Molière.

6. I shall expand on the discourse of subjectivism in chap. 5, in order to put forward a formal refutation of it.

7. Jacques, *Dialogiques 1,* 40.

8. Valéry, "Fragments du Narcisse," *Charmes, Oeuvres* 1, 128.

9. *Ibid.*

10. This is the recognition of the body through its mirror image, which is not to be confused with the perceived or the conceived body.

11. For more on the iconophile's discourse it is well worth consulting Baudinet, "L'Incarnation, l'image, la voix."

12. Valéry, "Fragments du Narcisse," *Charmes, Oeuvres* I, 130.

13. Bachelard, *L'Eau et les rêves,* chap. I.

14. *Ibid.,* 45.

15. Valéry, *Cahiers* 29 (Paris: Gallimard, 1973–4), 200.

16. Montaigne, *Essais* 2:8.

17. Benveniste, *Problèmes de linguistique générale,* 238.

18. Jules Vallès, "Le Testament d'un blagueur," in *Oeuvres* I (Paris: Gallimard, 1975), 1097–1138; also "L'Enfant" in *Jacques Vintgras* (Paris: Editeurs français réunis, 1969). In addition to Philippe Lejeune's work on autobiography, M. Beaujour's *Miroirs d'encre* (Paris: Seuil, 1980) and particularly L. Martin's *La Voix excommuniée* (Paris: Galilée, 1981) should be mentioned here. The review by Bertrand Poirot-Delpeche in *Le Monde* (24 October 1980) is also worth reading.

19. Sterne, *The Life and Opinions of Tristram Shandy, Gentleman.*

20. *Ibid.,* book 5, chap. 5.

21. Karlsruhe, Kunsthalle.

22. Montaigne, *Essais* 2:5.

23. In the three different cases, explains Genette in *Figures 3,* the narration is respectively hetero-, homo-, and auto-diegetic (251).

24. Montaigne, *Essais,* "To the Reader."

25. Quoted by Montaigne, *Essais* 2:8.

26. *Ibid.*

27. Augustine, *Confessions,* 11:1.

28. Montaigne, *Essais* 2.

29. Montaigne, *Essais* 2:8.

30. Cardinal Newman, *Apologia pro sua vita.*

31. Rousseau, *Rousseau, juge de Jean-Jacques.*

32. Helen Keller, *The Story of my Life.* (London: Hodder and Stoughton, 1904).

33. Henry Adams, *The Education of Henry Adams* (New York: Twayne Publishers Inc., 1906).

34. Stendhal, *La Vie De Henry Brulard* (Paris: Garnier, 1953).

35. Mayoux, *Sous de vastes portiques,* 21.

36. Poirot-Delpeche in *Le monde des livres* (24 October 1980).

Chapter 5. The Heart of the Subject

1. Montaigne, *Essais* 3:8.

2. Descartes, "Règles pour la direction de l'esprit," *Oeuvres* 12.

3. Nietzsche, Friedrich, *The Gay Science* (Vintage, 1974), 277.

4. Descartes, "Réponses aux 5e objections," *Oeuvres* 8, 358–359.

5. Beyssade, *La Philosophie première de Descartes,* 137–139; 163–164.

6. Sartre (*Critique de la raison dialectique,* 39) warns against the incorrect tendency to assimilate the structure of reflexive and nonreflexive acts.

7. This point is developed in *Dialogiques 1*, second investigation, 117ff.

8. Descartes, "Preface to the Reader," *Oeuvres* 7 : 9–10. Earlier, the author points out: "nec tantum mihi arrogo ut confidam me omnia posse praevidere quae alicui difficilia videbuntur." Cf. also *Discourse on Method* and *Letter to Mersenne* of 25 November 1630.

9. Buber states the problem in the same way, but as Rotenstreich remarks, he wavers as to the correct attitude to adopt.

10. One way of doing away with the apparent problem of the unconscious here is perhaps to see it not as one thing hiding behind another, but as a certain way in which the self is or is not in a relation with itself. The "unconscious" would then cease to be an anthropological structure of subjectivity and become instead a pragmatic structure of communicability with the self.

11. Montaigne, *Essais* 2 : 8.

12. Amiel, *Journal intime*, 3 March 1857.

13. *Ibid.* (my emphasis).

14. *Ibid.*, 10 March 1857.

15. *Ibid.*, 25 June 1856.

16. Valéry, *Lust, la demoiselle de cristal* in *Oeuvres* 2.

17. Gen. 12.1; 22.3.

18. Armengaud, "L'Impertinence excommunicative ou comment annuler la parole d'autrui."

19. That is the objection raised by Geach in *God and the Soul.* In response, I would argue as I did in the first section of the present chapter.

20. For that reason I cannot agree with Habermas' definition of communicational activity (in *Technik und Wissenschaft als "Ideologie"*) as an interaction mediated by symbols. The interlocutive relation is primary; it is not blind and has no need to invest itself in a secondary manner in signs. Wittgenstein's critique of private language is of course crucial here.

21. On this distinction, cf. *Dialogiques 2: L'Espace logique de l'interlocution.*

22. Fichte said as much in 1797: "The individual's consciousness is necessarily accompanied by that of someone else, and is possible only on this condition." So did Hegel, in *Phänomenologie des Geistes:* "Self-consciousness only exists as a self if it can see itself in another self-consciousness." It is always in this "mirror" relationship that the double comes into consciousness.

23. Peirce, *Collected Papers*, vol. 6, sec. 338; vol. 5, sec. 421. Compare Valéry, *Cahiers* 2, 793: "All mental processes are simply question and answer."

24. Guéroult, *Descartes selon l'ordre des raisons* 2, appendix 1, 311.

25. Scholz, "Uber das Cogito, ergo sum," 126–147; cited by Hintikka, "Cogito ergo sum: Inference or Performance?" in *Knowledge and the Known*, 98.

26. This is the objection of Hintikka in particular. *Ibid.*, 100ff.

27. Descartes, *Second Meditation*, par. 3.

28. As Robinet puts it in *Le Langage à l'âge classique*, 100.

29. On this point my argument follows Recanati, *La Transparence et l'énonciation.*

30. Hintikka, *Knowledge and the Known*, 3–32.

31. Augustine, *De Trintate*, 15:10, 17: "*intra se atque in corde suo dicere, id est, cogitando dicere.*"

32. Valéry, *Mélange* in *Oeuvres* I, 314.

33. Valéry, *Cahiers*, note of 1931. Note the dubious positivity which the author confers on communication with the self. Dubious from both a chronological and a logical point of view.

34. In the manner of Hegel (*La Phénoménologie de l'esprit*, 155): "For self-consciousness, there is another consciousness of self which appears to it as something coming from outside."

35. In the expression used by Husserl in his *Krisis*. Valéry, author of *Monsieur Teste*, (*Oeuvres* 12) frequently makes the same claim. Cf. *Cahiers* 24, 624.

36. "La Structure de l'énoncé," reprinted in Todorov, *Mikhaïl Bakhtine, Le principe dialogique*, 295.

37. On the discussions between Einstein and Born, see in particular their *Correspondence 1916–1955* (Paris: Seuil, 1969). On the debate between Einstein and Bohr, see M. Jammer, *The Philosophy of Quantum Mechanics* (New York: John Wiley & Sons, 1974), 121–158. Also Hübner, *Kritik der Wissenschaftlichen Vernunft*, 138–144.

38. In particular, the rules of correct formation are determined by the pure morphology of meanings; the rules for linking propositions are laid down by a logic of coherence; the theory of possible forms of theory is seen as the *ideal* of the deductive sciences, an ideal which, for Husserl, transcends their actual development, because he maintained it even after the theorems of Löwenheim-Skolem, Church, Gödel, and others on the limitations of formal systems.

39. Arnauld and Nicole, *La Logique ou l'art de penser*.

40. *Ibid.*, end of introduction to part I.

41. To that extent, I would not claim that the term "private experience" is an empty one, or, like Max Black, that we cannot even understand what the skeptic is saying when he insists on introducing the idea of an experience accessible to him alone. See Black, "Linguistic Method," *Philosophy and Phenomenological Research* 8, 635–649.

42. Ryle, *The Concept of Mind*, chap. 4, sec. 4.

43. On this last point, see G. E. Moore, *Wittgenstein's Lectures, 1930–1933*, reprinted in *Philosophical Papers*, 252–324.

44. Wittgenstein, *Blue Book*, 67.

45. Wittgenstein, *Philosophical Investigations*, sec. 398. See also his "Notes for Lectures on 'Private Experiences and Sense-data,'" 277–278.

46. Wittgenstein, *Philosophical Investigations*, sec. 351.

47. Wittgenstein's proof of this (*Ibid.*, secs. 258–280) is well worth reading and reflecting on.

48. Empirical confirmation of this is provided by the psychologists: Cf. Hora, "Tao, Zen, and Existential Psychotherapy," 237. For a comparable pragmatic analysis of "I believe that *p*," see my *Dialogiques 2: L'Espace logique de l'interlocution*, chap. 3. An analysis of "I mean" will be found in chap. 6, below.

49. In this approach, thought is considered to occur outside language, which remains a matter of expression.

50. On this point, see Wittgenstein, *Philosophical Grammar*, 193.

51. Though to some extent, I certainly am: see below.

52. On the term "communicative competence" as it is used by linguists, see Lyons, *Semantics*. And below.

53. This coincides with one of the Christian motivations of philosophy discussed by Bruaire, *Pour la Métaphysique*, 258ff.

54. Note that this includes communication with animals, rediscovered by Solomon. On this point, see *Dialogiques I*.

55. Kant (*La Religion dans les limites de la simple raison*, 31–2.)

56. 1 John 4.9, 16.

57. The General Council of Latran IV (1215) proclaimed that the absolute divine essence was identical to the relative Persons. In God there is both an Absolute and a set of Relations, and the Absolute is a Relation. Cf. the commentary of Franzelin S.J., *De Deo trino*, 339.

58. Levinas, "Un Dieu-Homme" in: *Qui est Jésus-Christ?*, Cahiers du C.C.I.F., *Recherches et Débats* (1968).

59. Isa. 55.1, 11.

60. Levinas, "Un Dieu-Homme."

61. Which, it seems to me, is not without relevance to the meaning of the revelation of the Burning Bush as shown to Moses. Should the famous: "I am that I am" be taken as the starting point for a reflection on the being and essence of the divinity, as Gilson proposes? Or should we follow Rashi who, like Halévy and Nachmanides, interprets it in accordance with the oral tradition, rather than "philosophically": the omnitemporality of the divine Being is the omnitemporality of His communication and Alliance with His people. I am the Eternal, your God. I shall be with them in their present distress, and also in their servitude under future empires.

62. John 15.26.

63. 2 Cor. 3.15–17.

64. Gal. 3.14.

65. Heb. 2.11; Col. 1.18.

66. Gal. 4.4–7. Cf. also the prayer of Saint Simeon, the New Theologian, to the Holy Spirit: "Come, you One alone, to one alone, because you see, I am alone. . . . Come, you who yourself have become desire in me, who have made me desire you. . . ." Quoted by Y. Congar, Notre-Dame de Paris, 7 December 1980.

67. Prologue to the Gospel of John.

68. R. E. Brown, *The Gospel According to John I–XII*, 172 n 4.

69. Cf. Simone Weil, *La Connaissance surnaturelle*.

70. Thus Zimmerli, *Das alte Testament als Anrede*.

71. Thomas Aquinas, *De Potentia* 9:4.

72. Valéry, *Charmes* in *Oeuvres* I, 137.

73. *Ibid.*

74. Shakespeare, *Troilus and Cressida*, IV:4.

75. St. Thomas makes the parallel point that the evil caused does not come from an act of nonconsideration of the rule, but rather from a non-act of consideration of the rule (he throws in this gem in passing). *Summa Theologiae* 1:49, 1–3; 1–2:75, 1–3; also *Summa contra gentiles* 3:10.

76. Hervé Bazin, *La Mort du petit cheval* (Paris: Grasset, 1961).

77. See, e.g., R. Stalnaker, "Logical Semiotics," 439–456.

78. Césaire, *Les Armes miraculeuses* (Paris: Gallimard, 1970).

79. Naming is an act of recognition ("I name you" is a performative), an acceptance rite which leads the named person to the classificatory crossroads of several social frames of reference. That is why anthroponymy confirms the social order, and sometimes its conflicts.

80. The use of proper names is only completely determined by the conjunction of these three pragmatic functions when an individual assumes fully his or her personal status. Which means that names of persons have a privileged relationship with the pronouns of all *three* persons, and not just, as some commentators have claimed, with those of the first and second persons. Note that the function of descriptive identification is still a pragmatic one in that it concerns the named person as a member of a speaking community.

81. Weil, *L'Enracinement,* 9.

82. Kant, *La Religion dans les limites de la simple raison,* 45.

83. On this point, see my *Dialogiques 2: L'Espace logique de l'interlocution,* and below, Conclusion.

84. Kant, *La Religion,* 46ff.

85. See my definition in *Dialogiques 2: L'Espace logique de l'interlocution.*

86. Should we accept the objection that these aspects can be explained by a simple theory of performance? That would exclude, for the sake of a methodological simplicity which is close to being a mere artifice, a number of aptitudes which are regularly seen at work in real linguistic communication. A semantic model that depended for its autonomy on shutting out these aptitudes would be just as inadequate today as syntactic models of the recent past which sought to exclude any sort of semantic approach. This represents a considerable extension of the linguist's task.

Chapter 6. Difference and Differentation

1. Pierre Emmanuel, *L'Autre* (Paris: Seuil, 1980).

2. Don D. Jackson, *Family Process,* 1–20.

3. Unless it runs away with itself, endangering its very existence: the result is breakdown or disaster.

4. On the notion of open systems, see Atlan, *L'Organisation biologique et la théorie de l'information.*

5. Watzlawick, "Patterns of Psychotic Communication."

6. Bateson, "Communication."

7. Molière, *Le Misanthrope,* trans. D. M. Frame (New York: Signet, 1968), 4:3.

8. *Ibid.,* 5, final scene.

9. *Ibid.*, 4:3.

10. On the extension of the mutuality relation, see *Dialogiques 1*, fifth investigation.

11. As the author's resume explains, this book can be read as the end of a story which begins with *Una* and continues through *Duel*. Pierre Emmanuel has also translated the *Poems* of Karol Wojtyla into French (Paris: Le Cerf, 1980).

12. A comparable attempt can be seen in Michel Tournier's novel *Les Météores* (Paris: Gallimard Folio, 1974), 421.

13. Emmanuel, *L'Autre*, III.

14. Irigaray, *Ce Sexe qui n'en est pas un*, 30.

15. Deleuze, *Différence et répétition*, 71.

16. Remember that St. Bernard obtained the condemnation of Abelard at Sens in 1140 on a similar point. Abelard wanted to attribute power to the Father, wisdom to the Son, and goodness to the Holy Spirit "specially, and as to their own," whereas they are attributes common to the three. "That is false! For the Father is just as truly wisdom, and the Son power. Whoever asserts as much is absolutely irreproachable." *Patrologiae Latina* 182 (Paris: Garnier, 1879).

17. Jacques, *Dialogues 1*, fourth investigation.

18. Wittgenstein, *Lectures and Conversations*, 53.

19. I define and analyze the "peremptory" attitude in *Dialogiques 2: L'Espace logique de l'interlocution*, chap. 4. It should not be confused with the authority of speech (see chap. 5).

20. La Bruyère, *The Characters of Jean de la Bruyère*, 130–131.

21. This is the classic idea of the unconscious as the literally *unknown*, the presence within us of "thoughts" that we do not know. We know neither what these thoughts are, nor what they are in us. I have sketched out a pragmatic conception of the unconscious, above (see chaps. 1 and 2).

22. On the technical question of pragmatic pertinence, see *Dialogiques 1*.

23. Cf. Armengaud, "L'Impertinence excommunicative, ou comment annuler la parole d'autrui."

24. Lewis Carroll, *Alice's Adventures in Wonderland and Through the Looking-glass* (London and Glasgow: Collins, 1939), 187.

25. On this conclusion, see *Dialogiques 2: L'Espace logique de l'interlocution*.

26. In *Ontological Relativity* (26–27), Quine reminds us that John Dewey realized the same thing in the 1920s: "Soliloquy is a product and a reflection of conversation with other people."

27. Wittgenstein, *Philosophical Investigations*, secs. 258–280.

28. On this paradox, see above. In Austinian terms, a "phatic" act, in which the speaker knows that the sentence he or she is uttering has a meaning, is not the same thing as a "rhetic" act, in which the sentence is uttered as having a *particular* meaning. For that it would have to be addressed to someone in context.

29. Remember the meaning of the Latin *sermo, sermonis:* conversation, exchanged speech; from *sero, serer, sertum:* to interweave, plait.

30. Dostoyevsky, *L'Idiot* (Paris: Gallimard, 1953); my emphasis.

31. "For although I am thinking about these matters with myself, silently and without speaking. . . ." *The Philosophical Writings of Descartes* 2:21.

32. See also *Letter to Elizabeth*, 28 June 1643.

33. Descartes, *Oeuvres* 7:31–32. I am most grateful to Marcel Lamy for pointing this text out to me, and for his comments on it.

34. On reference to possible worlds in dynamically exchanged speech, see *Dialogiques I*, fourth investigation.

35. I am leaving out free indirect speech, of which a partial treatment is given in *Dialogiques I*.

36. Authier, "Les Formes du discours rapporte," 51.

37. *Le Monde du dimanche* (28 February 1982).

38. On this point, see the inventive article of Authier, "Paroles tenues à distance," 127–142.

39. The two functions should therefore not be confused. See my critique of Benveniste in the Introduction, and below in the present chapter.

40. Interview between F. Core and Lech Walesa (6 April 1981).

41. Valéry, *Cahiers* 14:390.

42. Valéry, *Cahiers* 8:38.

43. Dostoyevsky, *L'Idiot*, 669.

44. Wittgenstein, *The Blue and Brown Books* 5.

45. *Ibid.*, 41.

46. Jacques, "La Mise en communauté de l'énonciation."

47. Mayoux, *Sous de vastes portiques.*

48. Carroll, *Alice's Adventures in Wonderland,* chap. 7, 65.

49. Searle, "Indirect Speech-Acts," 30–37.

50. Benveniste, *Problèmes de linguistique générale*, 2, 85.

51. We should remember that the formal structure of questions demands the construction of a double location system, as Culioli subtly reminds us in "Valeurs modales et opérations énonciatives," 59 n 31.

52. Jacques, *Dialogiques I.*

53. On this point I diverge from Kerbrat-Orrechioni, *L'Énonciation de la subjectivité*, 15.

54. Aeschylus, *Agamemnon*, 42–44.

55. Augustine, *De Trinitate*, book 8.

56. It should be remembered that the word *autobiography* only appeared in the dictionary of the French Academy in 1842, modeled on the English term.

57. There are exceptions, among them *Le Miroir de Venise*, by Vuillemin. On this book, see my review, "Le Moi, l'eau, et la parole," in the *Revue de Métaphysique et de Morale.*

Conclusion

1. According to the etymology of "Abel," as André Neher has pointed out.

2. See Husserl, *Formale und Transcendentale Logik*, sect. 103.

3. *Ibid.*, sec. 96.

4. Kant, *Anthropologie in pragmatischer Hinsicht*, book I, sec. 2.

5. Todorov, *La Conquête de l'Amérique*, II, 135.

6. Jacques, *Dialogiques 2: L'Espace logique de l'interlocution.*

7. See my lecture to the Société française de Philosophie (26 April 1980).

8. Weizäcker, *Who is the Knower in Physics?* (unpublished lecture). See also Desanti, *Les Idéalités mathématiques.*

9. This is confirmed by the institutional aspect revealed by studies of speech acts. Language is presented in them as an activity governed by a system of constitutive rules which are precisely at the service of the joint activity of signification.

10. Varela, *Autopoiesis and Cognition.*

BIBLIOGRAPHY

Aeschylus. *Agamemnon.* Trans. G. Thomson. Cambridge: Cambridge University Press, 1938.

Albritton, Rogers. "On Wittgenstein's Use of the Term 'Criterion.'" *Journal of Philosophy* 56 (1959).

Alexandre, Michel. *En souvenir de Michel Alexandre.* Paris: Mercure de France, 1956.

Amiel, Henri Frédéric. *Oeuvres complètes.* 3 vols. Geneva, 1948, 1953, 1958.

———. *Journal intime: L'Année 1857.* Paris: Union Générale d'Editions, 1965.

Anscombe, G. E. M. *Intention.* Oxford: Blackwell, 1957.

Anscombre, Jean-Claude, and Oswald Ducrot. "L'Argumentation dans la langue." *Langages* 42. Paris: Larousse, 1976.

Aristotle. *Nicomachean Ethics.* Trans. J. Warrington. Everyman's Library 547. London: Dent; New York: Dutton, 1963.

———, *Poetics.* Trans. L. J. Potts. Cambridge: Cambridge University Press, 1953.

Armengaud, Françoise. "L'Impertinence ex-communicative ou comment annuler la parole d'autrui." *Degrés* 28–29 (1981).

———. "Le Visage animal." In *Du Visage.* ed. M. J. Baudinet. Presses Universitaire du Livre, 1982.

Arnauld, Antoine, and Pierre Nicole. *La Logique ou l'art de penser.* [1662]. Paris: Presses Universitaires de France, 1965.

355

Atlan, H. *L'Organisation biologique et la théorie de l'information*. Paris: Hermann, 1972.

Augustine, Saint. *Confessions* and *De Trinitate*. In *Works*. Trans. S. McKenna. Washington, D.C.: Catholic University of America Press, 1981.

——. *Selected Sermons*. Trans. Q. Howe. New York: Holt, Rinehart, and Winston, 1966.

——. *Sermones*. In *Patrologia Cursus Completus, Series Latina*. 221 vols. Paris: J. P. Migne, Garnier Freies, 1844–1904.

Aulagnier, Pierre. *Le Désir et la pérversion*. Paris: Seuil, 1967.

——. *La Violence de l'interprétation* Paris: Presses Universitaires de France, 1975.

——. *Savoir, faire, espérer; Les Limites de la raison*. Brussels, 1976.

Authier, J. "Les Formes du discourse rapporté, remarques syntaxiques et sémantiques à partir des traitements proposés." *Documentation et recherche en linguistique allemand contemporaire*. Centre de Recherches de l'Université de Paris 8. Paris: Editions du CNRS 964:17 (1978).

——. *Paroles tenues à distance*. Paper read at conference on "Matérialités discursives" (24–26 April 1980), Université de Paris 10, Nanterre. Proceedings pub. Presses Universitaires de Lille, 1981.

Ayer, A. J. *The Concept of a Person and Other Essays*. London: Macmillan and Co., 1963.

Bachelard, Gaston. *L'Eau et les rêves*. Paris: José Corti, 1942.

Bakhtin, Mikhail. *Problems of Dostoyevsky's Poetics*. Trans. R. W. Rotsel. Ann Arbor: Aedis, 1973.

Bateson, Gregory. "Communication." In *The Natural History of an Interview*. Ed. N. MacQuown. Chicago: Chicago University Library, 1971.

Baudinet, M. J. "L'Incarnation, l'image, la voix." *Esprit*, special no. on "The Body" (Feburary 1982).

Beaujour, Michel. *Miroirs d'encre*. Paris: Seuil, 1980.

Bell, Daniel. *The Coming of Post-Industrial Society*. London: Heinemann, 1974.

Benveniste, Emile. *Problèmes de linguistique générale* 1 and 2. Paris: Gallimard, 1966 and 1974.

——. *Problems in General Linguistics*. University of Miami Press, 1973.

Berkeley, George. *An Essay Towards a New Theory of Vision* [1709]; *A Treatise Concerning the Principles of Human Knowledge* [1710]; *Three Dialogues Between Hylas and Philonous* [1713]. In *Works*. Alexander Campbell Fraser, 1871 and 1901.

Bernard, Saint. *Cantica Canticorum: 86 Sermons on the Song of Solomon*. Trans. J. Eales. London: Stock, 1895.

——. *De Diligendo Dei* [On the Love of God]. London: Mowbray, 1961.

Beyssade, Jean-Marie. *La Philosophie première de Descartes*. Paris: Flammarion, 1979.

Black, Max. *Caveats and Critiques*. Ithaca: Cornell University Press, 1975.

Blum, R. "La Perception d'autrui." In *La Communication*. Proceedings of the fifteenth Société philosophique de langue française congress. Montreal: Editions Montmorency, 1971.

Brentano, Franz. "Die psychische Beziehung in Unterschied von der Relation im eigentlichen Sinne." *Psychologie* (1911), appendix I.

Brown, R. E. The Gospel According to John 1–12. New York: Doubleday, 1966.

Bruaire, Claude. *Pour la métaphysique*. Paris: Fayard, 1980.

Buber, Martin. *Dialogisches Leben*. Zurich: Gregor Mülder, 1947; *La Vie en dialogue*. Paris: Aubier Montagne, 1959.

Butler, Bishop Joseph. "Of Personal Identity." In *The Works of Joseph Butler*. Oxford: Clarendon Press, 1877.

Canguilhem, Georges. *Essai sur quelques problèmes concernant le normal et le pathologique*. Clermont-Ferrand: La Montagne, 1943.

———. "La Théorie cellulaire," In *La Connaissance de la vie*. Paris: Vrin, 1965. 5th ed. 1975.

Carney, J. D. "Private Language: The Logic of Wittgenstein's Argument." *Mind* 69 (1960).

Casteñeda, Hector Neri. "The Private Language Argument," In *Knowledge and Experience*. Ed. C. D. Rollins. Pittsburgh: University of Pittsburgh Press, 1962.

Chisholm, Roderick. *Perception and Personal Identity*. Proceedings of the 1967 Oberlin Colloquium in Philosophy. Cleveland: Case Western Reserve University Press, 1969.

Church, Alonzo. "A Note on the Entscheidungsproblem." *Journal of Symbolic Logic* I (1936).

Clair, André. "Communication et communicabilité. A propos du livre de Francis Jacques: *L'Espace logique de l'interlocution.*" *Revue des sciences philosophiques et théologiques* 70 (April 1986).

Clavreul, Jean. "Le Couple pervers." In *Le désir et la perversion*. Paris: Seuil, 1967.

Cook, John W. "Wittgenstein on Privacy." *Philosophical Review* 74 (1965).

Culioli, A. "Valeurs modales et opérations énonciatives." *Modèles linguistiques*, I. Lille: Presses Universitaires de Lille, 1979.

Culioli, A., and Jean-Pierre Desclés. "Systèmes de représentation linguistiques et méta-linguistiques." Collection ERA 42, special no. (1981).

Deleuze, Giles. *Difference et répétition*. Paris: Presses Universitaires de France, 1968.

Dennett, Daniel. "Conditions of Personhood." In *The Identities of Persons*. Ed. Amélie O. Rorty. University of California Press, 1976.

Desanti, J. T., *Phénoménologie et praxis*. Paris: Editions sociales.

———. *Les idéalités mathématiques*. Paris: Seuil, 1968.

Descartes, René. *Oeuvres*, Ed. Charles Adam and Paul Tannery. 13 vols. Paris: Cerf, 1897–1909. Selections trans. J. Cottingham et al. as *The Philosophical Writings of Descartes*. 2 vols. Cambridge: Cambridge University Press 1984.

———. *Entretien avec Burman*. Ed., trans., and annotated by J. M. Beyssade. Paris: Presses Universitaires de France, Collection Epiméthée, 1981.

Desclés, Jean-Pierre. "Recherche sur les opérations constitutives du langage." *Cahiers Fundamenta Scientiae* 95. Strasbourg: Université Louis Pasteur.

Descombes, Vincent. *L'Inconscient malgré lui*. Paris: Minuit, 1977.

*Dialogue pour l'identité culturelle.*First International Conference on Cultural Identity. Paris: Anthropos, 1982.

Du Portal, G. F. "L'Humanisme dialogique de Francis Jacques." *Archivo di Filosofia* 15 (1987).

Einstein, Albert, and Max Born. *Correspondence 1916–1955.* In M. Jammer, *The Philosophy of Quantum Mechanics.* New York: John Wiley & Sons, 1974.

Fernandez–Zoïla, A. "Présence à soi et espace sémantique: La Fonction d'asymétrie en psycho-pathologie." In *Psychiatrie et société.* Paris: Erès, 1981.

Foucault, Michel. *La Volonté de savoir.* Paris: Gallimard, 1976.

Franzelin, J. B., S. J. *De Deo trino.* Rome, 1881.

Fraser, T., and André Joly. "Le Système de la déixis; Esquisse d'une théorie de l'expression en anglais." In *Modèles linguistiques* I. Lille: Presses Universitaires de Lille, 1979.

Frondizi, Risieri. *The Nature of Self; A Functional Interpretation.* Southern Illinois University Press, 1953.

Fuchs, Catherine. "Les Problèmes énonciatives." Documentations et recherches en linguistique allemande contemporaine 25 (1981).

Garver, Newton. "Wittgenstein on Private Language." *Philosophy and Phenomenological Research* 20 (1959–60).

———. "Wittgenstein's *On Criteria.*" In *Knowledge and Experience.* Ed. C. D. Rollins. Pittsburgh: University of Pittsburgh Press, 1962.

Geach, Peter T. *Mental Acts.* London: Routledge and Kegan Paul, 1957.

———. *God and the Soul.* London: Routledge and Kegan Paul, 1969.

Genette, Gérard. *Figures 3.* Paris: Seuil, 1972. Selections in: *Figures of Literary Discourse.* Trans. A. Sheridan. New York: Columbia University Press, 1982; and in *Narrative Discourse.* Trans. J. Lewin. Oxford: Blackwell, 1980.

Gochet Paul, and D. Giovannangeli. "Une Philosophie de la communication: Les Dialogiques de Francis Jacques." *Communication and Cognition* 15 (1982), no. 2.

Gödel, Kurt. "Uber formal unentscheidbare Sätze der Principia Mathematica und verwandter Systeme." *Monatshefte für Mathematik und Physik* 38 (1931), 173–198.

Granger, Gilles-Gaston. *La Théorie aristotélicienne de la science.* Paris: Aubier Montagne, 1976.

Gregory of Nazianzus. *The Five Theological Orations of Gregory of Nazianzus.* ed. A. J. Mason. Cambridge: Cambridge University Press, 1899.

Grice, H. P. "Utterer's Meaning and Intentions." *Philosophical Review* (April 1969).

Grunig, Blanche Noelle. "Pièges et illusions de la pragmatique linguistique." *Modèles linguistiques* Lille: Presses Universitaires de Lille, 1979.

———. "Plusieurs pragmatiques." *Documentations et recherches en linguistique allemande contemporaire* 25 (1981).

Guéroult, Martial. *Descartes selon l'ordre des raisons.* 2 vols. Paris: Aubier Montaigne, 1953.

Habermas, Jürgen. *Technik und Wissenschaft als "Ideologie".* Frankfurt am Main;

Suhrkamp, 1969; *La Technique et la science comme idéologie*. Paris: Gallimard, 1973.

Hagège, Claude. Review of *Différence et Subjectivité*. In *Bulletin de la Société de Linguistique de Paris* 78 (1983), no. 2, 40–43.

Hart, H. L. A. "Are There any Natural Rights?" *Philosophical Review* 64 (1955).

Hegel, G. W. F. *Phänomenologie des Geistes* [1807]; *The Phenomenology of Spirit*. Trans. A. V. Miller. Oxford: Clarendon Press, 1971; *La Phénoménologie de l'Esprit*. 2 vols. Trans. J. Hippolyte. Paris: Aubier, 1939–1941.

———. *Encyclopädie der philosophischen Wissenschaft* [1817]; *Encyclopédie des Sciences Philosophiques*. Paris: Vrin, 1952.

Hintikka, Jaakko. "'Cogito ergo sum': Inference or Performance?" In *Knowledge and the Known*. D. Riedel, 1974.

Hobbes, Thomas. *Leviathan* [1651].

Hofstadter Douglas R. *Gödel, Escher, Bach: An Eternal Golden Braid*. Hassocks: Harvester, 1979.

Hora, T. "Tao, Zen, and Existential Psychotherapy." *Psychologia* 2 (1959).

Hübner, K. *Kritik der Wissenschaftlichen Vernunft*. 2d ed. Freiburg/Munich: Karl Alber, 1979; *Critique of Scientific Reason*. Trans. P. Dixon and H. Dixon. Chicago: University of Chicago Press, 1983.

Hume, David. *A Treatise of Human Nature*. London: Longmans, Green, 1890.

Husserl, Edmund. *Cartesianische Meditationen; Cartesian Meditations: an Introduction to Phenomenology*. Trans. D. Cairns. The Hague: Nijhoff, 1988.

———. *Formale und transcendentale Logik*, Husserliana 17 (1974); *Formal and Transcendental Logic*. Trans. D. Cairns. The Hague: Nijhoff, 1969.

———. *Ideen zu einer reinen Phänomenologie und phänomenologischen Philosophie*. Vol. 1 [1950]; *Ideas: a General Introduction to Pure Phenomenology*. Trans. W. R. Boyce Gibson. London: Allen and Unwin; New York: Humanities Press, 1967.

———. *Die Krisis der europäischen Wissenschaft und die transcendentale Phänomenologie*. Husserliana 6 (1954).

Irigaray, Luce. *Ce Sexe qui n'en est pas un*. Paris: Minuit, 1977; *This Sex Which Is Not One*. Trans. C. Porter et al. Ithaca: Cornell University Press, 1985.

Jackson, Don D. *Family Process* (1965); reprinted in Watzlawik, P., and J. H. Weakland, *The Interactional View*. New York: W. W. Norton and Co., 1977.

Jacques, Francis. *Dialogiques 1: Recherches logiques sur le dialogue*. Paris: Presses Universitaires de France, 1979.

———. "L'Espace logique de l'interlocution." *Bulletin de la Société de Philosophie* 26 April 1980.

———. "L'Explication dans les sciences humaines: Entre le Déterminisme du comportement et la détermination de l'action." In *L'Explication en psychologie*. Paris: Presses Universitaires de France, 1980.

———. "Les Conditions dialogiques de la compréhension ou le paradoxe de Narcisse." In *Meaning and Understanding*. Ed. H. Parret and J. Bouveresse. De Gruyter, 1981, 353–388.

———. "L'Interrogation, force illocutoire et interaction verbale." *Langue française* 52 (December 1981), 70–79.

———. "L'Analyse des énoncés théologiques." *Initiation à la théologie.* Paris: Cerf, 1982.

———. "A quelles conditions un dialogue des cultures est-il possible?" In *Dialogue pour l'identité culturelle.* Paris: Anthropos, 1982.

———. "La Dimension dialogique en philosophie du langage." *Philosophie et langage.* Brussels: Editions de l'Université de Bruxelles, 1982.

———. "Le Schéma jakobsonien de la communication est-il devenu un obstacle épistémologique?" In *Languages, connaissance et pratique.* Ed. N. Mouloud and J. M. Vienne. Lille: Presses Universitaires de Lille, 1982.

———. "La Mise en communauté de l'énonciation." *Langages* June 1983, 47–72.

———. *Dialogiques 2: L'Espace logique de l'interlocution.* Paris: Presses Universitaires de France, 1985.

———. "Du dialogisme à la forme dialoguée: Sur les fondements de l'approche pragmatique. In *Dialogue—An Interdisciplinary Approach.* Ed. M. Dascal. Philadelphia and Amsterdam: John Benjamin, 1985.

———. "De l'intersubjectivité à l'interlocution. Un Changement de paradigme?" *Archivo di Filosofia* 14 (1986), 195–218.

———. "La Réciprocité interpersonnelle." *Connexions* 47 (1986), 109–136.

———. "La Promesse et le paradoxe." *Archivo di Filosofia* 15 (1987), 317–350.

———. "Entre conflit et dialogue." *Autrement* 102 (November 1988).

———. "Dialogisme et argumentation: Le Dialogue argumentatif." *Verbum* 12, (1989), no. 2.

Jankélévitch, Vladimir. *Traité des vertus.* Paris: Bordas, 1947.

———. *Le Paradoxe de la morale.* Paris: Seuil, 1981.

Jones, J. R. "Self-Knowledge." *Aristotelian Society Supplementary Volume* 30 (1956).

Kant, Immanuel. *Kritik der reinen Vernunft* [1781, 1787]; *Critique of Pure Reason.* Trans. N. Kemp Smith. New York: St. Martin's Press; London: Macmillan, 1968; *Critique de la raison pure.* Trans. Tremesaygues and Pacaud. Presses Universitaties de France, 1944.

———. *Die Religion innerhalb der Grenzen der blossen Vernunft* [1793]; *Religion within the Limits of Reason Alone.* Trans. T. M. Greene and H. H. Husdon. New York: Harper and Row, 1960.

———. *Anthropologie in pragmatischer Hinsicht* [1798]; *Anthropology from a Pragmatic Point of View.* Trans. M. J. Gregor. The Hague: Nijhoff, 1974; *Anthropologie d'un point de vue pragmatique.* Trans. M. Foucault. Paris: Vrin, 1964.

Kenny, Anthony. *The Five Ways.* London: Routledge and Kegan Paul, 1969.

Kerbrat-Orecchioni, Catherine. *L'Énonciation de la subjectivité dans le langage.* Paris: Armand-Colin, 1980.

Klein, Melanie. *Envy and Gratitude and Other Works, 1946–63.* 3 vols. New York: Free Press, 1984.

Kuratowski, Kazimierz. "Sur la notion d'ordre dans la théorie des ensembles." *Fundamenta Mathematicae* 1921: 161–171.

Labarrière, P. J. "La 'Réciprocité interlocutive' ou la 'canonique du dialogique': Sur la philosophie de Francis Jacques." *Archives de Philosophie* 51 (1988), 431–440.

La Bruyère, Jean de. *Les Caractères de Théophraste traduits en français avec les caractères ou moeurs de ce siècle* [1688]; *The Characters of Jean de la Bruyère*. Trans. H. van Laun. London: Nimmo, 1885.

Lagache, Daniel. "La Fascination de la conscience par le moi." In *La Psychanalyse*. Paris: Presses Universitaires de France, 1957.

———. "Modèle psychanalytique de la personnalité." In *Les modèles de la personnalité*. Paris, 1965.

Laing, R. D. *Self and Others*. Penguin, 1981.

Leibowitz, N. *Studies in Bereshit*. Genesis, 1972.

Levinas, Emmanuel. "Le Temps et l'autre." In *Le Choix, le Monde, l'Existence*. Arthaud, Cahiers du Collège philosophique, 1949.

———. "Un Dieu-homme." In *Qui est Jésus-Christ?* Cahiers du C.C.I.F., Recherches et Débats, 1968.

———. *Totalité et infini, essai sur l'extériorité*. The Hague: Nijhoff, 1961; 4th ed. 1980; *Totality and Infinity*. Trans. A. Lingis. Pittsburgh: Duquesne, 1969.

———. *Les Noms propres*. Montpellier: Fata Morgana, 1976.

———. *Autrement qu'être, ou au-delà de l'essence*. The Hague: Nijhoff, 1974; *Otherwise than Being or Beyond Essence*. Trans. A. Lingis. The Hague: Nijhoff, 1981.

———. "Ethique et Infini; L'Intinéraire philosophique d'Emmanuel Levinas." Radio interview with P. Nemo. France-Culture, 11 March 1981.

———. "La Croyance." Paper presented at the Colloque international d'Albi. July 1981.

———. *Du Dieu qui vient à l'idée*. Paris: Vrin, 1982.

Locke, John. *An Essay Concerning Human Understanding*. Oxford: Campbell Fraser, 1894.

Lyons, John. *Semantics* 1. Cambridge: Cambridge University Press, 1977.

Lyotard, Jean-François. *La Condition post-moderne*. Paris: Minuit, 1979; *The Postmodern Condition*. Trans. G. Bennington and B. Massumi. Manchester: Manchester University Press, 1984.

Maine de Biran [Marie François Pierre Gonthier de Biran]. *Journal*. 3 vols. Ed. Henri Gouhier. Neuchâtel: Editions de la Baconnière, 1954–1957.

Malcolm, Norman. *Dreaming*. London: Routledge and Kegan Paul, 1962.

Malinowski, Bronisläw. "The Problem of Meaning in Primitive Languages." In *The Meaning of Meaning*. 10th ed. C. K. Ogden and I. A. Richards, eds. London: Routledge and Kegan Paul, 1923–1949.

Marin, Louis. *La Voix excommuniée*. Paris: Galilée, 1981.

Mayoux, Jean-Jacques. *Sous de vastes portiques*. Maurice Nadeau, Papyrus, 1981.

Meiland, Jack W. "Meaning, Identification, and Other Minds." *Australian Journal of Psychology and Philosophy* 62 (1964).

Meinong, Alexius. *Gesammelte Abhandlungen.* 2 vols. Leipzig: J. A. Barth, 1929. Republished in *Meinongs Gesamtausgabe.* Graz: Akademische Druck und Verlagsanstalt, 1971.

Merleau-Ponty, Maurice. *Phénoménologie de la perception.* Paris: Gallimard, 1945; *Phenomenology of Perception.* Trans. C. Smith. London: Routledge and Kegan Paul, 1962.

———. *Le visible et l'invisible.* Paris: Gallimard, 1964; *Visible and Invisible.* Trans. A. Lingis. Evanston: Northwestern University Press, 1969.

———. *La Prose du monde.* Paris: Gallimard, 1969; *The Prose of the World.* Trans. J. O'Neil. Evanston: Northwestern University Press, 1973.

Mink, Lewis Otto. "Philosophical Analysis and Historical Understanding." *Review of Metaphysics* 21 (1968), no. 4.

Montaigne, Michel. *Essais.* Vols. 2 and 3. In *Oeuvres complètes.* Paris: Gallimard, La Pléiade, 1963; *Montaigne's Essays.* 3 vols. Trans. C. Cotton, ed. W. H. Hazlitt. London: Reeves and Turner, 1877.

Moore, G. E. *Wittgenstein's Lectures 1930–1933.* Reprinted in *Philosophical Papers.* London: Allen and Unwin, 1959.

Mounier, Emmanuel. *Le Personnalisme.* Paris: Presses Universitaires de France, 1949.

Mounoud, P., and A. Winter. *La Reconnaissance de son image chez l'enfant et l'animal.* Paris: Delachaux et Niestle, 1981.

Newman, John Henry, Cardinal. *Apologia pro sua vita.* 1864.

Nicole, Pierre. *Traité de la connaissance de soi-même.* Vol. 3 of *Essais de morale.* Paris: Desprez, 1725–1735.

Nora, Simon, and Alain Minc. *L'Informatisation de la société.* Paris: Seuil, 1978.

Ortigues, Edmond. "Quelqu'un, identité et personnalité." *Dialogue* (December 1977), 605–628.

Paillard, Jacques. "Le Corps situé et le corps identifié; Une Psychophysiologie de la notion de schéma corporel." *Revue Médicale de la Suisse Romande* 100 (1980).

Pascal, Blaise. *Pensées.* Ed. Léon Brunschwicg. Paris: Boutroux, 1923; Trans. F. W. Trotter. New York: Dutton; London: Dent, 1940).

Peirce, C. S. *Ms. 1903.* In *The Collected Papers of C. S. Peirce.* vols. 1–6. Ed. C. Hartshorne and P. Weiss; vols. 7, 8 ed. A. Burks. Cambridge: Harvard University Press, 1931–1935 and 1958.

Penelhum, Terence. "Personal Identity." In *The Encyclopaedia of Philosophy.* Ed. P. Edwards. London and New York: Macmillan, 1967.

Petit, J. L. Critical notice on Francis Jacques, *L'Espace logique de l'interlocution.* In *Logique et Analyse* 30 (May–June 1987), 155–165.

Philosophica 27: Pragmatics and Philosophy. Special issue. Ed. L. Apostel and A. Kasher, 1981.

Plantinga, Alvin. "Things and Persons." *Review of Metaphysics* 14 (1961).

Plato. *Complete Works.* 6 vols. London: Bohn, 1848–52.

Putnam, Hilary. "Dreaming and Depth Grammar." In *Analytical Philosophy.* Ed. R. Butler. Oxford: Blackwell, 1962–1965.

————. "Other Minds." In *Mind, Language, and Reality*. Cambridge: Cambridge University Press, 1975.

Quine, W. V. O. *From a Logical Point of View*. Cambridge: Harvard University Press, 1953.

————. *Ontological Relativity and Other Essays*. New York: Columbia University Press, 1969.

Récanati, Françoise. *La Transparence de l'énonciation*. Paris: Seuil, 1979.

Rey-Debove, Josette. *Le Métalangage*. Paris: Editions Le Robert, 1978.

Robinet, André. *Le Langage à l'âge classique*. Paris: Klincksieck, 1978.

Rorty, Amélie. "A Literary Postscriptum." In *The Identities of Persons*. Ed. A. Rorty. Berkeley: University of California Press, 1976.

Rotenstreich, Nathan. "Buber's Dialogical Thought." In *The Philosophy of Martin Buber*. Vol. 22 of *The Library of Living Philosophers*. Ed. P. A. Schilpp. La Salle, Ill., 1967.

Rousseau, Jean-Jacques. *Rousseau juge de Jean-Jacques*. In vol. 1 of *Oeuvres complètes de Jean-Jacques Rousseau*. 4 vols. Paris: Gallimard; Bibliothèque de la Pléiade, 1959–1969.

Russell, Bertrand. *Problems of Philosophy*. [1912]; Oxford: Oxford University Press, 1967.

————. "The Philosophy of Logical Atomism." *Mind* 28 (1918).

————. *Logic and Knowledge*. London: Allen and Unwin, 1956.

————. *My Philosophical Development*. London: Allen and Unwin, 1959.

Russell, Bertrand, and Alfred North Whitehead. *Principia Mathematica*. 2d ed. 3 vols. Cambridge: Cambridge University Press, 1925–1927.

Ryle, Gilbert. *The Concept of Mind*. London: Hutchinson, 1949.

Sartre, Jean-Paul. *L'Etre et le néant*. Paris: Gallimard, 1960; *Being and Nothingness*. Trans. H. E. Barnes. London: Methuen, 1969.

————. *Critique de la raison dialectique*. Paris: Gallimard, 1960; *Critique of Dialectical Reason*. Trans. A. Sheridan-Smith. London: NLB, 1976.

————. *La Transcendance de l'ego, esquisse d'une description phénoménologique*. Paris: Vrin, 1981.

Schiffer, Stephen. *Meaning*. Oxford: Oxford University Press, 1972.

Scholz, Heinrich. "Über das Cogito, ergo sum." *Kant-Studien* 36 (1931).

Searle, John R. "Indirect Speech-Acts." In *Semantics and Syntax*. Ed. Cole and Morgan.

Shakespeare, *Troilus and Cressida*. London: Methuen, 1982.

Shannon, Claude E., and Warren Weaver. *The Mathematical Theory of Communication*. Urbana: University of Illinois Press, 1949.

Stalnaker, Robert. "Logical Semiotics." In *Modern Logic—A Survey*. Ed. E. Agazzi. D. Reidel, 1980.

Sterne, Laurence. *The Life and Opinions of Tristram Shandy, Gentleman*. [1759] London: Macdonald & Co., 1949.

Tarski, Alfred. "On the Calculus of Relations." *Journal of Symbolic Logic* 6 (1941).

Tertullianus. *Adversus Praxean.* In *Patrologia Cursus Completus, Series Latina.* 221 vols. Paris: J. P. Migne, Garnier Frères, 1844–1904.

Thomas Aquinas, Saint. *Summa Theologiae;* Trans. into French A. D. Sertillanges. Paris: Editions du Cerf.

———. *Summa Contra Gentiles, Compendium Theologiae,* and *De Potentia.* In *Sancti Thomae Aquinatis Opera Omnia.* 34 vols. Paris: Vivès, 1871–1880.

Todorov, Tzvetan. *Mikhaïl Bakhtine; Le Principe dialogique.* Paris: Seuil, 1981.

———. *La Conquête de l'Amérique.* Paris: Seuil, 1982.

Torris, G. *L'Acte médical et le caractère du malade.* Paris, 1954.

Touraine, Alain. *La Société post-industrielle.* Denvel, 1969.

Tournier, Michel. *Les Météores.* Paris: Gallimard, 1974.

Valabrega, J. P. *La Relation thérapeutique.* Paris: Flammarion, 1962.

Valéry, Paul. *Charmes.* With commentary by Alain. Paris: Gallimard, 1952.

———. *Cahiers.* 29 vols. Paris: Gallimard, 1973–4.

———. *Oeuvres.* 2 vols. Paris: Gallimard; Bibliothèque de la Pléiade, 1959–1960.

Van Peursen, C. A. "Edmund Husserl and Ludwig Wittgenstein." *Philosophy and Phenomenological Research* 20 (1959).

Varela, Francisco J., with Humberto R. Maturana. *Autopoiesis and Cognition.* Dordrecht: D. Reidel, 1972.

Vigarello, Georges. "Le Laboratoire des sciences humaines." *Esprit* 2 (February 1982).

Vuillemin, J. *Le Miroir de Venise.* Paris: Juilliard, 1966.

Wallon, Henri. "Syndrôme d'insuffisance psycho-motrice et types sensori-moteurs." *Annales médico-psychologiques* 5 (1932).

Watzlawick, Paul. "Patterns of Psychotic Communication." In *Problems of Psychosis.* Ed. P. Doucet and C. Laurin. Amsterdam: Excerpta Medica, 1971.

———. "Structures de la communication psychotique." [1979]; trans. into French Y. Winkin. In *La nouvelle communication.* Paris: Seuil, 1981.

Watzlawick, P. and J. H. Weakland. *Sur l'interaction: Une nouvelle approche thérapeutique.* Paris: Seuil, 1977.

Weil, Simone. *L'Enracinement.* Paris: Gallimard, 1949.

———. *Attente de Dieu.* Paris: Editions de la Colombe, 1950.

———. *La Connaissance surnaturelle.* Paris: Gallimard, 1950.

Wellman, C. "Wittgenstein and the Egocentric Predicament." *Journal of Philosophy* 58 (1961).

Williams, Bernard. *Problems of the Self.* Cambridge: Cambridge University Press, 1973.

Wittgenstein, Ludwig. *Tractatus Logico-Philosophicus.* [1922] London: Routledge and Kegan Paul, 1961.

———. *Philosophische Bemerkungen.* [1930] Ed. Rush Rhees. Oxford: Blackwell, 1964; *Philosophical Remarks of Ludwig Wittgenstein.* Trans. R. Hargreaves and R. White. Oxford: Blackwell, 1975.

———. *Philosophical Investigations.* Ed. G. E. M. Anscombe, Rush Rhees, and G. H. von Wright. Oxford: 1953.

————. *The Blue and Brown Books.*Oxford: Blackwell, 1958.

————. *Lectures and Conversations on Aesthetics, Psychology, and Religious Belief.* Oxford: Blackwell, 1966.

————. *Zettel.* Oxford: Blackwell, 1967.

————. "Notes for Lectures on 'Private Experiences and Sense-Data,'" in *Philosophical Review* 77 (1968).

————. *Philosophische Grammatik.* Ed. Rush Rhees. Oxford: Blackwell, 1969; *Philosophical Grammar.* Ed. Rush Rhees, trans. Anthony Kenny. Oxford: Blackwell, 1974.

Wittgenstein and the Problem of Other Minds. Ed. Harold Morick. New York: McGraw-Hill, 1967.

Zimmerli, Walter. *Das Alte Testament als Anrede.* Munich: Chr. Kaiser, 1956.

INDEX